Language Policy and Language Planning

Other books by Sue Wright

LANGUAGE AND CONFLICT: A Neglected Relationship (*edited*)

LANGUAGE, DEMOCRACY AND DEVOLUTION IN CATALONIA (*edited*)

LANGUAGE POLICY AND LANGUAGE ISSUES IN THE SUCCESSOR
STATES OF THE USSR (*edited*)

WHOSE EUROPE? THE TURN TOWARD DEMOCRACY (*edited with D. Smith*)

COMMUNITY AND COMMUNICATION

Language Policy and Language Planning

From Nationalism to Globalisation

Sue Wright

palgrave
macmillan

First published 2004 by
PALGRAVE MACMILLAN
Houndmills, Basingstoke, Hampshire RG21 6XS and
175 Fifth Avenue, New York, N.Y. 10010
Companies and representatives throughout the world

PALGRAVE MACMILLAN is the global academic imprint of the Palgrave
Macmillan division of St. Martin's Press, LLC and of Palgrave Macmillan Ltd.
Macmillan® is a registered trademark in the United States, United Kingdom
and other countries. Palgrave is a registered trademark in the European
Union and other countries.

ISBN 0–333–98641–5 hardback
ISBN 978–0–333–98642–4 paperback

This book is printed on paper suitable for recycling and made from fully
managed and sustained forest sources. Logging, pulping and manufacturing
processes are expected to conform to the environmental regulations of the
country of origin.

A catalogue record for this book is available from the British Library.

Library of Congress Cataloging-in-Publication Data
Wright, Sue, 1947–
    Language policy and language planning : from nationalism to globalisation /
  Sue Wright.
       p. cm.
    Includes bibliographical references.
    ISBN 0–333–98641–5 – ISBN 0–333–98642–3 (pbk.)
      1. Language planning – History. 2. Language policy – History. I. Title.

P40.5L35W75 2003
306.44'9'09—dc21   2003056399

Printed and bound in Great Britain by
CPI Antony Rowe, Chippenham and Eastbourne

For Colin, Tom and Anna

Contents

Acknowledgements   ix

1   Introduction   1

Part I   Community and the Role of National Language   17

2   From Language Continuum to Linguistic Mosaic:
    European Language Communities from the Feudal
    Period to the Age of Nationalism   19

3   Language Planning in State Nations and Nation States   42

4   Nation Building in the Wake of Colonialism: Old
    Concepts in New Settings   69

Part II   Transcendence and Language Learning   99

5   Transcending the Group: Languages of Contact
    and Lingua Francas   101

6   French: The Rise and Fall of a Prestige Lingua Franca   118

7   English: From Language of Empire to Language of
    Globalisation   136

8   Language in a Postnational Era: Hegemony or
    Transcendence?   157

Part III   Renaissance and Revitalisation in Small Language Communities 179

9   New Discourse, New Legal Instruments and a New
    Political Context for Minorities and their Languages   181

10 The Fragmentation of the Old Nation States and
    the Rise of Small Nations   201

11 Endangered Languages   218

12 Conclusion   244

Notes   252

Bibliography   283

Index   306

Acknowledgements

This book, like all academic work, owes much to the ideas and arguments of all the people that I have worked with over the past decade. I am extremely grateful to all those who have given their time to discuss the ideas in this book. In particular, I would like to thank Christina Bratt Paulston, John Joseph, Dario Castiglione, Dennis Ager, Henry and Kate Miller, Charlotte Hoffmann, Elizabeth Erling, Dennis Smith, John Rex, David Block, Helen Kelly Holmes, Laksmi Holland, Miquel Strubell, Sue Wharton and Julian Edge for reading and commenting on various chapters. I would like to express my gratitude to all my colleagues in the Department of Language Studies at Aston who covered my sabbatical and were a constant source of support, both moral and intellectual. I am indebted to my postgraduate students whose reactions have been of great assistance in working out my ideas. I am also grateful to the Aston Modern Languages Research Foundation for the grants they awarded, which allowed me to commission the translation of primary material in languages that I cannot read. Finally I would like to thank my daughter, Anna, for all her help on the index and general preparation for publication. All mistakes remain of course my own.

1
Introduction

This is a book about language planning and language policy, and naturally deals with the core issues of the discipline. There is, of course, much on the legal process of making a language official (status planning). There is also discussion of the linguistic changes planned in language institutes or among elite model givers (corpus planning). There is inevitably consideration of the policy measures and management, which ensure that the chosen and planned language is taught and learnt in school (acquisition planning). However, there is also more. There is reflection on political events and social processes, that are not always seen as within the scope of the subject. My argument is that, although formal language policy making and language planning is a relatively recent development in terms of human history, as an informal activity it is as old as language itself, plays a crucial role in the distribution of power and resources in all societies, is integral to much political activity and deserves to be studied explicitly from this political perspective.

My thinking on language policy and language planning (LPLP) developed from hearing M.A.K. Halliday give his seminal 1990 lecture at the Ninth World Congress of Applied Linguistics. He suggested that

> Language planning is a highly complex set of activities involving the intersection of two very different and potentially conflicting themes: one that of 'meaning' common to all our activities with language, and other semiotics as well; the other theme that of 'design'. If we start from the broad distinction between designed systems and evolved systems, then language planning means introducing design processes and design features into a system (namely language) which is naturally evolving. (Halliday 2001: 177)

This led me to wonder at what point there is conscious use of certain language forms for particular ends. It seemed to me to occur very early on in the language making process. From such a perspective it seemed possible to broaden out from LPLP interpreted narrowly as status, corpus and acquisition planning to see it as a field of enquiry that can range over the whole human activity of making meaning and conveying our meaning one to another. Studying the discipline from this perspective starts one on a journey where the limits are difficult to define.

One can argue that 'natural' language always has an element of 'design', at least in the sense that language is rule bound. Without being in agreement on the semantic load of our phonemes we could not communicate. Language works because all the members of a speech community accept the conventions. The choices that have been made are arbitrary. The links between signifier and signified are sustained by normative behaviour (which invests these sounds with these meanings within a particular community) and prescriptive behaviour (which differentiates the language of one group from the language of another and which avoids fracture within the group). A language exists ultimately because the community wills it, and the distinction between 'naturally evolving system' and 'designed system' is quite difficult to mark.

From a social perspective, we could also say that communities exist because they have the linguistic means to do so. In other words, language is the means by which we conduct our social lives and is foremost among the factors that allow us to construct human communities. The importance of language for human beings as social animals is that it opens up the future to planning, it permits the past to become shared experience from which learning can take place and it allows cooperation in joint ventures, with all the advantages of scale that implies. As such, language plays a major role in the constitution of groups, and normative behaviour (observing language rules) and prescriptive behaviour (enforcing language rules) are essential to the process.

It is in this broad sense that I am interested in LPLP and want to investigate how human beings have acquired, manipulated and negotiated language varieties to further their purposes, to consolidate their groups and to celebrate their individual characters. I want to respond to Ó Riagáin's criticism of sociolinguistics:

> The power of state language policies to produce intended outcomes is severely constrained by a variety of social, political and economic structures which sociolinguists have typically not addressed, even though their consequences are profound and of far more importance than language policies themselves. (Ó Riagáin 1997: 170–1)

In order to respond to this challenge, it will be necessary to enquire within the political and social sciences, acquire information from economics and law, and set the events and processes that affect language choice and change within a historical framework. The approach needs to be highly interdisciplinary. We all know how risky it is to go beyond one's own training, but perhaps, as Ó Riagáin points out, in the LPLP context, it may be even riskier not to do so.

1.1   What is language?

There are, however, perhaps two preliminary areas of enquiry to engage with before moving to the main concerns of the book. The first is to ask 'what is language?' One school of thought sees language as a cultural construct. Edward Sapir (1921: 7) described it as a 'purely human and non-instinctive method of communicating ideas, emotions and desires by means of a system of voluntarily produced symbols'. The words and utterances we use refer to common experience. In this interpretation we share knowledge about facts, ideas and events and fit them into a pattern of knowledge about the world which is replicated to some extent by each member of our group. The language of the group expresses its social and cultural reality, and, indeed, forms it as well. This was the central idea in the work of Sapir and his pupil, Benjamin Whorf, and has been termed linguistic determinism.

In its strong form, the belief that we are imprisoned in our language is discredited. The learning of foreign languages, the elaboration of new terms and translation all contradict the idea that our thought processes are bounded by our mother tongue. However, in its weak form the Sapir–Whorf hypothesis is more widely accepted. It seems reasonable to intuit that we are more likely to perceive, process, discriminate and remember in the ways that our language makes readily available.

The constructivists seem on first consideration to hold an opposing view. Rather than believing that the natural world shapes language, they contend that the way human beings use language frames the way they experience the natural world. Halliday provides a clear statement of the constructivist position:

> Language does not passively reflect reality: language actively creates reality ... The categories and concepts of our material existence are not 'given' to us prior to their expression in language. Rather they are construed by language, at the intersection of the material with the symbolic. Grammar in the sense of the syntax and vocabulary of a natural language is thus a theory of human experience. It is also a principle of social action. In both these functions, or metafunctions, grammar creates the potential within which we act and enact our cultural being. This potential is at once both enabling and constraining: that is grammar makes meaning possible and also set[s] limits on what can be meant. (Halliday 2001: 179)

The constructivist definition takes into account that language is inevitably dynamic. New facts, ideas and events necessitate new language. New ways of looking at old ideas, facts and events will cause speakers to recalibrate the ways of talking about them. Meanings are constantly renegotiated. Thus the language of our group is constantly creating cultural reality as well as simply expressing it. We are both formed by and form our language. Interestingly, in the final sentence of this definition, Halliday reveals that the constructivist position actually shares some ground with the weak form of the Sapir–Whorf hypothesis.

Not all would agree with this thesis. The universalist view is that all languages are the products of evolutionary development that took place in early human history. Stephen Pinker in his book, *The Language Instinct*, takes the view that the human ability to use language is no more a cultural invention than the ability of human beings to walk upright:

> The universality of complex language is a discovery that fills linguists with awe, and is the first reason to suspect that language is not just any cultural invention but the product of a special human instinct. (Pinker 1994: 26)

This was the view of language held by Charles Darwin, who came to the conclusion in *The Descent of Man* (1871) that language is an innate ability. Much recent work has set out to corroborate this. Current research in neuroscience aims to show that it is so, although the evidence is not yet assembled. Without a great deal of empirical data,[1] Noam Chomsky subscribed to the idea and theorised that human beings are endowed with a very rich and explicit set of mental attributes that make them genetically predisposed to learn language. His theories of generative grammar derive from a belief that

> (I)t is difficult to avoid the conclusion that whatever its function may be, the reliance on structure-dependent operations must be predetermined for the language-learner by a restrictive initial schematism of some sort that directs his attempts to acquire linguistic competence. (Chomsky 1972: 63)

A different school of thought holds that language is a necessary product of the society and the people that use it. This was the Marxist position, which saw language as dependent on the economic bases it served. Therefore, language necessarily changed as human beings moved through the economic modes of production of primitive communism, slavery, feudalism and capitalism. This corresponds to the Marxist idea of culture being a super structure on economic life. Language adapts itself inevitably to the new ways of being. This definition removes agency and is strongly determinist in a similar way to the strong Sapir–Whorfian position.

My own view leans to Halliday's definition, where language is the principal means of our socialisation into our group and the principal means of our meaning making and it is this definition which underpins the arguments of this book. We are moulded by the ways of meaning developed in our society and by the processes in which we elaborate those meanings within and for that society. I would also agree with some of the more nuanced ideas that Sapir developed. External environmental influence on language is never direct. Nature is mediated through society and culture. It is only where a group is interested in an aspect of the external world that it makes the effort to name it. It is only when precision serves the group that such naming is qualified (Sapir 1921).

Whatever the origins of the human language ability turn out to be, wired in the human brain or entirely learnt in a social setting, the definitive answer to the question will not fundamentally alter the present argument. Language may be partly a biological phenomenon and not simply a social construct or a cultural artefact. Nonetheless, it is *also* a social construct and a cultural artefact and it is an understanding of the processes at work here that will allow us to have a full understanding of the field of language policy and planning.

1.2 Why are there so many languages?

One of the empirical grounds for concluding that individual languages are social constructs is the wealth of languages that exist in the world. Some put the figure as high as 6809 (Ethnologue 2000). Moreover, many languages existed in the past that no longer exist today. This brings us to our second question. If language is the prime means by which human beings became social animals, what is the origin of the extreme and profligate diversity of human languages? George Steiner wonders:

> Why does *homo sapiens* whose digestive tract has evolved and functions in the same complicated ways the world over, whose biochemical fabric and genetic potential are, orthodox science assures us, essentially common, the delicate runnels of whose cortex are wholly akin in all peoples and at every stage of social evolution – why does this unified though individually unique mammalian species not use one common language? (Steiner 1998: 52)

Why do human beings speak thousands of different, mutually incomprehensible languages? The disadvantages are clear. Steiner (1998) mentions just three: tribal societies that have withered inwards, isolated by language barriers even from their near neighbours; contempt, fear and hatred caused by the inability of human beings to understand each other; linguistic atomisation in Africa, India and South America which prevented them making common cause against foreign invaders. There are others: a brake on the transmission of ideas and technologies; the opportunity costs where plurilingualism requires translation and interpretation; difference that can be made to serve discriminatory systems. In this view, the 'destructive prodigality', the 'implausible variety' and the 'crazy quilt' of our linguistic systems creates 'zones of silence' and 'razor edges of division' (Steiner 1998: 56–8).

How can we explain the fact that human beings of identical ethnic background living on similar terrain under similar climatic and ecological conditions, often organised in similar communal structures, with similar kinship systems and beliefs speak entirely different languages? Steiner says that he puts the question repetitively because, for a long time, no linguist seemed to find the question worthy of discussion or comment. One scholar who has attempted an answer is Peter Mühlhäusler. Mühlhäusler maintains that different languages cause different perceptions of the world and reflect 'thousands of years of human accommodation to complex environmental conditions' (Mühlhäusler 1996: 270). The insights within each language, acquired over millennia, are complementary according to this interpretation. Each language may be understood as a provisional interpretation of 'a world so complex, the only hope for understanding is to approach it from as many different perspectives as possible' (Mühlhäusler 2001: 160). Although the argument is attractive, the supporting evidence is thin. The examples that Mühlhäusler and others give of different ways of perceiving the world are never radical and always appear translatable, for example, different perceptions of colour, different ways of expressing kinship and showing respect in social relationships, different ways of expressing number and mass.

Another response to Steiner's question comes in the work of D.C. Laycock. He suggests that languages are different simply because people prefer it that way. A distinct and singular language contributes to their sense of self. Amassing evidence from Melanesia, he shows how change in linguistic usage is initiated within groups to differentiate one from another. The most telling example of how diversity is planned rather than accidental is the case he cites of the Uisai dialect of Buin where all the anaphoric gender agreements have been switched, so that female become male and *vice versa*. There is, he suggests, no known linguistic mechanism that would explain this; it must have been done deliberately to create particularity. Such desire to differentiate may also explain why relatively small groups in Melanesia appear to have little difficulty in preserving their language. Laycock suggests that:

> Once the process of diversification was well under way, Melanesians cannot but have become conscious that linguistic diversity had advantages as well as disadvantages, in clearly distinguishing friend, acquaintance, trading partner and foe. (Laycock 2001: 171)

The idea that language can be a tool for inclusion and exclusion is central to this book. Language builds human societies, solidarity and cooperation but it also plays a crucial role in the distribution of power and resources within a society and among societies. In non-democratic societies it serves to mark class and caste acquired through non-linguistic means; in democratic societies it is power itself, since authority in a democracy derives ultimately in a leader's ability to *persuade* the electorate to accord that authority.

1.3   Identity and communication

Steiner was focusing on the communicative purpose of language in his essay; Laycock was emphasising the role language plays in group identity. These two functions of language can be complementary. With their ability to communicate, human beings can build communities, which then provide, among other things, a powerful source of identity for their members. If the group with which one needs to communicate is also the group to which one belongs then there is no conflict and these two functions can work symbiotically. This may be the case in small traditional communities which are self-sufficient, do not seek to break their isolation and have no contact imposed by the wider world. It may be the case among those who feel patriotic allegiance to their nation state, speak the national language and do not need to move out of national circles for any of the key activities in their lives.

For many, however, the communicative and identity functions are not fulfilled by one and the same language. Where economic or political pressures cause the speakers of one language group to come into contact with the speakers of another and then to function at whatever level within the latter's linguistic environment, the former group is constrained to some form of linguistic accommodation, either language shift or societal bilingualism. Throughout history, conquest and colonisation have led to situations where one group has imposed language use on another to incorporate them or to exploit them. Indeed Appel and Muysken (1987) argue convincingly that the political history of the world can be retold in terms of language contact and conflict. At the present time the phenomenon of globalisation has meant that increasing numbers of people find themselves needing to communicate or access information outside their primary language group. This is leading to a situation where increasing numbers are functionally bilingual, with their language of group identity not the language that they need in most of their acts of communication.

One can argue that the desire to ally communicative competence and group identity lies at the heart of language planning whether it is conceived as overt policy making or develops informally in the general governance of social groups. Such a desire is central to nation building, where national leaderships encourage linguistic convergence and assimilation within national groups and regulate their permeability to outsiders. Such a desire is key in the campaigns for maintenance and revitalisation of threatened languages, where activists advance the argument that language is a vital component in a group's identity. This search for congruence is also at the heart of the issues that arise when groups come into contact, and linguistic accommodation is necessary. Those who have to acquire the language of the other or a hybrid language of contact will see the relationship of their identity and communicative competence altered.

1.4   The development of LPLP as a discipline

As a subject of academic enquiry LPLP appeared first in the age of nationalism. Language planning was an integral part of nation building and, in the eighteenth and nineteenth centuries, intellectuals in the United States, France, Germany, Italy and to a lesser extent Britain produced a rich literature on the subject. The work of the Germans, Herder and Fichte, was particularly influential in the elaboration of the role of language in ethnic nationalism. Renan in France convincingly reconciled language and the theories of civic nationalism. The ideas of German Romantic nationalism and the theories of French Republicanism inspired a ferment of interest among those who aspired to the status of independent nations. Language was at the heart of nationalism. In the struggle for independence, it could be enlisted to define the ethnicity of the group and, after independence, it could be fostered to provide the statewide community of communication that nationalism seemed to require. Scholarly activists in the many groups seeking to exit from the rule of the British, Ottoman, Russian or Austro-Hungarian and French Empires laboured to codify, standardise and disseminate a single language for the group, which could then be presented as part of the evidence for its claim to a separate polity. After independence was achieved, it was the role of the schools to eradicate dialectal differences and to promote this single 'national' language as the medium that permitted the business of the state and united its citizens in a single community. Naturally, this body of language policy and planning literature is highly committed, and the work should be interpreted in the context of its campaigning and polemic origins and purposes.

After the Second World War, LPLP established itself in the universities as a recognised subject of academic enquiry. The language needs of the new 'nations' founded in the wake of decolonisation brought about renewed interest in the philosophy and strategies of nation building. The concept of 'one language, one people, one state' was, of course, particularly problematic in the postcolonial world. All frontiers are to some extent arbitrary, but those in postcolonial states were often completely arbitrary, following lines of latitude and longitude rather than natural barriers and long-standing tribal borders, and bringing together groups who were rivals for power and had no basis for conceiving themselves as a single people. Among the many and complex problems left by the departing colonial powers were a requirement to solve the logistics of communication in order to govern, an urgent need to weld disparate groups into a homogeneous whole and the necessity to modernise, to provide the minimum needs of the population. Each of these seemed to have a language dimension and to need speedy intervention in terms of LPLP to produce a solution. Joshua Fishman, a key figure in LPLP studies who began his work in this era, thought the fluidity of the situation in the recently decolonised countries made them 'an indispensable and truly intriguing array of field-work locations for a new breed of sociolinguists' (1968: 11). As Fishman predicted, the developing countries were of great appeal to sociolinguists who were 'interested in the transformations of group identity in general and societal (governmental and other) impact on language-related behaviour in particular' (Ricento 2000). In the discipline during this period there was a general belief in the effectiveness of LPLP. Joshua Fishman along with Joan Rubin, Björn Jernudd, Jyotirindra Das Gupta, Wilfred Whiteley and Einar Haugen, other leading LPLP researchers of the era, exhibited a degree of optimism[2] that 'language problems' could be solved. In this they reflected the contemporary tendency to believe in the solubility of problems and in the power of planning.

The second phase in postwar LPLP research was framed by a reaction against too optimistic a belief in progress. In many states newly freed from colonial government, modernisation and democratisation stalled and led to a rejection of Western solutions seen as neo-colonialist. In the West itself, a widespread questioning of the establishment and of hierarchical structures took place. All established traditions seemed to be under attack. In the academic world, research methodologies, in particular, came under scrutiny. Were they the tools of white racists, capitalists or male supremacists promoting worldviews, which confirmed their position? Those who thought they were and who saw themselves as marginalised by the dominant ideologies in the international research community developed methodologies to reflect their own worldview.

New disciplines: Feminist studies, Black studies, Cultural studies, Development studies, appeared on the curriculum. Within the established disciplines, there was a critical analysis of approaches, which led to change. In LPLP, the focus on the linguistic dimension of modernisation and nation building was eclipsed, and many researchers and scholars turned their attention to the social, economic and political effects of language contact, concentrating particularly on issues of advantage/disadvantage, status and access. In accordance with the mood of the times, there was a fundamental review of the terms of the discipline. Many were seen to be ideologically laden. In many ways the questioning of assumptions was helpful, and concepts such as bilingualism, multilingualism and diglossia were made more useful through thorough discussion. There were also excesses, and those who unreflectingly employed terms such as immigrant, minority, mother tongue speaker and linguistic competence were (sometimes unjustly) attacked as racist.

The massive migrations of the second half of the twentieth century had an immense effect on language behaviour as large numbers of speakers of diverse languages came into contact. These migrations[3] seemed to produce different linguistic behaviour from that which had frequently been witnessed in the past. There was a greater desire to maintain the language of the country of origin and full linguistic assimilation was often rejected. A very active group in the LPLP field, Jim Tollefson, Joe Lo Bianco, Michael Clyne, Tom Ricento, Colin Baker, Jim Cummins, David Corson, Nancy Hornberger, Nancy Dorian, Li Wei, was concerned with the issue of bilingualism/multilingualism among migrant groups, particularly in education, and suggested alternatives to the assimilationist policies of the past. Some governments revised their policies, abandoned the strong form of assimilation and began to view the varied origins of their immigrants as a potential resource, and the maintenance of the linguistic and cultural traditions as an opportunity rather than a threat. Canada and Australia, for example, both formulated policies in the direction of a more tolerant pluralism.

The third phase had its origins in the postwar era and the Cold War division of the world. A bipartite globalisation linked states within the two ideological and economic blocs, and flows and exchanges in each led to a growth in the knowledge of Russian in the one camp and English in the other. With the demise of Communism at the beginning of the 1990s, the sole remaining macro socio-political framework was American dominated globalisation which spread, in its economic form at least, to most parts of the world. At the same time, some political power seemed to be leaching away from the nation state to inter- and supranational bodies, as the United Nations, NATO and alliances of Western powers intervened in one polity after another, and international courts ruled that there were limits to state sovereignty. The economic autonomy of the state diminished significantly as the IMF, the WTO and other capitalist interest groups pressed for a global market place without tariffs and quotas. The idea that a national economy could stand alone or be protected was no longer tenable. Culture increasingly crossed frontiers; few national film and music industries continued to produce only for their own domestic market, and the US product penetrated most markets. The revolution in information technology allowed an unprecedented volume of information to circulate at an unprecedented rate, at least among the societies and classes able to afford the hardware. And as this is a phenomenon which is not yet fully realised and whose potential is only just beginning to be tapped, it is difficult to know the extent to which it will affect language behaviour in the long term. One can predict, however, that the effect will be substantial.[4] And it is not only virtual contact that increased, but real contact too. Improved transport communication put the major cities at a few hours flying time from each other and at a price that a growing number could afford.

As globalisation has brought people into association and caused the need for a medium of communication, the general solution has been to use English as a lingua franca. Even where political association, global market and cultural convergence are not dominated by native English speakers, there has still been widespread adoption of English as the medium of contact. From the end of the Cold War, the hegemony of English in political, economic, cultural and technological spheres has remained unchallenged. One strand of LPLP has responded to this with a critique of Anglophone dominance (Tollefson 1991; Pennycook 1994; Canagarajah 1999), termed linguistic 'imperialism' by some (Phillipson 1992). This tradition uses the critical social theories of the Frankfurt School, in particular Jürgen Habermas, and the French cultural theorists, in particular Pierre Bourdieu, as a springboard to understanding and exposing the role of language in power relationships.

Regional supranational groups have arisen alongside globalisation and in a complex relationship with it. They are themselves a form of globalisation in that they relocate power at the supranational level, but their genesis also stems from a desire to build a counterweight to American led global structures. The member states of the European Union, for example, concede some authority to the supranational level of governance in Community institutions and laws, and hope by pooling power to weigh more heavily in global forums.

One of the spillovers of globalisation and regionalisation seems to be a certain renaissance of local political organisation. This was unexpected, although, viewed with hindsight, it can be seen as a logical development, which dovetails with and profits from globalising forces. There has been a reaction among groups who were previously incorporated into nation states and constrained to learn the language of the capital; citizens against their will, many had never accepted the situation as being irreversible. In the era of high nationalism there seemed little that could be done. However, as the nation state came under attack from above and the locus of political power grew more confused, some groups seized the opportunity to demand autonomy or independence from 'below'. The Catalans, the Scots, the Flemings, the Slovaks, the Estonians, are just a few of the European groups who have acquired autonomy or an independent state in Europe in the last two decades. The break up of the USSR and Yugoslavia has derived from similar aspirations, even if, particularly in the case of the constituent states of Yugoslavia, the process has been bloodier.

Outside Europe, there are also many examples of the process. In Indonesia, for example, groups on the periphery of this massive state, such as the Acehnese, are trying to break away. Militants from the Kurdish minorities in Syria, Turkey, Iraq, Iran and the Caucasus want independence and reunification with Kurds in other states.

In LPLP the 'minority' issue has spawned a body of work on linguistic human rights. Together with scholars in the legal field, linguists have been working within UNESCO, the Council of Europe, the Organisation for Security and Co-operation in Europe and the United Nations towards framing agreements on recognition of and respect for linguistic rights for those speakers who want to distinguish themselves from the national communities of communication into which they are incorporated.

Another aspect of LPLP interest in minority issues is the growing commitment to the preservation and restitution of languages with small and diminishing numbers of speakers. This area has always attracted linguists, but in the past the study of small languages was primarily in the cause of linguistic understanding; it was felt that the cataloguing of all human languages would reveal evidence for universal grammar or would illuminate the working of the human linguistic faculty. The focus now has evolved to encompass the rights issue alongside conservation. A number of scholars, including Tove Skutnabb-Kangas, Fernand de Varennes, Nancy Hornberger, Miklós Kontra, have used their sociolinguistic work to support the right of speakers of these languages to continue to use them. The success of such academic militancy will depend very much on the societies themselves. Where members are making the decision to shift to other languages that appear to serve their life chances better, it is unlikely that revitalisation will be successful in the long term. The disappearance of languages is not a new phenomenon, and more languages are thought to have disappeared in the course of history than exist today (Steiner 1998). At a certain point of demography and in a situation of interpenetration and contact, loss may be inevitable unless the speakers have exceptionally high motivation for maintenance.

The field of ecolinguistics[5] has developed from the concern felt for the disappearance of small languages. Ecolinguists are both activists for maintenance and recorders of disappearing ways of making meaning, many of which, they argue convincingly, could open the eyes of the developed world to the mistakes it is making in regard to non-renewable resources and pollution.[6] Scholars in the discipline argue that the diversity of language is self-evidently good and worth preserving, by analogy with the evident need to preserve diversity in the natural world. This is, of course, a metaphorical rather than actual comparison and it is hard to support the case for linguistic diversity purely with the arguments for preserving the diversity of species. Language is behaviour and has no existence outside the speaker, writer, listener or reader who uses it. The speaker can shift language and survive and may incorporate the old ways of perceiving into the new language. Full evidence for the ecolinguistic argument is not yet in place.

1.5   The perspective and outline of the book

In the first part of the introduction I said that I would be working within a very broad of definition LPLP. I see it as the discipline that enquires into all aspects of the language arrangements of all human societies. LPLP can examine how elites use language to define the group, and encourage solidarity and consensus within it. It can explore how language is employed in hegemony, to coerce, to regulate and to maintain boundaries. It can scrutinise how the permeability of language borders is regulated, how contact and incorporation are allowed or discouraged and how language plays a critical role in exclusion and disadvantage. It can investigate whether the group that is denied the opportunity to use its own language in key domains is denied a fundamental human right.

Of course, this view of LPLP makes its possible scope enormous. One book could not cover more than a small proportion of the field. I have chosen what I consider to be three major themes in the field: first, how language has been used as an organising principle and mobilising force in nation building; second, what is happening as the processes of globalisation bring citizens of these nation states into ever greater contact; third, how groups whose languages have been eclipsed in nation building or through unequal competition with the languages of those more politically and economically powerful are engaged in reviving these languages in what could become a postnational era. These three themes seem to be both interconnected and topical. Understanding them seems to me to give a framework[7] for dealing with language policy and language planning at a meso or micro level.

Part I examines nation building. For over two centuries the nation state has been the way groups are organised politically or the way they aspired to be organised. Throughout this period, intellectual and political elites, with very few exceptions, strove to achieve the congruence of cultural nation and political state. There were many reasons for this, but one of the most important was the new and revolutionary societal arrangement of democracy. It was clearly necessary for the community to acquire both the linguistic means and institutional forums for consultation. The nationalist planning that achieved this was often heavy handed: status planning promoted the language of the dominant group(s) to the exclusion of all others; corpus planning prescribed and proscribed; acquisition planning caused cultural and linguistic assimilation. The tension between the very laudable aspiration to include all citizens in the national community of communication and to ensure their participation, and the very destructive means by which nationalist policy makers and planners achieved unity, has never been resolved. The tensions and contradictions inherent in building large communities of communication were as evident in the first wave of nation state building in the early Modern period, as in the second wave that followed the adoption of the principle of self-determination in 1918, as in the third wave after the end of colonialism in Africa and Asia. Despite these evident tensions and contradictions, however, many national elites achieved their goals of convergence and assimilation, and many citizens shifted to the national standard language.

Part II of the book begins with a consideration of how linguistically disparate groups who come into contact manage to communicate. Where there is peaceful coexistence and a desire for the exchange of goods, technologies or ideas, there is the need for a common medium to permit this. Where the contact is coerced, conquerors and colonisers require subject peoples to accommodate, at least enough to fulfil the economic roles that are imposed on them. Groups drawn into the orbit of others, whether willingly or not, develop patterns of social diglossia and personal bilingualism to manage the situation. Speakers from groups that are politically, economically or culturally dominated are under pressure to accept a total shift to the language of the dominant group. Currently globalisation is producing worldwide social diglossia and ever extending personal bilingualism. Whether there will be massive language shift or not is not yet known.

So, at the present time, we are experiencing two phenomena in tandem and in competition. First, the national communities of communication promoted to provide cohesion and solidarity within the state and differentiation among states now coexist with a globalising world where flows of goods, services, money, people, information and culture constantly cross national borders and cause the spread of a global lingua franca. Second, the supremacy of the nation state as a form of political organisation has been challenged by a multitude of supranational, international and transnational institutions and regimes, and many attributes of the sovereign nation state are disappearing. The distinct linguistic mosaic of the national era may be one of them.

Part III explores the recent renaissance of the languages of small groups. I argue that language revitalisation may be a phenomenon which coexists more easily with globalisation than with nation states. Those who were incorporated politically into nation states but were not culturally and linguistically akin to the dominant national group have often been in a perilous position. Where they assimilate, they lose their particularity and distinct identity. If they do not assimilate they are often disadvantaged because of their marginal position and tend to become the object of national suspicion. However, as political and economic power moves from the national capital to the more distant and more dispersed sites of global power, it may be that one effect will be that space opens up for minorities. This is a difficult development to predict in its entirety because we are only at the beginning of the process. However, it is not inconceivable that as power moves away from the national to the supranational level, that some balancing mechanism will return an element of control to the local. In parallel, it is not inconceivable that as intergroup communication happens increasingly in English, speakers from the smaller language groups will move from being bilingual in their own language and the national language to being bilingual in their own language and English. This latter bilingualism might be more stable than the former; certainly there is little likelihood of pressure from the English-speaking centres for wholesale language shift to English monolingualism in the way that national centres pressed for the monopoly of national languages. There is equally little likelihood that a functional lingua franca, such as International English, could replace group languages as the sole medium of identity.

In short, the book looks at the making and unmaking of the nation state and the actual and possible language consequences.

Part I

Community and the Role of National Language

2
From Language Continuum to Linguistic Mosaic: European Language Communities from the Feudal Period to the Age of Nationalism

This first section of the book examines how the world was constructed linguistically before the era of nationalism and then investigates how patterns of language practice and use altered fundamentally in the Modern era, as those engaged in nation building recognised that altering the language landscape was one of the key elements for the successful accomplishment of their ambitions. The focus in this and the next chapter is Europe, because this is the continent where the concept of the nation state first took root. In Chapter 4 there is a consideration of how language has contributed to nation building on other continents.

The ideal of nationalism, that cohesive national groups should strive to have their own state, was and remains immensely problematic as a way of organising groups politically. No European country naturally matches the ideal of congruence between territory and people, except perhaps Iceland, where a small and unified cultural and linguistic group inhabits the clearly defined territory of an island. In all other situations the congruence of nation and state has only been approximated through strategies to assimilate divergent elements.

There have been two quite different ways in which political elites have attempted to achieve such congruence. In the first model, which could be designated *state nation*, the polity came first. The limits of a kingdom were set as a dynasty acquired land through conquest, dowry and inheritance. Thereafter, as the concept of national group developed, rulers set out to mould the populations within their borders to be cohesive on a number of continua, including language. In the second model, a group that saw itself as a cultural and linguistic entity, or at least whose leaders saw it as such, sought to acquire territory, which would be exclusively for the group. This we could term the *nation state*.[1]

However, as we shall see below, when we come to examine these two ways of working towards the congruence of nation and state, they reveal themselves as not very different. The national group is largely a construction, whether it is created from groups that start out as very disparate in linguistic and cultural terms or from groups that are adjacent on a linguistic and cultural continuum.

2.1   Language in Medieval Europe

This point becomes clearer if we start by examining societal organisation before the advent of the state nation and the nation state. In the Medieval period,[2] the linguistic landscape was both more local and more 'international' than today.

The vast majority of Europeans were settled agriculturalists. Singman (1999) and Fossier (1970) estimate that more than 90 per cent of the population were engaged in producing food.[3] These farmers were tied to the land, and lived and died in the villages and hamlets where they were born. This was as true of free peasants and freeholders who were materially bound to the land as it was of serfs and villeins, whose freedom to move from their birthplace[4] or marry out of their group was limited by their legal status.[5] Assigned a place in a rigid social order with little social mobility, members of this class rarely ventured far unless they were forced to go on military campaign by their feudal lord or were among the few to go on pilgrimage.

Living in small groups and travelling little, most would have been monodialectal, or at the most bidialectal, a language repertoire that would have been enough to satisfy their communication needs in their very restricted networks. This seems a reasonable claim although it is difficult to substantiate from contemporary evidence. As Singman notes:

> Although the peasantry constituted the largest part of the medieval population they remain its most elusive component. (Singman 1999: 99)

They were not literate and, unlike other classes such as the clergy and the nobility, have left no record of themselves and their lives.[6] However, I would argue that it is legitimate to extrapolate from the anthropological knowledge of non-literate peasant farming cultures which persist in the present time and draw parallels to build a picture of medieval peasant communities. In addition there is also a legacy of folk stories. From these two sources we can surmise that these were highly contextual societies, where knowledge came through the oral tradition, where communication was face to face, where the main preoccupations of life were food, its consumption and production, sexuality, birth and death (Rietbergen 1998). When the stories of the medieval countryside were not occupied with these matters that conditioned daily life, then the subject matter was usually what the group feared and could not understand in the natural world, and that was legion:

> Indeed fear in the face of this world which presented itself as chaotic and unruly was perhaps a central emotion in this Europe. (Rietbergen 1998: 166)

Because groups tended to be turned in on themselves and to consider all outside the village as strangers and outsiders (Bourin and Durand 1998), a medium for intergroup communication was not a major preoccupation.

However, because of the linguistic development of Europe, the means for communication with most immediate neighbours was available. The majority of Europeans spoke a dialect from one of the major Indo-European phyla: Romance, Germanic, Celtic, Slavic, Baltic. Adjacent dialects along these continua would have been mutually comprehensible from the linguistic perspective. Given the desire to communicate, good will and a little effort by the two parties in the speech act there should have been no block to communication. In the south of Europe, where Muslim groups had settled, dialects of Arabic and Turkish were also present. Islands of Finnish, Hungarian, Greek, Albanian and Basque speakers dovetailed into these dialect continua or existed at their edges.

The major difference between the language landscape at this period and in later centuries was that the dialect continua were not clearly truncated by the political allegiances of speakers. A traveller disembarking in Portugal and trekking across the Iberian peninsula to the Mediterranean coast, then eastward to the Alps, down into the Italian peninsula to the island of Sicily would have found as a general rule that the inhabitants of each village could understand the inhabitants of the next. There were no major breaks in the Romance language continuum although minor changes added up so that groups at a distance could not easily understand each other, and those at the end of the continua were unlikely to recognise the relationship of their two languages at all. Geographical barriers such as mountains and wide rivers caused some dislocation, but it was not disjunction to the same extent as was to develop in later centuries. For example, the difficult passes in some parts of the Pyrenees correlate quite closely with significant dialect divergence (Nordman 1998), but this never approached the scale of linguistic difference that now exists along that border and which derives from the political division between the French and Spanish states.

Of course the ability of adjacent groups to communicate or not was dependent to some extent on whether they chose to recognise similarities or underscore differences, but this depended on social rather than linguistic criteria. In the medieval period, it was only on the cleavages between language groups from different phyla that there were clear linguistic borders, a break in the communication continuum and difference that participants could not *decide* to overcome. On these linguistic frontiers some bilingualism among individuals would have been necessary to ensure exchange and contact.

The narrow linguistic repertoire of the peasant in the village was extended if s/he was among those who went to markets in towns and whose dialectal knowledge had to be multiplex to deal with the population mix of the town. Also awareness of linguistic variety must always have been present in a society which was constantly exposed to the sacred language in church. Nonetheless, the majority of medieval peasants were members of extremely small communities of communication and, from the dismissive portraits painted by other classes and by analogy with isolated communities today, it does seem legitimate to argue that the vast majority of peasants in medieval Europe were monodialectal, in a dialect which differed in only minor ways from its neighbours.

On the other hand, the opposite end of the social spectrum was far from being monolingual. The feudal[7] ruling class was 'European' in that the most powerful families chose marriage partners, gave allegiance and inherited and waged war on a pan-European scale and on a continental stage. At the pinnacle of the hierarchy, marriages and alliances were contracted among a very small number of royal dynasties. The consequent mixing promoted complex family multilingualisms.

A brief history of the Bohemian court in the fourteenth century will illustrate the intricate networks within medieval royal families and the extensive language repertoires they needed to function in all the settings in which they found themselves. The last king of the Premyslide dynasty that ruled in Bohemia died in 1306 with no obvious heir.[8] After a power struggle, the House of Luxembourg secured the throne when Heinrich von Luxembourg arranged the marriage of Jan, his ten-year-old son, to a sister of one of the Premyslide kings. King Jan had little interest in Bohemia, was not often in the country and was killed at the battle of Crécy in 1346, fighting for the French king. His son, Karel, raised at the French court, had, however, learnt to speak Czech from his mother. He chose Prague as his capital city when he became Holy Roman Emperor and set about making it an artistic and intellectual centre. He founded the first university in central Europe in 1348 and initiated a massive building programme to improve the city. Foreign architects and artists were brought to Prague. Polish- and German-speaking scholars were invited to the university. Following the feudal tradition, he secured marriage partners for his children to cement relationships and in the hope of advantageous inheritance. His younger son, Sigismund, was married to a Hungarian princess and eventually inherited both thrones, adding Hungarian to the dynasty's languages. His daughter, Anne, was married to Richard II of England. The consequences of the contacts brought about by this marriage are particularly interesting, since it seems that members of her retinue met John Wyclif and were influenced by his ideas for reforming the Catholic Church. After Richard's murder, Anne and her court returned to Prague, where Wyclif's philosophy circulated, apparently influencing Jan Hus and his followers and contributing to the Hussite Reformation and the wars that it provoked. Other siblings and cousins married and inherited in German-speaking Brandenburg and Sorb-speaking Lusatia.

The fourteenth-century House of Luxembourg was by no means exceptional; similar patterns of marriage, inheritance, alliances, exchange and contact can be traced in any of the major dynasties, and with comparable linguistic and cultural effects. Moreover, it was not only the major dynasties, the Habsburgs, the Capetians, the Spanish and English royal families, who underwent these experiences and were multilingual in consequence, the practice extended to the lesser nobility as well. This is clear from any number of biographies.[9]

In the feudal system, these dynasties were the focus of political organisation. Their subjects were not linked definitively to the polity, and they and the territory in which they dwelt could be passed from the stewardship of one great family to another, depending on how alliances were brokered, marriages contracted or wars won or lost. Loyalty was rather to the individual ruler not to the idea of nation or territory in the political sense (Davis 1988). The feudal system promoted the ideology of the king as God's steward and elaborated a system of personal debt and honour which held alliances together. In a situation where the rule of law was yet to be secured, it was essential to enlist divine assistance. The sacralization of the dynasty meant that loyalty to the king often became synonymous with Christian piety. This process is particularly clear in France where the kings adopted the title, *le roi très chretien*, but most monarchies emphasised the link between service to them and service to God (Greenfeld 1992).

Like the feudal aristocracy, the clergy of the Catholic and Orthodox Churches had patterns of identities and allegiances which transcended the local. However, they were in a very different situation from the perpetually shifting power structures of feudalism. Of course, the upper echelons of the Christian hierarchy were drawn from the aristocracy but when they became part of the church they entered tight hierarchies controlled from Rome or Byzantium and the 'international' networks to which they belonged had a stability deriving from the institutions of the Catholic and Orthodox Churches.

Rietbergen (1998) argues that the Christian church was the heir to the Roman Empire in many respects. It took on its bureaucratic structure, gave a framework for the loosely organised kingdoms of the medieval world and employed its languages as sacred lingua francas. In the west of the continent, Latin was the language of worship and contact. In the east, Greek played the same role as sacred language and lingua franca of the Orthodox Church, until the missionaries who went into Slavic lands decided to use the vernacular. From the tenth century on, Church Slavonic was a further sacred language and lingua franca.

The religious orders were all bilingual to a degree. Even the lowliest priest mastered enough words of the great sacred language to officiate at religious services, although there is anecdotal evidence that some parish priests memorised the liturgy and recited it without full understanding of what they were saying (Nicholas 1999). Despite individual failings, literacy and scholarship were the province of the clergy. It was the 'information caste'

(Rietbergen 1998). Those in western Europe who could read and write would have been educated by monks or priests through the medium of Latin. However, few outside religious orders were literate even among the ruling aristocracy. The tendency for state bureaucrats to be recruited from religious orders until the late Middle Ages illustrates the point (Nicholas 1999). In the east, Greek and Church Slavonic played a similar role.

This brief summary of the linguistic dimension of the European medieval world highlights how that society differed from the society that would follow it in the next era, that of the nation state. First, medieval Europeans saw themselves as members of Christendom,[10] as members of families, as inhabitants of a region or as subjects of a ruler. Since territory changed hands frequently, by succession, marriage or conquest, they did not see themselves as members of polities, as members of states with unchanging borders and a single state language, with stable laws, political traditions and symbols.[11] These attributes of modern states only appeared at the very end of the Medieval period (Davis 1988) and took a very long time to become general. Although a number of scholars of nationalism believe that the Hundred Years War between France and England marks the beginnings of nationalist affiliation in those two countries (cf. Duby 1987 and Hastings 1997), there are also studies that show that national and ethnic identity were not understood or accepted by all, well into the twentieth century. Zaniecki found that peasant groups on the Polish–Ukrainian border classified as ethnically White Ruthenian had no understanding of their classification (cited in Fishman 1971: 6). The concept of national and ethnic identity grew very slowly.

Second, in the medieval context, the modern concept of linguistic minority had no meaning. There was no majority to define minority. Where peoples could be gifted in marriage contracts, inherited by distant princes, won and lost in military struggle, there was little stability and thus little opportunity for feelings of political allegiance to develop towards a single dominant cultural group. Society remained fractured with group membership understood mostly in local terms. There were few societal forces that encouraged linguistic convergence within the dialect continua and many that favoured fragmentation. This is not to say that those who spoke differently might not attract resentment, aggression or persecution, but rather that where communication was highly contextualised and face to face, almost everyone was technically a minority in that they came from a small linguistic group. The existence of a scholarly lingua franca blocked any tendency towards convergence of the vernaculars among the intelligentsia.

Third, because there were no pressures for linguistic homogenisation or convergence, rulers of territory of any size always governed multidialectal if not multilingual populations. The communication problems this occasioned were minimised by a feudal structure that included a second tier of nobility that held the land in trust and swore allegiance to the great dynasties. The sons of this local noble class were educated in the houses of the ruling elites and became the bilinguals who ensured communication from the centre to the periphery. It was such bilinguals who maintained vertical lines of communication in situations where rulers and ruled often had no common medium. This seems of major importance in societies where neither aristocrat nor peasant were literate and all orders had to be given orally and their execution controlled personally, but is rarely commented on in the scholarly literature. Rulers too showed little interest in the linguistic behaviour of their people, and not until the end of the Medieval period was this vertical truncation seen to be problematic.[12] The king's subjects were akin to chattels; they were not citizens who needed to be consulted. Monarchs rarely appealed to the masses for support.[13]

The forces that would aid linguistic convergence did already exist, but as yet had exerted little influence. In future centuries, towns and armies would be linguistic melting pots for the majority. We should beware, however, of overestimating the influence of either in this early period. Towns grew slowly. At the end of the medieval period (fifteenth century) Europe only had some 20 000 towns (Hohenberg 1995). Even as serfs were freed in western Europe, the solidarity and stability of the village were not substantially affected for a considerable period (Bourin and Durand 1998). The demographic pressures building during the twelfth and thirteenth centuries which would have resulted in a move from the monodialectal village to the more linguistically complex town came to an end when plague in the fourteenth century reduced populations by up to a third. After the plague there was land for all and the move to the towns was postponed (Fossier 1970). Even the lesser linguistic influence of trade between town and country was affected by this catastrophe. Records show that although by 1300 a majority of farmers in most parts of western Europe was producing small surpluses for markets, this fell back as both town and countryside were depopulated (Nicholas 1999).

Although the ability of fighting men in multilingual armies to maintain lines of communication must have been an issue, it touched relatively small and shifting numbers. There were no standing armies.[14] Moreover, the feudal chains of command kept different elements of the army relatively separate. The main exception to this appears to be the Crusades where there is some circumstantial evidence that a lingua franca evolved. Lingua Franca, which became the language of contact and trade for the Mediterranean for several centuries, is likely to have played a lingua franca role for the Crusaders. The etymology of its name suggests this, as does its base language, which is from the Romance continuum.

2.2 From language continuum to mosaic of languages

Between the sixteenth and eighteenth centuries the feudal system crumbled in the countries of western Europe. Dynasties fixed the limits of their territory and the integrity of national space was increasingly respected. The idea of national identity also took root, particularly after the Reformation and the Wars of Religion in the sixteenth century concluded with the agreement that there should be national homogeneity. As the belief in the divine right of kings was challenged, a new conception of the *state* appeared, deriving in part from the Classical model but developing far beyond that base. Economic expansion and commercial integration underpinned the institutional expansion of the state (Nicholas 1999).

In the new concept of political power, legitimacy derived from the people. Given that society at the beginning of the Modern period was fractured linguistically and lacked any cohesive national identity, these legitimating peoples had yet to evolve as distinct entities. Nationalist scholars would dispute this, arguing that nations are primordial and exist in latent forms even where their distinctiveness is not widely recognised. Modernist scholars of nationalism, on the other hand, would see in centralisation, urbanisation, industrialisation and education the processes through which disparate groups were welded into cohesive nations.[15]

Understanding the nation state, its genesis and development is essential if one wants to understand the linguistic landscape of present day Europe, how it came about and why majorities in all populations have developed deep attachments to the standardised national languages introduced and disseminated by the state.

2.2.1 The state nations

2.2.1.1 *Borders, religious unity and print capitalism*

The rulers in Spain, Portugal, France, Britain, Sweden, Denmark and the Netherlands were the first to begin to fix the boundaries of their kingdoms and to constitute themselves as state nations (Hroch 1985).[16] It was a long process, which was not fully completed until the end of the Second World War,[17] but the general shape of the countries was set at this time. The territory of the Spanish monarchy increased as the Reconquista was accomplished. The border to the south became the sea in 1492 when the Muslim state of Granada fell. The border between Spain and Portugal was established during the campaigns of the twelfth century.[18] The French monarchy established its western frontier on the Atlantic seaboard at the end of the Hundred Years War (1337–1453).[19] The Treaty of the Pyrenees (1659), which settled hostilities begun during the Thirty Years War, drew the border between France and Spain. The northern and eastern frontiers of France took more time to establish definitively.[20] The Treaty of Teusina in 1595 established the border between Russia and Sweden–Finland and the Stromstad Treaty of 1751 defined the Norwegian–Swedish border. The border between Denmark and Sweden was drawn following the break up of the Nordic Union in 1520 and then redrawn in 1660 after a series of wars, to follow the Sound. These treaty agreements lasted because they were made at the period when the belief began to spread that peoples should not be transferred from master to master like herds of cattle without consulting their wishes or considering their interests (Rousseau 1762).

At the time of drawing these political borders, however, this philosophy had not gained general acceptance and they were decided by high politics with no thought of keeping cultural and linguistic communities together and many groups were split by arbitrary frontiers.[21] That most of those living on the state periphery came to accept a distant capital as the focus of their loyalty and the source of their identity is an indicator of how potent the concept of nationalism was to become and how successful nation building strategies were in bringing disparate groups together into national communities. Once the boundaries of the state were reasonably stable, this process of homogenising the peoples living on the territory of the state began.

Religious unity was the first preoccupation of the European leaders. This was of course no new departure. Medieval monarchs had always lent support to Christian supremacy and exclusivity in Europe with a long history of killing, expelling or forcibly converting other religious groups, such as Jews, Cathars, Hussites and Muslims.[22] What was new was that the violence was among Christians, as the Protestant Reformation caused a schism in western Christianity. The Peace of Augsburg (1555) introduced the rule *Cuius regio eius religio*, which stipulated that subjects and their king should share the same religion. Whichever religion people chose to follow decided the kingdom in which they could reside. Or conversely, if they wished to live in a certain country, they were constrained to follow the version of Christianity espoused by that monarchy. A contemporary French commentator shows how religion was the main locus of loyalty, taking precedence over nascent national allegiance:

> I would rather be a Spaniard so that I can practise my religion and ensure my salvation, than remain a Frenchman and condemn my soul to hell. (*Dialogue du Maheustre et Manant*, cited in Lebrun 1980: 94. Author's translation)

National identity would develop in part from this unity of populations in religious practice.

The Treaty of Westphalia (1648), which marked the end of the Thirty Years War, reaffirmed the principle of religious unity within the kingdom. It also, and perhaps just as importantly, introduced the new political philosophy that there should be mutual recognition of integrity and autonomy among states.[23] This enshrined the move away from feudalism and shifting alliances in an international agreement. The boundaries of the state were increasingly accepted as fixed and inviolable and, thenceforth, for the next three centuries, European politics was largely concerned with maintaining the balance of power on the continent.[24] Under the principles of integrity and sovereignty no external authority would interfere within state boundaries. This had many effects, not least the severing of links along the dialect continua, as groups were split by borders and discouraged from maintaining links in the interests of building national solidarity.

The religious conflicts of the sixteenth and seventeenth centuries had a marked effect on the standardisation and spread of the vernacular languages. The Protestant challenge to the Catholic Church was circulated in religious treatises and tracts. In the early period these were written in Latin in the tradition of all religious scholarly texts, but widespread interest in and demand for access to the ideas meant that key texts were soon translated into the vernaculars. Martin Luther's theses were rendered into German and circulated throughout the German-speaking world in a matter of weeks of his nailing them to the church door in Wittenberg (Febvre and Martin 1976). Jean Calvin originally wrote *Institutes of the Christian Religion* (1536) in Latin. However, the book was very swiftly translated into French (1541) and it was in this version that it circulated in France and had widespread influence. It was clear that it was not simply the clergy and its intellectual challengers who were reading these works. A growing lay readership, which included women and the merchant class who had not traditionally learnt Latin, was engaging with religious literature. For works to be accessible to this new type of reader they had to be translated into the vernacular. And as one of the key rights claimed by Protestants was the right to dispense with the priest intermediary between them and their God, there was a growing desire for direct access to the Bible in translation.

The introduction of printing coincided with this period of intense religious interest and fervour and Protestantism, always fundamentally on the offensive, made good use of the burgeoning vernacular print market to spread its message (Anderson 1983). For the first time in Europe there was a mass readership and a popular literature with mass appeal (Febvre and Martin 1976). This had profound linguistic spillover. Printers used the language of the urban centres in which they were based, centres which in the state nations were those of court and monarch. Since printers were primarily commercially motivated and concerned to find large markets for single products, they were not predisposed to change language variety to accommodate dialectal difference. Thus they became promoters of standardisation of vernacular languages, principally because it gave them bigger markets than the splintered linguistic landscape of the dialect continua (Anderson 1983). Given that, before this period, few would have had the option of owning an expensive handcopied book, accommodating to the language variety used by the printers seemed a small concession to make to own an affordable copy of important religious texts. Thus works in the language of the capital, particularly the Bible and other religious writing, were sold outside the geographical heartland of the dominant language variety, and helped to spread this dialect of the language.[25] The written form of the language of the monarchy and the capital were accepted throughout the kingdom and reached many social levels as literacy grew through Bible study.[26]

2.2.1.2   Absolutism, centralisation and the language of state bureaucracies

The wars, rebellions and repressions caused by religious dissension affected society in a profound way. The rise of Absolutism can be seen as both ruled and rulers' reaction to the violent upheavals of the period: the monarchs' desire to regain control led them to claim unrestrained freedom of power, granted by God; their subjects fearful of anarchy mostly accepted this claim. This was a basic change in patterns of governance. Feudalism had depended on a monarch's ability to retain the support of the great nobles to remain in power. Absolutism meant the monarch ruled alone. The first theorist of Absolutism is generally held to be a Frenchman, Jean Bodin. In his 1577 text, *Six Books on the Commonwealth*, he argues that the monarchy's absolute, perpetual and indivisible power is held directly from God and is unbounded and unrestrained. Another Frenchman, Jacques Bossuet, further elaborated the theory of the divine right of kings, supporting it with evidence from the Bible (Bossuet 1709). Much had prepared the way for populations to accept the sacred nature of the monarchy. The medieval sacralization of the king and his bloodline was increasingly expressed in royal iconography as, from the mid-sixteenth century on, monarchs commissioned statues and paintings of themselves as deities.

From this period the authority of the monarch is increasingly presented to the population as spectacle and a discourse develops where loyalty to the monarch and the dynasty begins to be expressed as patriotism[27] (Strong 1973; Greenfeld 1992). The country personified in the king appears increasingly as a focus for identity.[28] For those sovereigns of state nations engaged in colonialism there was a new and important source of revenue (Braudel 1972). The wealth, which the voyages of discovery brought back to Europe, allowed royalty to fund pomp and ceremony to impress the people, to construct lavish palaces as monuments to its own greatness and to support artistic endeavour for its greater glory. The prestige of the monarchies seemed to fan patriotism, as populations enjoyed the pleasures of being part of successful polities where there was growing wealth and power. Breuilly (1982) has argued that such growth is one of the prime reasons for the growth of nationalism, and that this relationship is discernible even when the state was still essentially the absolute monarch.

Different dynasties had different degrees of success in persuading their subjects of their divine right to rule and Absolutism was longer lasting in some settings than others, but all the Absolutist monarchs encouraged centralisation and set up bureaucracies that reported directly to the monarch. This was the case in England under the Tudors and in France from François I to Louis XIV.[29] The growth of the state bureaucracy had a profound social effect because these societies acquired the mechanism for limited social mobility for the first time in centuries. Kings did not recruit their bureaucrats from the old feudal aristocracies whose powers they wished to limit. They preferred able members of the new professional middle classes or of marginalised elites in conquered or annexed territory. With many from outside the old feudal aristocracies rising to be administrators of royal power, larger sections of the population were drawn into public life (Seton-Watson 1977).

Bureaucracies became one of the chief instruments of administrative centralisation and another powerful agent of linguistic unification within the state as bureaucrats increasingly employed the language of the capital and the monarchy in place of regional vernaculars or Latin (Anderson 1983). In France, use of Latin in commercial and state business had begun to diminish in the fifteenth century even before the advent of printing. At the beginning of this shift, there had been some use of the local language (one of the dialects of the Langue d'oil (Picard, Normand Burgundian etc.) or one of the dialects of the Langue d'oc (Provençal, Languedocien, Gascon etc.) in place of Latin in legal documents, legal proceedings and commercial correspondence. However, the French king, François I, wanted to ensure that if Latin was being replaced by the vernacular, it was replaced by the vernacular that represented his power. The Edict of Villers-Cotterêts (1539) ordered that all judicial and administrative documents be written 'in the maternal French language and no other'.

In Britain, the use of English was imposed in the law courts in Celtic Wales at much the same time. Those who could not speak English could not hold public office. The Act of Union (1536) stated:

> that all justices, Commissioners, sheriffs, coroners, escheators, stewards and their Lieutenants, and all other officers and ministers of the law, shall proclaim and keep the sessions, courts … in the English tongue, and all oaths of officers, juries and inquests and all other affidavits … to be given and done in the English tongue; and also that from henceforth no person or persons that use the Welsh speech or language shall have or enjoy any manner office or fees within this realm of England, Wales or other the King's Dominion upon pain of forfeiting the same offices or fees, unless he or they use and exercise the English speech or language. (Rees 1937: Appendix)

This clerks' language did not permeate deep into the rural heartlands of western European states. Those who worked the land were still in the linguistic situation that had pertained for centuries. The difference in the linguistic landscape came from a growing, largely urban, middle class that was increasingly fluent and literate in the language of the capital and the court.

2.2.1.3 *Revolution, democracy and the need for consultation*

Absolutism was too extreme not to cause rejection and reaction. Where the absolutist monarch slid towards the arbitrary exercise of power, there was growing support for the rule of law to be sacrosanct and to take priority over the right of kings to such power. Once the divine right of the sovereign to rule had been disputed, it was necessary to find an authority to put in its place. In France, Montesquieu (1748/1961) and Voltaire (1734) presented the idea that the people should be a brake on the monarch's will. Rousseau (1762/1972) a French-speaking Swiss, developed the idea of the will of the people (*la volonté générale*), which was supposed to transcend individual egotisms and secure what was best for society in general. In Britain, Locke (1679/1967) developed the idea that consent of the governed should be an integral part of government. The English, American and French revolutions embodied these ideas in action. The legitimacy of any claim that a government had the right to rule independent of the will of its subjects had been challenged (Hechter 2000).

For our study, the growing importance of the 'people' is significant. Feudal and Absolute monarchs do not need a linguistically cohesive population; decrees and orders can be handed down from on high to subjects through the bureaucracy and where there is linguistic difference a small group of bilingual bureaucrats can ensure communication. Linguistic diversity is a different matter in any polity when the people move from being subjects to being citizens. Where the people are to be consulted on matters of state and where a consensus has to be achieved on the direction these matters will take, there have to be two-way channels of communication. Democracy and nationalism appear to be in a dialectic relation (Fishman 1971) because nationalism can help create the cohesive community of communication that democracy seems to need.[30]

Communication was a major problem confronting the French revolutionaries in 1789. How were they going to inform the people in whose name they were taking power? How, without the channels to reason and persuade, could they carry the people with them? In the first phase, the revolutionary message was spread in the various languages and dialects of France. The need to understand the extent of the linguistic diversity with which they were dealing led to a language census carried out by the Abbé Grégoire in 1790. This revealed that only three million French spoke French as their first language. A further three million had some competence in the language and the rest of the 25 million population spoke some other language and had minimal or no competence in French (Grégoire 1794).[31] When the Jacobins emerged as the victors in the struggle between centralists and federalists, it was clear that tolerance of diversity, including linguistic diversity would be halted. From this time on proclamations from the centre to the provinces were in French and it became a patriotic and revolutionary duty for citizens to learn and use French:

> In a democracy each citizen must keep a watch on the government. To carry out such a role one must know one's government and above all one must understand the language it uses. (Barère 1792. Author's translation)

The other languages of France were demonised and linked to anti-revolutionary forces and factions:

> Breton is the language of federalism and superstition; German is the language of those who hate France and have abandoned it; Italian is the language of those who oppose the revolution; Basque is the language of fanaticism. We must destroy these harmful instruments, which lead the people into error. (Barère 1792. Author's translation)

The French government has maintained its support for monolingual public life and much of its nation building has set out to achieve this (e.g. mass education). It has also come about as a side effect of other measures (e.g. general conscription). The argument for monolingualism has always been that only a single language can foster the solidarity and fraternity needed for a welfare state and that only a single language can ensure the equality of opportunity needed for a meritocracy.[32]

2.2.2 The nation states

2.2.2.1 *The myth of the past*

The concept of the sovereign people spread in the wake of the English, French and American revolutions and in the aftermath of Napoleon's challenge to the old dynasties. The influence was evident in both emulation and reaction. In the Greek struggle for independence from the Ottoman Empire, French revolutionary ideas inspired several leaders including Adamantios Korais (1748–1833) and Rhigas Pheraios (1760–98), and links between these men and France were strong. In the German-speaking world, on the other hand, there was a growing interest in the idea of the congruence of state and nation, but a growing rejection of the French model. Klopstock (1724–1803), Voss (1751–1826), Herder (1744–1803), Hamann (1730–88), Fichte (1762–1814) and the von Humboldt brothers (Alexander 1769–1859 and Wilhelm 1767–1835) questioned the rational humanism and the universalism promoted by the theorists of the Enlightenment. They were less interested in the French, American and British philosophers' use of the concept of sovereign people as a limit to the power of the monarch and state apparatus and more attracted to the idea of the people as a mystical and primordial blood brotherhood that had a destiny to be together in a polity.[33] The theory of ethnic nationalism as it was developed by Herder[34] and those who followed him held that humanity was divided into national groups, that these nations were differentiated in profound ways and that their distinctiveness dated from the beginning of time. Each culture was moulded by the particular experience of the group. The language spoken by the group caused it to conceptualise the world in a certain way and a way that was different from speakers of other languages. The biology of the group made it unique. Ethnic nationalists are thus essentialists, believing that nations are a natural phenomenon whose linguistic and cultural cohesion derive from a common past and whose destiny is to be a single political unit.[35] Ethnic nationalism has proved to be a very powerful doctrine and this belief that each nation has an explicit and peculiar character (Breuilly 1982) has been adopted in many struggles for political autonomy since the work of these German philosophers promoted the concept.

Not unexpectedly Germany was one of the first sites of nationalist mobilisation based on such a belief in primordial unity. The discourse elaborated among German-speaking intellectuals, citing commonality of history and descent, language and culture, as evidence of the existence of a German nation, was adopted by German politicians as the rationale for the creation of a German nation state. This discourse had to be highly selective. There was little common history or culture from which to draw. Prior to the nineteenth century, the area which was to become Germany was a collection of over 350 small states and cities, with no internal cohesion. Customs barriers, the lack of a common currency and a common system of weights and measures divided these states in the economic sphere. Geographical variation made their agricultural practices extremely diverse. An acceptance of *Mehrstaatlichkeit*, multi-state particularism, divided them politically. Culturally the German-speaking peoples were split by religious difference; the north was mainly Protestant, the south Catholic. Commonality which marked them as a distinct group was thus difficult to find. The nation builders returned to a distant and mythical time of unity during the *Völkerwanderung*, when the Teutonic tribes moved west to colonise and conquer (Behn 1963) and where, a cynic might note, discrepancies in the construct were not so apparent.

2.2.2.2 Language – a problematic marker of national boundaries

The only incontrovertible commonality seemed to be language, but this too posed problems as a criterion in any predefinition of the nation. The Germanic dialect continuum is much more extensive than the groups involved in German unification. On the north-western and south-western reaches, the reasons why the Dutch, the Alsatians and the Swiss were not candidates for incorporation were political not linguistic. To the south, the German-speaking Austrians posed a problem. The inclusion or exclusion of Austria, debated at length in the constitutional assembly held in Frankfurt in 1848, was eventually decided by Prussian military victory over Austria in 1866. The Prussians excluded the southerners from the new German state. The complex reasons for this were, in part, because the Prussians wanted no rivals. Without the Habsburgs, they would be the unchallenged leaders. In part, it was a matter of ethnic-cultural identification. The Austrians would have brought the Hungarian and Slavic peoples of the Habsburg Empire into the new state and diluted its teutonicity. Thus, cultural and linguistic considerations were overridden in the exclusion of Austria, but they remained, nonetheless, a key element in German unification, and, although language may not have been sufficient reason for a group to be included, it was held to be a prerequisite.

In addition to the problems of defining the external boundaries of the ethnic group, there were also problems of internal linguistic cohesion. There was great linguistic variety within the Mid- and East Germanic dialect continuum that made up the proposed German state, arguably as great as that in the North Germanic dialect continuum that crosses Sweden, Norway and Denmark. However, in one respect there was an element of unity. Speakers on this continuum who were literate possessed competence in Hochdeutsch,[36] the common literary standard, promoted by the forces of print capitalism and religious democratisation discussed above. Thus there was internal linguistic cohesion, at least in written language. Hochdeutsch was, of course, not the exclusive preserve of the German nation state. The Swiss and Alsatians also acquired literacy in it. Hochdeutsch acted as an internal unifier but not as a boundary setter.

A close study of German unification illustrates that, for the ethnic nation state as for the state nation, the boundaries of group identity are ultimately indeterminate until they are located in institutions (Schlesinger 1986), and so, despite the rhetoric, until the political elite begins the process of nation building, the ethnic nation is a fiction to a large extent.

The process of Italian unification which was happening concurrently and with much of the same philosophical underpinning confirms this. Here too political imperatives could readily override cultural and linguistic identity.[37] The remark attributed to Massimo d'Azeglio, the Piedmontese politician, at the time of Italian unification, 'We have made Italy now we must make Italians', suggests that nationalists themselves knew that primordialist nationalist theory, which claimed the existence of a national group, prior to its political expression, was a construct. There may have been some feeling of identity within the Italian-speaking world, but this had largely been a phenomenon restricted to a narrow intellectual elite.

2.2.2.3   *The spread of the ethnic nationalist model*

The idea that each national group is unique and needs its own state to be truly authentic was taken up and used throughout the nineteenth and twentieth centuries by numerous groups particularly within the Ottoman, Russian and Austro–Hungarian Empires. Nationalists campaigned for recognition of 'nationhood' and for their own sovereign state on their own inalienable territory (Taylor 1989), presenting the process as natural (Smith 1995).

They adopted and adapted the argument that one was born into a nation as one was born into a family, that each nation had natural unchanging frontiers, a special origin and a peculiar character, mission and destiny (Smith 1992, 1995). Greek independence, achieved in 1830, had fuelled this ideology since the claim for Greek national identity was particularly suitable for being presented in this way. Contemporary reality was actually a fractured group that had not been distinct for centuries. To mobilise this group it was necessary to link it with a time in the past when it could be seen as a cultural if not a political whole. Archeologists and linguists played major roles in reminding Greeks of their Classical Golden Age. The promotion of Katharevousa, a form of Greek purged of borrowings from the Ottoman period and closer to Classical Greek than the Demotic generally spoken was one strand of the process.

In the early phases of all nineteenth-century national movements the middle-class intelligentsia had the function of reminding the group of its origins. They did this in many ways: by collecting and publishing the folk songs and stories of the group, writing histories in which the group was presented as a single unit, promoting group heroes and elaborating group symbols such as anthems and flags. The nations of nineteenth-century Europe were to a greater or lesser extent the ideologised products of educated elites who moulded their populations to fit the criteria for national self-determination (Seton-Watson 1977).

Nowhere was the nation builder's task more pressing than in the case of language. Prior to mass education there could only have been the 'local dialectal idiosyncracy' (Gellner 1983) discussed above. This lack of linguistic cohesion within the dialect continua was felt to be an impediment. If, as Nairn (1977) suggests, the intellectual class had to 'invite the masses into history', then they had to send the invitation card in a language that the people could understand.[38] Where there was no national language community this message would have to be in the different languages of the state.[39] Such recognition of pluralism was at odds with nationalist claims to be language communities with the distinctive and unique ways of thinking that Herder had suggested. An early objective in the nationalist project was thus to achieve linguistic convergence within the group and to differentiate the national language from all allied dialects on the continuum. Nationalist campaigns therefore included language planning both pre- and post-independence. A codified form establishing a standard for the dialects spoken on the territory claimed as national created a national community of communication. A written form and literary tradition contributed to national standing and pride, as well as providing a medium for government and administration. Linguists and writers played a key role in the elaboration of cultural and linguistic traditions that contributed to establishing a separate and unified national group and this is discussed in more depth in Chapter 3.

2.3 The First World War and national self-determination

The Westphalian system, in which the balance of power was carefully maintained through strategic alliances and the sovereignty of states respected, worked well for a long period in Europe, allowing states to avoid major conflict. This ended with the First World War. This war was the war of high nationalism. The events that triggered it were part of the fight for national autonomy in the Balkans. The rivalries that pulled so many into the conflict were fuelled by national ambitions. In its final resolution, the Treaties of Versailles, Sèvres and Trianon, national self-determination was the paradigm for the peace settlement. The American president, Woodrow Wilson, was sympathetic to the doctrine of self-determination. Groups should decide themselves on whether they wished to be independent or part of a larger polity. Thus the claims of many of the small nations of Europe were treated sympathetically. This acceptance of the ethnic-nationalist argument was not disinterested. It gave a better reason for dismantling the Ottoman and Austro-Hungarian Empires than victors' revenge. Groups such as the Irish and Catalans who were trying to secede from the old state nations were not offered the same opportunities.

The principle of self-determination was not adhered to strictly in 1919 since in the era of high nationalism, it was felt that nation states had to be a certain size in order to survive as economic units, in order to be able to raise armies large enough to ensure their defence, and in order to be able to weigh politically in the community of nations. Thus, although ethnic nationalism underpinned the creation of the post First World War states in Europe, the criteria of 'a single language', 'a single culture', 'a single history' and 'a single belief system' were often interpreted very generously or disregarded entirely.[40]

This explains why disparate groups such as the Czechs and Slovaks were joined together in states that were supposedly being constituted on the ethnic nation model. It was only to achieve necessary critical mass that the state of Czechoslovakia contained both Czechs and Slovaks. Their histories had been very different. Protestantism, industrialisation and influence from the German world were part of the Czech heritage; the Slovaks were a far more pastoral group, whose Catholicism had been undiluted and who had long been a cultural and political backwater of the Austro-Hungarian Empire. The only item on the list of criteria for the ethnic nation that they really had in common was the possession of languages very close on the Slavic dialect continuum.[41] It also explains why Slovenians, Croats, Serbs, Macedonians, Montenegrins and others were combined in Yugoslavia.

2.4 The modern nation state system in Europe up to 1945[42]

The map of Europe thus became a chequer-board in the nineteenth and twentieth centuries, a mosaic of states. Frontiers became real barriers, and people were separated from each other by borders that became increasingly difficult to cross. Each state had its own national market, labour force, mass culture, army and system of values. This separation was not only physical but psychological too, as nationalism became the dominant ideology. Patterns of identity had changed. At the height of the nationalist period people saw their main loyalty as being to the nation, that is, to a much more extensive group than had been the case in the past. These developments were intimately linked with changing patterns of language use which can be seen as being both cause and effect within the nation-building process.

2.4.1 Economic solidarity, labour mobility and the changing nature of work

National economies were isolated by tariffs, quotas and other forms of protectionism. Customs and border controls made contact between nation states physically difficult and expensive, while links within the state were promoted through the abolition of internal controls and tolls. Economic behaviour that was competitive internationally and cooperative intranationally was encouraged. In times of economic crisis problems would routinely be exported in what came to be known as 'beggar thy neighbour' policies.[43] It became natural to show preference to fellow nationals to the extent that buying their products came to be seen as a patriotic duty. In linguistic terms these policies had greatest effect along the frontiers.[44] Producers no longer sent to the nearest market if it was across the border and trans-frontier communication was reduced.

This impermeability of frontiers also affected labour mobility. Recruitment of labour to the industrialising areas of Europe was first and foremost from within the state and migration across borders slackened even where geographically this would have been more logical. For example, those southern French who had traditionally gone south to Catalonia in years of bad harvest started to make the longer journey north to Paris and the industrial areas of northern France. There were numerous reasons. National transport infrastructure made the journey to the capital easier, and often neglected routes across frontiers. For example, train tracks in neighbouring countries could be different gauges. Education in the national languages began to break down the mutual comprehensibility that speakers in adjacent areas had enjoyed. For example, the southern French, speaking Languedocian and Gascon, had been able to communicate in Catalan-speaking areas. There had been no serious language barrier to finding work. This was no longer true as the shift to French gathered pace.

Industrialisation was another factor in national economic consolidation and also an important agent in linguistic unification. Gellner (1983) argues that industrialisation requires an education system where there can be generic training for all to ensure the basic level of skills and the flexibility that is required for a workforce in a technologically advanced and evolving situation. This is too expensive an undertaking for any group but the state. Education thus becomes the business of the state and a state institution. Like other state institutions, parliament, courts, and so on, its medium is the national language.

Industrialisation also promotes linguistic convergence because industries attract the workforce they need from a large national catchment area and the resulting towns become linguistic melting pots. The shift to the national spoken standard is much more likely in this urban setting where there is greater need to communicate in multilingual or multidialectal groups than was the case in the stability of country networks.

2.4.2   Political solidarity, welfare and war

The growth of respect for state sovereignty made contact across boundaries politically difficult and interference within the affairs of one's neighbour unthinkable. The growth of nationalist ideology made contact psychologically difficult. The citizens or subjects in the adjacent state were constituted as the Other. The total wars of the age were possible because of nationalism and they of course fostered it; the foreign national was constituted as Enemy. Clausewitz (1780–1831), the German military historian and tactician, understood the importance of nationalism in warfare at an early stage (1830/1997). The feeling of national identity that developed within the nation states made it possible to mobilise the whole nation in its defence in a way that he did not believe had happened since the Teutonic invasion of the Roman Empire. More recent writers on nationalism have wondered how nationalism became so powerful a doctrine that it could be used to justify great sacrifice, even that of one's life (Hechter 2000). The ethno-nationalist belief that one is part of an organism dating from time immemorial and stretching into the future may explain the citizen's acceptance of sacrifice for the collective. There may also be a modernist explanation. Economic prosperity, life chances and well-being are all seen to be bound to the survival of the state, which promotes the citizen's interests. As the state provides order, justice, social welfare and defence (Hechter 2000), it may be worth individual sacrifice to ensure its survival.

For whatever reasons nationalism proved such a potent mobilising force, the linguistic outcome is clear. Ideologically, use of the national language became a patriotic act, and the process was circular; as the linguistic community developed so too did the feeling of belonging, which was necessary for patriotism. Practically, defence of the nation gave the reason and the opportunity to use the national standard rather than the local dialect. As general conscription of all young men took them away from their primary language groups and mixed them together, a common medium was necessary. The experience of conscription built on the apprenticeship in the national language that had begun in the national education system.

Times of crisis underlined both the practical and the psychological need for a community of communication. In war, linguistic convergence was very marked as both issues of identity and the need for clear channels of communication were of utmost interest and importance. Letters from French soldiers written during the trench warfare of the First World War show a rapid shift to French. In the general population, the surge of patriotism from that era was a key step in the Francisation of the French (Baconnier *et al.* 1985).

In times of peace, political solidarity was expressed in the development of social welfare. Citizens accepted that they would be taxed in order to support co-nationals. This too was easier in a community of communication where, although one would never see all one's fellow citizens, one knew that should one meet there would be the possibility of communicating with them.

2.4.3   Literacy, mass media and the feeling of community

Benedict Anderson (1983) has suggested that the nation can be defined as an imagined community:

> because the members of even the smallest nation will never know most of their fellow members, meet them or even hear of them, yet in the mind of each lives the image of their communion. (1983: 15)

He argued that certain acts allow individuals to conceive of themselves as members of a nation even though they never know or meet the rest of the group in face-to-face interaction. Reading the daily national newspaper was one such means of constructing national consciousness. This daily habit allowed the members of a society to come together in a virtual community. Individuals knew that their own reading was part of a mass national activity, taking place separately but concurrently, a knowledge that Anderson termed 'calendrical consciousness'. Where national newspaper reading spread throughout the population, as it did in the United Kingdom, a new kind of press developed. Before the 1880s the British press had been largely Liberal, provincial, rational, middle class and intellectual. With the arrival of the yellow press in the last two decades of the nineteenth century this tradition was sidelined (Cannadine 1983). The new papers, the *Daily Mail*, the *Sketch*, the *Mirror*, the *Daily Express*, were sensationalist, nationalist and popular. They were agents of nation building in a number of ways: they fostered nationalist sentiment, they treated their readers as a cohesive group and they promoted the standard language. Their growing readership meant a large proportion of the population were habitually exposed to the written standard and had regular daily practice in it. The nationalist philosophy of the papers reinforced acceptance of borders and the concept of insiders and outsiders, as journalists presented the world as either national or foreign, and refracted world events into the specific world of vernacular readers (Anderson 1983). National radio stations had the same effect in that co-nationals listened 'together' to news bulletins that were presented in a national context and from a national perspective. Broadcasting had further important linguistic consequences in that it encouraged convergence of the spoken language or, where individuals resisted losing their distinct accent, at least ensured that the standard pronunciation of the state language was familiar and understood. After 1945, television would continue the process.

Anderson (1983) also argued that the novel whose plot unfolds in a 'recognised common space' was another means of fostering a sense of belonging to a national group. Fiction too promoted the written standard language. Where the writer presented the readers with biographies of fellow members of their society, readers were alerted to the parallel lives of other citizens coexisting with them in time and in national space.[45]

Eric Hobsbawm (1983) has shown how governments made conscious efforts to promote feelings of community and solidarity through the organisation of national celebrations, the elaboration of national ritual and national symbols. He demonstrated how very few nationalist 'traditions' have long pedigrees and suggested that they were introduced consciously to achieve social stability and political loyalty in a period of rapid political change and increasing political democracy. Pomp and ceremony for state occasions, imposing public buildings and proliferation of statues, flags and national symbolic representation had become more complex since the Absolutist period. Their main purpose was still the promotion of patriotism but this was now allied to a concern for vertical integration:

> Glory and greatness, wealth and power, could be symbolically shared by the poor through royalty and its rituals. (Hobsbawm 1983: 283)

The aim was no longer simply to dazzle and persuade the ruled of the rulers' relation to the divinity (Cannadine 1983). In the nationalist period, public ceremonies, parades and ritualised mass gatherings were to encourage the national public to believe in the essential cohesion of the group, its common past and its common destiny. The statuary of the town and village, the allegorically decorated and beflagged public buildings and the proliferation of national symbols employed by the post office, transport and other nationally owned utilities were to demonstrate the rootedness of national heritage and the stability of national institutions. Billig (1995) has demonstrated the importance of the daily experience of the semiotics of nationalism, to its continued vigour as an ideology. He terms this 'banal nationalism'.

2.5   Conclusions

If we compare this description of society in the heyday of the European nation state before the Second World War with the organisation of medieval Europe described earlier in the chapter, it is clear that the tendency to horizontal, Europe-wide integration of the ruling class and the clergy gave way to vertical national integration of all those within national borders. Class divisions certainly remained but were sometimes overcome or ignored to promote solidarity in the national interest. Language played a key role in this process. The elaboration and spread of a national language provided the community of communication necessary for the functioning of the nation state and was an important element in the construction of national identity. As this chapter has shown, linguistic unification was both planned and unplanned, often occurring as the side effect of other nation-building strategies or simply as a spin-off of economic or political actions, not conceived primarily to contribute to linguistic convergence. However, whether consciously willed or not, the achievement of a community of communication was central to all nationalism and nation building. The next chapter investigates the role overt language planning and policy played in nation building and examines the immense contradictions inherent in the idea of a single standard language.

3

Language Planning in State Nations and Nation States

The history of the politics of nation state building reveals how the conscious promotion of language convergence was part of the development of the nation state. The national language takes on a number of important roles in the nation building process. First, it has a utilitarian role. It becomes the medium of communication which permits the nation to function efficiently in its political and economic life, particularly as democracy develops. The citizens of the nation state are trained in their national education systems to be both able and willing to assent to this; they possess the language because they are taught through the language, and it is hoped that self-interest will persuade them to accept dialect convergence, or even language shift, since it is the means of social promotion and necessary for employment in the mainstream. Second, a unified language is held to promote cohesion, allowing the nation to develop a shared culture. There is a symbolic dimension to this: to know and to use the national language is part of the definition of belonging to the nation; to speak the language is a badge of inclusion; to refuse to know the language is to refuse the community and is seen as schismatic and unpatriotic. Third, if it can be demonstrated that the language of the group is both different from that of neighbours and with some measure of inner cohesion, this can be used as one of the arguments in any bid to be treated as a separate nation. Thus the political leaders of the nationalist era of both actual and aspirant nation states believed that it was essential to encourage a single community of communication. Leaders concerned themselves with language to a far greater extent than hitherto. The ways in which they intervened in the language choices and behaviour of their citizens were categorised as status planning and corpus planning by the Norwegian–American linguist, Einar Haugen, (1968) to which Cooper (1989) has usefully added the classification, acquisition planning. These three categories of LPLP provide the framework for this chapter.

3.1   Status planning

3.1.1   Status planning in the state nations

Status planning concerns itself with the choice of the varieties that will become the official language(s) of the state, in particular the medium of its institutions. Chapter 2 demonstrated how in the state nations this was mostly an organic process that began with the growth of the political and economic supremacy of a group within a particular territory. The language of exchange was inevitably the language of this dominant ruling group and the language of the capital. The language took root and spread because national laws dictated it and because national bureaucracies, education systems and armies adopted it. Usage and spread were reinforced because those who were ambitious learnt the language of power and social mobility, because greater contact among fellow citizens changed language custom and practice, because the written language was unified through print capitalism and growing literacy and, most of all, because the ideology of nationalism persuaded the majority of the national group to accept this convergence. In the state nations the language element was important and central to the process even if not always overtly so. There was a great deal of implicit and informal language planning and some of the sociolinguistic *faits accomplis* that took place are not made explicit, even in the scholarly literature. Formal language planning was always *post facto*, after the formation of the state.

Acceptance of developing standard national languages depended to some extent on the permeability of elites and their willingness to adopt a very broad definition of what it meant to be a member of the nation. Where the centre allowed lateral ethnies (Smith 1991a) to enter power networks then the official language of the centre was often accepted and learnt (Joseph 1987). Where peripheral groups were excluded from power, such exclusion produced a centrifugal force that encouraged separate and dissenting development. Where was the incentive to learn the language of the centre? Szporluk goes further, contending that permeability alone is inadequate for cohesion:

> Historical evidence suggests that the unity of multi-ethnic polities depends largely on the willingness of the dominant element not to think of itself as an ethnic category. It is not enough for the state to seek to assimilate its diverse groups; the dominant element in the state has to dissolve itself within and identify itself with a broader territorial, political and/or ideological concept as well. And so we have Americans, not WASPs; Ottomans not Turks; British not English; Spaniards not Castilians. (Szporluk 1990: 17)

We might argue with Szporluk on the extent of this dissolution; such integration was only partial and elite groups remained firmly in power, even where they opened to a limited number of newcomers. Nonetheless, vertical integration was both a tool and an outcome of nation building[1] and linguistic convergence and language shift can be seen as part of the process. Thus it does seem erroneous to present the development of a standard language as a tool of class differentiation, as is often the case in current sociolinguistics.[2] If anything the reverse is true. If privilege is bound with membership of a certain group and if a language variety is associated with membership, then privilege must become less secure where the prestige variety becomes accessible and acquirable. Class differentiation was always there. The development of the standard and provision of access to it may attenuate it in some settings and contribute in a minor way to promoting social mobility.[3] Although Bourdieu (1982) is right to state that a standard always legitimises the class from which it stems, the absence of a standard does not reverse this. The dialects of those without power will never constitute cultural capital and the argument that a standard is more easily acquired than an in-group variety that is not codified is legitimate. Language here cannot be seen as a *cause* of intra group difference and disadvantage.

Where the other languages/dialects present on the territory of the state nations survived the pressures of nationalism, they mostly retreated to the private domain, were not taught in schools and were not permitted in any contact with the state. At the very least, use of other languages in place of the state language was disbarment to employment and inclusion in state life; at the worst, it could occasion persecution, if the government saw it as an act of defiance against the state. Nationalist ideology discouraged minority language use with a variety of sanctions from mockery to punishment. This nationalist stance survives to this day. It is still possible to be persecuted for using a dialect or language considered to be threatening to state power. Thus Kurdish speakers in Turkey, Iran, Iraq and Syria are still battling for the right to use their language.[4] Macedonian speakers have been recently prosecuted by the Greek state.[5] Russian speakers in Estonia are denied citizenship until they acquire some competence in Estonian.[6] It is still the case that states see a cohesive linguistic group as essential for the well-being of the state. The English Only Movement in the United States employs these arguments. The Conseil constitutionnel in France[7] did so recently too. Given the centripetal pressures of nationalism it is remarkable that so many languages survived in the private domain. In Part III we shall consider the renaissance of a number of these survivors.

Thus, in summary, for the state nations, the term status 'planning' is really a misnomer. The official language was not imposed by planning diktat. The variety that became de facto the dominant language on a territory did so principally through a protracted political process, developing with the political and economic strength of the speakers of that language and their influence. Status 'planning' here is the legal acceptance or recognition of a status quo. In many states in western Europe the official language has actually never been explicitly designated as such. This is the case in the United Kingdom. The French government only declared the language of the Republic to be French in 1992[8] and this legislation had little to do with promoting the cohesion of the nation and much to do with the perceived threat of English and globalisation.[9]

3.1.2 Status planning in the nation states

On the other hand, in the ethnic nation states, status planning has been much more overt and, from the earliest stage in the struggles to achieve separate statehood, the question of 'national' language was central to consciousness raising within the group and to the gaining of recognition from others, and was thus a focus for conscious policy making. The nationalist movement had to build a case to demonstrate that the group was distinct and should be treated as such. The need to create a feeling of solidarity within the group was equally essential. Making the case that a language was separate and coherent was a powerful strategy in the bid for independence and sovereignty. Johann Gottlieb Fichte, the German Romantic nationalist, put the point most forcefully: wherever a separate language was to be found there was also a separate nation, which had the right to manage its own affairs and rule itself (1808/1908: 25). Possessing its own language helps define a group. They are X because they speak X. This is a desideratum of nation building even in the cases where the national language never actually comes to be widely spoken. Nationalist movements understood this, and it is significant how many organised congresses of language and language planning in the very first phase of national mobilisation to plan differentiation from allied varieties and to promote general acceptance of a norm (Fishman 1993).

A strong reaction to this developed among political scientists. A significant group of scholars takes the position that language is contingent in nation building (cf. Hobsbawm 1990, Brass 1991, Kedourie 1960). In the European context, Switzerland and Ireland are often cited as evidence of this. The first is held to prove that a multilingual nation is possible and the second to show that a national group does not always see the need to differentiate itself linguistically. There is some truth in this since the formation of groups and polities is not part of the natural world and is, therefore, not subject to incontrovertible laws of nature. There can always be divergence from what normally happens. However, these exceptions do not contravene the general observation that nationalist movements usually concerned themselves with language and sought to differentiate theirs from others, nor that nation states seek linguistic convergence where they can. In the case of Switzerland a number of variables explain why its multilingualism has survived: the important political unit is the canton, and these are monolingual except for three (out of 26);[10] the confederal organisation of the state allows a high degree of autonomy; the mountainous terrain reinforces a number of the political and linguistic boundaries; it became an independent republic long before the era of high nationalism. Switzerland was well established at the time of the intellectual enthusiasm for nationalism and thus unconcerned with the ethnic nation model of state formation. It is perhaps more difficult to explain why it never followed the model of the old state nations and how it avoided centralism. Perhaps the lack of a single dominant centre and its particular geography are partial explanations. In any case, the general observation that the political community in any kind of democracy tends to language convergence is not contravened in the case of Switzerland, because the largely monolingual canton is the main political unit, which maintains its own constitution and legislates for itself.

In the Republic of Ireland, Irish is the national language and carries immense symbolic significance as one of the variables that mark the Irish as different from their neighbours in the other parts of the British Isles. All Irish school children learn some Irish. However, only a minority of Irish citizens speaks it regularly or competently. Here the symbolic language did not become the sole official language in which all contact between state and citizen takes place. English, the language of the former occupying power, has remained as the second official language, alongside Irish. The language shift to English seems to have been accepted partly because of economic and opportunity cost considerations, partly because English in Ireland is a distinct variety of the language,[11] and partly because there is a prestigious literature in both the literary standard as well as in dialects of Irish English. There is, in fact, a strong argument to be made that English has established itself as one medium for the expression of Irish cultural identity. The Irish illustrate that nationalist planning to reinstate a former language of the group as the language of power and as a distinct marker may not be accepted in practice. This has also been the case in a number of postcolonial states, where the language of the political process and state bureaucracy has remained that of the colonial power, either in place of or alongside the national language which is symbolic of independence from that power.

These cases underscore the duality of language, the fact that language is not only an element of identity but also a means of communication. Thus, although there is a symbolic element in the choice of an official state language, its utilitarian purpose always transcends the symbolic in the way that other symbols such as flag and anthem do not. In bi- or multilingual settings the different functions of symbol and communication may be fulfilled by different languages. Whether such an arrangement can remain stable or not is questionable. Certainly societal competence in a language which comes to be highly symbolic but which is little used in communication is not secure.

Because language has this symbolic function it can be immensely difficult to gain accurate data about the languages spoken in a polity. Claiming may have more to do with wishing to identify with the group that speaks the language than actual competence in it. Individuals may also categorise themselves as X for strategic reasons of inclusion and to bolster the numbers in the group, rather than to reflect actual language skill. The difficulty of collecting data may explain why status planning does not routinely include a language census. The other reason may be that a census can provide data that may be unwelcome to the state. It can reveal the actual lack of cohesion in the group, as was the case in the 1790–91 language census in France. And it can help maintain intrastate difference. Can there be any significance in the fact that states such as the USSR, whose censuses regularly recorded what citizens spoke, and Yugoslavia, whose censuses asked citizens for their ethnic affiliation, have turned out to be fissiparous in contrast to those states that rejected recognition of difference in public life? France, for example, never repeated the language census,[12] and the elite and the mainstream population have maintained a vigorous intolerance of diversity up to the present day. I am not arguing direct cause and effect here but again simply noting the variables that often accompany nation building and national cohesion.[13] In the imagined community, the belief that one could potentially communicate with all one's fellow nationals was immensely potent.

3.2 Corpus planning

Achieving and maintaining cohesion requires effort. Bakhtin (1981) argued[14] that standardisation goes against the natural tendency towards diversification as a speech community grows in size. Speakers are constantly pushing the language of their group in the direction of heteroglossia. Where there is no systematic prescription or pressure to maintain cohesion there is the likelihood of the development of differentiation within sub-groups of the speech community, as individuals engage in the creation of terms and forms which suit their purposes and act as the cohesive glue for their sub-groups. It is the process we witness in contemporary developments of jargon and slang, for example. To counter fracture within the speech community, prescription is employed as a means of maintaining solidarity and mutual comprehensibility. Solidarity is seen to be served by stability and an agreement on norms, and intergenerational continuity by conscious monitoring of children's acquisition. Such prescription is not just a conscious activity of literate societies, as Bloomfield (1927) illustrated in his study of the practices of the Menomini Indians. Although theirs was a purely oral society, it had an acutely developed awareness of what was good linguistic practice and acceptable style and this was policed by the elders. However, although acceptance of norms may have always acted as social glue, the process becomes systematic and ideological in nation building, and the refinement and homogenisation of the language and its dissemination throughout the nation a patriotic duty. In the nationalist view, promoting the standard language within the country is seen as the concern of all, as well as needing the attention of expert linguists. In consequence, institutes for corpus planning have often been established in the early phase of nationalism.[15]

Corpus planners had a number of overlapping aims. They set out to differentiate the national language from that of other national groups to mark group boundaries. Sometimes they distanced themselves linguistically from one group in order to approach others, which they saw as their natural allies or models. They encouraged convergence within the national community of communication with the aim of minimising variation in form and maximising variation in function (Haugen 1966) or, alternatively, minimising misunderstanding and maximising efficiency (Milroy and Milroy 1985). They elaborated the language so that it could be used in all domains. Although this language intervention was primarily top-down, it was largely successful. This was and is unusual. As subsequent chapters will illustrate, most top-down LPLP is very ineffectual. The goal was achieved in this setting because LPLP was in accord with, and in support of, the dominant ideology. Where people accepted nationalism they tended to adopt the national language, since it was the emblem of national communities and national pride and had acquired a symbolic function, in addition to its pragmatic role in building national communities of communication.

3.2.1   Differentiation

Kloss (1967) coined the terms *Ausbau* and *Abstand* to explain the linguistic dimension of difference among languages. *Abstand* languages have no close relatives in linguistic terms. To be labelled a language rather than a dialect on this criterion, 'an idiom must show a considerable amount of internal disparity from all related languages under which it might conceivably be subsumed' (Joseph 1987: 2). Speakers of such languages are on linguistic islands and thus if one wants to use the language to draw boundaries around the group it is comparatively easy to do so. There are, however, only a minority of languages that are isolates. In Europe, Basque, the only pre-Indo-European language to have survived in the West, comes into this category; so too do Hungarian and Finnish, distantly related Finno-Ugric islands in the Slavic and north Germanic continua; and Albanian which is an Indo-European language but in a branch on its own. For the political purposes to which language is put in nationalism these languages are well placed. There are no other idioms with which they are mutually intelligible; they are clearly identifiable as languages separate from those around them.

Ausbau languages, on the other hand, started out as dialects on a continuum. If they have come to be recognised as languages distinct from dialects adjacent to them, it is because they have experienced a process of elaboration and extension in a number of domains and registers that has not happened to neighbouring varieties. Languages of power are typically those that are distinguished from adjacent varieties, as they acquired more extensive vocabularies and domains of use. They become 'a standardised tool of literary expression' (Kloss 1967: 290), a language of administration and the law and the language for economic exchange. This was the case for Castilian, for Francien, the dialect of the Ile de France, and for the dialect of London and the south-east Midlands. The political power of their speakers established them as the regional dominant language variety and the uses to which they were put distinguished them structurally from other varieties on the Romance and Germanic continua.

National linguists in language groups where the desired political boundaries were also language boundaries (e.g. Basque, Finnish, Romanian, Irish and Hungarian etc.) concentrated mostly on elaboration, developing their languages to give them the terms and registers necessary for their use as languages of government, education and science. They did not need to develop the language to make it a border marker. On the other hand, national linguists whose languages were clearly part of dialect continua where mutual intelligibility across borders was often as great as mutual intelligibility within the state (e.g. Czechs, Croats, Serbs, Norwegians, Catalans, etc.) also worked on differentiating their variety from others, to realise the political goal of separate national community. The *Ausbau* process which is differentiation through elaboration and development was thus right at the heart of many nineteenth-century nationalist projects.

Planning for difference rather than convergence was not simply a strategy undertaken by aspirant ethnic nationalist groups that understood the need to stress their cultural and linguistic particularity in their bid for statehood. It was also an activity of many national groups that already had states, but felt obliged to underline their cultural as well as their political distinctiveness. The process can be monitored as soon as there are written literary forms of the vernaculars, and the example of Scandinavia is a good illustration of the point. The North Germanic continuum starts to split into national languages with the dissemination of translations of the Bible. The holy texts, widely read and immensely important to Scandinavian Protestants, became the models for usage. In Sweden, the translations of the New Testament (1526) and then the complete Bible (1546) were quite archaic and consciously emphasised differences between Swedish and Danish.[16] In Denmark, in contrast, the translation of the Bible was modernising, and the translator, Christiern Pedersen, decided to acknowledge recent phonetic developments that the Swedish version ignored. This conscious defining of the two states' languages coincides chronologically with agreement on the border between them. Here political boundaries, nascent national identity and the interests of domestic print markets seem to have reinforced each other. In the nineteenth century, a short-lived Nordic solidarity arose, perhaps to oppose increasing German influence or perhaps fired by Romantic interest in a common Norse heritage. For whatever reasons, a growing pan-Scandinavian spirit in the nineteenth century led to a meeting (1869) where linguists and scholars tried to come to an agreement on a common orthography for the Scandinavian languages. There was some consensus but the political will to implement the recommendations in both countries was lacking (Karker 1983). After 1905, the date of Norway's secession from Sweden and the beginning of the Norwegian language reform, the written standard was fractured again, first into three and then into four.[17] The mutual intelligibility of the Scandinavian languages declined.

Ausbau corpus planning can even take place at sub-state level, where one region wishes to signal its rejection of the centre's nation building activities. The Slovaks were never reconciled to what they perceived to be their inferior status in Czechoslovakia (Karpat 1993). Within the Czechoslovakian constitution there was one unified people and under the Language Act one unified language, 'deemed to consist of two literary languages, Czech and Slovak' (Karpat 1993: 150). However, the dominance of Czechs in the civil service in both parts of the country, their adherence to their linguistic norms and their refusal to accommodate Slovakian was an irritant for the Slovaks. Significantly, Slovakian linguists continued cataloguing and underscoring the linguistic differences between them and speakers of Czech after 1919, a Slovak nationalist project that worked against Czechoslovakian nation building (Salzmann 1980). These two sets of speakers could have converged if there had been the will to nation build together, but there was not.[18] Of course, language was not the reason why Czechoslovakia failed to survive as a state but the language issue was a litmus paper that predicted that scission might happen.

Ausbau corpus planning can also come after the achievement of independence to underscore that independence. For example, in the wake of American Independence, Noah Webster set out to promote an American variety of English 'for the 500,000,000 of citizens destined to occupy the vast territory within our jurisdiction' (Webster 1828).[19] The most recent example of corpus planning for differentiation is in former Yugoslavia. Bosnian and Croatian linguists are currently engaged in the production of grammars and dictionaries which undo the planning for a single form for the south Slavic continuum that took place between 1919 and 1990 (Clyne 1997; Katičić 1997).

3.2.1.1 Alphabets

One indisputable marker of linguistic distinction is alphabet. Where one dialect on a continuum uses one alphabet and the adjacent dialect another, there is a clear break between the two.

The pan-Slav movement that had existed throughout the nineteenth century had often faltered because of conflicting ambitions and the union that the Croats and Serbs came to in the Balkans in 1917 was largely tactical.[20] The two groups were divided by religion with the Serbs belonging to the Orthodox tradition and the Croats to Catholicism. Their histories had separated them, the Serbs having been under Ottoman rule and the Croats in the Habsburg Empire. The only element of the ethno-nationalists' objective criteria that the Serbs and Croats possessed in common was language. Although there are differences between the two varieties, they are clearly adjacent on the dialect continuum, and there is arguably as much difference among dialects classed as Serbian or Croatian as there is between the two 'languages'.[21] They were, however, written in two different alphabets. This divergence stems from ancient times. The Glagolitic[22] script was devised for translations of the liturgy and other religious texts, because Greek did not have the necessary number of letters for the phonological pattern of Slavonic. Orthodox Slavs started to replace the Glagolitic alphabet with the Cyrillic from the twelfth century. From the late fourteenth century onwards, the Croatians moved from Glagolitic to the Roman alphabet (e.g. the Šibenik prayer) although they continued to use Glagolitic as well, if less widely, until the nineteenth century. Thus although the Serbian and Croatian languages have many areas of similarity, and indeed from 1919 to 1990 were treated as if they were a unitary language, the fact that they had been written in a different alphabet for centuries underscored difference. Although linguists planned for linguistic convergence in the nineteenth century, in preparation for future independence and although there was actual convergence during the time the two groups shared a state in the twentieth century, neither group was prepared to give on alphabet change.[23]

Changing alphabet can also be a way of reaffirming identity or signalling new orientations. Adopting an alphabet may indicate the associations which a group of speakers wishes to claim. Romanian speakers were subjects of either the Ottoman or Austrian Empire. When their elite began to mobilise them as a nation claiming autonomy, language difference was a major argument advanced in support of their case. The Romanians of Wallachia and Moldavia presented themselves as a discrete group, different from the surrounding Slavs, and not part of the eastern traditions of the Ottoman Empire. Central to their bid for independence was the provenance of the Romanian language, which is part of the Romance language family, and, therefore, not related to any of the languages of neighbouring groups. In 1778, Samuil Micu wrote the first history that represents the Romanians as descendants of a Roman and Dacian fusion. This relationship had not been particularly salient before this period.

Up until the eighteenth century Romanian in Wallachia and Moldavia had been written in Cyrillic. In 1779, Micu published the *Prayer Book for the Piety of the Christian* using the Latin alphabet. In 1780, he and Gheorghe Sincai published the first printed grammar of the Romanian language which set out to demonstrate the Latin roots of the language and which maintains that Roman is the appropriate alphabet for the language.

In 1859, after the events of the Crimean War, the Romanian-speaking provinces, Moldavia and Wallachia, were united and given some autonomy, although remaining under the nominal rule of the Ottoman Empire. In 1860–62, the Roman alphabet was introduced as 'an affirmation of national identity' (Serban 1983: 222. Author's translation). When Transylvania, formerly part of the Habsburg Empire, was united with the other two provinces, use of this alphabet was confirmed. Using the Roman alphabet emphasised the Romance tradition from which Romanian ethnicity drew and was a key marker of difference underscoring the break with Bulgaria to the south and Ukraine to the north. It accompanied the strong Romanian purist movement discussed below.

The case of the Turkish alphabet reform is remarkable. The Republic of Turkey, founded in 1923, was to be a secular and monolingual nation state on the European model to replace the theocratic, multinational organisation of the Ottoman Empire. The Ottoman Empire had been highly multilingual with groups speaking languages from three vastly different language families: Turkic (Turkish etc.), Indo-European (Persian etc.) and Semitic (Arabic etc.). Kemal Atatürk had two goals: nation building and modernisation. Moving to the Roman alphabet signalled a desire to break with the tradition of the Ottoman Empire and to turn Turkey towards Europe. On 1 January 1929, the old alphabet was abandoned and the new Roman one adopted. That this radical piece of planning was successful was perhaps due to the low levels of literacy among the Turkish population at the time. It was a change that did not affect the majority, although it was a massive blow to the small class that was literate and that became, in effect, illiterate overnight (Ahmad 1993). There is no doubt that this iconoclastic reform had a levelling effect and aided the reorientation of patterns of identity:

> It brought about the decline of pan-Islamic patterns of cultural identity and replaced it with a cultural nationalism which set out more or less deliberately to make contact with the pre-Islamic past of the Turks in Central Asia. (Bazin 1983: 175. Author's translation)

3.2.2 Codification, standardisation and prescription

The second desideratum of national corpus planning is that citizens should exhibit minimal variation of form and maximum variation of function. In other words there should be a minimum of misunderstanding within the community of communication and a maximum of efficiency in all areas of national life. Those engaged in linguistic unification became aware very early in the process that the national and official language of the state would be spread most efficiently to non-speakers in the population if its written form was stable and if there were clear rules on its grammar, syntax, lexis and orthography, that could be taught formally in the education system.

Imposition of the national standard throughout national territory is most easily achieved through codification and standardisation of orthography and grammar by central bodies. Codification and standardisation are thus usually state initiatives, undertaken by prestigious language academies at the behest of government or sovereign. In a minority of settings, however, there was more organic development as literary and intellectual groups provided models that permeated vertically through society in an unplanned way, the side effect of literary exemplars and their dissemination by printers. At first, standardisation had most effect on the written language. Generations of children passed through national education systems and learnt of the state's 'intolerance for optional variety' (Milroy and Milroy 1985). With the development of audio–visual media, a larger proportion of the population was influenced by models from the centre, since television and radio penetrated even where literacy was not a well-rooted or much practised skill. Lepschy and Lepschy (1988), following de Mauro (1963), suggest that Italian only became generalised with the advent of television.[24]

Standardisation is, as Voloshinov (1929/1973) has pointed out, a highly political and ideological business, which relies on the imposition of arbitrary norms of usage by authority. The point made in the introduction that language is the means by which we build our social groups is pertinent here. Voloshinov argues that:

> Every ideological refraction of existence in process of generation, no matter what the nature of its significant material, is accompanied by ideological refraction in word as an obligatory concomitant phenomenon. Word is present in each and every act of understanding and in each and every act of interpretation. (Voloshinov 1929/1973: 52)

The deeper relationship of standardisation and nationalism is made explicit here. Adopting the standard language is not merely behaviour that ensures communication within the national group (although it is this too), it is also practice that has an ideological dimension. Accepting the standard is, according to Voloshinov, inextricably linked to socialisation into the attitudes typically and habitually expressed within the community of communication that uses it.

Standardisation is in part a fiction. We have imagined languages in the same way that we have imagined communities. In our national groups we are designated as speakers of X, although the reality is always a degree of heteroglossia and a tendency to develop more. There is a perpetual tension as centripetal forces of convergence compete with centrifugal forces of differentiation (Bakhtin 1981). The political and institutional influences that lead us to acceptance of standardisation (education, conscription, bureaucracy, patriotism etc.) are in constant contradiction with the individual's decision to employ poetic and creative styles that deviate from the imposed norm and the group's choice to employ codes, registers or jargons that mark it as distinct.

The claim that a standard language is fiction perhaps needs some elaboration. After all, every language is a construct that depends on its speakers' support of its conventions and all language is needful of constant attention to maintain those conventions. Thus Milroy and Milroy's (1985: 23) statement that a standard language is 'an idea in the mind rather than a reality' could be claimed as equally true of any language.[25] However, their point is useful in drawing attention to the particular difficulties of maintaining the cohesion of large language groups, those which are imagined and where the vast majority of speakers will never interact. A standard language is the means by which large groups become and remain communities of communication. The norm is decided and codified by a central group, disseminated through the institutions of the state such as education and then usage is constantly policed and users dissuaded from divergent practices, both formally and informally. We could designate all the activity concerned with maintaining the 'fiction', LPLP, whether formally presented as such or not. Such a description clearly situates teachers in the classroom as integral to language planning.

3.2.2.1 Academies

Academies were key institutions for conscious planning for standardisation. The first, the Accademia della Crusca, set up in Florence in the sixteenth century,[26] codified and promoted the archaic Tuscan vernacular used by Dante (1265–1321), Petrarch (1304–74) and Boccaccio (1313–75), the first three influential writers to write in the vernacular instead of, or as well as, in Latin. In France the highly influential Académie française was established in 1635 at a time of intense linguistic awareness and an increasing acceptance among the elite of regimentation and control of language use (Rickard 1989). The Bourbon king, Philip V, founded Spain's Real Academia Española in 1713, on the model of the French academy. The Svenska Akademien was founded by Gustav III in 1786, and charged with the task of promoting the 'purity, strength and sublimity of the Swedish language'. The Prussische Akademie für Sprache und Dichtung was set up by Frederick II in 1779, and there had been numerous Sprachgesellschaften in Germany from the seventeenth century on (Thomas 1991). The Hungarian Academy began in 1830. The Russian Academy (1783) was singular in having a woman, Ekaterina Dashkova, as its first president. In the twentieth century, academies continue to be established to promote a national language on national territory. The institutes for the standardisation, elaboration and promotion of Hebrew, Swahili and Indonesian stem from the concept of the older European academies although they are, arguably, less elitist and archaising. A few academies also have the remit to stem divergent tendencies among different national varieties and maintain an internationally mutually comprehensible standard of a language. The Academia Española is linked to the other academies in South America for this purpose. The Arabic academies also have this function. In general, however, academies are primarily for national language planning for national groups.

Academies have usually come into existence through the interaction of cultural and political elites. The early academies tended to be literary groups founded to discuss stylistic issues. This was the case for the Accademia della Crusca, which was at first a literary society. The Medicis soon recognised the value of having it under their patronage and instituted an officially sponsored academy in 1572. The members of the Accademia, schooled in the unchanging norms of Latin and Greek, wanted to attain a similar ideal for Tuscan, fixed for all time. This ambition made the Academicians both purist and highly prescriptive, and when the Accademia della Crusca produced a dictionary (*Vocabolario degli Accademici della Crusca*) in 1612, the illustrations of usage drawn from medieval and contemporary texts were often doctored to reflect and reinforce the conventions that they wished to impose (Hall 1974).

In the same way, the Académie française started as an independent literary group dedicated to 'purifying' and promoting a literary standard (Thomas 1991). Richelieu too saw the utility of harnessing such a force for the purposes of the monarchy and adopted it on behalf of the king. The Académie exercised a strong influence from the outset and was an important influence on French respect for the norm[27] and acceptance of conformity (Caput 1986). By the 1830s, just four decades after Grégoire's census had recorded that only a small minority of the French had any competence in French and five decades before the advent of general primary education instilled it in all French children, the population had accepted that mastery of standardised spelling was necessary for any employment within state institutions (Caput 1986). The French really took to heart the importance of mastery of the standard language. It was not simply enough to accept French as the language of the state, it had to be spoken and written correctly for the user to be accepted as part of the group. And this hyper-respect for the standard persists, demonstrated, for example, by the current popularity of the dictation competitions whose finals are a major television occasion.[28] The prestige of the Académie developed and persists despite the fact that its actual forays into corpus planning have been largely unsuccessful. Its dictionaries have never been the most influential nor most highly regarded, and its grammar which took three hundred years to appear was considered a 'scandalously poor piece of work' (Hall 1974: 181).

3.2.2.2 Intellectual elites

Even where there has been no formal academy there has still been corpus planning, in that dictionaries and grammars have been produced by elites at the centre to promote the norm throughout the territory. There has been no formal language planning agency in the English-speaking world with a brief to codify and standardise the language. Jonathan Swift (1667–1745) recommended that an official body be set up first to 'improve' the language and then to 'ascertain' (or standardise) it. He argued 'the need of a developing nation and colonial power to have relatively fixed language for the practical purpose of clear communication over long distances and periods of time' (Milroy and Milroy 1985: 34). The idea did not find favour, however, in official circles or among other intellectuals. Samuel Johnson in the preface to his dictionary claimed that academies were ineffectual. He was of the opinion that far from French being protected and preserved, it had 'visibly changed under the inspection of the academy' (Johnson 1755 cited in Thomas 1991: 111). Thus, in Britain, it was left to private individuals to undertake the tasks of the academy. Johnson hoped that his *Dictionary* (1755) would secure English 'from corruption and decay' (Johnson 1755 cited in Thomas 1991: 111). Grammars by Bishop Lowth (1762) and Lindley Murray (1795) were influential.

Johnson's dictionary was in the tradition of most lexicography up to the end of the twentieth century. His aim was to present an idealised representation of the language, to show how it should be, rather than how it actually was. He drew examples from the recognised canon of national literature and from usage in his own intellectual and upper-class London circle, giving English speakers and would be speakers an elite model on which to base their choices.

Benson (2001) argues that not only did the monolingual dictionary fix language and provide a model for use but that it also developed a particular form of representation of the standard. In its etymological presentation of lexis, the dictionary makes the present form of the language appear as if it were destined, the inevitable result of a historical process, the only possible outcome of human interaction within the speech community. It is as if interaction among the citizens of the nation leads inexorably to the language of the dictionary, where it is documented in its perfected form. The lexicographers' presentation of a language makes it easier to understand the preoccupation of purists who sought to purge forms that they saw as undesirable from the final and frozen configuration of the national language. Benson's analysis makes clear how dictionaries are part of nation building.

Recently there have been significant developments of philosophy and practice in dictionary making. Lexicography is always a mixture of prescription and description but the balance between the two seems to have shifted in recent decades. The early tendency was to be both archaising and prescriptive. The Accademia della Crusca dictionary did not include contemporary works among its examples. Despite early criticism of such omission (Beni 1612), reliance on the canon continued for the next three and a half centuries of lexicography. In recent times, however, the advent of technology that permits the collection of enormous corpora of spoken and written language and its electronic interrogation has changed this practice. Today lexicographers can report on usage among a wider range of speakers of the language, and show some of the actual variety in language use within a speech community.[29] This development happened in part because it became technically possible, but also because it became psychologically possible. Standardisation has come to have negative connotations, in that it is at loggerheads with the current tendency to demand respect for difference. Prescriptivism seems part and parcel of a nationalist philosophy that has been questioned in an increasingly postnational era. It is becoming rare to find mainstream linguists engaged in the prescriptive activities described in this chapter. However, acceptance of difference and variety has not been wholehearted. Where lexicographers have refrained from evaluations of acceptability (e.g. *Webster's Third New International Dictionary* 1961), the public has been hostile (Milroy and Milroy 1985). Permissive attitudes towards language in general and dictionaries in particular have generated controversy in the media (Hartmann 2001).

3.2.3 Purism

Nineteenth-century nationalists' belief that each nation had a singular history and destiny and a particular idiom for their expression makes it is easy to explain why they saw a need to police the language. Herder's idea that a language embodies the soul of a nation made all those in the language industries, linguists, writers and poets, the guardian of that soul. Thus in many settings there was the conviction that language could only become an authentic tool for the group if it was purged of terms borrowed from other languages. Borrowings had to be replaced and neologisms coined by recourse to national sources: the dialects of the people or classical and ancient literatures where these existed. Purging of words of foreign origin served the twin purposes of corpus planning. It differentiated the language from its neighbours and reinforced internal cohesion. Purism originated from both within and without the academies and, as Milroy and Milroy (1985) show, often has much support within national communities.

Purism is not solely a phenomenon of the nationalist period. Purism is a feature of all languages in so far as speakers of that language will reject what hurts their feeling of self (Thomas 1991). Written languages with a literary canon will occasion purist attitudes as scholars and teachers hold up literary models for emulation. This is particularly true of 'the poetics of languages like Hebrew, Sanskrit, Latin, Greek and Arabic' which have served as media for the world's major religions (Thomas 1991). However, purism does appear to be at its most intense in nationalist periods. Thomas even argues that 'the periodisation of purism can be calibrated with that of nationalism' (1991: 138). This claim of interdependence can be supported by evidence. Although purism appears in most national groups and in most times, independence movements and newly constituted nation states have been the settings for the most active campaigns.

The French concern with the flow of Italian lexis into French in the sixteenth century coincides with the first fixing of borders and the early stirrings of French national identity. Several contemporary works set out to persuade French speakers to avoid these foreign loan words (Rickard 1989).

Purism was a conscious choice of German speakers in nineteenth-century Prussia where there were overt nation-building ambitions. This is particularly marked when Prussian usage is compared with that of German speakers in Switzerland and Austria (Thomas 1991) where national unification was not an issue.

Nineteenth-century Finnish linguists condemned borrowings and advised that neologisms should be constructed from a root already existent in one of the Finnish dialects, which were seen as an authentic source. Thus, at the beginning of the twentieth century, Swedish *telefon* was rejected in favour of *puhelin* from *puhele* 'to chat' (Sauvageot 1983).

The Estonian population are said to have spontaneously rejected a number of words of German and Russian origin when they gained their independence in 1918 (Tauli 1983). In their linguistic choices they marked their new political identity.

In Turkey, early twentieth-century planners sought to make the lexis more 'authentic'. The Turkish people were asked to suggest Turkic equivalents for the words that were to be shed from the lexis. They could borrow and adapt from old Turkish texts, from Turkish dialects within Turkey or from allied Turkic languages and dialects. By 1934 a vast number of equivalents had been found by both professionals and the general public. Published under the title, *Tarama Dergisi*, 1300 pages of terms to be replaced and the Turkic equivalents were presented to the Turkish public (Bazin 1983).

Purism can also be a reaction to nation building in other states. In nineteenth-century Sweden, there was some fear of the large state forming to the south. Anti-German feelings were expressed by calls to resist Teutonification as, for example, in Vikto Rydberg's polemical article, *Tysk eller nordisk svenska?* (1873) calling on Swedes to desist from borrowing (Karker 1983).[30]

Purist planners have been very aware of language groupings and have often turned to affiliated languages for new coinings. Thus in Estonia, the key language reformer, Johannes Aavik (1880–1973), suggested that neologisms should be drawn from dialect sources or from old Estonian. If these failed to provide the necessary roots, he advised turning to Finnish because of the pan-Finno-Ugric relationship (Tauli 1983).

In a similar way, Romanian linguists rejected Slavic, Greek and Turkish borrowings in favour of terms of Latin, Italian or French derivation, seeing the Romance group as their natural home and France as a particular model. This pan-Romance purism caught the imagination of the Romanians and was extremely successful (Serban 1983).

European Fascists were particularly prone to supporting purism. It fitted with their conceptions of racial purity and foreign 'pollution'. In Italy, promotion of standard Italian had at first entailed action against dialect words in the belief that the national language was menaced by competing varieties of Italian rather than by any language from the outside. However, in the first half of the twentieth century there was a change in orientation and a growing concern to protect the national language from foreign influence and borrowing. The Fascist regime (1922–45) applied an authoritarian policy of economic, cultural and political self-sufficiency and unity. Linguistic purism was one strategy along with racial purification by which these aims were to be achieved. Foreign borrowings, dialects and the languages of linguistic minorities were under attack and all lexis betraying foreign origin was purged. The names of towns, surnames, hotels, public signs and advertisements were particular targets. Legislation was passed to repress anything which would jeopardise 'not only the concept of national language but the idea of nation itself' (Zanichelli quoted in Pulcini 1997: 77–85). Although the repression under the Fascists was extreme, some commentators believe it built on the purist attitudes to be noted since unification in 1861 (Lepschy and Lepschy 1988).

In Fascist Germany the ideas of linguistic ethnic nationalism were also adopted and adapted to support the Nazi philosophies of race and predetermination. There was an enormous amount of nationalist linguistics in the universities for this purpose (Hutton 1999). Among the mass of people a kind of popular purism was also prevalent, revealed particularly in the choice of old Germanic names for the generation born 1933–45. Surprisingly, however, purism was not expressly promoted by the Nazi leadership and where lower echelons engaged in doing so, Goebbels and Hitler are reported to have become impatient of such petty bourgeois, romanticising 'Deutschtümelei' (Thomas 1991).

At the beginning of the twenty-first century the reaction among purists in many parts of the world is to the incursion of English terms, along with the concepts of US-dominated globalisation and as a consequence of the contacts and networks it occasions. Corpus planning in state institutions attempts to counter this by the conscious development of terminology to provide language in areas where new concepts are entering national life in such areas as scientific research or democratic governance. However, prescription was always dependent on the people's acceptance of linguistic patriotism and their relative isolation in their respective nation states. Neither of these phenomena pertains today. Even in the nation states of eastern Europe, newly liberated from the Russian domination of the Soviet era and in many cases engaged in active and overt nation building after recent independence, it is unlikely that there will be even the limited success of former times in stemming borrowings.[31] While nationalism certainly continues to be a potent force and nation states are still able to command the loyalty of those who see themselves as their nationals, there are also immense differences. It is inconceivable that state institutions could police language use in the way that they used to do[32] or that people would accept it. The circulation of ideas, information and techniques aided by the new technologies of internet and satellite television is too extensive not to have an effect on borrowing, and is not easily censored. Those using these new media tend to accept new vocabulary when they see it as appropriate.[33] Moreover, borrowing is now on the whole judged in the academic literature to be a sign of the vitality of a language rather than a pathology. The general consensus (Laitin 1996) is that the hegemony of one standard language on one territory will be less successful than in former times.

3.2.4   Diglossia

As foreign borrowings were banned at the height of purism new terms had to be found. This led in a number of cases to the conscious promotion of language from an earlier era, particularly where this was held to be the Golden Age of national cultural and political achievement. Thus the Greek linguists of the Independence era returned to Classical sources. Adamantios Korais (1748–1833), the key figure in the introduction of Katharevousa, the variety of Greek based on the Classical language, consciously expunged Greek of foreign imports and returned to Classical texts to coin neologisms, find models for syntax and usage of lexis. In consequence, the chasm between the high literary written language and the spoken language, which was already an issue in the Byzantine period, was deepened, since the spoken language (Demotic) had not undergone this purification. The language question in the young Greek state was highly politicised. Acquisition and use of Katharevousa was presented as patriotic and its advocates attacked those who supported Demotic as 'enemies of the Nation' (Clairis 1983: 354. Author's translation).

A similar fissure opened up in Italy between the literary language, based on the archaic Florentine dialect of Tuscany, and the great variety of dialects used in the Northern and South-Central Italian dialect continua. Because the writings of Dante, Petrarch and Boccaccio commanded immense prestige and because the Accademia della Crusca had accepted *le tre corone* as a model, the Italian printing industry adopted Tuscan as the norm even though the most important printers were actually located in Venice. At the time of unification, the writer, Alessandro Manzoni (1785–1873), supported the choice of Tuscan as the basis of the written language, but argued that it should be the modern language of the educated bourgeoisie in Florence rather than the historic language. The linguist, Graziado Ascoli (1829–1907), countered this, suggesting that Italians follow the German model and maintain a standard largely based on their literary tradition. This would protect the spoken dialects against an indiscriminate offensive. He viewed them as the 'repositories of a local ethos worth saving' (de Mauro 1963: 82. Author's translation). Ascoli's solution was adopted mainly because it could be presented as a neutral solution that did not favour the Florentines as much as the Manzoni proposal. However, the decision meant that archaic and highly sophisticated written Italian was quite distant from the regional spoken idioms, and a general situation of diglossia developed (Kramer 1983), which lasted until the advent and spread of audio–visual media began to cause some shift from the dialects.

LPLP can have contrasting effect for continuity and access to historical texts. An individual who knows modern written Italian can read fourteenth-century authors. Knowledge of Katharevousa gives easier access to Greek Classical authors. In Turkey, on the other hand, language planning has cut the modern Turkish speaker's link to the past. The alphabet is the greatest hurdle but the replacement of words of Persian or Arabic provenance by coinages from Turkic roots means that Turks cannot easily read the literary works produced during the Ottoman Empire when a Turkish–Persian–Arabic synthesis had developed (Bazin 1983). Both enterprises are in the full tradition of nationalist linguistics: the first a desire to evoke a national 'Golden Age', the second a desire to embrace Modernism and secularism.

3.2.5 Cosmopolitanism and universalism

The philosophical underpinning of nationalist linguistics came under attack wherever there were currents of cosmopolitanism, internationalism and universalism. Linguistic purism, brought into disrepute through the support accorded it among National Socialists and Fascists, declined as a respectable activity for linguists to engage in. It has disappeared from mainstream scholarship, even if purist attitudes lingered longer among the general public.

3.3 Acquisition planning

Spread of the national standard throughout national territory came with the spread of literacy, because a written language can be standardised and monitored more easily than spoken interaction. Imposition of the national language comes with education for all in the national education system in the standard. Acquisition planning is the term generally employed to describe the policies and strategies introduced to bring citizens to competence in the languages designated as 'national', 'official' or 'medium of education'.

3.3.1 Nationalist ideology

It is of course a truism to remark that the young of the group are always socialised into the ideology prevailing in the group. It is therefore unre-markable that national education systems in nationalist times inculcate nationalist attitudes along with and through the national language. One of the clearest expositions of what a nationalist education system should aim to be comes from Fichte. In *Reden an die deutsche Nation* (1807–08) he rejected the individualism and cosmopolitanism of the Enlightenment and urged the Germans to create a new national state through a new kind of education that would be uniform, national and German (Weimer 1963). Fichte explicitly advocated the vertical integration of society, with a comprehensive system in which streaming is through merit. Hegel (1770–1831) also conceived education to be the business of the state, a national affair needing a national system (Weimer 1963). There was some enthusiasm for these ideas in the Prussian government and the Süvern plan (1817) included proposals to increase literacy and promote social integration (Rowlinson 1974). The whole package proved, however, too revolutionary for the Prussian hierarchy and Süvern's ideas were never fully implemented, although participation in education and literacy did grow. By 1838, one in six of the Prussian population was in education, and a high proportion of the population could read and write because of the heavy emphasis on literacy in the nine years of mainstream schooling (Arnold 1865–67/1964). However, the division between Gymnasium, Realschule and Volkschule maintained rigid class divisions, and in the Gymnasium the continued stress on Greek and Latin preserved a certain linguistic differentiation, and protected the cultural capital of the elite.

In early nineteenth-century Britain, Henry Brougham (Lord Brougham) advocated a national primary school system, and tried to introduce it through his Parish Schools Bill (1820). His philosophy differed from Fichte's in that he was not advocating vertical national integration through education. In fact his Bill was based on his 'Report on the Education of the Lowest Orders', and it is clear he approved the binary line which maintained the class divide between state and private schools. However, his remark that 'education of the poor is the best security of morals and the peace of nations' (cited in Pollard 1956: 165) makes it clear that he too had the idea that social cohesion can be served by national education. Brougham's crusade was, of course, unsuccessful and it was not until 1870 that state education for all was introduced in the United Kingdom.[34]

One of the clearest expressions of an ideological stance on language and nationalism comes from the French Convention. Talleyrand declared that the curious situation which saw the French language become an ever spreading international language but remain unknown to many French citizens should be understood in part as a strategy of the ruling classes. He promised that:

> Elementary education will put an end to this strange inequality. In school all will be taught the language of the Constitution and of the Law and this mass of corrupt dialects, these last vestiges of feudalism will be forced to disappear. (Talleyrand 1791: 472. Author's translation)

Brunot (1967) sees this speech as heralding an era during which 'national unity would be achieved through the school'. It was, however, a long process and progress was slow. In the early part of the Revolutionary period (up until 1794) there was some tolerance for bilingual education to provide a transition to French in the non-French speaking areas. This paralleled the concession in the early years of the Republic (between 1790 and 1793) that governmental decrees be translated for the citizens of these regions. However, after the Vendée Revolt, these concessions were withdrawn and non-French speakers could expect harsh treatment. Any bureaucrat or official who failed to use French could be imprisoned.

In reality, education, whether bilingual or monolingual, remained a pipe dream. A project to train teachers in an Ecole normale (training college) and produce materials appropriate to the new era was abandoned in 1795 (Brunot 1967). The Comité d'Instruction publique was not able to recruit enough French speakers to fulfil Talleyrand's promise of a primary teacher in every parish (*commune*) and in any case, faced with a war, could not have afforded it. In 1833, the government passed an Act designed to move towards the goal of free primary education for all. However, there was no funding for this provision from central government and it was left to the parishes to pay for it. Thus, the law was a statement of intent rather than a reality in many areas of the country. Literacy was far from universal; in 1855, 32 per cent of bridegrooms could not sign their names on the register (the percentage of illiterate brides was no doubt even higher) and 38.9 per cent of conscripts were illiterate (Kemp 1989).

Arnold (1865–67/1964) had been impressed by the inculcation of French national values and culture after visiting schools on a study tour in the 1860s and publicised the ideas in Britain. French education was education to be a French national.[35] Any student getting to the final years of the lycées would have been fluent in French, acquired a comprehensive knowledge of the canon of French literature and had full exposure to a history of the French nation which presented them as a cohesive group since pre-Roman times. When national education became available to all at last in 1880–81, its most immediate effect was to spread the French language and to encourage a sense of French citizenship throughout the territory.[36]

In all the national education systems, acquisition of the national language was interwoven with other aspects of socialisation into national life and the acquisition of national identity. The language was both medium and message. Bakhtin explained that it could not be otherwise because of the ideologically saturated nature of language and the societal construction of meaning. Talking of national, standardised, unitary languages he says:

> What we have in mind here is not an abstract linguistic minimum of a common language in the sense of a system of elementary forms (linguistic symbols) guaranteeing a minimum level of comprehension in practical communication. We are taking language not as a system of abstract grammatical categories, but rather language conceived as ideologically saturated, language as a world view, even as a concrete

opinion, insuring a maximum of mutual understanding in all spheres of ideological life. Thus a unitary language gives expression to forces working towards concrete verbal and ideological unification and centralization which develop in vital connection with processes of sociopolitical and cultural centralization. (Bakhtin 1981: 74)

3.3.2 Modernity

The provision of education for all in nineteenth-century nation states was not simply a result of governments' desire to develop national identity, citizenship and a national community of communication. There was also the move to industrial forms of production that demanded a revolutionary change in education (Gellner 1983). Gellner argues that the knowledge necessary for work could no longer be learnt through emulation, as had been the case in an earlier, slow changing, agricultural society. In an industrialising society there had to be a period of generic education to prepare the individual for the flexibility needed in the shifting roles that industrial processes and evolving technology demanded.[37] It was only the state that was in the economic and strategic position to offer such generic education. It was also clearly in the economic interest of the state to do so. Since state education was in the state language, it also had the effect of promoting the linguistic homogenisation of the nation, although in the modernist explanation this was not its prime purpose. There does not seem to me to be any contradiction here since language choice, language shift and language convergence always appear to have several different and coinciding explanations. The successful spread of the national language because of pressure from industry and commerce does not seem to me to be at odds with the argument that national education systems set out to socialise future citizens. It is likely that educational policy makers hoped to promote both national identity and economic well-being. These different pressures and motivations worked in tandem;[38] top-down policies decided by the state were reinforced by the changing needs of those who moved from subsistence farming to become industrial workers in urban settings and those who employed them.[39]

Industrialisation reinforced nation building. Prussia can serve as an example once again. As the country industrialised, the state poured funds into education and literacy in the standard language. There was great expansion in scientific and technical education from 1840 onwards (Kemp 1969). The Prussian government encouraged the study of technical subjects in a society where Classics had always dominated higher education. The strategy was successful. The use of Latin as a language of scholarship was eclipsed and German not only moved into new domains at the national level but also became an international language for science in the following century. At the other end of the spectrum, primary school funding increased and education became the norm for all. By the time of German unification, illiteracy had nearly been eradicated in Prussia (Kemp 1989).

In contrast, where industrialisation and nation building came later the spread of literacy too was delayed. In 1920 only 50 per cent of the Bulgarian, Romanian and Yugoslavian population was literate (Teichova 1989).

3.3.3 Minorities in nation building

The final point to be made about language in education in the era of high nationalism is that few groups espoused the right of the group to learn and use its own language as a universal human right. It was difficult for groups to reconcile respect for the aspirations of others with their own project. This was, and remains, the fundamental problem of nationalism, particularly ethno-nationalism. Groups do not sustain self-determination as a general principle and a universal entitlement, but as a right they ask for themselves.

Of course it was unlikely that the governments of the old state nations would encourage separate development within their borders, given their tradition of centralisation and homogenisation. There was no space for the languages of minorities in their national education systems. Anecdotal stories, passed down through families in the United Kingdom, France and Spain whose language was other than the national standard, recount punishment and humiliation in the classroom for those who would not or could not make the shift demanded.

The history of the Hungarians' fight for nationhood is interesting in that it reveals this basic dilemma within ethno-nationalism. Even a group that recognised the rights of others intellectually eventually felt constrained to repress them in its own interest.

Within its nineteenth-century borders, Hungary had a population that was highly diverse. In addition to the Hungarians descended from the Magyars, there were Germans,[40] Croatians,[41] Romanians,[42] Slovaks,[43] Greeks and Armenians. Each of these groups had retained its specificity to a large degree whether protected by statutes or simply by custom. There had been no centralisation from a strong monarchy on the state nation model, mainly because the country had been under Turkish occupation and then annexed by the Habsburgs. The Magyar nobility was highly conservative and used the Hungarian Diet largely to maintain aristocratic privilege. The most important families were holders of posts at the Habsburg court, and had little connection to Hungary except in so far as their estates provided their wealth: they spoke German (or French) in Vienna, Latin at the Diet, and Magyar only when dealing with their peasants.

Up to the end of the eighteenth century, much secondary education had been organised by the Jesuits,[44] and was thus in Latin.[45] In 1777, however, the empress, Maria Theresa, had removed education from the Jesuits (*Ratio Educationis*) and instructed that education was henceforth to be in German and in the mother tongue of the respective nationalities, with content following the model of Austrian textbooks. The bureaucracy, for whom the medium had also been Latin, underwent Germanisation as well. This offended the Hungarians who were used to contact with the state in Latin or Magyar.

At the end of the eighteenth century the lesser nobility and the professional classes were fired by the ideas of the French Revolution. The first Magyar-language newspaper was published in 1780, helping to create Hungarian national identity by its use of the language and popularising the idea of self-determination. In 1848, the Hungarians rebelled against the Habsburgs. The April laws promoted Hungary as a Magyar state and discriminated against minorities, in particular making the franchise partially dependent on competence in Magyar. When Austria retaliated to put down the Hungarian revolution, some of the Slav-speaking Hungarians fought with the Austrians, fearful of any ethnic Hungarian success for their own national aspirations.[46] After their defeat, the Hungarians lost all autonomy and were ruled as part of Austria, with German as the language of administration.

Twenty years later, the Hungarians were eventually granted a certain degree of autonomy when the Habsburgs needed their support after military and political disasters in other parts of the empire. According to the 1867 Compromise (*Kiegyezes/Ausgleich*) Hungary became a nominally sovereign state, even if it was in an anomalous position of also being subservient to Austria in the person of the Habsburg monarch. It is at this point that the minority policies of Hungary become interesting. Nothing in the immediate past made it seem as if the Hungarian elite would be accommodating to minorities. There had been progressive Magyarisation up until the 1848 rebellion.[47] However, the Nationality Act of 1868 explicitly recognised the ethnic diversity of the country. It declared that the citizens of Hungary constituted a homogenous nation 'of which every citizen regardless of nationality was a full member with equal rights'. This was the civic nation model of citizenship based on *jus soli* rather than the ethnic nationalist ideal of *jus sanguinis*. The state nations, in particular France, when faced with this kind of heterogeneity, had developed towards cultural homogeneity through a number of interlocking policies and processes, some intended to promote unity and some producing it as a by-product. In the process they had ridden roughshod over any groups wishing to maintain their specificity. Given the previous tendency to Magyarisation, this might well have been the decision of the Hungarian government. On the contrary, however, there were concessions. Under the Nationality Act, each group had the right to use their minority language in official documents, administrative matters and in communications with the government, wherever one fifth of the representatives of the region demanded it. The Act also gave every church, community or group of individuals the right to establish and maintain schools using any language for instruction. The Public School Act (1868) made provision for state schools in the different languages of the communities. József Eötvös, the minister of religion and public education, did not attempt to establish Hungarian as the medium of education for all citizens. This planning for separate development was without precedent in Europe at that time (Hevizi 2002).

It was not to last long, however. For the minorities, these concessions were not the territorial autonomy or independence that they wanted and they continued to mobilise to achieve their political ambition. The Magyar majority felt their situation precarious and started Magyarisation once again; the nationalities were to be incorporated. By 1876, a new, unified and centralised administrative regime had been set up. In 1879, an Act was passed requiring Hungarian tuition for all trainee teachers and competence in Hungarian as a prerequisite for gaining a teacher's certificate. In 1896, the 1000th anniversary of the Magyar state was celebrated as a national occasion with a high degree of pressure to participate. This was much resented by the nationalities. In 1907, the Apponyi Act required school children to have at least four years' tuition in the 'national' language. In other words, the Hungarian government retreated from its short-lived but liberal multilingual and multicultural position to a programme of nation building closer to the norm set by other governments of the time.[48]

3.4 Conclusion

For both categories, state nation and nation state, national linguistic homogenisation was encouraged, because a single linguistic group could be enlisted in claims for national self determination or for continued national sovereignty. Nation builders saw that national education and national service would create a single community of communication in addition to their primary purposes of training the workforce and the military. Actual and imagined communication would build national identity and solidarity.[49]

Linguistic differentiation was welcomed because it reinforced borders. Where the citizens on either side of a political border spoke the same language there was always fear of irredentism at worst or a dilution of national identity at least.[50]

A national language is presented as a natural attribute of and a prerequisite for the nation by ethno-nationalists and as both constructed and contingent by modernists, but the actuality lies somewhere in between. A group which is too large for communication to be face-to-face does not naturally share a single language because the centripetal forces inherent in human language use tend to fracture the language across space and time. A unified language for such a group depends on the development of a standard language, and its widespread dissemination through compulsory education, universal literacy and widely available print media. A national language is thus a construction. The political class understands the role of language and oversees the standardisation and dissemination processes.

The spread of standard national languages has been seen in two conflicting ways. It is widely held to be a requirement as soon as the political legitimacy of the state derives from the people, because it provides a forum and a means for political participation. It is also considered as a means of achieving social cohesion and social mobility.[51] From another perspective, a standard language is seen as an imposition from a hegemonic centre, which destroys diversity as it is promoted throughout the state. As other languages are eliminated along with the cultures they carried, there is personal loss in those particular communities since they no longer have access to the language-borne cultural heritage of the group. There is general loss for humanity if the insights provided by particular ways of meaning expressed in the languages of those communities are lost along with the language.

In recent scholarship the whole nation building process has been challenged and the heteroglossic aspect of language foregrounded. Many question the stability of the socially constructed ethnic identities of the nationalist era (Özkirimli 2000). Much recent work on language and nationalism has also shown how problems that are presented as language problems are very rarely to do with language but rather indicative of competition, tension and conflict in other fields. These challenges to nationalist Linguistics will be explored in Part III.

However, nation building continued in the twentieth century and seems set to persist through the twenty-first. As colonies gained their independence at the end of empire they were left in a situation that is similar to that of the state nations, that is, they had set borders with disparate groups within them. Many postcolonial countries adopted the one language one state philosophy of nation building or at least set out to reduce to manageable proportions the sociolinguistic complexity in which they found themselves (Blommaert 1996). The postcolonial period was the heyday of conscious language planning. It is this highly functionalist and modernising period in the development of language policy and language planning that is the focus of the next chapter.

4
Nation Building in the Wake of Colonialism: Old Concepts in New Settings

The dissolution of the European colonial empires in the second half of the twentieth century resulted in another postwar period where many new states were constituted. Liberation movements had invoked the ideal of the nation in the fight against the colonial powers and, having gained independence, took the nation state as the model for sovereign statehood. Although the leaders of the newly liberated countries were in very different settings from their counterparts in the earlier waves of nation state formation, the basic problems were felt to be much the same. On the linguistic and cultural front, the challenges were the ever intractable issues: how to achieve national unity, how to ensure independence, and how to educate the national population effectively.

4.1   The legacy of the colonial period

It may well turn out that Europe's most enduring legacy to the regions it colonised in the rest of the world will be the tradition of the nation state as an organising principle. This form of political organisation was inherited, however, by groups where there was little cultural and linguistic cohesion or other factor that could be employed in an ethnic construction of nationality. As we have seen in previous chapters, there was rarely neat coincidence of 'nation' and state in Europe. But what was already fiction in Europe became doubly so in postcolonial Africa and Asia.

In postcolonial Africa, there was extreme heterogeneity within states and arbitrary borders between them. The imperial delegates to late nineteenth-century conferences had carved Africa up according to the power balances among European states and drawn state boundaries that were often geometric and that rarely took notice of ethnic groupings. The rationale for borders was simply that competing colonial powers were blocked in their advance by each other; 'they reflect spheres of influence and trade carved out by the precursors of European colonialism' (Fardon and Furniss 1994: 11). In consequence, societies that had been highly unified in terms of language and culture were divided and groups that were immensely disparate were joined together.

Despite this, after independence, there was no move to redraw the map. The member states of the Organisation of African Unity agreed to live with their boundaries. But, although these frontiers were not actually contested, they were highly contentious, since they left governments with disparate linguistic populations within their borders and a high risk of irredentism where groups that had been dissected desired to regroup. Independence from colonial rule gave the African continent a mosaic of states that its autochthonous inhabitants had never willed and borders that it had never contributed to drawing.

Federalism and loose association would perhaps have been the best resolution in many cases, but the majority of newly independent states did not make that choice, instituting instead regimes where power was concentrated in the capital and where the people were treated as a single group. The nineteenth-century European model of political organisation, which promoted the ideas of a single unified group on a single territory, total sovereignty and self-reliance, was immensely influential. This was a logical development in many ways since the anti-colonial liberation movements had adopted nationalist ideology as a mobilising force and retained the philosophy after independence as the founding principle for the state (Nyerere 1999).

The end of empire thus left many governments in the same position as the state nations of Europe in the sixteenth and seventeenth centuries; that is, they had fixed boundaries, heterogeneous populations and centralised political systems. Rulers and governments saw a pressing need to unite their populations and mould a more homogenous citizenry. The nation state was the normative response. Planning for unity was undertaken consciously and in haste. The difficulties inherent in introducing the old ideal of 'one people, one language, one state' into the kind of diversity described above did not stop politicians from trying.

This one party, one language, one nation project was typical of nation building in the postcolonial period. Bamgbose has categorised it in the African situation as 'obsession with the number one':

> It seems that we are obsessed with the number 'one'. Not only must we have one national language, we must have a one party system. The mistaken belief is that in such oneness of language or party we would achieve socio-cultural cohesion and political unity in our multi-ethnic, multilingual and multicultural societies. (Bamgbose 1994: 36)

4.2 The single 'national' language

Finding the one language that would purportedly promote unity and solidarity within the state was not a simple task. The heterogeneity of the populations presented no simple indigenous solution. In some states there were literally hundreds of different languages. Indonesia, one of the most linguistically diverse states in Asia, has more than 731.[1] Nigeria, one of the most linguistically diverse states in Africa, has an estimated 400 languages (Elugbe 1994).[2] In both Nigeria and the Indonesian archipelago the languages are spread across different language phyla which means that, although there are dialect continua where some mutual comprehension is possible, on the cleavages between phyla there is no possibility of passive understanding. Even within phyla, speakers may not necessarily achieve comprehension through mutual passive understanding.[3] Indonesia and Nigeria may be extreme cases of diversity, but most African and Asian postcolonial states are linguistically heterogeneous to some degree.

From the perspective of governments, the case for rationalisation was not difficult to make. Faced with extreme multilingualism, recognition of the rights of citizens to use their language in public life, in particular their interaction with state institutions, was considered unfeasible. Pluralism was blocked, practically, by the logistics of implementing policy and, psychologically and ideologically, by commitment to the nation state model. Post independence ethos was firmly against recognition of ethnic diversity. The identification of cultural and linguistic difference was seen as retrograde, a pandering to a tribalism that had to be transcended in the modern state. In contrast, the embedding of different 'tribes' and groups into the nation was seen as progressive. There was optimism that this could be done through commitment to nationalist ideology, the charisma of the new leaders and universal education, all of which would provide 'the nurturing for the integrated growth of these new nation states' (Laitin 1992: 8).

The third argument against multilingualism was that it was antithetical to development and economic growth. Research had been produced which suggested that states that were highly heterogeneous in terms of language were characterised by low or very low per capita GNP (Banks and Textor 1963). Pool (1972: 216) reported a general acceptance of the opinion that 'language diversity breaks down occupational mobility and thus slows development'.[4]

Multilingualism was also held to be unworkable if the aims of basic education and literacy for all were to be met. Sub-Saharan African languages had not generally been written down until contact with Europeans (Mazrui and Mazrui 1998)[5] and, therefore, producing basic teaching materials in the vernaculars depended on whether they had undergone what Charles Ferguson (1968) has termed graphisation. Only some of the vast number of languages had been codified, given an alphabet and elaborated so that they could function as media for modern education systems. It would be a mammoth task to undertake provision of teaching in every mother tongue (Ansre 1970; Elugbe 1994).[6]

In their introductions to policy statements and constitutions, governments may have lauded the linguistic skill of multilinguals coping with numerous languages in their daily encounters (Fardon and Furniss 1994), but they took little notice of this multilingualism in the substance of their laws which were aimed at national integration and efficiency through the imposition of a national language. The ethos was for national unity, and multilingualism was seen to be promoting what divided the nation and held it back from development and modernity and was rejected. Thus, in the early days of independence, no state made provision for bureaucratic and political interaction or education to be in all the language varieties found on the territory or even envisaged doing so.

Within the framework of wanting to designate one official language for a multilingual population, the problem then became the actual choice of language. There was always the possibility of using the language of the former colonial power. Supporters claimed that it was both neutral and provided a link with the wider world.[7] Such a choice was, of course, problematic. The former colonial language could not be indexical in the way that is desired for national languages. The proposition was anathema to those who wanted to break with the colonial past. According to many who were looking for a new beginning, the imposition of the colonial language had already inculcated a sense of inferiority:

> The language of an African child's formal education was foreign. The language of the books he read was foreign. Thought in him took the visible form of a foreign language … (The) colonial child was made to see the world and where he stands in it as seen and defined by or reflected in the culture of the language of imposition. (Ngugi 1986: 17)

To continue to use the language of that colonialism was to ensure a continued sense of inferiority.

Nonetheless, the government of many postcolonial states did just this. But most states were in a bind; their heterogeneity appeared to allow them no other solution than the language of the colonial power that had brought them together and their espousal of nationalist ideology meant that the pressure to find a single national language was strong. The former colonial powers backed this solution since it kept their lines of contact and influence open. English was promoted because it could be adopted

> as a politically neutral language beyond the reproaches of tribalism. (Moorhouse (1964) cited in Mazrui and Tidy 1984: 299)

The promoters of French noted that:

> le rôle privilégié que le français joue au niveau de la population est dû au fait qu'il apparaît comme non marqué ethniquement. (Daff 1991: 152)

The British press found it 'remarkable that English has not been rejected as a symbol of colonialism' (Moorhouse (1964) cited in Mazrui and Tidy 1984: 299). The French were equally self-congratulatory (Conac *et al.* 1987). These reactions rather ignore the fact that given the disparate populations left by colonialism no other solution readily presented itself to a would be unitary state.[8] The adoption of English and French can be best explained as the least bad solution in the circumstances rather than by any claim that they could be politically neutral.

Finding a national language from the country's own tradition that would not promote the interests of one group over the others was the ideal solution. Ansre, writing just after decolonisation and at the time of the great language debate, noted that the ideal in the search for the single national language would be to identify one that was:

> indigenous because it can then engender a sense of national pride, facilitate the promotion of the indigenous cultural heritage and provide a certain amount of loyalty at the emotional level. (Ansre 1970: 2–3)

The revolutionary and socialist figures in decolonisation favoured this solution. Frantz Fanon stressed the link between language and culture:

> To speak means to be in a position to use a certain syntax, to grasp the morphology of this or that language, but it means above all to assume a culture, to support the weight of a civilisation. (Fanon 1967: 17–18)

Ngugi (1986) taking a very Whorfian position, argued the corollary of this. He maintained that those Africans who forsook their mother tongue for English or French would be inevitably westernised. The alien language would carry alien ideologies.

Choosing this ideal national language remained the problem. The languages of the larger groups were rejected as official languages of power as their adoption would have fuelled fear of domination and caused rejection of the unitary state. The 'national' language had to be one that would be acceptable to all sections of the 'nation'. Few states had any ready made solution.

In both Tanzania and Indonesia, however, there was such a language that could be employed for the purpose. These countries had three linguistic influences from which to draw: the indigenous languages, the language of an earlier regional power and the language of the European colonial period. The languages of the earlier regional power, Swahili in Tanzania and Malay in Indonesia, seemed to fit all the requirements for a national language. They were indigenous and so would have a symbolic dimension that would signal a new beginning after colonialism. They were not the languages of any politically prominent single ethnic group and so could promote unity within the state. They would foster a distinct identity on a regional basis since they were both regional lingua francas. They were languages with historical links that could be used to build a sense of national belonging and continuity. The only serious disadvantage was that they would need to be imposed by planning diktat, top-down, since they were not spoken by the majority of future citizens, but as this was a time of general optimism and belief in technocratic solutions this was not held to be an insuperable difficulty.

The new nation states of Africa and Asia became the laboratory for conscious language planning with a mushrooming of university and policy groups committed to explaining how it could be done. Scholarly teams from Western universities (Fishman, Ferguson, Das Gupta 1968; Jernudd and Rubin 1971; Fishman 1974; etc.) analysed the experiences of the recent European nation building past and employed the knowledge to suggest frameworks for the postcolonial nation building future. They were quite optimistic that language change could be orchestrated:

> Planning includes indicative, regulative, productive and promotional functions. The indicative aspect of language planning consists of assessing the language situation in terms of social developmental requirements and prescribing certain courses of change. The regulative aspect calls for authoritative action in the form of public measures accompanied by sanctions for encouraging specific uses of selected languages for defined domains. The productive aspect attends to the task of developing the capacity of a language to cope with the increasing demands likely to be made on it from the domains ... Planning authorities are likely to engage in active promotion of the products and standards among the potential user publics, including the administrative, educational, news media and other modes of language use. (Das Gupta and Ferguson 1977: 5)

Language planning scholars stretched along a continuum of opinion from those who believed that a decision could be taken centrally and imposed top-down through education to those who began to wonder whether language practice could be influenced greatly at all. Jernudd and Rubin posed the question (1971) 'can language be planned?' and concluded that some studies 'convincingly show the absence of planning from language planning' (Jernudd and Das Gupta 1971: 201). Haugen (1966) reported the incremental force of individual decisions and suggested that top-down policy only succeeds when bottom-up patterns of behaviour are (or can be brought to be) in accord with it.[9] Other scholars and most policy makers were less cautious; they believed that language policy could be introduced top-down through the agencies of the state and citizens persuaded of the utility of the rationalisation. Ansre records the advice contemporary policy groups were giving:

> For the purpose of national unity and progress it is necessary to have a language or major languages which can be used widely throughout the

country not only so that government can communicate with the governed, but also that it could serve as the medium of national interaction at all levels. Governments are, therefore, exhorted to formulate and implement language policies for the nation as a whole. (Ansre 1970: 2)

The political elites in both Tanzania and Indonesia instigated language planning on all the formal levels (status, corpus and acquisition) and engaged in a massive ideological campaign to convert the 'nation' to the national language. Formal language planning institutes continued the work on codification, standardisation and elaboration. The following sections narrate how partial success was achieved in each country and explain why that success was never more than partial.

4.3   Language planning in Tanzania: the introduction of Swahili

Tanzania came into existence on 26 April 1964, when Tanganyika united with Zanzibar to form the United Republic of Tanganyika and Zanzibar, renamed the United Republic of Tanzania on 29 October. Tanganyika had first been a Germany colony, and then, after the First World War, control of most of the territory passed to the United Kingdom under a League of Nations mandate. After the Second World War, Tanganyika became a UN trust territory under British control. In 1961, Tanganyika became an independent state under the presidency of Julius Nyerere.

Zanzibar came under Portuguese domination in the sixteenth and early seventeenth centuries but was retaken by Omani Arabs in the early eighteenth century. The Anglo-German agreement of 1890 made Zanzibar and Pemba a British protectorate which the British ruled through the sultan. Zanzibar gained independence from Britain on 10 December 1963. One month later, the sultan of Zanzibar was overthrown and replaced by representatives of the Afro-Shirazi Party (ASP) with Karume as its head of state. Karume signed an Act of Union with Nyerere and the two countries combined later that year to form the modern state of Tanzania.

Tanzania's 1964 frontiers brought together a number of disparate groups: tribes that were still hunter–gatherers; nomadic herders; a large, illiterate peasantry; seafaring traders; a sophisticated urban intelligentsia. They also aggregated more than 120 ethnic groups with different cultures and languages. The larger groups (the Sukuma, Haya, Nyakyusa, Nyamwezi and Chaga have more than 1 million members) are Bantu-speaking peoples. Groups of Nilotic or related origin include the nomadic Masai and the Luo, whose territory straddles the border with Kenya, thus making them citizens of different states. Two small groups speak languages of the Khoisan family peculiar to the Bushman and Hottentot peoples. Cushitic-speaking peoples, originally from the Ethiopian highlands, are also present on the territory. Much of the African population on Zanzibar came from the mainland. The

Shirazis, however, trace their origins to the island's early Persian settlers. The small Asian community includes Hindus, Sikhs, Shi'a and Sunni Muslims and Goans.

In the first decade after independence Nyerere's government consciously aimed at creating political hegemony and a unified nation with a common national culture based on the 'best of the traditions and customs of all the tribes' (Nyerere 1967: 187). The Arusha Declaration of 1967 introduced the policy of *Ujamaa* (familyhood) and sought to apply socialist principles to the African context. This included a one party system, with the democratic structure of competing interest groups rejected as divisive.

In Africa, the languages associated with the Islamic tradition (Hausa, Fulfude and Mandinka in West Africa and Swahili, Somali and Nubi in East Africa) had long played a historic role as regional lingua francas (Mazrui and Mazrui 1998). Swahili is a Bantu language, from the north-east branch of the phylum (Hinnebusch *et al.* 1981) with a significant proportion of lexis taken from Arabic along with some features of pronunciation. Although the language is coloured by its association with the former conquerors of the area, the memory of this earlier domination had faded and, for Tanzanian nationalists searching for a language for nation building, it had the advantage of being an indigenous language.[10] Swahili had a double function in East Africa: it was the lingua franca of regional commercial relations, accompanying trade inland, as far as the great lakes of Central Africa and beyond, and it was also the mother tongue of the peoples of the coastal strip and a language associated with Islam and the Muslim population (Ansre 1974). It was a particularly suitable choice as Tanzania's national language since its Bantu base made it an accessible medium for the 94 per cent of the population whose languages are Bantu related (Whiteley 1971).

Swahili had been used in state institutions throughout the colonial period. German colonial administration adopted the regional lingua franca as the language of contact with the populations they ruled in East Africa. The other two possible media for communication were rejected: the local languages were too numerous and each group of speakers too small for the contact role (Whiteley 1971); the colonial language was little used for inter-group contact as both the Germans and the British, who replaced them after the First World War, subscribed to a doctrine of distinction and Swahili served as a way of keeping the African population and the colonial class separate (Ansre 1974).[11] This was most evident in the three-tiered education system developed in British East African territories, with Swahili medium education from 1925. Those of the autochthonous population that went through primary education did so in Swahili (Mazrui and Mazrui 1995). The British and the Asians had their own schools.

Swahili was a language of religion. Originally associated with Islam, it gradually became the medium for Christian missionary work in the second half of the nineteenth century. Its adoption was uneven since some missionaries were opposed to Swahili because of its associations with Islam and some churches adopted local languages as a surer way of making contact with those they wished to convert (Whiteley 1971). However, Swahili slowly gained ground.

The codification of the language was problematic. That traditional agent of standardisation, the translation of the Bible, was less influential than it had been in European settings, because the translator, a Lutheran called Pastor Roehl, not only came from outside the Swahili speech community but also set out to purge the language used in the translation of all Arabic influence. This purism imposed from outside, for religious purposes, was ill received. The resulting text was difficult to recognise as a written version of the varieties of Swahili actually spoken and Ansre reports:

that native Swahili speakers who heard Roehl's variety always asked: 'Where is this Swahili spoken?' (Ansre 1974: 384)

The main work on codification and standardisation was undertaken by European linguists in the 1920s and 1930s.[12] Again local spoken varieties were very different from the written form, and again, the standard was not universally recognised or accepted by mother tongue speakers (Ansre 1974).[13] A further difficulty for Swahili as national language were the two scripts: those educated in mission schools were literate in it in the Roman script and those educated in the Muslim tradition learnt to write it in the Arabic.

The defining period that ensured the spread of Swahili was the 1950s. Swahili[14] was the language of political mobilisation against colonialism. TANU (Tanganyika African National Union), the main organisation of the Tanganyikan independence movement, used it as its medium from its founding in 1954 onwards. Thus by independence 'Swahili had already acquired the status of a party or national language' (Whiteley 1971: 146) and was thereafter associated with the socialist ideology of Nyerere. After independence, Swahili was the language in which the *Ujamaa*[15] policies were introduced; the language and the political ideology reinforced each other. The introduction of Swahili as the national language in 1966 has been described as:

an ideological imperative inducing a state of mind towards the language as one of the behavioral corollaries of the national ethos. (Whiteley 1971: 151)

Interestingly for a language that was being promoted as a national symbol, it was also presented as a language of Africa. This was consonant with Nyerere's stance as the great supporter of pan-Africanism. Whiteley records how Swahili was promoted on several accounts: its African pedigree, its role as the medium of mobilisation against colonialism, its indexical function as the language of freedom, socialism and the nation. He notes that the

Tanzanians were exhorted to:

> use Swahili on such grounds as 'it is an African language', 'it played a crucial role in our struggle for independence', 'it is shameful to use the language of the colonialists and neo-colonialists' or 'it is the language of the people'. (Whiteley 1971: 151)

From 1967 an education policy based on *Ujamaa* socialist principles (*Elimu ya Kujitegemea* or education for self-reliance) introduced primary education for all in Swahili. Secondary and higher education continued to be through the medium of English but the plan was that they should also undergo Swahilisation at a later date (Blommaert 1994a; Mafu 2001). A national literacy campaign sent young activists out into rural Tanzania where Swahili was both the medium for information on new agricultural methods, health issues, political education, and a language whose acquisition in both its written and spoken forms signalled commitment to the nation and the *Ujamaa* project. Literacy programmes were based on primers promoting new ideas on the production of maize, wheat, rice, cotton, cattle or fishing and on political education (Buchert 1994).

Swahili thus spread to become the language of the public space in Tanzania (Blommaert 1994b) principally because it was the medium for a political philosophy that had a degree of acceptance, and *vice versa*. *Ujamaa* mobilisation of a majority of the country could not have happened without Swahili, the national language as symbol and medium (Mazrui and Mazrui 1998). Language engineering always has greater chance of success where there is ideological underpinning for new patterns of language use. Certainly, the Tanzanian government achieved a considerable degree of political participation through Swahili in the first twenty years after independence. Politics conducted through Swahili meant that a wider group could contribute than in countries which had retained the colonial language as the language of government[16] (Mazrui and Mazrui 1998). Education for self-sufficiency through Swahili also ensured a more democratic distribution of knowledge than in the postcolonial education systems where English and French continued to be the medium of primary schools (Blommaert 1994b).[17]

Tanzania has been a comparatively stable state compared to many other postcolonial states and in some senses this is an indication that nation building policies, including the spread of the national language, were largely successful. Nyerere (1999), himself, claimed that language had played a key role in the cohesion and stability he achieved:

> The Arusha Declaration and our democratic single-party system, together with our national language, Swahili, and a highly politicized and disciplined national army, transformed more than 126 different tribes into a cohesive and stable nation.

If we were to stop this account of language planning for national cohesion in Tanzania twenty years after independence, it would be possible to present Swahilisation as a successful intervention in the nation building tradition and contrast it with what happened in Kenya and Uganda where English persisted and vertical integration was not so far advanced (Bratt Paulston 1992). Many commentators contend that Swahilisation held ethnic and religious divisions in check for forty years (e.g. Gasarasi 1990). However, the situation has not remained stable. *Ujamaa* was not able to deliver economic prosperity and this coupled with the external economic pressures from the 1970s onwards led the Tanzanians to abandon socialist solutions. During the 1980s, socialism and the policies designed to foster self-reliance, equality and national identity, although still officially supported by the government, were abandoned under the impact of the structural adjustment programmes which were implemented in many 'developing' countries in the wake of worldwide recession. These programmes set new goals for 'development' in Tanzania, replacing the former emphasis on equality and participation with economic and political reform (Buchert 1994). Bowing to pressure from the World Bank and the International Monetary Fund, the Tanzanian government adopted domestic policy measures that were at odds with the previous philosophy. The major *volte-face* was the change from a state dominated socialist economic system to a market economy with a blending of public and private enterprise.[18] This had an immediate impact on education. The emphases on mass education in Swahili, on widening access, on increasing equality and fostering social cohesion, which were the mark of the *Ujamaa* period, waned. In its place, the goal of the education service became the development of excellence in science, technology and vocational training as means of modernising and developing the country, but not necessarily for all. The education of a small qualified technical and commercial elite became the focus. The concern was not to expand and democratise education but to ensure high standards for a limited group. There was no significant expansion of secondary education and the language of provision remained English. Only a tiny minority progressed from primary. Both the language in which it was delivered and the limited number of secondary places available ensured this (Blommaert 1994a; Mafu 2001). The World Bank and the IMF had reinforced the decision to postpone the Swahilisation of secondary education, by making clear their preference for English (Mazrui 1997). Widespread English competence had practical advantages for them and, as Mazrui suspects, there was probably an ideological dimension to the pressure. As aid was an increasing component of the education budget, the cash-strapped Tanzanians[19] felt they had little choice but to concur.

Among sociolinguists and planners the early euphoria evaporated. The flow of papers from the 1970s that stressed the relationship between corpus planning and national development, language acquisition and national cohesion began to dry up in the national language policy and planning literature (Blommaert 1994a). Swahili, the motor of national development and the language of liberation and Africanhood, appeared to have been eclipsed in key domains by a growing tendency to employ English. Even Nyerere, the champion of Swahili, conceded in 1974 that it would 'be foolish to reject English' (quoted in Blommaert 1994a: 219).

The period of austerity meant that education budgets had to be slashed, and, although the numbers in education in the previous period may have not been as high as the near 100 per cent literacy and school attendance subsequently claimed by Nyerere (1999), there is no doubt that numbers declined sharply (Danish Ministry of Foreign Affairs 2002). The proportion of the government spending devoted to education fell from 11.7 per cent in 1980–81 to 2.5 per cent in 1995–96 (United Nations 2000). School attendance fell from 70 per cent in the early 1980s to 60 per cent in the late 1980s (Buchert 1994). Buchert also reports that adult literacy is likely to have fallen in the period 1980–94, suggesting that, the idealism of *Ujamaa* that linked literacy with political education and social change had disappeared. The young activists who had breathed life into the scheme were replaced with teachers doing paid overtime and without the same motivation or time to commit to the activity. The learners too had different motivations; increasingly literacy and education came to be seen as the means for individuals to improve their economic situation rather than as giving value to the community. The vertical integration of the population that had started to occur, with Swahili as part of the process, was slowing

Then, as state schools, accused of having unsuitable curricula and too few and poorly trained teachers (Danish Ministry of Foreign Affairs 2002), appeared increasingly unable to provide for the aspirations of the elites, a parallel system of private academies began to develop to which the middle classes sent their children. Significantly these schools are English medium or place a heavy emphasis on English (Boyle 1999; Mafu 2001) and charge a rate that is out of reach of all but a very narrow elite class (*Tanzanian Observer* 12/01/03, p. 3).

In the state sector, there was no longer full commitment to free and compulsory education for 7–13 year olds made in the 1978 Education Act. Parents were asked to pay fees and other school related costs that had once been assumed by the government. The fall in school enrolment was inevitable and the government had to reconsider the policy in 2002. However, only primary school was made free for all; there were still fees for secondary and tertiary levels (Vavrus 2002) which exacerbated the binary divide between the basic level of education (potentially for all) in Swahili and the secondary fee paying level with instruction in English for a small minority. As Mazrui and Mazrui (1995) point out, English medium was not necessarily intended as elite closure, but, associated as it is with fee-paying, it has had that effect in both the public and private education systems.

The situation in Tanzania is echoed in the rest of Africa (Boyle 1999). As recession took hold, state schools suffered from chronic underfunding and the children of the urban poor and the rural periphery were most affected. Those who can flee the system do so, and more and more children of the professional and political elites are now educated in private schools (Boyle 1999). In consequence, education and literacy have ceased to be agents of vertical integration and horizontal language spread. There has instead been increasing stratification as the young of the rich are educated in English medium elite academies (less frequently French), the majority educated in cash strapped public schools[20] and the young of the very poorest effectively deschooled by urban or rural poverty. The growing number of street children in urban centres is a growing problem (United Nations 2000).

It seems that in Africa:

(t)he era of bold solutions, by the choice of single African languages in order to pursue only the goal of national unity, has generally been abandoned as impractical or self-defeating in its own terms. (Fardon and Furniss 1994: 13)

This holds true even for Tanzanians where the commitment to introduce and spread a distinct national language had been very clear. The movement towards linguistic unification within the state has stalled; citizens are not all *Waswahili* (Swahili speakers) despite claims to the contrary (Blommaert 1994b; Fieldwork Tanzania 2003). Swahili has not replaced local languages outside the main urban areas and has not replaced English in all prestige domains. Studies have recorded a relentless antipathy to further Swahilisation of education among the middle classes (Mafu 2001). They want to preserve the English medium secondary education system that they feel gives them the advantage Bourdieu defined as cultural capital (Bourdieu 1982).[21]

In the African states where English or French was designated the official language, the ideal of the single language is, unsurprisingly, even further from being realised. The numbers of English and French speakers remain small and competence in these languages distinguishes the political elite class. The variables that pushed European populations inexorably towards convergence and the realisation of a national community of communication did not all develop in the African context or were cut off before they took effect. Linguistic unification has been shown to be interrelated with the centripetal forces that create, spread and police a unified literacy (printing, education, bureaucracy, national media etc.) and the social arrangements that merge national populations (statewide programmes, conscription, social mobility, centralisation of decision making, investment in infrastructure). In the last three chapters I have been arguing that linguistic unification is a construct that needs to be supported by a prevailing nationalist ideology to make individuals feel constrained or moved to realise it in their practice. The evidence from Africa seems to point to a collapse of many of the contributing variables in the construct. Given that we might now be moving into what I shall argue can be seen as a postnational era in many respects, it may be that the process of achieving a single language for a single people in a single state will not be realised in the African postcolonial contexts and will become irrelevant. In a speech in Accra in March 1997, Nyerere himself expressed the opinion that the nation state model had proved unworkable in the African context and that with hindsight he was relieved:

> I reject the glorification of the nation state that we inherited from colonialism, and the artificial nations that we are trying to forge from that inheritance. We are all Africans trying very hard to be Ghanaians or Tanzanians. Fortunately for Africa we have not been completely successful. (Nyerere 1997)

So there are alternative conclusions to the story of the efforts of the Tanzanian language policy makers and planners to impose Swahili top-down on a diverse population in order to encourage feelings of national unity and solidarity. The first claims that the policy achieved a limited success on its own terms. Status planning worked in so far as Swahili became the language of the state institutions and the language that citizens mostly used when interacting with or working within these institutions. Corpus planning worked in the sense that Swahili was codified, standardised, elaborated, disseminated and accepted widely enough for mutual comprehension to be preserved. Acquisition planning worked to the extent that large numbers of children had engaged with Swahili as they were educated in the national education system and many learnt enough to use it easily in their daily lives. The alternative assessment has begun to appear more and more frequently in the literature and in political discourse over the past two decades. This very different perspective states that after two decades of planning for development, the lack of expansive economies to pay the social costs of national integration brought about a discrepancy between formulated and implemented policies in Tanzania in particular, as in Africa in general. Indeed rather than growing at a rate that could cover costs, economies contracted under pressures from internal problems and external forces.[22] The realisation of policies to ensure cohesive national development, particularly through education, was simply not possible in much of Africa, prevented by wars, droughts, heavy debts and a host of other economic and political crises and natural environmental and health disasters. Globalisation and the imposition of a market economy caused the horizontal fracturing of society with elite education increasingly through English.

4.4   Nation building in Indonesia: the role of Indonesian

The other case study in this chapter, Indonesia, provides some evidence that what happened and is happening in Africa is happening elsewhere. Indonesia is also an example of the kind of tensions rising within multi-ethnic states between the centripetal efforts of the nation building centre and the centrifugal pressures of independence and autonomy movements.

4.4.1 The historical and political context

Indonesia is also a country that was arbitrarily united by a colonial power. Consisting of more than 13 000 islands and stretching more than 5000 kilometres along the Equator, Indonesia is even more heterogeneous than Tanzania, although, with few land borders, fewer groups had been summarily divided by colonialism (Grant 1996). Today Indonesia has a population of 203.4 million people, making it the fourth largest state in the world. The vast majority of the population (70 per cent) lives on the islands of Java and Sumatera (2000 census).

Indonesians were never ruled as a single group prior to Dutch colonisation. There had been empires in the area before the Dutch conquest, but they were never coterminous with present day Indonesia.[23] The Dutch built the colony from several territories and never attempted to unite the peoples in any way. The Dutch East Indies were inhabited by very diverse peoples ranging from those who lived in highly civilised societies in which sophisticated technologies and philosophies had developed prior to the arrival of the Europeans (e.g. at Yogjakarta and Surakarta, the political centres of Central and Eastern Java) to societal organisation at a very simple level (e.g. the hunter–gatherer societies of Irian Jaya/Papua[24]). Their diversity was recognised, very belatedly in the colonial period, in a quasi-federal system set up by the Dutch in the final years of their rule.

At independence the new government had to deal with this diversity. The new nation would be composed of the hundreds of ethnic groups, recognised in the census. The groups differ wildly in terms of size. The Javanese community is the largest, followed by the Sundanese, Madurese, Minangkabau, Buginese, Batak and the Balinese. Smaller ethnic groups include the Ambonese, Dayaks, Sasaks, Acehnese. And apart from these indigenous communities, there are other communities, which originated outside the archipelago (Chinese, Arabs, Indians, Europeans). Despite this mix, federalism was rejected by the nationalist movement, and the new Indonesian government declared Indonesia a unitary state in 1949. The model for nation building was necessarily civic, although leaders sometimes evoked ethnic arguments for association:

> The national state is only Indonesia in its entirety which existed in the time of Shrivijaya and Majapahit and which now too we must set up together. (Soekarno quoted in Drake 1993: 19)

Notwithstanding the rhetoric, Indonesians had no common history to draw on except for the experience of Dutch colonialism (Drake 1993); they had no common language; they did not subscribe to a common religion.

The choice of national language for Indonesia had been made at the very start of the independence struggle. In a congress of nationalist youth organisations in 1928, Soekarno and others proclaimed their now celebrated 'Pledge of Youth' which called for 'one territory – Indonesia, one nation – Indonesian, one language – Bahasa Indonesia'. The choice of language was politically astute. Bahasa Indonesia (Indonesian) is closely related to Malay, the lingua franca of the sea-faring commercial community that had been used throughout the archipelago for centuries (Ricklefs 1993). Thus it was a language rooted in the area and familiar to many. It was also a language with historical links to Islam, the religion of the majority in Indonesia. The Islamic courts of Sumatera had been Malay speaking (Johns 1996). At the same time, it was not the mother tongue of any of the dominant groups in the nationalist movement.

Malay also had a long history as the language of literacy in the archipelago. The earliest written records of the language are the seventh-century Buddhist inscriptions on Sumatera (Ferguson 1977). Certainly from AD 671[25] and perhaps even earlier Srivijaya was a centre of Buddhist scholarship and Malay the medium of learning (Hunter 1996). Ninth-century inscriptions show that the language was in early use on Java as a language of literacy. Muslim missionaries who arrived in the twelfth century adopted Malay as the language of their missionary work and, as areas converted, Malay came to be written in Arabic script. The new religion brought new ways of thinking, and much Malay vocabulary in theological, spiritual and legal domains clearly derives from Arabic. Malay was thus the language of prestige in the area for several centuries, and when Europeans came to the archipelago they found the language in widespread use in political and commercial lingua franca functions in almost every coastal region of the Indies (Ferguson 1977). Pigafetta, who accompanied Magellan, compiled a glossary of Malay words in the Moluccan islands for the use of explorers. The Dutch navigator, Huygen van Linschoten wrote in 1614 that Malay was so prestigious among the peoples of this part of the Orient that for an educated man not to know it was like an educated Dutchman not knowing French (Kana 1994). In the following centuries, the Christian religious organisations that arrived in the wake of European adventurers and colonists used Malay as the main language for their missionary work.

After Dutch rule was established, it was usual policy to use Malay rather than Dutch in the education system for the various autochthonous groups, as this practice maintained the distance that the Dutch also favoured in their colonial arrangements.[26] This did not affect the majority of the population, however, since formal education was only for a select few.[27] In 1918, the Volksraad (People's Council) formally recognised Malay as the second official language after Dutch. It replaced Dutch as the medium of education in 1942, and in 1945 the Japanese accepted it as the official language of the colony. At independence, Malay was the evident choice as Indonesia's national language. Its long history as regional lingua franca and administrative language alongside Dutch and its prestige as the language adopted and promoted by the independence movement made it the prime contender (Drake 1993). Its long association with Islam, the main religion of the area, gave it further status. Most importantly, its choice as official language of the state prevented inter-ethnic competition for linguistic dominance, which would have resulted, most probably, in the imposition of Javanese on the rest. Javanese speakers were by far the largest group in the country (47.8 per cent of population at independence), and one that attracted a high level of resentment for their perceived dominance in political and economic domains (Moeliono 1994). Javanese could never have played the role of single national language and mobilising force for unification. Malay, on the other hand, the mother tongue of only 5 per cent of the population, was conspicuously unattached to any politically salient ethnic community. In its Indonesian variety, Bahasa Indonesia, it was related quite transparently to the institutions of the state, yet at the same time retained enough historicity to stand as a unifying symbol with appeal to most Indonesians. Bahasa Indonesia was thus a perfect nation building language, able to add an iconic dimension to its practical function (Errington 1998) and provoking few ethnic tensions. In the first decades of the new state the ideological importance of Indonesian as a symbol of unity and the basis for ethnic and cultural identity was enormous. Together with the national flag and *Indonesia Raya*, the national anthem, Indonesian became the symbol of national independence. In its practical function it enabled the political system, the army, the education system, the bureaucracy to function as national institutions and it acquired high status as elite groups used it increasingly among themselves and in their professional capacities (Drake 1993). Policymakers were optimistic that it would allow a community of communication within the new nation (Moeliono 1994).

Indonesia's first president, Soekarno, saw his overriding priorities as national unity stability and development (Eldridge 2002). A short period of parliamentary democracy during the 1950s was attacked within national political circles as having failed to achieve either prosperity or stability, and rebellions in West Sumatera and South Sulawesi appeared to threaten national integrity. Soekarno's solution was to incorporate the army in government and administration, to return to the 1945 constitution and to institute his system of Guided Democracy, which curtailed the ability of different groups to present and defend their interests, as is the tradition of liberal–pluralist democracy. The guiding principles underpinning the polity were enshrined in *Pancasila*,[28] a philosophy which prioritised the values of consensus and group unity. Decisions were to be resolved on the basis of deliberation and consensus. Competitive voting and the recognition of majority or minority interests would be avoided. An integralist discourse downplayed individual and group rights and presented the nation as a large family. The result was a paternalist, monolithic system, allowing for no opposition (Eldridge 2002).

Soekarno fell from power after an alleged left wing coup in 1965 which was put down by the army. General Soeharto assumed full presidential powers in 1967 and proclaimed a 'New Order' in Indonesian politics, which, although its main focus was economic rehabilitation and development, maintained the integralist aspects of *Pancasila*. Although Soeharto's rule was extremely authoritarian, it was to last more than three decades and was accepted by the majority because it was accompanied by a steady increase in living standards.[29] However, those who wanted political freedoms or who contested the highly centralised nature of the Indonesian state were to suffer. Soeharto's regime imprisoned many left wing militants and regional activists, many of whom died in prison from ill treatment and torture.

During this period, the fragile coalition of different peoples, religions and territories that formed Indonesia was only kept together by military force. A policy of resettlement of people from crowded Java on less densely inhabited islands was seen as a melting pot strategy, but was often unwelcome to host groups and sometimes had to be enforced by the army. In many areas independence movements gathered strength, for example, in Aceh on Sumatera and on Irian Jaya/Papua. East Timor was a particular case, a sovereign state that Soeharto had invaded in 1975 and annexed the following year.[30]

Despite the corruption, nepotism[31] and human rights abuses of his government, Soeharto remained in power until 1998. His grip on power only loosened as the Asian financial and economic crisis hit Indonesia in mid-1997, accompanied by the worst drought in the region in fifty years. The *rupiah* plummeted, inflation soared and investors withdrew their capital, provoking a swift plunge into recession. Food shortages, bankruptcies and the suspension of Indonesian banking led to hardship and insecurity. The Indonesians protested and rioting gradually intensified, despite brutal police efforts to stem protest. After several months of clashes, students occupied the country's parliament grounds, demanding the president's resignation. On 21 May 1998, Soeharto bowed to the pressure and resigned, naming vice president Habibie as his successor.

Indonesians' expression of their dissatisfaction with the economic situation widened to become general discontent with their political class Although Habibie pledged to lift restrictions on political parties and hold open elections as part of a package of reform measures intended to liberalise political life, violent rioting continued and with it an increasingly harsh response from the government. Many died. In the elections in June 1999 Habibie was ousted and Abdurrachman Wahid of the National Awakening Party, PKB, became president. Wahid was unable to combat the soaring inflation, unemployment and poverty rates and was in turn forced to step down. In June 2001, Megawati Soekarnoputri, Soekarno's daughter leader of Indonesian Democratic Party of Struggle, PDI-P, took over.

Criticism continued. General awareness that corruption had directed the fruits of economic growth to the few rather than the many had caused a profound change in attitudes towards the leadership.

The veneer of national unity was breaking down, primarily caused by economic tensions although 'ethnic' and religious factors appeared to be growing in importance. In a number of centres there was mounting friction between Muslims and Christians, resulting in rioting where the (mostly Muslim) crowd's anger was directed against the small business and shop-keeper class (mostly Christian). Inter-ethnic tension mounted. Many who had been happy to be part of the Indonesian project in more hopeful times now turned away. Various independence movements such as the Free Aceh Movement (GAM), the Irian Jaya/Papua separatists and the East Nusa independence movement increased their power base and now seriously threatened the integrity of the state. Tengku Hasan di Tiro, the leader of the Aceh separatists, expressed the position of those in the various independence and autonomy movements:[32]

> The problem is Indonesia. Indonesia is not a country at all; it is the empire of the Dutch. Sooner or later, Indonesia is bound to break up because the people want to go their separate way. (*Jakarta Post* 21/12/00, p. 1)

Since East Timor had broken away from Indonesia in 1999, the possibility of rejecting Indonesian nation building seemed a more attainable goal. In response to these developments the government proposed the introduction of limited autonomy in Aceh and Irian Jaya, hence to be called Papua, as it had been formerly. 1 January 2002 this came into force. Since then, those intent on independence rather than autonomy have continued their campaign against Jakarta, particularly in Aceh, and Megawati authorised an intensification of military reaction, which escalated in May 2003 into a full military offensive against the rebels.

This brief history gives the framework for the language policy and planning work that took place in Indonesia in the second half of the twentieth century. There was strong support for the adoption and spread of the language from all those who supported the nationalist project. A political system that declares that it values consensus needs a forum and Indonesian was the language promoted as its medium. As in the other case studies in this book, Indonesia's postcolonial experience suggests that language policy and planning alone is unlikely to be very effective. But when it coincides with other factors that promote national cohesion then it works in tandem with them, both to permit and to promote unification. Thus Indonesian linguistic unification has come about largely where national integration has taken root. Such integration was made possible in part by a growing economy. The feeling of solidarity in a situation where there was wealth to be distributed meant that only a minority was set against nation building.

When the boom ended then fractures appeared. How this will affect the spread of Indonesian remains to be seen.

4.4.2   Indonesian language planning

4.4.2.1   *Status planning*

The spread of Indonesian as the language of state throughout Indonesia was to be one of the key means of achieving the national unity that was key in both Soekarno's and Soeharto's vision. Indonesian was enshrined as the official language of the state by Article 36 of the constitution. It became the language designated for use in government, administration, the army and all education after the first three years. The former colonial language had no function in the new system and was not employed in domains where it would challenge Indonesian (Dardjowidjojo 1998). Other languages of Indonesia were guaranteed respect where they were 'well preserved' by the people (in a note appended to Article 36) but were to play a very limited and minor role in the public domain.[33] In 1972 the status of Indonesian was reaffirmed by President's Resolution 57 which gave further clarification on the domains of formal public life and state business where it had to be employed. The national language continued to have a dual function: it was both the language of literacy, modernisation and social mobility and the language of national identity and patriotism. It became the civic duty of speakers of languages other than Indonesian to become bilingual and societal arrangements ensured that it was to their advantage to do so. With this carrot and stick approach, the language spread. In 1971 40.5 per cent of Indonesians claimed to know Indonesian. This rose steadily with the decennial census reporting approximately 50 per cent knowing the language in 1981 and 60.8 per cent in 1991.[34] This is, of course, self-reporting, and so should be treated with some caution as the replies often show as much about loyalty and identification as competence. More 'objective' monitors of competence may be the state exams for civil servants and for school leavers, although there are claims that scores here are manipulated to allow citizens through to higher education or employment (Sugiyono and Latief 2000).

4.4.2.2   *Corpus planning*

There had actually been a formal language planning agency for Indonesian since the early 1940s. During the Occupation, the Japanese set up an Indonesian Language Committee to create modern terminology for science and technology and write a grammar of Modern Indonesian. Indonesian independent language planning built on this and the National Language Council was set up in 1947. This became the Centre for the Development and Preservation of the National Language (PPPB) in 1975. Language planners saw themselves as having a key role in both nation building and modernisation: the language had to be standardised to maximise internal intelligibility and provide a medium for education; it had to develop in new lexical domains if it was to be a tool in the general drive for modernisation and development. Indonesian corpus planning was a classic top-down operation, typical of the technocratic 1960s and 1970s, and has kept some of that ethos to the present day.

The standard developed and promoted by the language planning agency was based on Johor–Riau Malay, the classical literary language, rather than on Bazaar Malay, the koine or lingua franca developed for use in inter-group communication. This has caused a situation of diglossia. Indonesian is the high form (H) used for state affairs, literature, education, administration and all written functions and Bazaar Malay is the low form (L) used in the street, the market, in casual exchange and in popular entertainment. Thus, although the national language is related to a koine that many citizens either speak as a first language[35] or master to some degree, that koine may differ widely from the standard. In addition to the H/L difference there is much difference among dialects. The diversity within the L language is to be expected given its development in several centres over several centuries.[36] The phonological, semantic and syntactical variation exhibited by speakers of the different varieties mean that some dialects listed as Malay are probably not inherently intelligible to Standard Malay or Indonesian speakers.[37]

Thus the advantage of having a unifying national language based on a lingua franca that many already knew has turned out to have drawbacks as well as advantages. Those who speak one of the L varieties predictably have a false sense of security with regard to their knowledge of Indonesian, the H form. Some resistance to acquiring the standardised version is to be noted in diglossic situations, and there is always a tendency to introduce idiosyncratic features of the L variety into the H language. In the Indonesian situation, extreme pluricentrism of the L form means diversity is imported into the H form as learners transport features of their dialect.

Even when learners of Bahasa are not affected by a regional variety of Malay, there is still distinct regional difference. Given the size and spread of the population and the hundreds of different first languages, it is inevitable that when Indonesians learn the national language in school there is great divergence in pronunciation, linked to interference. Major regional differences can be traced to the regional languages. For example, Javanese, Sundanese, Madurese, Balinese, Toba Batak and Acehnese each provoke distinctive features of lexis and pronunciation (Moeliono 1994).

The valuing of variation within pluricentric languages that has entered the discourse of language planning in recent decades (Clyne 1984; Canagarajah 1999) has not made inroads in Indonesia where belief in the goal of a unified, centralised state frames the approach of planners. Sugiyono and Latief (2000) report on the various efforts to promote the standardised language and the clear understanding of the aim to build mutual comprehension and national identity. They report how the government actually ran a campaign in 1988 urging Indonesians to speak 'Good Indonesian'.

The second problem is a more recent development and stems from the way that Indonesia's diglossia is evolving to become societal cleavage not personal bilingualism. It is becoming less usual that a single individual will use the H form in one setting and the L form in another. Educated Indonesians tend to use the H in an ever-increasing number of settings (Moeliono 1994; Fieldwork 2001, 2002). Thus the H form becomes the language of the elites, differentiated from the morphologically less complex language of the poor, Bazaar Malay,[38] and from the hybrid variety developing among the young. The work done by British scholars (e.g. Trudgill 1983) shows how speakers of English may be socially and economically disadvantaged when their dialect variety is different from English Received Pronunciation (RP), and that, in this situation, it may actually be better to be a Gaelic or Welsh speaker. Thus we might expect that L speakers in Indonesian society will also be disadvantaged. Despite speaking a form of the national language, they are pigeonholed for speaking a non-prestigious variety and could be categorised as socially inferior with attitudes towards them more contemptuous and dismissive than towards mother tongue speakers of major regional languages such as Javanese, Sundanese, Madurese, Balinese, Toba Batak and Acehnese whose Indonesian is learnt in the classroom (Kana 1994).

4.4.2.3 Acquisition planning

The education system was charged with ensuring the spread of the newly standardised language, but in the first decades after independence the Indonesian education department simply did not have at its disposal the numbers of trained teachers with fluent standard Indonesian needed to implement its national language policy.[39] So before teaching the new generation Indonesian, a cohort of teachers had to be brought to the required levels of competence themselves, and, most importantly, kept at those levels when they returned to live among non-native speakers of Indonesian. Teachers acquiring the language at the same time as their pupils could not even draw on a bank of materials in the standard. It took some time to rewrite all basic textbooks in Indonesian from the fourth year of schooling through to university particularly given that the pool of people competent to create core texts and new materials in every area was limited and the important role that language planning was felt to have in early nation building was eclipsed by the political crises of the 1960s.

In the face of these difficulties of introducing standard Indonesian into the classroom, little attention was given to the fact that children were studying through a second language (Rubin 1977). The preparation for Indonesian medium education for the children who did not speak it at home was only one hour per week in the year before they moved to Indonesian as the only medium of education. The education service had not decided whether it was teaching Indonesian as a second or foreign language, nor what the consequences of this would mean for pedagogy (Rubin 1977). Moreover, for those who did have some competence in Malay before the fourth grade, there were also problems. Pupils were not always aware of their language needs and deficiencies. Those who had acquired Bazaar Malay in an informal way regularly overestimated their competence in Indonesian. They were not fully conscious of the functional differentiation between the H and L varieties of the language and were resistant to attempts to plug what they could not recognise as a gap in their knowledge (Rubin 1977). Both foreign commentators like Rubin and Indonesian academics like Moeliono called for research and action.

Some of the problems have disappeared with time. There is currently no difficulty in finding teachers who are fluent in Indonesian. Standardisation of the language has been completed and is accepted. Curriculum development and materials production have improved as the teacher training agency in Jakarta[40] has worked on projects and disseminated good practice through courses. But the others persist. Until 2002, the education system remained highly centralised, run from Jakarta on a single model. This has meant 'one size fits all' solutions to individual situations in very different provinces. One dilemma remains, the modalities of introducing Indonesian as the medium of instruction. Since the cities, particularly Jakarta, are progressively moving to monolingualism, the education system now assumes that it is the first language of the pupils in the towns and adapts pedagogy appropriately. In the countryside and on the periphery of the archipelago, Indonesian remains a second language and different approaches have to be adopted. Problems still arise, however, as these students ultimately have to compete with monolinguals in a single system. The introduction of Indonesian as a compulsory subject from the first grade onwards and a creeping tendency to use it as a medium of instruction from the third grade are seen as ways of minimising differences (Fieldwork 2002).[41] More Indonesian in the classroom means a reduction in education through the mother tongue, which is widely seen as unwise in the bilingual literature in terms of child development and may be felt as a loss among groups that continue to value their linguistic and cultural heritage.[42]

Increasingly, a proportion of students fail to master the scholarly variety of Indonesian necessary for study and use a hybrid variety that mixes low and high forms of the language in its place. Most students are not fully aware of their lack of linguistic competence, educators have difficulty persuading them of it and although students are alerted to diglossic variety, there is, so far, no clear resolution in terms of changed language behaviour and increased differentiation.[43] In the teacher training and language policy literature there is evidence of tension between a purist movement that wants to police the language (e.g. the 'Speak Good Indonesian' campaign) and individual speakers who are making it their own. However, one could also see these problems as deriving from the heteroglossia that is inevitable when a population of more than 200 million people moves to a common language. They furnish, perhaps, a convincing reason to believe that Indonesian is increasingly a first language and not merely a H language learnt in school for formal purposes.

4.4.3   Centrifugal forces

The republican belief in the necessary unitary nature of the state is still supported by the majority of Indonesians (who live on Java). There is widespread backing at the centre for a hard stance when the periphery demands devolved power. There is still a strong patriotic attachment to Indonesian and the Youth Pledge is often quoted in the letters, editorials and articles in the Jakarta based newspapers that reveal how capital based opinion is strongly opposed to pluralism or devolution. A letter to the *Jakarta Post* exemplifies such attitudes:

> Any wish to secede from the Unitary Republic of Indonesia is tantamount to rebellion and must therefore be subject to firm measures. We have the Youth Pledge and this must be upheld at any cost. (*Jakarta Post* 13/12/00)

4.4.3.1   *The end of integration*

However, there are signs that the Indonesians have ground to a halt on their trajectory towards homogenisation and linguistic unification. Indonesian in its iconic role as symbol of national unity, as facilitator of the national community of communication and as the medium of social mobility may be in retreat. A number of political and economic developments are likely to have a profound effect on the status and use of Indonesian.

The unravelling at the centre comes from a fracture within education. The economic crises of the late 1990s left the government impoverished and the political crises left it preoccupied. One of the casualties was public education.[44] Faced with underfunded and failing schools, the professional and middle classes have increasingly opted for private schooling. As in Africa, private education is often English medium or part English medium. This added a further reason for exiting the state system since parents were anxious that their children be in a position to participate in the increasingly transnational nature of much economic activity. They wanted to prepare their children linguistically for roles, not necessarily at national levels of activity but at global. The increase in private education underscores the deep class divisions already apparent in Indonesia, and the children of the elite group are increasingly differentiated from the rest by their language repertoire, which includes good English skills as well as knowledge of the national language.

Globalisation has also affected policy in the state sector. The 1997 economic crisis illustrated graphically the vulnerability of domestic markets and the power of external influences. Government agencies that had seen the spread of Indonesian as key to achieving economic and technological advance now rethought their strategy and decided that the needs of the knowledge economy meant that Indonesians should also acquire competence in English (Huda 2000). However, although English teaching increased, the gap between private and state provision has not closed significantly. Public schools are not in a position to rival the private sector. First, the state system is under-resourced. The highly centralised education system which foregrounds national unity and equality of educational experience for all students does not allow for differentiation and so English has become an obligatory subject for all students at Junior High and above. This has led to a thin spread of expertise. Teachers' own competence in English is deemed one stumbling block to effective teaching and learning (Fieldwork at PPPG 2000; Hamied 2000). Second, there are problems of motivation. A proportion of Indonesian students cannot at present see adequate reason to acquire English. In many of the islands they do not have contact with native speakers and do not see that their future roles will require knowledge of English as a lingua franca. The obligatory status of English has thus led to a high level of disaffection among certain groups of students who are already having to master one second language in education and are now being forced to learn another (PPPG 2000).[45] The evaluation of the teacher training agency that:

> Most high school graduates are unable to communicate in English although we have been teaching them for six years. (Soejoto 2000)

suggests that the English for all policy in the public sector cannot yet be counted a success (Fieldwork at PPPG 2000), and makes it feasible to believe that students in private schools will continue to be advantaged.

Indonesia has never been an egalitarian society but, after independence, linguistic divisions were being erased. Less economically privileged groups embraced Indonesian as the language of opportunity, which could contribute to their social mobility. Now they may feel that the linguistic capital that they believed they were acquiring is worth less to them than in past decades and this may fuel some disaffection. Laitin (1999) has noted how alienated people feel, when competition for the best jobs goes to those who are linguistically advantaged. It seems that those acquiring high levels of competence in English will be best placed for the most prestigious roles since private companies now regularly require English language qualifications before considering a candidate (Sugiyono and Latief 2000). Since the economic crises of the late 1990s an English-speaking elite in Jakarta has increasingly turned outwards to grasp opportunity. In such a context, differentiation in linguistic skills and repertoire works against vertical integration and causes resentment.

At the other end of the economic continuum there is another aspect of the economic crisis that is also blocking national integration. The very poor have grown poorer and there are increasing numbers of street children in the urban centres who are not in education at all. Demographic pressures combined with diminishing resources have made it even more difficult to provide universal education and ensure attendance. Such exclusion is likely to produce a disaffected and disenfranchised class that sees itself outside the national group. This was already apparent in the riots of the late 1990s. Although different political groups may have been at the heart of the opposition, the scale of the protests was due to the mood among the very poorest. And whereas the former were targeting corruption in the Soeharto family and demanding political reform, the latter saw the Indonesian–Chinese commercial class as their main target and attacked and looted their shops and businesses. The scale of the attacks and the clear, ethnically defined target has been a blow to integration.

One of the many outcomes of the riots has been an increasing tendency among the Chinese community to send their children to Mandarin classes and to the People's Republic of China (PRC) to study. There is a strong sense that as a group they should be forward planning for migration and be ready to move if necessary (Fieldwork 2001). This seems a logical decision and very interesting to note in a period where English is so often seen as the medium to acquire for migration.[46]

The last and perhaps one of the most significant factors contributing to any unravelling of the community of communication might well be coming from government opposition. The opposition that ranged against Soeharto accused him and his New Order government of masking and manipulating facts (Fatah 2000). Indonesian was the medium for distortion and slogans and this may have some consequences for individuals' language choice and patterns of allegiance. Where the state has been rejected as authoritarian and/or corrupt, the language with which it is so closely associated could lose some ground.

4.4.3.2 Secession at the periphery

In addition to these fissiparous trends at the centre, a number of regions on the periphery are rejecting their incorporation in the Indonesian state. Several movements for secession and independence are active and there are a number of on-going ethnic and religious conflicts within Indonesia. Not all protagonists are in pursuit of independence or significant devolution of powers. Some, for example in Central Sulawesi, where fighting between Christian and Muslims caused more than 2000 deaths in the Poso Regency in the three-year period 1998–2001, before the two sides called a truce (Malino Declaration), are about economic and political power distribution within the existing framework and are unlikely to end in calls for secession. Other groups, however, have independence as their goal. GAM, the Free Aceh Movement, has been engaged in guerrilla warfare since the mid-1970s in an attempt to create an independent Islamic state. Thousands have died in this conflict[47] and both GAM and the army have a history of extreme violence. In summer 2002 a special autonomy package was agreed for Aceh, although the referendum on independence for which they asked was refused (*Jakarta Post* 30/07/02). In 2003 violence flared again between Aceh separatists and government forces. Unsurprisingly, a breakaway education system operates in Aceh, where Islamic schools use Acehnese, and Arabic for Koranic study, in place of Indonesian. From January 2002, the Acehnese began the process of introducing Sharia law which can only widen the cultural and linguistic divide between them and the rest of the country (*Jakarta Post* 27/12/01).

The dissident Acehnese are an extreme example of the threats to Indonesian integrity, but the trend is discernible in other, quite unlikely, places. Many Javanese displayed great emotional commitment and predisposition to Indonesian as an indication of their support for the republic. To have their children acquire it and use it properly was a commitment to make the postcolonial regime work. The Javanese, a high status group which hitherto had been literate in one of the prestige languages of the archipelago, was willing for its children to be educated in the new medium, in an unusual forfeiture of privilege.[48] Now it seems there is some regret that the previous generation made that decision and an indication of a return to Javanese literacy[49] (Errington 1998). Warih (2001) expresses a growing band of opinion when he calls for Javanese to be taught as a subject within the education system to ensure that the younger generation are literate in the language, and for more newspapers and magazines to be published in Javanese.

In other areas there are also calls for a return to the ancestral language and one of the telling developments is the change of attitude to be noted. Populations that had reported feelings of shame when they could not express themselves in the national language, now are more likely to express pride in their ancestral language (Miehle 2001). The 1999 Act No. 22 on the autonomy of the regions gives them the authority to finance the preservation and development of their languages. This was previously the remit of the PPPB, which caused if not a conflict of interests, then certainly a conflict of agendas. Now regions have the right to standardise and then to introduce into the curriculum the languages that they choose to support and promote. This will depend a great deal on the funding available and public support (Mahsun 2000).

We can perhaps conclude here with a quote from the respected Indonesian scholar, Anton Moeliono, reflecting on the twin pressures on the national language discussed here. He remarks that from one direction Indonesian is under attack from the instrumental advantage conferred by English. Knowledge of English is increasingly seen to enhance the status of those who can speak it. Even the ubiquitous 'Hello Mister' has some element of this about it and is felt to give advantage to the street seller in a way that calling 'Tuan' to a potential customer does not. At the same time, he observes that the integrational pull of the various vernaculars of the Indonesian archipelago has not waned as the nation builders hoped:

> The lack of motivation to master the national language adequately, apart from the competitive influence of English is related to language attitudes of people towards Indonesian. ... We can say that people generally have a higher level of emotional commitment towards their mother tongue than towards Indonesian. (Moeliono 1994: 211)

Since Moeliono wrote these words in 1994, the cohesion of Indonesian society has been further challenged by economic crisis, constant scandals stemming from corruption in the political elite, ethnic tensions and conflict, the secession of East Timor and limited devolution. It remains to be seen what will happen to Indonesian if the national ideal falters further. Its long history and its continuing use as a regional lingua franca for Malaysia, Brunei, Singapore and Indonesia will ensure its survival but it may have reached its apogee and find its domains of use squeezed between the pressures of global English and vernaculars which reconquer some of the areas from which they disappeared in the nation building era. Of course, language grievances do not fuel separatism (Laitin 1999), but they are often an early indicator that groups are reacting to centralisation and nation building.

4.5   Conclusions: new conceptual frameworks

In the accounts given in this and preceding chapters, it has become clear that national language policy and planning is an activity, which was supported by those it targeted and had some measure of success, when it was in sympathy with prevailing nationalist ideology. With changing economic and political contexts and the new ideological frameworks that have developed with them, it is increasingly out of favour. At the present time there is a growing conviction that the very concept of language policy making and planning has become unacceptable. Language planning in one or other of its forms may still be taking place in the service of nation building in newly independent countries and newly autonomous regions, but it has been roundly challenged by contemporary scholarship in many other locations. Language planning procedures are now subject to far greater scrutiny and challenge than was the case in the preceding period. Today, scholars are likely to approach certain kinds of LPLP more critically than those in an earlier period, when the prevailing nationalist ethos made it rare for linguists to engage with the negative effects of the language standardisation and spread that they approved of and that they were often instrumental in developing and promoting. A branch of scholarship has grown up that monitors and analyses policy critically, and the objects of planning themselves are more alert, if not to the process itself, then to the issues accompanying it.

   This stems in large part from a paradigm shift which has occurred in the last few decades and which has made us both suspicious and critical of the nation building process. The new paradigm has been influenced by post-modern and postnational thinkers in other disciplines. Both postmodern and postnational schools of thought challenge all the concepts under-pinning the activity of language planning in the nation state. From the postmodernist perspective, language planning is a contradiction in terms. Christina Bratt Paulston's description of postmodernism gives an indication of why this is so:

> Postmodernism opposes the universalizing of arguments and positions; rejects metanarratives or any one privileged discourse, sees disagreements over meanings as integral to its own position and welcomes diversity and variety of analysis, which can only be approached by each observer from his or her opinion. (Bratt Paulston 2002)

National language planners are clearly in the opposing intellectual camp: in status planning, the aim has usually been to gain general acceptance for a privileged language variety (inevitably linked to a privi-leged group and to a dominant discourse) and to impose it on the rest of the community. Other media for making meaning are ousted as the national standard gains ground. In much corpus planning, particularly in the early period, the aim is to standardise, to fix language in a system, where meanings are defined by the academy or the dictionary makers rather than negotiated in interaction. In acquisition planning, the aim is to socialise the young of the group into the nation's language and the national discourse(s) and to direct usage in a quite authoritarian way.[50] The aim of nation building LPLP is convergence, not recognition of diver-sity. The postmodern paradigm challenges the basis of such activity, and the two cannot be reconciled.

The paradigmatic change that postmodernism brought to sociolinguistics has produced a scholarly literature informed by the belief that diversity is inevitable and incontrovertible and that the policies of nation builders were both utopian and doomed to failure. In the African context this new model has been widely assumed. Academic opinion has now veered towards view-ing 'multiculturalism, pluralism and multilingualism as facts of African life (that) have to be seen positively as resources upon which development must build and not as impediments to national unity and development' (Fardon and Furniss 1994: preface). Policymaking has taken the same route, and is exemplified most clearly in post-apartheid South Africa's rejection of the unitary model and its government's decision to designate eleven languages used within the state as co-official.

A parallel, post-structuralist current questions the objectification of language inherent in language planning and suggests that it is a total myth that any unitary structure equates to Indonesian, Swahili or any other lan-guage. There is, of course, much truth in this. Where Malay is described as being the language used in certain settings, what set of linguistic practices does that mean? Malay as a lingua franca changed both over time and over space. Substrata of autochthonous languages influence usage and both Dutch and Portuguese interacted with it to produce distinct varieties. Add to this the variety arising from different stages of acquisition of what is mostly a second language, and the result is extreme diversity. There are, therefore, a disparate set of language practices that shelter under the name Malay. There is no denying this; the interesting point is, of course, that language planners expected to counter this, did objectify language and set out to produce a community where there was 'minimal variation'.

As the new schools of thought gained ground in the 1980s, both theorists and practitioners made the case for multilingualism, and researchers set out to reveal the traditional ways that groups overcome the uncomfortable linguistic discontinuities inherent in any societal organisation that includes diverse linguistic groups. The research also began to concentrate on individual liberties and rights rather than social cohesion, to focus on the disadvantages of linguistic convergence and to look for means to accommodate multilingualism within institutions.

The other new theoretical framework that altered the landscape in LPLP was postnationalism. In the political sciences, nationalism became a focus of interest and a body of literature began to treat it almost as a pathology. There seemed to be new and different ideologies that were perhaps eclipsing old style nationalism, new societal forms of organisation that were evolving and that were antithetical to the nation state.

There is, however, a challenge to nationalism inherent in postnationalism which could itself be categorised as nationalist. There is a growing tendency for states to break up into smaller units, with a continuum of political accommodation from limited autonomy through to full secession. Campaigns for the devolution of power are usually attended by a renaissance of interest in regional languages and demands for their reinstatement in the education system, very much in the nationalist mould.

The last two parts of the book explore the new nexus of power and association that accompany globalisation and the new awareness of rights and recalibration of identities that come with the demands for minority recognition, both of which appear to be undermining nation statism and affecting language attitudes and behaviour and both of which entail rethinking of language policy.

Part II

Transcendence and Language Learning

5
Transcending the Group: Languages of Contact and Lingua Francas

5.1 Languages of contact and lingua francas

Part I of the book focused on how there are pressures within communities to move towards linguistic homogeneity. The argument was that speaking in the same way is an act of identity as well as an act of communication. The language policymakers and planners of the nation building era understood this and, recognising that language is a very powerful social glue in the constitution of groups, systematically and rigorously encouraged the creation of a single community of communication within the polity. Because they sought to change behaviour top-down, the very activity of language policymaking has come to be seen as inherently repressive (Brumfit 2002). But it should not be forgotten that they mostly succeeded because there was consensus from below. Nationalist ideology was accepted by large majorities within populations for a significant period, particularly in Europe.

In Part II, the book turns to the question of contact among speakers from different speech communities and discovers how communication is achieved across language borders. Humans solve their communication problems in one of two ways: either by developing an interlanguage which both sides employ, or by one group, or a section of one group, learning the other's language. The likelihood of one solution rather than the other stems from the reasons for the communication and power relationships. A wish to trade and benefit economically from contact, a need to bow to political pressure, to accommodate to a conqueror, an aspiration to identify with the ideology or religion of another group and have access to its sacred works, a desire to access new ideas, new art, new technologies in order to adopt them, are immensely different reasons for contact and will each have a different linguistic outcome and provoke different behaviour and practices.

One of the crucial differences in language learning derives from whether the language has a written form or not. Where the target language only exists in the spoken form, it can only be acquired through direct contact with its speakers, and this is how language learning happened throughout most of human history, as need arose through new face-to-face contact with outsiders. To become fluent in the language of an oral society meant to live among the group that spoke that language. Once the language was written, however, it could be detached from its speakers and learnt as a system outside of their physical presence, although considerable phonological and semantic distortion might occur.

The motivations for learning a language are also affected by literacy and the circulation of information in written form. Once knowledge can be disseminated through the written word, then a second language may be learnt to gain access to sacred texts and ideological works, to new technologies or to language-borne culture. Transfer can be depersonalised and access to knowledge does not depend on the agreement of the authors once they have committed the knowledge to public record. In the past, formal learning of a written language was usually restricted to a small, literate, elite class charged with assuring translation and interpretation between groups for transfer of cultural or technical knowledge.

Now we are entering a new phase in human association. With the advent of audio-visual media, face-to-face contact is reproduced in virtual form for millions of people. With the vast growth in the knowledge now stored and disseminated in electronic formats, the number of people concerned with the retrieval of written information in other languages has increased exponentially. With the rise of global regulation, systems and regimes, the world operates as a unit in an increasing number of domains, and communication among the parts needs to be achieved. Learning the languages of others is no longer the affair of a small cosmopolitan elite or a bilingual clerical class, traders or travellers. A far larger proportion of the world now wants or needs to communicate across language borders.

This chapter briefly reviews the history of language groups in contact and discuss some of the lingua francas and pidgins that have arisen in the past when two groups came into contact. The linguistic solutions for trading relations do not appear to be so different from those following conquest and occupation when the conquered have to accommodate to serving the conquerors. This gives some insight into the similar pressures that economic superiority, greater political power, cultural prestige, or technological supremacy exert in the choice of language. The second part of the chapter focuses on the acquisition of a codified and standardised language of a group seen to be prestigious. Here learners are not always under direct pressure to acquire the language, but see the access to information that it will bring and the prestige association that it permits as advantageous both to them and to their society.

Traditionally, there has been much less conscious language planning to achieve intergroup comprehension than for intragroup. Until the recent past, societal acquisition of foreign languages was not necessarily the affair of the state. Foreign language learning was more likely to be a personal decision and undertaking. Trading lingua francas and pidgins and the creoles of colonisation were never the focus of education systems; they were not documented nor consciously taught. The people that needed to use them learnt them without direction, according to need. There was little state planning to ensure communication across linguistic borders even where imperial powers required a class of competent bilingual bureaucrats. It was often elite groups among the conquered groups themselves that made sure their children acquired the prestige lingua francas that would allow them to be part of governance in the new order, and the ruling group did not need to take action itself. However, if ruling elites did not often learn the language of those they ruled, they usually learnt the languages of powerful neighbours. At the very highest level of political hierarchies, there is frequently a cosmopolitan elite able to act on an international stage. The general rule of instrumental language learning seems to be that one learns the language of the group with more power than one's own. This is true whether it is coerced learning in situations of conquest and colonisation or foreign language learning undertaken to promote life chances.

The existence of a hierarchy of languages had always been appreciated. Rulers realised that use of one language rather than another reflected the state of power relationships in economic, political, cultural and technological terms and thus promoted their own in negotiations. However, it took somewhat longer for them to understand that there is actually little that can be done to persuade others to use one's language, if the reasons for doing so are not present anyway. Chapter 6 tracks the rise and fall of French as a lingua franca. The spread of French occurred with little conscious promotion of the language, and resulted as a by-product of other processes. The chapter concludes with an account of recent policy initiatives undertaken by the French government to protect the position of French as a lingua franca and to halt its contraction, all of which have had little effect. The general message from this case study is that language policy makers are largely powerless to control or even influence the spread of lingua francas.

5.2   Trading languages

Perhaps trade and empire do not represent a dichotomy but a continuum with a gradual development from mutual benefit by exchange without coercion through to gross exploitation of one group by another. Certainly there is no clear dividing line between the linguistic solutions developed to deal with the different situations. In both trade and imperial settings there may be the development of a simple pidgin, a utilitarian language of contact stripped of everything except that which contributes to the bare necessities of communication. '(Pidgins) come into being where people need to communicate but do not have a language in common' (Bakker 1995: 25).

A pidgin is not used here in the detrimental sense found in many dictionary definitions but following the technical definition of linguists:

> Pidgins result from the communicative strategies of adults who already have a native command of at least one language. Pidgins have therefore been called 'auxiliary' languages because they are needed by their speakers in addition to their own native language, to bridge a communicative gap with speakers of some other language. (Sebba 1997: 14)

Thus, by definition, pidgins have no native speakers. At its most simple, a contact language is a jargon where what is complicated is left out (Mühlhäusler 1986) and where the tiny vocabulary reflects the reason for contact.[1] A jargon becomes a stabilised pidgin when the language of those communicating settles into a conventional pattern. The two sets of speakers in contact borrow conventions from their first languages. Several things can happen. In the first possibility, one language is the matrix providing the grammatical and syntactical structure and the other the lexifier, providing most of the vocabulary. Where clear superstrate and substrate languages are not identifiable, the term adstrate is used (Sebba 1997) to indicate a kind of cross-language compromise of the languages in contact (Thomason 2001). One school of thought holds that pidgin structure is 'negotiated' and highly influenced by the universals of second language learning (Bickerton 1975).

A pidgin is always a reduced language. The grammar of the pidgin is always simpler than the grammar of the source language (Sebba 1997). There is maximum use of minimum lexicon (Mühlhäusler 1986: 171). A basic pidgin has no expressive functions, restricted lexis and a low degree of iconicity, that is, lexical items do not acquire the same degree of connotation in the pidgin as they do in the mother tongue. Interestingly, pidgins are generally not mutually intelligible with their source languages (Sebba 1997).

Trading jargons and pidgins that do not move away from their primary function are purely utilitarian language and remain an additional language for each of the groups using them (Romaine 1988). They are a practical solution for trading purposes because they serve specific and very limited needs (Le Page and Tabouret-Keller 1985). Because of their utilitarian and spoken nature, pidgins often leave little historical trace. People are not literate in them. They are not recorded in topography. They must have proliferated in prehistory but we do not have any account of them. Even the forms of those used in the recorded past are difficult to describe. For example, we know of the existence of a Romance-based pidgin used extensively in the Mediterranean by traders, sailors and crusaders and their contacts from AD 1000 until the early nineteenth century, but we do not know enough to reconstruct it accurately. Only a few anecdotal quotations in the writings of travellers or observers and an incomplete French/Lingua Franca vocabulary (1830) meant for settlers in Algeria have survived (Corré 2000).[2] Its lexifier seems to have been either an Occitan or Northern Italian dialect but the base language is unclear. It is known both as Sabir and Lingua Franca, and the second name is of course the origin of the current term to denote a language of contact for two or more groups. Another early recorded pidgin is Maridi Arabic mentioned by the Arab geographer, Abu Ubayd al-Bakri, in a book he wrote in 1068. This pidgin was used in the Maridi region to allow trade between Arabs and Africans.

Most European trading pidgins were based, unsurprisingly, on the languages of the seafaring nations. A Basque–Icelandic and a Basque–Algonquian pidgin existed in the sixteenth and seventeenth centuries as this maritime people explored the Atlantic rim and traded (Arends *et al.* 1995). Russenorsk was a trading language used in sporadic summer commerce along the northern coast of Norway, Finland and Russia in the eighteenth and nineteenth centuries. Its first documented occurrence was in a lawsuit in 1785 (Romaine 1988).

These five European pidgins died out when the contact they enabled no longer took place (Naro 1978). This is normal. Trading languages regularly vanish when the economic relations that cause them disappear. This is illustrated quite graphically by Russenorsk which disappeared immediately after the Russian Revolution when the political and economic isolation of the USSR caused commerce between the groups to cease (Romaine 1988).

We can assume that the adoption of a trading language like all other language use is not neutral. It is unlikely that there will have been equal effort from both sides of the language divide to bridge it. The economically and politically weaker will have made the major effort. This explains how pidgins can come to dominate over a large area as lingua francas; they are most heavily influenced by the group that is travelling and trading, where that group has some political and economic clout, and their language becomes the lexifier of the pidgin. Through their common semantic core, the different varieties retain some mutual comprehensibility. In south east Asia, Bazaar Malay functioned as a lingua franca for the Malay peninsula and for much of the Indonesian archipelago for centuries.[3] Chinese traders along routes on land and sea left a legacy of Chinese based pidgins (Arends *et al.* 1995).

Thomason (2001) gives a number of examples where a pidgin was developed to prevent outsiders learning the group language and thus acquiring membership. The Nez Percés in North America used two languages, the language that they considered and termed 'proper' and a 'jargon' which differed so much that there was no mutual comprehension between the two. The jargon was a pidgin originating in basic communication with the prisoners that they had taken in war and was kept in order to maintain social distance between the ruling class and the slave group (Thomason 2001). In the colonial and missionary period there are also instances of pidgin development to keep newcomers at arm's length. As the Chinese came into contact with Western, specifically English, traders and colonists, Chinese Pidgin English was developed, because, Hall (1966) claims, the Chinese were disdainful of the English, were unwilling themselves to learn English and did not want the English to learn Chinese. The Hamer in Ethiopia and the Motu in Papua New Guinea also withheld knowledge of their language to prevent others from entering their society (Thomason 2001). In parallel, the British and the Germans in East Africa used Swahili to maintain distance between themselves and those they had colonised.

Exogamy and trade also seem to have created what Trubetzkoy first noticed and termed *Sprachbund* (1928–29). Where there is regular association there may be the development of similar linguistic phenomena as one set of language users starts to adopt the syntactic structures and lexis of the other. Although there is no actual formation of a new language of contact, the outcome suggests that pidgin-like communication may have taken place and provoked a real similarity. *Sprachbunde* have been recognised in the Baltic area, the Balkans, South Asia, different regions of Africa and North America among languages that have no linguistic affiliation but geographical proximity and a history of exchange (Winford 2003). This is, of course, the contact which promotes congruence among different language speakers and which purists try to stem in an effort to maintain clear boundaries between groups.

There is a continuum from trading language to imperial language. Some trading may be backed by military force and involve a high degree of coercion. There may then be a seamless continuum into settlement and the forced labour of colonisation. For example, the pidgins which began as trading languages between European adventurers and the peoples of the countries they visited in the sixteenth century soon became languages to maintain a power imbalance. Such contacts were different in kind from those for which Russenorsk, for example, was developed, where the groups were equals in the exchange. As the European powers colonised, the pidgins became the languages of inter-ethnic contact and the medium of command between the new masters and those made to work manually on farm or plantation, in mine or factory. It appears that imbalance in the relationship is reflected in the development of pidgins. The lexifier is overwhelmingly the language of the dominating group. In Russenorsk, in contrast, the lexicon was equally drawn from both groups (Holm 1989; Sebba 1997).

Russenorsk was not a stable pidgin, because the Norwegian and Russian groups in contact were likely to be different with every season's fishing and trading. Holm (1989) suggests that it was probably recreated every year. Pidgins become stable if the groups in contact maintain a long-term relation. Pidgins become more complex as they extend into new functions. Pidgins spread where they are taken up by third parties as a useful language of contact. Where a pidgin becomes the first language of a group it is then termed a creole. When creoles come to be used by whole communities as their main or only language, they become semantically and syntactically more complex.[4] In the dislocation that colonialism caused in many societies, many pidgins became creoles, that is, the principal languages of many groups whose ancestral languages were eclipsed. This is particularly true of the Africans taken to the Americas to work on plantations. Family and tribal groups were broken up, often intentionally to weaken the ability of the slaves to organise resistance. The only languages available to heterogeneous slave communities were the contact pidgins, which subsequently developed into creoles.

Indeed many major official standardised languages probably developed in this way as simplified languages of contact which were subsequently adopted as the only medium of a group.[5] Many of the national languages of southern Europe may have originated in this way, developing from Vulgar Latin fusing with the substrata of languages spoken in the territories before the arrival of the Romans and influenced by the mother tongues of invaders who arrived later (Le Page and Tabouret–Keller 1985).

Before moving from the subject of pidgins and creoles there is a point to be made about the marked similarities of all the pidgins associated with European colonialism. In one of the theories that explain this, the monogenetic theory, linguists suggest that a very early contact pidgin based on Portuguese or Sabir and used along the West African coast, provided the model for the other pidgins of colonialism. The hypothesis is that this basic pidgin spread west where it became the basis for the creoles used by the slaves in the New World plantations. Here it underwent relexification depending whether the masters were French, English or Spanish (Perl 1984; Goodman 1987). It is also suggested that the same basic pidgin existed in the Indian and Pacific regions where it was subsequently relexified under the influence of Dutch, French and English colonisers who followed the Portuguese (Whinnom 1956). Some evidence for this theory comes from a nineteenth century study of Tok Pisin in New Guinea where German relexification of an English based pidgin was noted (Hesse-Warteg 1898, reported in Mühlhäusler 1986).

The other theory about pidgins is universalist and is based on the possibility discussed in the Introduction that human beings are biologically programmed to acquire language rather than a particular language. Todd (1990) suggests that:

> the programming includes an innate ability to dredge our linguistic behaviour of superficial redundancies where there is a premium on transmitting facts, on communicating, as it were, without frills. It is not being suggested that we are consciously aware of how we adjust our language behaviour. But the fact that we do adjust and the fact that people of different linguistic backgrounds adjust their language behaviour in similar ways, suggests that the behaviour is rule-governed and may be the result of linguistic universals. (Todd 1990: 40)

Others suggest that the evident similarities of pidgins derive from the way speakers, whether of African, American, Melanesian or Chinese mother tongue, took similar linguistic material from the Indo-European contact language, and then used it in the same way in the similar physical, social, political and economic settings imposed by colonisation (Bickerton 1975; Hancock 1986; Arends *et al.* 1995). If this were so, it would be more powerful evidence that the language of groups is dictated by the power relationships that pertain.

The key point to note for a study of language policy and planning is that phenomena such as *Sprachbunde*, pidgins and creoles develop organically. They arise typically among groups that are not literate. It seems unexceptional to expect that speakers of languages that have not been presented as discrete systems will be less likely to compartmentalise languages. Certainly, evidence from speakers of languages not yet codified and standardised in both West and East Africa shows that multilinguals with such languages in their repertoire do exhibit a greater tendency to move among all their languages with less differentiation than, for example, the bilingual who masters two languages from Standard Average European (Fairhead 1994; Magbaily Fyle 1994). Codeswitching seems to be less tolerated by speakers of standard languages who have a highly developed understanding of their language as *system* where all borrowing may be seen as undermining the 'integrity' and 'purity' of the language.[6] However, where a language is not presented as an objectified system in a classroom, it may not seem necessary to organise it separately from all other communication strategies and choice is more fluid and less rigidly constrained (Fairhead 1994; Haust 1995).

However, care is needed in all analysis here, since, as Slabbert and Myers-Scotton (1996) note in a study of mixed languages in South African townships,[7] bilingual mixed languages can also result from a highly conscious desire to mark a certain group identity. Abdulaziz and Osinde (1997) studying bilingual language creation in Kenya came to the same conclusion, that the fusion was willed rather than spontaneous, unplanned mixing. They found that Engsh, a mixture of Swahili and English with more English, had been developed as a marker for affluent urban youth. Sheng, a mixture of Swahili and English with Swahili predominant and other Kenyan languages interwoven, was the language of identity of poorer urban groups. In these examples, speakers are playing with the forms of highly standardised languages in a deliberate gesture of rebellion and self affirmation.

5.3   Languages of empire

The circumstances dictate what will be demanded of those who have to accommodate after conquest. There are different pressures. A conquered people forced to service the needs of a conqueror will split into two groups. There will be the mass of people expected to work for the benefit of the conquerors and a small group of bureaucrats recruited from the conquered aristocracy to manage that work.

5.3.1 Bureaucracy

If we define imperialism as exploitation of conquered territory for the benefit of the conqueror, it is evident why new rulers will want to resolve communication problems early in the process. Thus after an imperial power has conquered and pacified a territory, it typically recruits a small class from the subject people to provide the channels of command from the new masters. The Romans, the Chinese, the Turks, the Spanish, the British, the French, and the Dutch ruled their empires in this way, relying heavily on a small number of the conquered to acquire a high level of competence in the imperial language and to provide the clerks and foremen necessary for the smooth functioning of the imperial administration and economy. In such a setting a situation of classic diglossia develops (Ferguson 1959)[8] in which the language of the rulers (H) and the language of the ruled (L) are functionally differentiated with the prestige language (H) employed for all formal functions and conferring prestige on speakers; the L language is only used in informal settings and/or by those in the lower classes of the society. In many such settings the elite speaks only the H language and uses it for both formal and informal purposes. The L language becomes a marker of exclusion, poverty and political weakness. The bilingual class that provides the bridge is small in number.

The different phases in imperialism are associated with different rates of language spread. In the early days of empire, the imperial ruling classes tended to be reluctant to promote the standardised prestige form of the imperial language outside the elite, educated bilingual class. Access to it was seen as a privilege. This was so in the early Roman Empire, Latin was not the language of all until a fairly late date (Lewis 1976; Edwards 1994).[9] In the British, Dutch, German and French Empires, the numbers gaining access to the imperial language through schooling were always small even into the twentieth century.[10] The reasons for this policy are clearly illustrated in a number of British policy documents. In his famous *Minute on Education* (1835), Macaulay advised the British government to educate a class to be English in terms of language, tastes, opinion, morals and intellect and to provide the bureaucracy to administer British rule in India,[11] but to restrict this class in number. Later in the century, the inspectors of schools for the colonies repeatedly advised against the extension of English medium education to large numbers, which would produce a class 'unwilling to earn (its) living by manual labour' (Hill 1884).[12] As ideas on liberty, equality and representation developed among the working class in the English-speaking world, there was another reason to deter the acquisition of the standard language and the literacy in it which would have allowed groups to access the subversive writings that had influenced sections of the working class in the United Kingdom itself (Viswanathan 1989). Thus the spread of standard English and literacy in English were restricted during the major part of the British colonial period and really only gained momentum in its last decades (Brutt-Griffler 2002).

The case of Chinese as an imperial language and bureaucratic lingua franca is interesting in this context because it has actually been the written language that has been the homogenising agent permitting contact and chains of command. The Chinese organised a literate mandarin class to administer their territories. Since literacy in Chinese is mastery of a system of ideograms and since ideograms carry only semantic information and do not record phonetic data, it was possible for speakers of many different varieties of Chinese and of other languages to become literate in Chinese for intergroup communication without acquiring a common spoken language.

5.3.2   The army

In imperial societies, only a small class was recruited to the bureaucracy and to minor roles in industrial, mining and agricultural management, but colonial or conquered peoples also provided the soldiers of the imperial armies and here much larger numbers were involved. Armies are interesting linguistic melting pots. In the extreme situations of warfare, maintaining hierarchical status through differentiated language use would have been dangerous. Thus imperial armies have often proved to be the site of linguistic shift ahead of other sectors of the population. In some examples, the development of a pidgin throughout the army provided the means of communication; in others, the officer class learnt the dominant language of the imperial power in a situation with many parallels to that of the bilingual bureaucracies; in yet others, all ranks of soldier learnt the language of the state they were fighting for as a badge of allegiance.

The Mughal Empire provides an example of the first process. The linguistically diverse army of the Khan developed a classic pidgin, where the lexis of the ruling group (Persian) was grafted on Khariboli Hindi, the most widely spoken language of Northern India. This army language was called Zaban-e-Urdu-Muala, which means language of the exalted camp or court. In fact the word for such an immense army in English, *horde*, stems from the same root as Urdu.[13]

The armies of the Austro-Hungarian Empire are an example of the second structure. The rule was that all written communication between the army and the authorities and all commands in battle should be in German. The officers and NCOs were taught German if they did not come from German-speaking areas. Ordinary soldiers were taught Kommandosprache which comprised a number of command words for engagement. The daily life of the regiment was carried out in the Regimentssprache which depended on the provenance of the soldiers within it. The German variety used among non-German speakers in the Austro-Hungarian Empire has been termed Ärarisch Deutsch, or German for public use, a dialect of German developed for restricted use in limited institutional domains.[14]

The third possibility is exemplified by Napoleon's Grande Armée. The revolutionary wars mobilised the largest number of French soldiers up to that date. Recruits came from all parts of France and in the majority they speak French but one of the other languages of the French state (Ba, Gascon, Languedocian, Provencal, Corsican, Alsatian, Flemish, Breton ex Placed in battalions that deliberately did not take account of their origins (Hagège 1996), the young conscripts acquired French very rapidly, as the imperial forces swept across Europe. The army found itself bound by new ideology, the early exhilaration of conquest and then the shared misery of enormous losses. The medium through which this brotherhood was expressed was French, the language that had been declared the national language and the language of the revolution.

Imperial rulers were fully aware of how language and the sword could work together. Nebrija expressed the Spanish view in the introduction to his *Gramática Castellana* (1492). This is of course the queen's linguist writing rather than the queen herself, but given the context, it is likely that he set out to reflect her views:

> Illustrious Queen. Whenever I reflect upon aspects of the past that have been preserved in writing, I am always forced to conclude that language has always been the consort of empire, and shall forever remain so. Together they come into being, together they grow and flower, and together they wither … Our language followed our soldiers sent abroad to conquer. It spread to Aragon, to Navarra, even to Italy … the scattered bits and pieces of Spain were thus gathered and joined into one single kingdom. (Nebrija 1492: introduction. Author's translation)

5.3.3 Social promotion

Whether the language of the conquerors penetrates deeply into the conquered society (and remains as a legacy after the end of empire) depends on a number of factors. Fishman *et al.* (1977) suggest that the duration of the occupation, the linguistic diversity within the empire and the degree of social promotion permitted to the conquered are major factors in the spread and hold of an imperial language.

Dominated groups are likely to be assimilated over time unless extreme geographical or psychological isolation maintains distinction.[15] The disappearance of the Ligurian, Iberian and Gallic languages, spoken in the territory that is now France, Italy and Spain, by the end of the Roman Empire is an example of this, even though, as we noted above, at the beginning of empire assimilation of populations was not on the Roman agenda.

Extreme linguistic diversity may also be a factor in acceptance of the imperial language. Where an empire is very linguistically diverse the need for a lingua franca may be accepted pragmatically and personal competence recognised as advantageous (Fishman *et al.* 1977). Individuals will learn the language even if its mother tongue speakers are resented. The complex motivations at play here are recorded by a British historian commenting on Slavs

...ning German in the Austro-Hungarian Empire. He is ... of the First World War and at the apogee of nationalist ...s that

...(Magyars) fall back on German as a lingua franca, and can ...see German ousted from its pre-eminent position, however much and however justly they resent and resist the Germanizing spirit that used to prevail, and still lingers, in some high administrative quarters. (Steed 1914: 66)

The key factor in linguistic assimilation and consequent language shift may however be material advantage (Fishman *et al.* 1977). Where colonial regimes or conquering peoples allow some of the conquered to become part of the ruling economic and political elites there is often a language shift among those who desire social mobility and will accept incorporation into the imperial system.

In the main, however, colonial ruling groups wished to resist the general admittance of the conquered to their circles and thus restricted opportunity for learning the (H) language and actively discouraged acquisition by those not designated as eligible. This was the case in the Dutch East Indies where caste separation was seen to be aided by linguistic differentiation (Hall 1966). It was also the case of the Moors or Moriscos in Spain from the sixteenth century onward. They preserved their Arabic because they were marginalised in Christian society, were not educated and not socially mobile (Houston 1988). It was the case in the parts of the German-African Empire where Swahili permitted communication without permitting entry to the conquerors' culture. It was also the case in the British Empire, where only a small proportion of the colonised peoples were educated through English (Brutt-Griffler 2002). The colonised saw the withholding of education in the imperial language as one of the ways in which they were kept at arm's length from power and lobbied against apartheid education. It is not always appreciated that far greater numbers came to use English as a language of education in the postcolonial period than under colonialism.[16]

The presence of missionaries either in the wake or vanguard of imperial presence can have a variety of linguistic outcomes. Those involved in conversion are concerned to spread the language that gives access to the sacred texts. Thus Arabic ousted the other Semitic languages of Arabia and displaced Coptic and Berber in North Africa in large part because it was the language of the Koran (Fishman *et al.* 1977). Those involved in conversion needed a common idiom with those they sought to convert. Christian missionaries often learnt autochthonous languages to proselytise. They were often the first to provide a written form of some languages, doing so in order that the Bible and other sacred works could be made available in them. In Central and South America, Spanish-speaking priests wrote grammars and vocabularies of Amerindian languages and adapted them to the Latin grammar used in the Church (Mignolo 1995). However, since these Catholic missionaries were primarily intent on building linguistic bridges to bring the autochthonous populations to Christianity by whatever means, the ultimate effect of their proselytising was to aid the spread of Spanish, as the main language of that activity and the priest class that promoted it.[17] Missionaries in Africa had similarly diverse effects, sometimes providing the written form of languages but mostly contributing to a spread of the imperial language. Canagarajah (1999) reports how a colonised population used the linguistic possibilities that religion provided. Some young Sri Lankans trained for the ministry simply as a means of getting access to English language education which was restricted by the British imperial system.

5.4   Prestige lingua francas and voluntary language learning

There is, of course, a difference between a language imposed by conquest and a language acquired because it permits access to new ideas, to prestigious culture and to useful invention. In the event, however, the language may actually be the same, as powerful states engaged in military expansion have often proved to be innovative in the cultural and scientific domains as well. And the imperative to learn the language which is the medium of new ideas may be so strong that language learning can appear to the individual as a kind of coercion. Perhaps the dichotomy of forced and voluntary bilingualism is a false division and many voluntary bilinguals might argue that they actually had little choice in whether they acquired a second language or not.

5.4.1   Languages of ideas and culture

Those societies that break new ground in the philosophies that underpin our social and political lives and inspire our spiritual lives, or that develop the technologies that improve our material life, have always attracted interest from outside the speech communities in which they originated. Those who would gain access to innovation need to learn the language that will allow this. Thus Renaissance thinkers learnt the classical forms of Latin and Greek to access the philosophy and literature of the Ancient World. To understand the scientific concepts developed in the Caliphates, scholars learnt Arabic. To comprehend the ideas of the Enlightenment, intellectuals learnt French. To acquire the technical expertise developed in the Industrial Revolution, scientists acquired English. This is, of course, an elite phenomenon linked to literate elites with access to formal education.

The cultural sphere sometimes causes similar patterns of language acquisition. The prestige of a particular cultural centre motivates individuals to acquire its language in order to access its artistic life and literature. Again this is an elite phenomenon linked to literate elites. In Europe the influences and debts are easy to identify. A select and restricted group among the Roman elite learnt Greek. From the eleventh to the thirteenth centuries Limousin was the literary koine in southern European courts from Catalonia to Northern Italy.[18] In the sixteenth century Italian was the language of culture for its neighbours. In the seventeenth and eighteenth centuries the prestige of French derived from its Golden Age of literature encouraged by the patronage of Louis XIII and Louis XIV. In the Romantic era, English and German saw a rise in popularity as readers learnt these languages to gain access to the new literature. In the present day, a liking of the audio-visual productions of the United States contributes to the motivation to learn English.

5.4.2   Sacred languages

The motivation to acquire a second language is particularly strong where it gives access to a religion and or an ideology. In this context learning the language becomes an act of identity and even of worship as knowledge of the sacred language gives entry to the sacred texts. The motivation to acquire the language is extremely strong because linguistic competence aids salvation.[19]

The languages associated with religions that have spread widely throughout the world have all become lingua francas to a degree. In some cases, the priesthood of the religion has been the sole group to have access to the sacred language and this has limited the lingua franca role. The Parsees' sacred book, the *Avesta*, is said to have been destroyed during the invasion of Alexander the Great, but was retained for centuries in the memory of the priest class. Eventually written down in the ancient language, known under various names but perhaps most accurately as Avestan (i.e. the language of the book), the *Avesta* is inaccessible to all but the priest class because of the obscurity of its language. In other settings where education was dispensed by the priesthood in the sacred language, this became the language of literacy and scholarship and a lingua franca for the educated classes. Thus Latin provided a means of exchange within Catholic Europe for many centuries. Greek and Church Slavonic were used in the Orthodox Church. Arabic plays the same role in the Islamic world. Sanskrit is the medium for the Hindu Vedic scriptures, Chinese for Buddhism, Hebrew for Judaism.

This last is an interesting case; here a language which was purely a sacred idiom, used only in worship, was adapted for general and daily use by the linguistically disparate groups that came together to fight to establish a Jewish state. This sacred language has since become the official language of Israel, used in all domains and now the mother tongue of Israeli citizens born in the state.

In the modern secular world there has been a similar process associated with ideologies and their propagation. In the twentieth-century battle between Communism and Capitalism, the two camps proselytised through the languages of the leading exponents. The countries allied to Moscow or Washington put Russian or English on their school curriculum in order to prepare the population to be part of the respective military, economic and ideological bloc. As with the languages closely associated with different religions, English and Russian developed semantically and syntactically in symbiotic ways with the ideologies for which they were vectors (cf. Chilton *et al.* 1997). This observation brings us back to the discussion in Chapter 1 on the relationship of language and the construction of groups. Here we said that the words and utterances we use develop connotational layers deriving from common experience. We share knowledge about facts, ideas and events and fit them into a pattern of knowledge about the world that is replicated to some extent by each member of our group. We claimed that the language of our group expresses its social and cultural reality. We also maintained that new facts, ideas and events necessitate new language and that new ways of looking at old ideas, facts and events cause speakers to recalibrate the ways of talking about them. Meanings are constantly negotiated. Thus, we concluded, the language of a group is constantly creating cultural reality as well as simply expressing it. And this has been particularly evident in the media, for expression of belief in religions and ideology.

The Vietnamese are a particularly interesting group from the point of view of language learning as a barometer of ideological identification and bloc loyalty. The revolutionary movement that fought to liberate the country from French colonialism[20] had the backing of both the Russians and the Chinese, and its cadres were often educated in Beijing or Moscow. This produced a bilingual group able to liaise with the military support and political advisers provided by the Communist bloc. After the defeat of the French at Dien Bien Phu in 1954, Vietnam was divided and the civil war escalated to become a confrontation of the Communist and Capitalist worlds.

Between 1954 and 1975 the small proportions of North and South Vietnamese who had acquired some French in the colonial period now found little use for it. They needed to acquire some knowledge of the languages of the groups that were supporting them. In the North, both Chinese and Russian were useful at different stages. In the South, extensive American involvement up to 1973 made English the language of liaison. Many of the children of the southern elite were educated in English-speaking countries.

After the fall of Saigon and the end of the war, the Provisional Revolutionary Government and the National Liberation Front made it a key point in their programme 'to eliminate the enslaving decadent culture that destroys the old and beautiful traditions of the Vietnamese people' (quoted in Terzani 1997: 176). The vectors of this 'decadent culture' were of course English and French. Both disappeared from the education system and individuals who spoke them kept their competence hidden. Those who learnt them clandestinely could be punished and were immediately suspected of preparing to leave the country.

Chinese too was no longer on the curriculum as the Chinese and Vietnamese became estranged over border disputes and Vietnamese intervention in Cambodia. Russian was the only language formally acquired.[21] The Warsaw Pact countries were their sole allies and the only link with the outside world.

A need to trade to survive coupled with the fall of Communism in Eastern Europe forced Vietnam to open up to the outside world. Within the population there was little language competence to aid the process. The foreign language skills which educated Vietnamese had acquired were not useful in a world where Russia was no longer a major international player. Since 1986, the year of economic liberalisation, the Vietnamese education system has tried to respond to the need for transnational actors (Wright 2001). English and French have returned to the secondary curriculum.

5.5   Conclusions

The argument in this chapter has been that people learn the languages of other groups because they are constrained to do so by political forces or because they expect to profit materially, intellectually or spiritually from such learning. Foreign language learning is not the affair of any one social group; in one setting it may be the peasant or industrial worker who is forced to learn the language of new masters; in another, the elite may learn the language of a prestige group to gain access to new cultural or scientific production; in yet another, acquisition of the language may be associated with personal salvation or identification with an ideology. Where speakers acquire another language, it may be a pidgin if only limited knowledge is required (as in trading contacts) or it may be a standard language if the aim is to gain access to the goods, beliefs, ideas and inventions of a prestige group.

The overview suggests that where a group dominates in one or more of the following spheres: political, economic, technological, ideological or cultural, speakers of other languages will learn the language of the dominant group through a variety of pressures that are both overt and covert. Political ascendancy is the strongest coercive pressure. Conquest and occupation may give rise to a pidgin as large numbers of the conquered accommodate to menial service roles. Conquest will also bring into being a class who master the conquerors' language to near native speaker standard and provide the bureaucrats and officer class who mediate between ruler and ruled. Conquest and colonisation usually result in diglossia.

Economic advantage is another powerful pressure. Where a group desires to trade or a class looks for social promotion and language acquisition aids the realisation of the ambition, then languages are learnt. This category of motivation stands between coercion and choice.

Where there is pre-eminence in philosophy, literature, science, technology and so on within a speech community, desire to gain access to this knowledge motivates speakers of other languages to acquire the necessary language competence voluntarily. Where the acquisition of the prestige language is sufficiently widespread it becomes a scholarly lingua franca and permits circulation of ideas. Thus languages may continue as lingua francas of knowledge even when the political and economic preeminence which underpinned them and the belief systems which encouraged them have been eclipsed, as was the case for Latin, which continued as the major language of knowledge for centuries after the fall of the Roman Empire.[22] For the majority, however, lingua francas have clear lifespans, spreading as the native speaker group grows in power in some domain and receding as the group is no longer dominant. There is often a critical point where the advantage to the individual of acquiring a different lingua franca becomes clear and it eclipses the old. Since, apart from the sacred languages, lingua francas do not have the same deep psychological hold as the mother tongue, changing lingua franca is bound with utility and not with identity, and change may occur more rapidly in consequence.

The next chapters document the rise (and fall) of the two most recent European lingua francas, French and English. Since these languages were the languages of the two powers with extensive empires in the period of European colonisation, their spread has been worldwide. The questions of interest here are whether French and English differ in any significant way from the lingua francas that preceded them and whether it is possible to plan in this area. Can a government intervene to promote a lingua franca on the wane or to block a lingua franca that is spreading?

6
French: The Rise and Fall of a Prestige Lingua Franca

French has been both an international elite language and the language of a large empire and provides an illustration of many of the points made about lingua francas. Its rise and fall show the complex relationship that lingua francas have to power. Interestingly, its spread as the major European lingua franca in the seventeenth and eighteenth centuries predates its adoption as the national language of all those on French territory. Racine recounted in 1661 that he needed an interpreter in the south just as much as a Muscovite would in Paris (Dupuy 1987).

The reasons for the development of French as a lingua franca derive from a number of different ways in which the French dominated in Europe and beyond. First of all, France was an aggressive and successful military power. The monarchy and then the Empires and Republics maintained a policy of expansion over several centuries. The territory on the European mainland governed by Paris was extended steadily from the end of the Hundred Years War until the acquisition of Nice in 1860.[1] The royal family was able to ensure succession either through direct descendants or in collateral lines from the tenth century to the eighteenth, which made it the most stable dynasty in Europe. French spread among European elites as these high status royals married into other dynasties.

The international political standing of France was at its height in the long reign of Louis XIV. France's traditional enemies were weak or overcome. The British monarchy had been enfeebled by the Civil War and Charles II owed Louis for the support given him during his years of exile (Fumaroli 2001). Louis' expansionist policies had led to a number of wars that had extended French frontiers to the Rhine and the Pyrenees,[2] and the King insisted that the Treaties of Nijmegen (1678 and 1679) be negotiated in French rather than Latin.[3] French actually replaced Latin in the text of the Treaty of Rastadt (1714), which is particularly significant since this treaty was actually a restitution of some lands to the Emperor Charles VI (Hagège 1996). France was a dominant power in Europe, and despite some military reverses in the eighteenth century, French became the accepted language of diplomacy.

It is a legacy of this practice that French remains an official language of so many international organisations in the twenty-first century.

Second, France was an economic force with the most extensive territory and the largest population of western Europe in the early Modern period, the home of one sixth of all Europeans at the end of the seventeenth century (Rickard 1989). Some historians suggest that it may even have been over populated (Braudel 1986). And although metropolitan population growth slowed in the early nineteenth century, France was at the height of its power and spread in the nineteenth and first half of the twentieth century, with the French Empire spanning all continents. The number of French speakers grew at home as schooling was made obligatory for all. Not every colonial subject spoke the imperial language, but in each colony a small elite was educated through French and in some a larger workforce used French-based pidgins and creoles. Thus as French trade and colonisation increased throughout the seventeenth, eighteenth and nineteenth centuries, those who wanted to interact with important centres of commerce and industry were more and more likely to need French to do so.

Third, Paris was the major European cultural centre for several centuries. In the seventeenth century, Louis XIII and Louis XIV consciously developed the court as a centre of French aristocratic life (Fumaroli 2001). Their patronage of the arts, undertaken to confirm their prestige among their own nobility, had immense effect outside France. By the late seventeenth century, the courts of Berlin, Hanover, Dresden, Kassel, Darmstadt, Stuttgart, Munich and Vienna, the centres of political and intellectual life in the German-speaking world, had all begun to adopt aspects of French culture and to use French among themselves. French took over from Latin in education and became the language of literacy (Paulsen 1908) and scholarly writing. Leibniz (1646–1716) was an early example of the move from Latin to French in intellectual circles. Contemporary prejudice held that other vernaculars, such as German, were not adapted to scholarship. Perhaps more importantly and more accurately, French guaranteed access to a wide and international audience, much as English does in the international scientific community today.[4] We should remember, of course, that the shift to French was neither speedy nor uniform. Burke (1991) reminds us how long it took for Latin as a scholarly language to be fully eclipsed.

The Prussian royal family was one of the most prestigious and influential Francophone groups outside France. A nineteenth-century German historian says of Frederick II who came to the throne in 1740:

> The culture of his court was entirely French and, as far as he could, he surrounded himself with foreigners. (Paulsen 1908: 106)

Frederick II promoted French literature and French art, inviting Voltaire to his court and becoming the patron of the painter, Watteau. French became the language of correspondence within the family. He and his sister, Frederika Sophia Wilhelmina of Hohenzollern, wrote to each other in French. Prussian francophilia was longlasting. In 1782 the Berlin Academy set an essay entitled '*Qu'est-ce qui a rendu la langue françoise universelle?*' for its annual competition. Rivarol's often cited essay was the winning entry and was written, of course, in French.

Other monarchs were equally Francophile and Francophone. Christina of Sweden (1626–89) invited Descartes to Stockholm to tutor her. Catherine the Great of Russia who came to the throne in 1762 modelled herself on Frederick II. She also corresponded with Voltaire and was host to Diderot in 1773 who was charged with the mission of acquiring art for her. Gustavus III of Sweden, a nephew of Frederick, who ascended his throne in 1771, was another francophile and French speaker, who corresponded with his German relatives in French. Stanislas II, King of Poland from 1771–98, wrote his memoirs in French (Fumaroli 2001).

All sectors of European aristocracy tended to use French for international communication.[5] Lord Chesterfield (1694–1773) corresponded with a network of European grandees in French. Eugene, Prince of Savoy, used French to communicate with Marlborough at the Battle of Blenheim (Fumaroli 2001). Fumaroli (2001) gives the example of several highly placed members of the European aristocracy who conducted their love affairs in French.

France remained pre-eminent in cultural domains into the nineteenth and twentieth centuries with many significant European literary and artistic trends originating in Paris. This naturally caused some resentment. In 1927, Friedrich Sieburg is reported to have asked with some irritation whether God himself might not be French (quoted in Fumaroli 2001). French influence in Western art and literature continued in the decades immediately following the Second World War.[6] Then, slowly its influence was eclipsed, as New York, London and other centres were increasingly seen as the hubs for experimental work.

Fourth, the French were innovators in the political and natural sciences. The seventeen volumes of the *Encyclopédie* (1751–65) attempted to portray the whole spectrum of human knowledge and to present the new ideas developed in Europe in the eighteenth century. French influence dominated during the eighteenth-century Age of Enlightenment and French scientists and thinkers were central in the Positivist tradition that derived from it. French developed functionally to express new ideas in new disciplines. For example, Lavoisier's *Méthode de nomenclature chimique* dictated the way chemical elements and processes were described for three centuries (Beretta 1996). French influence increased with the spread of the universalist ideals of French Republicanism, as the French supported the American revolution, conducted their own revolution and established regimes throughout Europe during the revolutionary and Napoleonic wars. The French and American revolutionaries used French to communicate. Benjamin Franklin is recorded as a fluent speaker.

Fifth, French also spread as a language of religion.
which Calvin settled in 1536 and which adopted and p
was mainly French-speaking. Calvin himself was fro
Although his major work, *Institutio Christianae Religioni*
in Latin (1536), it was soon translated into French (
came to Geneva, and then returned as disciples to pro
country, where their activity and the widespread use oi ule ḍᴵᴰᴵᴄ ... .
vernacular contributed to the spread of French within France. The religious
conflict in France between Catholics and Protestants was supposed to end
with the Edict of Nantes which permitted Protestants to worship as they
wished. But religious dissension continued and Louis XIV revoked the Edict
in 1685 provoking a massive exodus of Protestants. This sent the French language into a number of new centres, as the Huguenots settled in Flanders,
Northern Ireland, Switzerland and the New World. At the same time, French
continued to be closely associated with Catholicism. Dubbed '*la fille de
l'Eglise*' by the pope, France under Napoleon III provided strong support for
the Holy See in particular and Catholicism in general. The strong links
between Paris and the Vatican strengthened the position of the language
and French is actually an official language of the Papal States.[7] The claim
that French is the ideal language of spirituality is still made today.[8]

Thus French was the main foreign language learnt in Europe for three centuries. In the German-speaking world French joined Latin and Greek as part
of the core curriculum in the Gymnasium in the eighteenth century. English
was the other main foreign language in the curriculum, but significantly
more usual in the vocational Realschule in the eighteenth and early nineteenth centuries (Paulsen 1908). In Britain, French had traditionally been
the main foreign language that was learnt. This had its origin, of course,
in Norman domination, but remained after the language shift in the
monarchy. In the sixteenth century, Giovanni Bruto advised parents that
French was a necessary part of any young gentlewoman's education. It
remained an essential part of the training of the cosmopolitan elite even
when relations with France itself were tense or suspended.

The spread of French outside the borders of France as a prestige lingua
franca and its position as the main foreign language learnt in many western
European countries have nothing to do with the qualities of the language
itself. We should reject a very common argument that languages have intrinsic qualities that make them particularly suited to be the language of science,
philosophy and so on.[9] This is nonsensical. The qualities that are cited, for
example, large and expressive vocabularies, come because the language is
used in a wide variety of domains by a large number of speakers. Any language used extensively in these same domains would eventually acquire the
same vocabulary and range.

The reasons for the spread of French as a lingua franca was not because
French speakers set out to promote the language as such. French was learnt

because its speakers had political, economic and cultural clout. The
of the language was a secondary effect. There was no policy action to
mote it as such, except when monarchs such as Louis XIV used language
hoice as a means of underscoring their power and insisted on the use of
French in negotiations and treaties. Now, the use of French as a lingua franca
is contracting. It remains for historical reasons in some international functions but the acquisition of French as a foreign language is generally in
decline.[10] And, it is now, in the period when French is shrinking as a lingua
franca, that its speakers are developing various language policy and planning initiatives to promote the language.

The second half of the chapter assesses how far LPLP can work in a different
direction from the political, social and cultural contexts that cause people to
adopt certain lingua francas at certain times. At the moment the French are
engaged in a threefold policy initiative. They have legislated to try and protect
the monopoly of French in the public domain in France. They have lobbied
within the European Union to promote a regime of linguistic diversity which
they believe will benefit French. They have funded language learning in the
countries belonging to the Francophone network to bolster the numbers
acquiring French. None of these policies has been overly successful, not
because those engaged in promoting the language have not striven to their
utmost, but because all the factors that caused the spread of the language in
the past are no longer in place.

6.1   Legislation to protect French in France

The French have a long tradition of using the law as well as social pressure to
influence language behaviour. This has usually been successful, but we should
remember that from the Edict of Villers–Cotterêts in 1539 to 1937, when the
Office de la langue française was set up to support the Académie and defend
the status of the national language, legislation was always underpinning the
spread of a language of a group in the ascendant; both law and social trends
were working in tandem. It is a different matter when the law sets out to cur-
tail and constrain language behaviour in contradiction to other social trends.
The date of the inauguration of the Office is quite revealing. That the French
should have felt a particular need to defend their language in the 1930s was
possibly an indication of an early understanding that the pre-eminence of the
French state and the French people was under serious attack.

By the 1960s, it was becoming ever clearer that French was losing ground
as an international lingua franca. De Gaulle replaced the Office with the
Haut Comité pour la Défense et l'Expansion de la Langue Française, a new
organisation with greater powers within France and a brief *to promote the
language abroad*. Of course, what was happening to the language was a
reflection of changing political and economic relationships. The status of
France had been diminished by defeat in the Second World War and

doomed military attempts to maintain the French Empire. English was in the ascendant. This was not because of the old rivals across the Channel. The British too were in period of retrenchment. Although they perceived themselves as having derived prestige from the war, they were profoundly impoverished. Preoccupied with rebuilding at home and dismantling empire abroad, they were not the group that the French viewed as the threat. The challenger was the United States which had taken on the mantle of leader of the capitalist camp in the Cold War and which, as the only major industrial power not profoundly damaged by bombing in the Second World War, was dominating world markets as others recovered (Gordon 2001).

Under the leadership of de Gaulle, France set out to restore its political and economic authority. De Gaulle's political agenda was to reestablish France as a major world player and to counter Anglo-Saxon (American) dominance. To this end he proposed French leadership for those states that rejected the Cold War polarisation of the USSR and the United States. He extricated France from NATO and ejected US troops from French territory. He made France a nuclear power with its own independent weapons capacity. He was the major opponent of Britain's application to the European Economic Community (EEC), which, had it been successful, would have endangered France's dominant position within the European movement. In his speeches, he quite deliberately adopted a discourse of celebration of French greatness designed to rouse the French nation in this endeavour of national self-promotion (Czerny 1980).

Protection and promotion of the French language were consistent with these policies. The Haut Comité fostered the use of French in international settings and promoted the idea of international Francophonie. Under de Gaulle's successor, Pompidou, the Loi Bas–Lauriol (1975) introduced legislation which made the use of French obligatory in commercial and industrial domains on French territory. All advertising and publicity, instructions for use of products and signs for the public were to be in French. All work contracts were to be in French. Terminology commissions were set up in every ministry from 1970 onwards, so that new technologies and systems would not be designated by English terms, henceforth prohibited.

However, despite these government actions for the promotion and protection of French, despite a constant railing among the Parisian intelligentsia against American cultural and linguistic imperialism, and despite a certain acceptance of de Gaulle's discourse of '*gloire*', the prestige of English was not diminished in the eyes of the mass of French nor the desire to learn the language and to borrow terms. A steady number of English words entered the French language[11] and there was relentless growth in the numbers wishing to learn English because of the entrée it provided to the networks and systems of globalisation.

The French government thus instigated further legislation. In 1992, the French constitution was amended to state that the language of the Republic was French. This decision to give *de jure* status to what had always been the case *de facto* should perhaps be seen as a symbolic act, taken in a precautionary mood in the light of greater European integration, rather than as a necessary move in the campaign to contain English. There was certainly no substantive threat to French as the language of the French on French territory. There was, however, creeping use of English as a lingua franca in the transnational situations in which the French were involved and extensive borrowing. To counter this and to reinforce the constitutional amendment, the 1994 Loi relative à l'emploi de la langue française (Toubon Law) strengthened the provisions of the Bas–Lauriol Law and extended obligatory use of French. In addition to further legislation in the areas of business and publicity, it identified education, the media and the scientific community as domains where use of English had increased. Academic conferences and colloquia on French territory had started to accept the use of English as the scientific lingua franca. Henceforth, conference organisers were to guarantee the right of participants to speak in French and have non-French papers translated or interpreted. In the elite sector of higher education, the Grandes écoles and the Écoles de commerce, the practice of teaching business subjects in English had become increasingly common. Henceforth, examinations and theses were only to be in French. Any official and subsidised publications were to be in French, and the use of public funds to disseminate scientific literature in English to the English-speaking international community were to be curtailed.[12] The role of French in national radio and television was recognised and the broadcasting of songs with lyrics in other languages was to be restricted to a set proportion of playtime.

The Toubon Law has widespread support from the elites.[13] Within government, language policy has a high profile and numerous committees are concerned with the subject: the Conseil supérieur de la langue française is chaired by the prime minister himself and has a broad policy making role; an inter-ministerial committee coordinates application of the law in the seven ministries concerned; the Délégation générale à la langue française is concerned with the general application of language policy and has a particular role in corpus planning and the development of terminology.

Within civil society, particularly among the Parisian intelligentsia, defence of the language is seen as vital to the protection of French interests and cultural independence. There are more than 200 lobby and pressure groups[14] set up to promote and defend the interests of French speakers. Three associations, Défense de la langue française (DLF), Avenir de la langue française (ALF) and Association francophone d'amitié et de liaison (AFAL), have the right to bring civil actions against those flouting the language laws.[15] Most of these organisations publish a variety of documents to alert the French-speaking world to the spread of English and to lobby both the government and the public to take action.[16]

In contrast to the elite, the wider public has not consented to the Toubon Law, where it sees it to be against its interests or its inclination, and infringements of the law are legion in certain domains. The rulings that restrict the language of conferences to French have never been applied except in a small number of high profile conferences in the mid-1990s when government subsidy underwrote the translation and interpretation costs. Since then, limited funding for language services and a drop in numbers of the international scientific community attending have had an effect. Use of English in all but the most formal of settings (e.g. the welcome address) is tolerated. The practice of holding conferences entirely in English has been brought to the attention of the courts but the Francophone associations complain of their lack of interest in following up the complaints (Association droit de comprendre 2001).

The practice of using English as a medium for some courses in higher education has continued and increased, particularly in business schools, where private sector flouting of the regulation has pressurised state-funded institutions to do the same. The subsidies for official publication in French have had a mixed effect; conceived to ensure that work is published in French, they actually seemed to have the contrary effect. Some authors decided to publish in English medium journals in order to secure an international readership (Truchot 2001). Some government departments actively flout the law, seeing it as counter to their principal interest. For example, the Direction de l'assistance publique in Paris decided that from 2000 onwards it would only count publications in English when assessing research output from its laboratories (Association droit de comprendre 2001).

The restriction on songs with English language lyrics has given space to French writers on national radio but with the proliferation of transnational audio–visual networks those who want to avoid the restriction have no difficulty doing so (Ager, 1999).

There is, of course, no language shift in France. The French are not abandoning their own language for English, indeed far from it. The prestige of French and the nation's affection for it are clear. France is still a country where newspapers and magazines run popular columns about various aspects of French usage, where the ability to use the language skilfully is highly valued and where acquiring the standard language is the key focus of primary education. But there is an acceptance of the move to English as a lingua franca, and the vast mass of the population has adopted a very utilitarian attitude towards English. The then education minister, Claude Allègre, reflected this current trend when he advised his countrymen to stop thinking of English as the purveyor of Anglo-Saxon culture and start regarding it as a means of participating in the networks and systems of global society. He was of the opinion that:

English had become a commodity, similar in kind to computers or the Internet ... The French have got to stop thinking of English as a foreign language. (Allègre, speech at La Rochelle, 30/08/1997. Author's translation)[17]

His thesis was to be challenged by many and he appeared to be in a minority in government circles and out of touch with the rhetoric in the editorial and letters pages of some newspapers.[18] The supporters of the anti-English legislation continued to see it as a way of protecting the French against themselves and persisted in trying to persuade them that accepting English as a lingua franca is not in their long-term interest (e.g. Hagège 1996). Allègre, however, seems to reflect the pragmatic view of an enormous silent majority of French, who have decided that they (or their children) will learn English for their own life projects and advancement.

This attitude is shown in the steady rise in the numbers studying English.

Secondary education (public and private sectors)	
Year	Percentage of secondary school children studying English
1980–81	83.8
1990–91	86.1
1999–2000	89.7

Source: Ministère de l'éducation nationale 2000.

This trend is reflected in other sectors. In higher education the percentage studying English out of all those studying for a language degree rose to 64 per cent in 2000–01 (Ministère de l'éducation nationale 2001a). In 1999–2000 80 per cent of primary school children studying a language were learning English (Ministère de l'éducation nationale 2001b).

By their choices, French parents and students provide a clear illustration of the futility of language policy in promoting foreign language learning which does not reflect the decisions made by individuals about what is to their advantage and in their interest. The attraction of a prestige lingua franca is clearly extremely strong and individuals will not accept the argument of national interest over their right (or their children's right) to acquire the language that they see as providing indisputable cultural capital. The French are not the only people to ignore their government on this. A number of other states provide case studies of parental and student desire for English at odds with state education policy.[19] The French situation is typical rather than extraordinary.

6.2   European policies to promote diversification in foreign language provision

The French establishment was, unlike the French population, not generally predisposed to support the education minister's call to accept English as a lingua franca in 1997. Many politicians lined up on the opposing side. They had the support of a number of their counterparts in the twelve other non-English speaking member states. It is perhaps not surprising that there should have been this stance, particularly among those most committed to the European project, since the origins of the European Union (EU) are, at least in part, rooted in a desire to provide a counterweight to US economic and political power. This would imply resistance to the proliferation of its cultural products and its language as lingua franca. In an interview with Hagège, Toubon explained that he saw the French fight for diversity in language use and learning as a blow against the free market philosophy and the cultural model promoted by the Anglo-Saxons (Hagège 1996).

Moreover, speakers of French, Spanish, Dutch, German have an understanding of the many advantages that a lingua franca always confers on those who speak it as a first language, because their languages have played the lingua franca role in different settings in the recent past. Their societies have first hand understanding of the advantages. First, mother tongue speakers of a lingua franca are spared the burden of having to acquire it to participate in multilingual settings and networks. Second, their society is economically advantaged in that it has no translation, no interpretation, no acquisition costs. Third, they are politically advantaged in that they have no communication barriers when putting their case and defending their interests in international forums. Fourth, they are even advantaged in less tangible ways. If we accept the weak Whorfian position that sees concepts moulded by the language available to express them, then the speakers of the lingua franca are conceptually advantaged because the modalities of their language frame international exchange. Finally, there is the question of prestige. A lingua franca is traditionally the language of a dominant group and so acceptance of the language is also in a sense a tacit acceptance of that dominance.[20]

The discourse that has structured resistance to encroaching English does not usually employ such arguments of self-interest and advantage overtly. The case against adopting English as the main or only foreign language in an education system has mostly been framed as a positive move; the need to safeguard the rich linguistic heritage of Europe is the lynchpin of the argument.[21] The discourse draws heavily on the tradition that conceives the EU as an association of sovereign states among which there will be no cultural (or linguistic) convergence. The commitment to protecting cultural diversity was enshrined in law in the Maastricht Treaty and translated into education policy in a number of initiatives to support diversity in foreign language learning. European interests were seen to be safeguarded and unity promoted through European school children learning each other's languages with no preference accorded to any one language. Promoting the teaching and learning of all the national languages of the EU within the various national education systems was an aim of the Lingua

Programme (1990–95). Its objectives were quite explicit:

> Priority will be given to projects which clearly set out to improve the quality of foreign language teaching and learning and which give support to the diversification of language provision and particularly to the teaching and learning of the least widely used and least taught languages of the Community. (Publicity leaflet for Lingua Programme, January 1990)

Many of the foreign language courses initiated in response to the unity in diversity principle and funded under Lingua and Erasmus (under Socrates post 1995) did not continue after initial funding. Europeans reacted unambiguously, refusing to be directed to language learning for any ideological reason. They would not learn foreign languages without clear evidence that this would aid social promotion and life chances. They were largely convinced that English was the most useful asset. Throughout the EU, the numbers of children learning English rose as a proportion of the school population.

English in secondary schools		
School year	Percentage learning English	Source of statistics
1991–92	83	Eurostat 1994
1992–93	88	Eurydice 1996
1996–97	89	Eurydice 1998
1998–99	91	Eurydice 2000

At the same time the other languages that had traditionally been learnt as foreign languages were in decline. French, the next most widely taught language in the secondary system was only learnt by 21 per cent of pupils in that sector in 1996–97 (Eurydice 2000), down from 25 per cent in 1994–95 (Eurydice 1997).[22]

These trends have occurred predominantly through parental insistence. It has been difficult for education systems to satisfy demand for English and has meant rapid training of large numbers of English teachers. The trend towards English seems to be confirmed by the early start programmes which offer foreign languages to primary school children in most European countries. They are overwhelmingly in English (Eurydice 2000) and this is principally fuelled by parent demand (TESOL teachers in Paris and Rome, private communications 2002).

The commitment to diversity has weakened. In subsequent Lingua publicity the commitment to diversity fell from prime position in the opening paragraph of information leaflets to a final sentence in the paragraph on guidance on applying for materials development funding:

> The development of language teaching materials for general use is supported; priority will be given to languages other than English, French and German. (Action V, 1991 onwards)

The present arrangements for supporting second language acquisition, now under the umbrella of the Socrates programme, are no longer presented with the same degree of commitment to diversity. The current presentation of the Comenius action (schools), the Grundtvig action (adult education) the Erasmus action (higher education) and the Lingua action (teacher education) does not press the diversity principle but speaks rather of language learning without specific reference to the language to be learnt.

Within European policy circles a central position developed which tried to weave a course between the market driven position that sees English as the only foreign language necessary, the idealists who want to discourage any idea of hierarchy among the languages of the European heritage and the self-interested groups that understand the advantage of others learning their language. The compromise was to support the learning of 'English plus'. Children would learn the languages of neighbours and of heritage in addition to the major lingua franca. Under the French presidency of the EU in 1995, the Council of Ministers (education) agreed on a Resolution that renewed a call for diversification of the foreign language curriculum and included a recommendation that every pupil have the opportunity to study two foreign languages (Council Resolution 31/3/1995).[23]

Statistics reveal that even this minimalist commitment to diversity is failing to capture widespread support. There must be a reason for learning a language and the popular view seems to be that one lingua franca will suffice. Where there are strong family traditions of contact and affective links, the two language policy has had some effect. The member states with large numbers learning at least two foreign languages usually have a historical reason that explains this learning. The following table shows the states with the largest proportion of school children taking two foreign languages:

Country	1st foreign language %		2nd foreign language %	
Belgium (French-speaking community)	70	(Dutch)	64	(English)
Belgium (Dutch-speaking community)	95	(French)	71	(English)
Denmark	100	(English)	76	(German)
Finland	99	(English)	93	(Swedish)
Luxembourg	98	(French)	92	(German)

Source: Eurydice 2000

It seems unlikely that the education ministries of Belgium, Finland or Luxembourg are responding to the two language directive. These states are carrying on a language learning tradition determined by the composition of their national groups. Denmark is the only state where the two foreign languages are true 'foreign' languages. It seems that where instrumental or integrative reasons for general application of the policy were not clear, it has not been widely supported. In 1996–97, over 20 million school children were enrolled in secondary education in the EU. Eighteen million of these were learning English, 4 million French and 2 million German.[24] The opportunity costs of language learning appear to Europeans to be too high to undertake it without clear objectives, and the supporters of the policy of diversification have not managed to win widespread support for their case.

European parents probably rejected the diversity policy and chose English as the main foreign language for their children for a raft of instrumental reasons. But there may also have been a lack of conviction that linguistic diversity is *per se* a good thing. The desirability of linguistic diversity is not the message from many European governments. Some are still pursuing a vigorous policy of eradicating diversity within their own state borders. To take the example of France once again, it is interesting to note that they are among the most enthusiastic supporters of diversity at the international level but have decided not to ratify the Charter for Regional or Minority Languages. The Conseil constitutionnel ruled that it would be counter to the constitutional declaration that '*la langue de la République est le français*' if other languages were admitted to public and official domains. Debate in 2001–02 over the public funding of Breton medium schools reinforced the point. Linguistic diversity within France has neither government nor majority support.[25]

So the desire of parents for their children to acquire what they deem to be the most 'useful' foreign language has worked against the policy of diversification and the policy of 'English plus' has not found overall acceptance, perhaps because of the opportunity costs. Once again the rule that language planning can only go with societal trends and not against them is upheld. This could have been foreseen; the utility of a lingua franca is greater, the larger the population that uses it as a lingua franca. To argue for a number of lingua francas does not seem logical and a significant group of Europeans appear to see this and have challenged the policy. Toubon's hope that in 20 to 25 years all European children would be capable of speaking three or even four European languages (interview in Hagège 1996) is unlikely to be realised.

6.3   Promoting French and strengthening Francophonie

The third arena where France is trying to counter the spread of English is outside Europe. The Francophone movement actually began as an African initiative in the early 1960s. French-speaking leaders of newly independent countries, Felix Houphouët of the Ivory Coast, Léopold Senghor of Senegal and Habib Bourguiba of Tunisia, proposed an association to promote association and common approaches to world politics. There was little support at first for this from de Gaulle who was concerned to free France from the weight of the recent colonial past (Déniau 1983; Ager 1996).

The outcome of these early debates were a number of private associations that promoted cooperation among Francophone broadcasting companies (1955), Francophone universities (1961) and Francophone politicians (1967). The Agence de Coopération Culturelle et Technique was set up in 1970 but had only limited powers and budget. It was not until Mitterrand came to power in 1981 that the French government began to take a serious interest at a high level. During Mitterrand's presidency, the first meeting of Francophone heads of state took place (1986) and a ministry for Francophonie was set up. The institutions of the Francophone movement multiplied and expanded. The series of intergovernmental meetings of Francophone states continued. By the end of the twentieth century the movement was providing educational aid from the richer French-speaking countries to the poorer, and was associated with the dissemination of agricultural, scientific and technical knowhow, cultural cooperation, including a common TV channel (TV5), development of French medium information technology, and the promotion of democracy, including the monitoring of elections.

By the 1990s, the French government had come to see the Francophone movement as the framework for a useful bloc in the fight for markets and as an arm in the battle against English and American influence (interview with Toubon, Hagège 1996). This was apparent in the policies and actions it developed towards Vietnam.[26] As we discussed in the previous chapter, Vietnam had been isolated from the Western world since the end of the Vietnamese–American war and had only maintained links with the USSR and the Warsaw bloc countries. As Vietnam's economic situation became progressively more difficult and the Communist regimes of Eastern Europe were in no position to help, Vietnam's leaders decided to follow the Chinese example and open up to trade and inward investment from the West even if they were not yet prepared for political rapprochement. France was the Western country that led the re-establishment of diplomatic ties.[27] In 1989, the minister for Francophonie visited the country. In October 1991 the French foreign minister came to Hanoi. A Vietnamese delegation visited France in June 1993. Vietnam hosted its first truly international meeting since the war, the Congress of French journalists, in November 1994.

The French president, Jacques Chirac, was quite explicit on French motivation at the 11th Francophone Summit, held in Hanoi. He was enlisting former Indo-China into the language bloc that might challenge Anglophone dominated globalisation:

Francophonie is perhaps above all a certain vision of the world. We are building a political association founded on a virtual community, that of the language that we have in common and which unites despite our cultural diversity ... Our raison d'être stems from a conviction that in the 21st century language communities will be key actors on the international political stage. (Chirac 14/2/1997. Author's translation)

French companies also led the way in re-establishing commercial relations as the 1987 Foreign Investment Law permitted foreign business to invest in joint ventures. By the mid-1990s, the Swiss and the French were the major investors from outside the region (Sadec 1996, 1999). However, the greatest volume of business was with neighbouring countries which accounted for 76 per cent of Vietnam's foreign investment as well as being the major (70 per cent) destination of most of its exports and the source of most of its imports at that time (Dickson 1998; Pham Ha 1998).

In the latter half of the 1990s the interest of foreign investors in Vietnam lessened (*Economist* 8/1/2000). But although flows of capital began to slow down overall, investment from France actually tripled. France's capital investment for the period 1988–95 was US$479 900 000 (State Committee for Cooperation and Investment figures 1996; Nguyen Tri Dung 1998). By January 1998 the number of projects in which France was involved had climbed to 89 and its total capital investment to US$1.4 billion (*Vietnam Economic Times* 1998). The French were also present in Vietnam as participants in a large number of non-profit-making cooperation schemes. A number of non-governmental organisations and private associations initiated contacts and projects in a number of fields, but principally medicine, psychiatry, dentistry, pollution control, environmental health and sustainable development.

Chirac, in his speech at the summit in Hanoi, had admitted that competence in French had been 'eroded' among the Vietnamese, even while enlisting them as members of Francophonie. He hoped that French could be reintroduced. His optimism was based in no small part on the generous funding and vigorous efforts that the French government was making to extend French medium education and French language learning in Vietnam. This initiative was very attractive to the Vietnamese since it injected funding to their cash-strapped education system.

The investment has been substantial. In the school year 1997–98 the Francophone agency, AUPELF–UREF, financed 14 000 school children in 491 bilingual (French–Vietnamese) streams. These classes were staffed by teachers from Francophone countries, principally France. Generous funding gave participants access to modern text books and the audio–visual and computer technology absent in much of the Vietnamese system. There were scholarships to help those whose families could not afford protracted education. Entry was by competitive examination and the scheme acquired a reputation for high standards and rigour. There was immense competition among the brightest and best students to be admitted. A further carrot was that the bilingual secondary streams led into a similar university programme in which, in 1997, 5000 Vietnamese students were being taught medicine, management, law, elementary science, agricultural science, engineering and computer science through the medium of French.

By 2000, the numbers in bilingual secondary streams had risen to 19 000 in Vietnam and 25 000 in former Indo-China as a whole. The first 43 *bacheliers* from the system graduated in 1999. Between 1998 and 2001, 597 Vietnamese students took a first degree under this system and 46 progressed to higher degrees (Agence universitaire de la Francophonie 2000–01). Ironically, France (as the major funder of these Francophone initiatives) is now educating a greater number of Vietnamese than when it was a colonial power. Given present data, it seems eminently likely that French will reinsert itself to some extent into Vietnamese society, because linguistic initiatives are supporting an economic trend fuelled by French investment, and is thus probably sustainable since there are evident instrumental reasons for learning the language.

However, outside the funded programmes, it is English as a foreign language which is on the increase both in the public and private sectors because it is increasingly the lingua franca of the ASEAN and APEC countries[28] with which Vietnam mainly does business. The Vietnamese Ministry of Education reports that it is now the most widely taught foreign language in the state system, the language that is generally most in demand and the language where the number of learners is increasing fastest in the burgeoning private sector (Fieldwork Vietnam 1999). It is doubtful whether French will retain its significant role as a foreign language within the Vietnamese education system if external funding is withdrawn and demand for French left to market forces.

6.4   Conclusions

6.4.1   The vigour of French

The discourses presenting and defending the policy reactions of the French to the spread of English often suggest that French is 'under attack'. But, as I argued above, English is not replacing the use of French among the French in France or other French-speaking territories;[29] it has only taken its place where the French are interacting in transnational settings or participating in transnational networks. The strong identification of nation, state and language continues in France and the use of French has been little affected among French speakers on French territory. Some borrowing is apparent, but, as Walter (2001) has shown, this is the sign of a healthy cultural community open to the outside world and in fact is not new behaviour among French speakers. And, significantly, although the French scientific community may use English in international settings, there is no indication at all that it does so within France. Success within the French research community depends heavily on achieving national recognition within the Centre national de recherche scientifique (CNRS) and this needs to be done through the medium of French. The argument here is that the reaction of the French elites is stronger than it would be if it were really only the use of language in France that worried them.

Joseph (2002) has argued that there has often been over-reaction to the perceived threat of English. From a series of quotes from diverse nineteenth-century sources (e.g. President Grant in his second inaugural address 1873; W.J.Clark a proponent of Esperanto in 1907 and the French writer A.L. Guérard in 1922) that rejoice in or bemoan the spread of English, Joseph assembles evidence to show how successive generations have predicted the eclipse of other languages. This is not happening, however, in the way or at the speed that any of these men predicted. The reason for this is the dual function that all languages possess, permitting communication and building identity. Joseph reminds us that there is a 'natural obstacle' (2002: 11) to language shift; speakers will not relinquish a language that is important for their identity to adopt a language which is merely utilitarian for them. This seems to describe the French exactly. For the present it is unlikely that the French will do anything more radical than adopt English as an additional language, to be used in highly circumscribed settings. For major language groups such as French speakers, the phenomenon of global English does not appear to be different in kind from the patterns noted in the history of previous lingua francas. The problem that English poses for the French is that it has displaced their language from the lingua franca role and this has been experienced with some pain in elite circles because of what it signifies:

> The status of a lingua franca depends most obviously on history's ups and downs: if the people who hold political and economic power lose their power their language is likely to lose its status for international communication. (Thomason 2001: 24)

The French case is interesting in the context of the present study because it illustrates clearly that it is not necessary for the agencies of the state to promote a lingua franca when it is spreading and not possible for them to legislate to counter its contraction. If the factors for lingua franca status are present, the language will spread. If not, there is no political action that can replicate them.[30] This is illustrated by the failure of the policies to promote French. All the initiatives to do so started at the moment that French was no longer pre-eminent as the international language in scientific, educational, political, cultural and economic spheres and have failed to stem the move to

English either in France or abroad. Toubon's call for a return to Babel (Hagège 1996) has been largely ignored as a foolish reaction in a globalising world. And finally, the French show that if individual members of a society wish to acquire the language they see as cultural capital, this cannot be countered. Only totalitarian states can legislate with any effect against language acquisition of which they do not approve.

Romaine (2002) makes it clear that laws regulating language matters either sanction what has already become practice or work in tandem with the sociological dynamics that are shaping practice. This explains the reasons why the French government's policies to promote French as a national language were successful and why campaigns to promote French as a lingua franca outside France have been a failure. In the first instance, the policy was in accord with other social pressures and in tune with the predominant ideology of the period; in the second the policymakers were at variance with all other social forces. Romaine (2002) argues that LPLP cannot fulfil a coercive function in a reasonably democratic society and the French experience illustrates this.

7
English: From Language of Empire to Language of Globalisation

This chapter looks at the reasons for the spread of English, the lingua franca that displaced French from that role and finds that there are many parallels between the biographies of the two languages. English first increased in numbers of speakers in the wake of British imperial power and trading success. However, the waning of English that would have accompanied the end of the British Empire and the decline of British economic and political power did not take place, because English was also the language of the United States, the next group to dominate. The reasons for the spread of this lingua franca are no different in kind from any of the lingua francas of the past, but the extent of its penetration as the language of globalisation outstrips that of any lingua franca of the past. It is this gigantism which makes it particular and its future development slightly more difficult to predict. One thing is quite clear, however; language planners at the national level can only respond to this phenomenon and not direct it.

7.1 English and the British Empire

English has only become a language of intergroup contact relatively recently.[1] Richard Mulcaster, writing in 1582 to promote the use of English in place of Latin, admitted that English was of little use outside a restricted heartland:

> Our English tung...is of small reatch, it stretcheth no further than this Iland of ours, naie not there ouer all. (Mulcaster 1582: 256)[2]

Even in the following century, after the start of English colonisation in the Caribbean and North America, English was still considered of little use as a language of contact. Richard Flecknoe advised English-speaking travellers in 1665 that they would not be able to rely on any outside Britain and its colonies speaking English. It was knowledge of French and Italian that would allow the traveller in Europe to converse with an educated elite throughout the continent. Dutch and Spanish were the languages most likely to serve the traveller in Africa, the New World and the Indies (Bailey 1991). Interestingly, at that time, the English had a reputation as good language learners. They had to be. To be understood outside the confines of the English-speaking world, they had to acquire another language. The seventeenth-century commentator, Richard Carew, was one of those who recorded that the English were accomplished language learners:

> Turne an Englishman at any time of his age into what countrie soever allowing him due respite, and you shall see him profit so well that the imitation of his utterance will in nothing differ from the patterne of that native language. (Carew quoted in Camden 1984: 40)

The currency of English outside Britain began to increase in the eighteenth century. In a revealing letter, David Hume[3] reproached Edward Gibbon for planning to write a work in French. Hume suggested that English would in time come to be a more widely used lingua franca than French, just as Latin had replaced Greek (Hagège 1996). By 1754, the Earl of Chesterfield could report that English was being studied more widely in the other parts of Europe (Bailey 1991). Growing interest in the language correlated with military victory, vigorous colonial expansion and increased trade abroad, industrialisation and political reform at home.

7.1.1 Colonial expansion

The soldiers, adventurers and colonists who established the British Empire ensured the spread of English. Where migrants from Britain took over land, ousting the original inhabitants, the language of the territory became English. Where autochthonous peoples survived the military onslaught, they were corralled in reservations or otherwise marginalised and saw their languages eclipsed along with the rest of their culture and social structures. This was the pattern in North America and Australasia.

Where colonists from Britain did not force out the autochthonous populations wholesale, but employed them as labour in plantations and mines, English was the language of the ruling classes and the language of contact between rulers and ruled. This was the pattern in Africa and Asia. A bureaucracy of competent bilinguals was trained and other interaction was usually a pidgin following the patterns described in Chapter 5. In these colonial situations the autochtonous languages survived alongside English as the L languages in a diglossic arrangement.

At the height of imperial expansion in the late nineteenth century a number of British commentators speculated that the spread of English would be extensive:

> As a vehicle of our institutions and principles of civil and religious liberty, it is belting the earth, pushing east and west, and extending over the five

great geographical divisions of the world, giving no doubtful presage that, with its extraordinary resources for ameliorating the condition of man, it will soon become *universal*. (Read 1849, quoted in Bailey 1991: 116. My italics)

The most extravagant projections, based on contemporary censuses in Britain and its colonies, estimated that the number of English speakers might grow to nearly a billion mother tongue speakers by the end of the twentieth century (Bailey 1991).

However these predictions and estimates from the imperial period overstated the case. Although English spread with imperialism, the great majority of those colonised in Africa and Asia did not acquire English under the British. Policy was not of a piece throughout the empire (Pennycook 2000a,b), but in very broad terms it can be described as reserving the colonial language for a restricted class in close contact with the British administration.[4] The imperial power needed 'to produce docile and compliant workers and consumers to fuel capitalist expansion' (Pennycook 2001a: 196), but for its purposes there was no need for these workers to learn English. British colonialism was similar to other imperialisms: the language change that it caused did not penetrate all classes. The nineteenth-century imperialists who claimed that the British Empire would effect language shift and the twentieth-century commentators who accept that claim (e.g. Phillipson 1992) have overestimated the extent of the spread of English language skills. Brutt-Griffler (2002) and Pennycook (2000a and 2000b) have both demonstrated the restricted provision of English medium education. The famous argument between the Orientalists who supported vernacular schooling and the Anglicists who proposed English medium education (Said 1978; Pennycook 2001) was not a debate about the medium for universal education but concerned schooling for the small class whose help the British needed for governance and management of farms, mines and factories. The acquisition of English was thus largely an elite affair, even if the elite became a numerous group in some settings (e.g. India).

7.1.2   Trade

Languages will spread widely if their use is perceived to be linked to material benefit. In the nineteenth century, English was gradually becoming the lingua franca of trade as Britain became the major overseas investor, and the biggest single exporter and importer of goods (Heaton 1963). The following quote from *Chambers's Journal* in 1855 may be in the contemporary tradition of vaunting and overstating the case, but the author's general understanding of the trend is accurate:

The language of the seas is already our own. Nine tenths of the commerce of the ocean is transacted through the copious and flexile medium of our tongue and claims the protection of the Anglo-American fraternity. (Quoted in Bailey 1991: 109)

7.1.3 Science and technology

Languages will also spread where their knowledge is a prerequisite for access to new technologies. The British went through a period of intense scientific creativity in the industrial revolution. Unsurprisingly, a technical elite outside the empire who wanted to be part of the phenomenon were motivated to learn English. A trawl through the biographies of any group of nineteenth-century scientists reveals examples of such learning. In Germany, a prominent example was the Siemens family. Three older brothers remained in Germany while William Siemens brought their inventions to England to find venture capital and manufacturers with the technology to develop them.[5] To achieve this, he became a fluent English speaker and lived for much of his life in the industrial Midlands.[6] However, despite this and further instances of English learning, the move from French to English as the language of science was only occurring slowly. In *Ostwald's Klassiker des exacten Wissenschaften*, a series of 22 books published during the first half of the nineteenth century in Leipzig by Engelmann, the ratio of French language sources to English language sources appears to be in the order of 4 : 1 and the French medium *Annales de chimie et de physique* were a key contemporary source for these two scientific disciplines.

7.1.4 Ideology and religion

Languages will also spread where they are linked to philosophies, ideologies and faiths that attract a following. Britain's role as a test bed for a kind of parliamentary democracy started to make English a language to be learnt for those who wanted access to political ideas developed within British society. In her typology of loan words, Henriette Walter (2000) charts the borrowing of ideas and the imitation of practice. She notes that French political writers of the eighteenth century use a number of terms such as *club, vote, pétition, majorité, opposition, motion, jury* and *verdict* at first for political processes as they originated in Britain and then for domestic political arrangements.

English was also one of the languages that gave access to the religion promised as a means of salvation by the missionaries who followed the explorers and colonisers. Christianity and Western languages arrived together. The extent of the English-speaking missionary movement was redoubtable. By the mid-nineteenth century more Bibles were being published and distributed in English than in all the other languages of Christendom combined (Read 1849 in Bailey 1991: 116).[7]

Imperial rule was often presented as promoting civilisation as well as salvation. Much scholarship in the postcolonial period has investigated the arrogant discourses of colonial thinking and analysed the way in which the theorists of British colonialism claimed an 'indelible link between a civilising mission and the promotion of the English language' (Pennycook 2001a: 202). The dominant discourse justified imperialism in terms of the access that it provided to both civilisation and Christianity. English was the medium that permitted access:

> Ours is the language of the arts and sciences, of trade and commerce, of civilisation and religious liberty. It is the language of Protestantism – I had almost said, of piety. It is a storehouse of the varied knowledge which brings a nation within the pale of civilization and Christianity. (Read 1849, quoted in Bailey 1991: 116)

Interestingly, these many and varied reasons were not considered adequate explanation for English spread, by contemporary commentators in Britain. As previously in the case of French, the dominance of English was often justified from a linguistic perspective and reasons found in the 'excellence' of its syntax and lexis for its adoption and spread. We should not need reminding that these are spurious arguments. Any language can become fit for a purpose if it is used in the appropriate domain. The German linguist, Jakob Grimm (1851), praised English for its 'richness, rationality, and close construction',[8] which fitted it for its role as international lingua franca, but he would have been more accurate if he had acknowledged that the growing political and economic clout of its speakers was the prime reason for its development as a language for international communication.

7.1.5 The waning of British power

The history of French as a lingua franca illustrated how economic, political, military, religious and cultural dominance leads to the spread of lingua francas and that when the conditions that brought them into existence disappear, such languages fall out of use as contact languages. All lingua francas of the past have had a defined life span and their decline can be linked to events and to diminishing power bases. After the Second World War, the primacy of English would probably have waned, as the economic and political power of Britain declined, and its science and technology became comparatively less prestigious and less sought after. The language was, as we have demonstrated, mostly an elite phenomenon, used as the auxiliary language for trade, administration and access to new ideas. If another language had been required to access these domains then English would have withered as a lingua franca.

During the period, 1946–97,[9] the British Empire was progressively dismantled. After decolonisation, it would have been quite possible for English usage to disappear or at least diminish in many of the newly independent states, in the way that languages of former empire usually do. It is no surprise that Russian was eclipsed in the Warsaw Pact countries after the fall of

Communism, or that Dutch withered in postcolonial Indonesia. The natural decline in the use of English was stemmed, however, because the United States, the rising power that was in its turn becoming economically, politically, militarily and culturally dominant, possessed the same language. Elites of the newly independent countries which had once been colonies in the British Empire saw an advantage in keeping alive skills in a language which would continue to be a major lingua franca and to provide a channel for contact with the wider world.

7.2   The spread of English within the United States

The United States had remained English-speaking after independence. In the immediate aftermath of the revolution there had been a lively debate about whether this should be so. Those who had rejected Britain, its culture and its politics were unenthusiastic about continuing to use its language. Eighteenth-century ideas on language and group made it seem essential for the new 'nation' to have a necessary, intimate and perhaps exclusive relationship with its language. There were suggestions that Hebrew, the language of the chosen, or Classical Greek, the language of democracy, should be adopted. Nothing came of these Romantic suggestions. It is a utopian undertaking to impose a language shift top-down, even where the enthusiasm of a revolutionary society might aid the endeavour. Most Americans[10] at the time of independence were English speaking,[11] and they remained so, and English continued to spread throughout the federation (Simpson 1986). There was, however, desire in some sectors to underscore that English in America was different from the language in Britain. In 1789, Noah Webster expressed this view and set out the pattern that his own work would take. He maintained that:

> customs, habits and *language*, as well as government should be national. America should have her own, distinct from all the world. (Webster 1789 quoted in Simpson 1986: 5)

Between 1780 and 1820 there was some support for an academy on the French model that could codify the particularities and present the language as national language (Baron 1982; Andresen 1990). However, nothing came of John Adams' formal proposal which was rejected by Congress as an assault on individual liberties (Crawford 1992). It was left to a small number of individual linguists to categorise the differences between the two varieties. The first dictionary of American English appeared in 1800, *The Columbian Dictionary of the English Language* by Caleb Alexander. Webster's first major attempt at a dictionary was the *Compendious Dictionary of the English Language*, 1806. He had already published a *Spelling Book* in 1783 that was widely used in primary schools. In 1828, he published the *American*

Dictionary of the English Language 'for the instruction of citizens' (Webster 1828: preface). These and other attempts to carve out a separate identity, and promote Americanisms as standard lexis within the state were not uniformly well received. Webster was not at first accorded the widespread respect and authority that he was later to gain, and even some American commentators called the new terms 'barbarous', 'vulgar', 'provincial', 'ridiculous' (Andresen 1990). In the event, those who were linguistically conservative reined in others' desire to exercise 'the right to coin new words as well as money' (John Adams quoted in Andresen 1990: 48).

Webster's dictionary did enshrine some differences in form and usage between the new standard for the new state and the British standard, but one could also argue that Webster's endorsement of eastern seaboard norms as 'the American way' was one of the influences that kept American standard English close to the British standard. Certainly a high degree of mutual intelligibility among British and American speakers of English was maintained, even though immigrants arriving in the country were increasingly from non-English-speaking backgrounds and had to acquire English as their second language.[12]

The United States was not an imperialist power in the European sense; there was no need to colonise abroad when there was so much scope for expansion within North America. Only the conquest of territory in northern Mexico (1848), the annexation of Hawaii (1893), and the acquisition of Guam, Puerto Rico and the Philippines[13] (1898) broke with this practice. And with such space and relatively few inhabitants, the United States was a magnet. The internal colonisation of the country, the opening up of the West, and its industrialisation were carried out by millions of immigrants. In language terms this has had interesting effects. In few other countries do settlers display the wide diversity of countries of origin as in the United States.[14] Partly because of this and partly because of the societal pressure from the prevailing 'fresh start', 'melting pot' ideology, immigrants mostly switched to English in as short a period as possible (Daniels 1990). This ideology was only enshrined in a formal federal requirement for English proficiency for citizenship in 1906.

Only groups of immigrants who came together and stayed together in rural settlements bucked this trend and sustained their language over time. The Germans, in particular, had a strong tradition of maintenance, enabled by their large numbers and concentrations in farming and their commitment to running German medium schools (Feer 1952). A series of pamphlets that defended German speakers against the prejudices of their fellow Americans record their attitudes to language conservation and give clues as to why it happened. Rush (1789) explains the high degree of language conservation among German speakers. An extreme piety led to a desire to access the sacred texts which were available in German. Those educated in German medium schools attained an unusually high level of literacy for agricultural populations. Commitment to their own religious practices made it unlikely that they would marry outside the group and so there was minimal shift within family groups. Rupp (1875) confirms the earlier picture of a pious, well educated, prosperous but impermeable society. German literacy meant that there were enough readers to support a number of German-language newspapers.[15] Laws were published in German in Pennsylvania in the nineteenth century. However, German speakers too were eventually unable to withstand the pressure to shift. During the First World War, German-language education contracted massively as the community was constrained to demonstrate its loyalty by accepting linguistic assimilation.[16]

7.3 The spread of English outside the United States

In the political domain, the United States was mainly concerned with domestic issues until the two World Wars of the twentieth century. The United States, reluctant to be drawn into an Old World conflict, was not a combatant in the First World War until 1917. However, its role in ensuring Allied victory guaranteed it an influential voice at the peace talks. The Europeans' acceptance of the Wilsonian principle of self-determination is widely acknowledged as one domain in which the authority of the Americans was felt (Saunders 1998; Bucklin 2001). It is less well known that Woodrow Wilson required that the Treaties of Versailles, Sèvres and Trianon be published in English as well as French. This, significantly, was the first occasion when the use of French as the language of European treaties was challenged. This beginning of the end of the supremacy of French as the language of European diplomacy went hand in hand with France's loss of influence. The French found themselves excluded from Anglo-American preparations for drafting the League of Nations covenant and their suggestions for military collaboration dismissed (Ambrosius 1987). The shift from the complete dominance of French as diplomatic lingua franca was a reliable barometer of the shift in centres of political power.

Domestic concerns, particularly the economic problems of the 1930s, led Americans to a policy of isolationism between the World Wars and in the political domain the United States turned in on itself again (Ambrosius 1987). Then for a second time European conflict escalated to become global and Japan's attack on Pearl Harbor eventually drew the Americans into the conflict. At the end of the Second World War, English was the language of the victors and of military might. The two other European languages that had been recently used as lingua francas were in eclipse. In defeat, German lost its role as a language of science and technology.[17] French had lost prestige through the Vichy government's capitulation and collaboration, and was ousted as the main language of postwar negotiations, treaties and diplomacy. In contrast to 1918, when the English speakers had to lobby for their language to be used, the French had to press their case in 1945–46 for

French to be included as one of the six official languages of the United Nations Organisation.

Russian, also a language of victors in the 1939–45 conflict, was the only competition to English as an international lingua franca. And, as the world divided into two ideological blocs, English and Russian were the two lingua francas that allowed intragroup communication within each camp. From 1945 to the fall of Communism in 1990, English was the language of the US led Capitalist bloc in the Cold War, promoted as the key to progress, modernity, prosperity and as a badge of affiliation to the Capitalist camp. Russian was advanced as the language of social engineering, the command economy, equality, fraternity and the Communist bloc.

7.3.1   Language, the Capitalist system and economic leadership

A key point to be made about the United States and the role that Americans play in the global economy is that it is actually much less than the rest of the world thinks it is, in terms of volume. From the 1870s to the mid-1970s America's foreign trade (both imports and exports) remained well under 10 per cent of GDP (Gordon 2001). From the Civil War until very recently the United States was largely self-sufficient and did not need to be overly concerned with exporting or importing. This is a surprising fact given the seeming prevalence of Coca Cola and McDonalds and similar American products throughout the world. However, the reality is that over the last century American exports to the rest of the world have stood within a steady 11–13 per cent range of the total global market. Only during the immediate postwar period, when other industrialised countries were in ruins and not in a position to export, did US exports rise (to take 22 per cent of the market in 1949). To put this into context, a comparison of world export market share in 1990 shows the United States with 12 per cent, Japan with 8 per cent, the emerging Asian economies with 10 per cent and the European Union with a massive 44 per cent[18] (Gordon 2001). The United States is the leading economic power, but cannot be said to dominate the market.

This is not to say that the United States does not have profound influence on the international economy. What is to be observed is an interesting relationship between actual and virtual global power. Free market principles and the neo-liberal paradigm derive directly from the United States, frame the Capitalist system and structure the inter-governmental organisations that ensure its survival. It is through the acceptance of its philosophy that the United States dominates. Inter-governmental Organisations (IGOs) such as the World Trade Organisation (WTO), the International Monetary Fund (IMF), the World Bank (WB), the Organisation for Economic Cooperation and Development (OECD) and the G7 are not exclusively American, but the interests and associated ideological preferences of the United States are the dominant influences on and in them. Moreover, voting strength in organisations such as the IMF and WB is based on the financial status and contributions of member states and since the United States is the biggest contributor to the IGOs, there is actual American power in these organisations as well.

The American private sector contributes to US governmental pressure on national governments worldwide to abide by the rules of the neo-liberal model and adopt free market philosophy. US bond rating agencies like Moody's and Standard and Poor's determine the credit-worthiness of governments. If they downgrade a government it has to pay higher interest rates on bonds, and it may be shunned by international lenders as a bad risk.

However, although the paradigm of the global economy is American, its power bases are not exclusively American and it would be as erroneous to depict economic globalisation as a worldwide network with the United States at the centre as it is to claim that the United States totally dominates world trade. First, the United States is not the main base of transnational corporations (TNCs). Out of the top 100 TNCs, ranked by their foreign assets, 50 per cent were actually EU based,[19] and only 26 per cent had their headquarters in the United States (WIR 2000). Second, the United States does not invest equally in all parts of the world. US FDI is directed very much towards the 'developed' world, with US hedge and mutual funds, bond and currency traders, US investment houses and banks and US venture capitalist providers investing a large proportion of their capital in a relatively small number of states. In 1998, an overwhelming 80 per cent of US FDI was invested in the industrialised countries of the 'developed' world. In 1999, this rose to 85 per cent as the financial crises of the late 1990s in South-East Asia, Eastern Europe and South America exacerbated the division. The United States is actually quite conservative as a world player, exhibiting a particular bias towards investment in the United Kingdom[20] (Deloitte and Touche 2001).[21] To summarise, we could say that, although it would be a simplification to see the financial networks of global Capitalism as US led or US dominated, global Capitalism can be seen as deriving from American led thinking and existing within a framework of institutions dominated by the United States and it is this framework that has led many to speak of ideological domination.[22]

In terms of choice of language, this ideological and actual domination has meant that economic globalisation has led to Anglicisation. The philosophical underpinning of globalisation has given birth to a growing international scholarly and business literature on the subject in English. The international organisations and institutions, where free market philosophy is translated into policy, use English as the language to express that philosophy and to negotiate and administer compacts among groups. In investment, where information flows must of necessity accompany financial flows, since success depends ultimately on knowledge, the public channels are largely anglophone. The biggest and most prestigious business news networks, such as Dow Jones and Reuters, have headquarters in the United States and

United Kingdom respectively and report in English. The IMF and the World Bank put pressure on client states to include English in their education systems as a part of development (Mazrui 1997).

Even where the United States is not in the lead in global Capitalism, as for instance in the ownership and geographical distribution of TNCs, the language effect of the process is still the steady spread of English. The case of Europe is particularly illustrative. The large group of TNCs that are based in Europe carry out much of their transnational activity within the common market of the European Union and thus need to communicate across language frontiers. Although Europe is traditionally an area where there has been fierce allegiance to state languages and resolute defence of national linguistic prestige in intergroup contact, a number of leading European TNCs have adopted English as the language in which the corporation talks to itself in-house.[23] Since transnational companies have economic weight that is greater than that of many states, and by their actions demolish national economic autonomy, it is perhaps understandable that TNCs no longer feel bound by national allegiance expressed by commitment to national language, and adopt a language for other reasons than national identity and loyalty.

Perhaps more surprisingly, this appears to be true of European business in general. A growing body of evidence suggests that English is increasingly the general lingua franca of business, even where native speakers are not dominant and where there is no direct pressure from powerful English-speaking interests to use English. This is a bottom-up, organic movement and made possible because European citizens have demanded that their education systems provide English as a foreign language for their children, often in direct opposition to official education policies which have striven to promote diversity of language learning, as we saw in Chapter 6. English is now the main foreign language of the region learnt by 91 per cent of European secondary school children (Eurydice 2000) and claimed as a skill by 41 per cent of European adults (Eurobarometer 2001). The statistics reveal that the older generations are much less competent in English than the younger and thus the spread of English as a lingua franca is on the increase in Europe. This is primarily utilitarian behaviour. Motivation is instrumental not integrative (Gardner and Lambert 1972) and European acceptance of the language may well be accompanied by a distinct dislike for any incursion of American culture, particularly among elite groups.

Outside Europe many non-English-speaking states have sought to improve the linguistic competencies of their workforce so that they can attract the knowledge industries of the new phase of industrialisation. Old style economic globalisation only needed a small bilingual class to provide a linguistic bridge between headquarters and producers in manufacturing plants sited in countries where wages and other costs were lower. New style globalisation will create a much larger bilingual force since much work now consists in the manipulation of information. Information gathering and dissemination can also be sited where labour is cheaper, but the demand on the workforce is linguistically greater. They must have high level skills in a language of international contact, usually English. In this new organisation of work, call centres for the United Kingdom, for example, are sited as far away as India and Sri Lanka. This and other similar clerical work now being farmed out around the globe will mean that there will be a much larger group than administrators and managers who will require or benefit from extensive knowledge of the lingua franca. This brings about a new situation on several counts. First, the elite nature of lingua franca is diluted. One cannot talk about the vast and growing numbers of those who have knowledge of English as a second language as an 'elite' in the usual sense of the word. Second, the balance of advantage is likely to tip towards those who acquire English formally in school, as a system, and from those who acquire it in contact situations and perhaps in pidgin forms. Third, the pressure to acquire English as part of training for economic activity has led to policies of 'English for all' in many education systems with results which may not be wholly beneficial (see Chapter 4).

The penetration and spread of English is aided by the psychological support given by the omnipresence of the language in the aggressive marketing and publicity to increase the consumption of the products produced by the TNCs. Cities in South-East Asia where English does not have a long history of presence, such as Bangkok, Jakarta, and even Hanoi, are bristling with adverts, signs and slogans in a variety of international English. The same thing is to be found in Poland, Hungary, the Czech Republic and other former Eastern bloc countries. Such usage of English does not significantly improve English language skills among a population but it may have a significant psychological effect, making English the normal and eventually the acceptable medium for the semiotics of the city. Already the hegemony of English in these regions is such that it is becoming the language of regional trading. The members of the Association of South East Asian Nations (ASEAN)[24] use English for group meetings and for negotiation among members (Nair-Venugopal 2002). In Eastern Europe, English is increasingly preferred to Russian for intragroup contact, particularly between Hungarians or Rumanians and the speakers of Slav languages.[25]

To sum up, English is the associated language of economic globalisation because the source of the paradigm was the United States. However, even where global economic activity is not connected with the United States, contact across linguistic borders is still likely to be in English. Indeed, English is even the language in which organisations that lobby and protest against the inequalities of the globalised market system and its environmental consequences organise their opposition.[26] To have voice, they accept the medium of English (Murphy 2002). The choice of English is also accepted as utilitarian by TNCs that do not feel strong allegiance to any single state and its language. English is seen as instrumental for individuals with ambitions to function within the economic domain, where it appears a necessary if not sufficient prerequisite for membership. Its role in the economic sphere pushes parents to demand provision for learning and state education systems to respond. Although economic globalisation principally benefits the developed world which is both the source and recipient of the large part of flows of investment, it is penetrating deeper and deeper into all national societies. Although globalisation and the attendant acquisition of English is predominantly an affair of the rich world and elites, this is no longer a small elite but a very large tranche of all national groups. Millions of individuals choosing or being directed to learn English widens its utility, reinforces it in the lingua franca role and increases the pressure to become skilled at speaking it.

7.3.2 Language and the political sphere

In the political sphere, the United States also dominates, both virtually and actually: virtually in the sense that the end of Communism allowed the undisputed victory of its vision of the liberal Western model of democracy; in the concrete sense in that, although it may not be overtly imperial in the same manner as the empires of the past, it does conceive for itself a role as global lawgiver and enforcer and tends to act unilaterally to impose its will. Of course critics would dispute any US claim that intervention was disinterested peacekeeping and argue that such action is taken cynically to serve American interests.[27]

Between 1990 and 2003, the United States intervened in a number of conflicts,[28] using a discourse of law and order and peacekeeping to explain and justify its actions to the rest of the world. This discourse was widely rejected outside the United States and among significant groups in the country itself. In the conflicting narratives that have been elaborated, the United States portrayed the 1991 Gulf War and the bombing of Iraq throughout the following decade as its legitimate pursuit of a dictator developing weapons of mass destruction; opponents saw it as part of a struggle for control of oil reserves and a need to appease certain factions in the United States. In 2001, the Afghan War was presented by the United States as the need to mobilise internationally to take police action against worldwide terrorism; the opposition believed the government's motivation to be more complex, involving a need to avenge the attacks on New York and Washington in 2001, a desire to extirpate a challenge to the United States and the seizing of an opportunity to deflect attention from economic problems. In the winter of 2002–03, the two narratives polarised even further, as an Anglo-Saxon led alliance sought UN Security Council backing for a war to disarm Iraq forcibly, whilst other governments, backed by a massive grassroots protest movement against the war, disputed the very concept of a just war. When, in 2003, the United States and its allies invaded Iraq, the cleavage in world opinion was even deeper and wider.

In this claim and counterclaim it is difficult to make a dispassionate judgement, but I think that for the purposes of the present argument it is possible to argue that the United States by virtue of its immense military strength does exhibit some of the aspects of old style imperialism in that it can use force to impose its will and to further its interests. And at the same time it could be argued that it does so in a less brutally self-interested way than the empires of the past, and that US intervention has been complex, mixing straight policing and clear promotion of self-interest. So, the next questions that present themselves are, first, whether there is a political superstructure developing that parallels the global reach of the economy and attempts to regulate it, and, second, if governance is taking place at a level above the state what the place of the United States might be within it. Functionalist theory suggests that:

> to the extent that national political systems can no longer fulfil today's requirements it is expected … that new more adequate political institutions will develop. (Zürn 2002: 82)

and that they will be supranational. Inter-governmental power theories oppose this functionalist reasoning and argue that it is only the support of a strong hegemon that will allow the elaboration of the institutions for governance (Zürn 2002), and that any global regulation will reflect that hegemon's interests. At the time of writing, in 2003, the way international and supranational political structures may develop seems particularly opaque, but perhaps it is defensible to venture the following as an analysis of the present state of affairs.

It has been generally held that the development of political structures to accompany and constrain economic globalisation are dragging (Strange 1996), and that the United States is keeping apart from the movement to build a political superstructure. Those who would support strengthening the ability of the international community to reprimand and control individual members point to the thick interconnectedness which now exists among states and argue that this brings about the need for negative international regulation and coordinated global public policy.

The United States is at present rejecting this. Its government does not have a good record on signing up to and abiding by agreements aimed at regulating Capitalism. Critics cite, for example, its refusal to ratify the 1997 Kyoto Protocol on climate change,[29] its lukewarm participation in the UN's World Summit on Sustainable Development (2002) which the American president did not even attend, and its promotion of the free market for the rest of the world while it continues to practise some protectionism.[30] Then when it flouted the will of the UN Security Council to go to war on Iraq it weakened the whole idea of the 'international community' as arbiter and forum. This seemed a reversal as there had been some move towards a more united and coherent international position on common threats[31] and individual abuses.[32]

Thus the Americans are part of the globalisation of political power, because they are the only super power and can and do impose their will. At the same time they are lagging in the political movements to develop the controls needed to react to the transnational nature of activities, threats and problems. And whereas other parts of the world are moving into the close cooperation of regional groupings that aspire to a political dimension and that are developing multilevels of governance,[33] the United States is holding back. As Gordon (2001) remarks, the United States is actively encouraging regionalism without itself becoming involved.

Whether the United States is actually the motor of political globalisation or a brake on its development, however, the linguistic effect is not in dispute. The increase in the practice of international 'policing' is another forum where English has become the medium. Where the Americans, the British and other English-speaking groups exercise power outside their national borders, their agents use English. More significantly perhaps, the other groups involved in the transnational teams also use English as the main lingua franca, whether or not English native speakers are involved. English is the language in which multinational peacekeeping forces communicate.[34] It is a language that predominates in the international courts and war crimes tribunals.[35] It is an official and the customary working language[36] of international agencies, governmental and non-governmental, that are involved in the growing intervention that takes place within weaker states. It is thus a utilitarian language of contact. It is at the same time the language of power, the language of international relations, increasingly employed in meetings between heads of state. Fewer and fewer key political figures are unable or unwilling to use it.[37] English has become the established lingua franca of the political sphere because it is the language of the most powerful players and of the dominating ideology, and is reinforced in this role because it allows the joint exercise of power within peacekeeping forces and courts.

7.3.3 Language and science

Similar patterns are to be observed in technological advance. The United States has achieved a certain position of dominance in the technological sphere, as competitors fell by the wayside, although it is not the sole provenance of new technology in a number of spheres. However, the language in which research on new technology is published is principally English, no matter what the origin.

The Russian challenge in the space programme and in weapons development withered as the USSR dissolved into its constituent parts. The United States spends $50 billion plus on military R&D,[38] incomparably more than any member state of the EU or Japan. Japanese manufacturers may have dominated for a period on the production of the hardware for the audio–visual and Information Technology revolution, but what goes onto the machines now largely originates in the United States. Gates' Microsoft achieved quasi-monopoly status in software at the beginning of the twenty-first century, with revenue reported at $25.3 billion for the fiscal year June 2000–June 2001 (www.microsoft.com/msft/earnings). In the biotech industries, American companies, such as Genentech, were the pioneers that led the field and produced breakthrough technology. This sector continues to be dominated by giant American corporations with Amgen the biggest with yearly worldwide sales of $3.2 billion in 2001 (Amgen 2002). The future in this sector seems set to be US dominated as innovative work continues to come from established American firms and as a host of new companies on the western US seaboard are mounting a growing challenge to them. In the development of pharmaceuticals, US firms such as Pfizer and Merck, Sharpe and Dohme compete with European based TNCs such as AstraZeneca.[39] Major US companies such as Motorola, Loral Space and Communications and Teledisc dominate the market to provide satellite-based telecommunication infrastructure for the whole world.

However, the United States is not without serious challengers in other industrial sectors. In car manufacture and precision instruments, German manufacturers are major innovators; the French nuclear and transport industries have taken a leading role in many developments; many smaller industrialised nations dominate in one small sector or another. Thus in the development of new technology, the United States dominates, but not exclusively and not in every sphere.

However, when we come to the medium in which the flows of information on cutting-edge science take place, then English does dominate exclusively and in every sphere. The research community has come to inform itself, debate and publish in English, even where the innovation originated in other speech communities.

Those who have stood out against the exclusive use of English in scientific conferences and journals have had a difficult task. As we have seen, the French government tried to stem the tendency for French research to be reported in English by refusing funding to conferences on French territory where French was not the language of the conference (see Chapter 6). However, under pressure from its own scientists whose work was not given the same prominence when the English-speaking international research community did not attend, and under pressure from its own Constitutional Council that ruled that such prohibition could be unlawful, it was forced to review the policy and tolerate English as a language of conference contributions.

There is little challenge to the hegemony of English in the scientific community. As governments work to integrate the research activities of foreign firms into their local economies and to maximise the domestic spill-over from their research activity, to encourage their nationals' participation in foreign centres of excellence and membership of international strategic alliances in science and technology, there appears to be no or little discussion of the medium through which the contact can be achieved. English is thus gaining its position as the lingua franca of twenty-first century technology almost without comment. A Catalan scientist invited to speak on English as the language of science expressed surprise that the question should even arise:

> I had never thought that the language used in such exchanges (scientific) would be a possible matter for debate. (Alberch 1996: 257)

The absence of comment on the medium of scientific exchange in much of the literature is what is perhaps most significant. For example, in international organisations for which technical transfer is key, language is rarely mentioned as a variable. In a trawl of OECD documents from 1995–2000 on the problems of research and development in the international community, I could find little on the language issue. And even when language is mentioned, there is no challenge to, no questioning of English as the accepted medium. For example, in the OECD 1998 report, *The Global Research Village: how information and communication technologies affect the science system*, there is only one allusion to language. It is remarked that email is preferred to telephone communication by collaborators in international teams whose native language is not English. It is understood without being discussed or commented upon that both email and telephone conversation would naturally be in English. Another OECD report (1999) on the difficulties inherent in the globalisation of industrial R&D is more typical. In this text language does not feature as a difficulty or a policy issue; indeed it is not mentioned at all.

There are clear reasons for the spread of English in this domain, deriving in part from the dominance of the United States in much leading technology now and in the recent past and building on the British legacy. However, as in the political and economic spheres, the consensual use of English is now so extensive, that it cannot be explained by American dominance in the field on its own. Once again the less powerful in the linguistic equation are willing to pay the opportunity and real costs for language acquisition to gain access to the scientific community of communication, its literature and its ability to confer international recognition. And as new scientists accept that they will read and publish in English, it becomes increasingly difficult for any other group or individual to do otherwise and resist the hegemony, as competing groups such as the French have found. Indeed there may well be resistance from within resisting groups as members who want their work to be known internationally break ranks (Alberch 1996).

7.3.4 Culture

The tremendous increase in trade in cultural goods over the last two decades has been one of the most important aspects of globalisation, in that the entry of cultural goods into a society may have a far greater effect in terms of ideology and language use than other trade and contacts. Between 1980 and 1998, the annual world trade of printed matter, literature, music, visual arts, cinema, photography, radio, television, games and sporting goods surged from US$95 million to $388 million (UNESCO 2000). However, if we interrogate the statistics we see that this was not global exchange in the widest sense. Most of that trade was between a relatively small number of countries. Five countries, the United States, the United Kingdom, China, Japan, Germany were the destination for 53 per cent of cultural exports and the source of 57 per cent of imports. And within these countries the flows are not reciprocal and equivalent; in 1994, US cross-border exports including affiliated trade of audio–visual services were about US$16 120 million, whilst imports were only US$136 million. And as UNESCO, the source of these statistics, notes, this is a likely underestimation of the imbalance because much intra-firm trade is not registered, and whether it is between overseas affiliates or foreign owned affiliates and head offices, major partners are likely to be American (UNESCO 2000).

The phenomenon is well illustrated by the film industry. Hollywood studios control film distribution networks throughout the world and ensure the distribution of their product globally. A non-American audience is far more likely to watch a US produced film than a US citizen to see a film originating outside the United States. The American cultural model in film prevails to such an extent that we are not surprised that an internal awards ceremony for the US film industry held in Hollywood should attract an annual global audience of over a billion. Icons of US popular culture such as Madonna, Michael Jackson, Tom Cruise, Cameron Diaz, Bruce Willis and other Hollywood stars receive global recognition.

The television screens of the world also have a disproportionate number of US made programmes. As with the film industry, this derives, in part, from the low cost of TV programmes originating in the United States, where the size of the domestic market allows producers to cover costs within that market and thus to offer the product very cheaply to the world. It is perhaps also a consequence of the experience built up within the US entertainment industry. Film-makers learnt to tell a story through image and gesture in the era of silent film. Then, in the early days of talkies, they were dealing with domestic audiences where large numbers would not have spoken English as a first language.[40] A number of genres in the American cinema rely heavily on the action and visual development of the plot and it is perhaps possible to trace their development to experience gained in these early years and established as a tradition. And, where dialogue is less crucial to understanding the plot, the American dubbed or subtitled product may be more accessible to audiences from other language backgrounds than films from traditions that place more emphasis on verbal interaction (Wright 1997). Thus for a number of reasons, commercial[41] and cultural, the US product has reached successfully into all parts of the world. However, once again we should remember that this is only so where there is electricity and hardware. Cultural globalisation is, like the other forms of globalisation, a phenomenon that splits the world into haves and have-nots.

This is not so true of culture which is not language borne nor linked to possession of technology. US food and drink styles have penetrated every corner of the globe; McDonalds burger bars are in the town centres of countries even when other forms of American culture are banned or rejected; Coca Cola is on sale in the most remote African and Asian villages. US fashion has also spread globally, even if it is an imitation Nike or similar brand and not the real article that consumers in the developing world eventually acquire. Status is often linked to the possession of US created symbols whether genuine or false. Youth culture, in particular, is characterised globally by an adherence to US fashion in music, clothes, food and drink, and statistics confirm the casual observation of any traveller that this is so. Because this aspect of cultural globalisation is very apparent it has attracted strong reaction from those opposed to globalisation. Such fashions do not, however, penetrate into indigenous culture in quite the same way as language borne culture. One can buy an occasional McDonalds and still eat traditional foods from one's own culture for most of the time. One can wear designer labels from global companies (or cheap copies) but still have some traditional items of clothing in one's wardrobe for particular occasions. However, language borne cultural products may be different in effect. Where one learns enough of another language to consume another society's cultural product, there may not be easy coexistence with home-grown culture, if language development in the mother tongue suffers as a consequence. There may be a zero sum effect where one is developing literacy in another language and not developing literacy in the mother tongue.

Recent trade figures show that, despite the evident widespread infiltration of burgers and fizzy drinks, it is nonetheless the export of language borne cultural products which is most important to the US economy in financial terms. In 1996 language borne cultural products (movies, music, television programmes, books, journals and computer software) became the largest US export sector, surpassing, for the first time, all other traditional industries, including automotive, agriculture, or aerospace and defence (UNESCO 2000). This has inevitable consequences for the spread of English, where the 'consumer' experiences the cultural 'product' in the original language, but the effect on English language spread may also be felt even where there is dubbing and translation. A translated text can promote Anglophone traditions of communication, if the underlying organisation of the material remains very close to the original. A dubbed English language film can still promote the ideologies and attitudes of its makers. So both written and audio–visual media provide the English language learner with the cultural connotations associated with certain lexical terms, with the way particular concepts are elaborated in the United States, with the social norms of communication of US society, particularly the method for presenting an argument. Even when accessed in one's own language, books and films originating in the United States can be a language lesson of a kind.

7.4   Conclusions and speculation

This analysis leads us to the conclusion that in many ways English is no different in kind from the lingua francas of the past. All the reasons why other contact languages acquired that status are currently at work in the case of English, that is to say that its spread and use derives from its speakers' dominance in military, political, economic, cultural and technological spheres.

However, there are also divergences from other instances of the phenomenon, which may prove significant. First of all there is the double provenance of its lingua franca status. English, the lingua franca of British colonialism, did not fade with empire, because the next power that came to dominance in the Western Capitalist world was also English speaking. The same language used by two different states and relying on two different sets of criteria for its lingua franca status entrenched use in a way that differed from lingua francas associated with a single polity. In this English is akin to Latin, which moved from being the language widely used throughout an extensive empire to being the sacred language of a major religion and the lingua franca of knowledge and secular law in medieval Europe. The double provenance of Latin was one factor in the long duration and wide spread of that language.

At the beginning of the twenty-first century some indicators seem to be suggesting that English may once again survive the framework that made it a lingua franca for a particular time and place. There are signs that the number of speakers has achieved a kind of critical mass which suggests English might persist in its lingua franca role even in a scenario where the United States was no longer the prime motor of globalisation. It might survive because it has become the purveyor of the discourses of the dominating ideologies of Western democracy and neo-liberal free market Capitalism, the common language of the international scientific community, and the main medium of the new audio–visual and info tech networks whether or not these are US dominated.

Once again there are parallels with Latin. The longevity of Latin in the lingua franca role long after the eclipse of the Roman Empire and the end of the exclusive dominance of the Catholic Church suggest that, where a language has achieved critical mass and plays the role of knowledge lingua franca, such survival can happen. Latin remained the lingua franca of knowledge and secular law in some parts of Europe well into the nineteenth century.[42]

In a similar manner, as the second language of millions of people who wish to operate in the transnational networks and systems of globalisation, English may have gained so much ground outside circles associated with or dominated by its native speakers, that it may be rooted as a lingua franca no matter what actually happens to the native speaker society. Where the tradition of learning the language is so widespread, its utility to all its speakers whether native speaker or not, ensures its continued use. Joshua Fishman is one who believes that this may be so:

> Although such utilization may have initially rested upon Anglo-American econotechnological might, it may well now surpass or transcend such origins. (Fishman 1996: 4)

However, in these speculative matters it always pays to be cautious. Andrew Conrad, writing in 1996, noted that only ten years earlier William Gage had felt able to write that Russian is 'the other super language' and 'second only to English as an avenue of access to modern science and technology' (Conrad 1996: 17). As the USSR fell from power and its influence withered, Russian was swiftly discarded as a lingua franca in many of its former strongholds. If there are indications that English might break the mould as it is accepted as a lingua franca in settings where there are no native speakers, there is still no guarantee that the normal rules will not prevail. If the next economic, political, technological and cultural centre is sufficiently powerful then the language effects will probably develop in the traditional way, English will be eclipsed, and the language of the new power will become the next lingua franca.[43]

Keeping this proviso in mind, it does seem possible to argue, nonetheless, that English is achieving a hegemonic critical mass. The millions of second language speakers and would-be speakers cannot be accounted for by straightforward coercion nor even through direction; the mass results from the incremental effect of individuals deciding that English is of advantage to them, as the prime language of social promotion in a globalising world. Thus we have a classic situation of hegemony in the Gramscian sense; those disadvantaged by their non-native speaker position contribute to their disadvantage by their consensual behaviour. If they all refused to acquire English, they would halt the imbalance that deprives them of the advantages of the native speakers. However, they perceive that to do so unilaterally would cut them off from global networks and systems that can bring political advantage, professional reward or economic benefit, and so do not make that choice. It is this new situation and the reactions to it that are the focus of the next chapter.

8
Language in a Postnational Era: Hegemony or Transcendence?

This chapter focuses on the apparent consensual acceptance of English as a lingua franca and examines its role as the medium of globalisation. It includes an analysis of globalisation which considers how far it can be said to be a new phenomenon which brings us into a postnational period where supranational and transnational structures have started to replace the national. There is a brief consideration of the sites which are resisting any move to postnationalism. The discussion then moves to the intellectual resistance to the spread of English and to the difficulties in countering the negative aspects of English language spread while retaining a language that can fulfil the lingua franca role.

8.1 The phenomenon of globalisation

Perhaps the first task in any discussion of language and globalisation is to establish whether there is any reason for believing that we are at the beginning of a new postnational, global period and to arrive at an understanding of what globalisation actually is. Investigating the phenomenon presents a number of difficulties. The first hurdle will be to decide which of the very many views of globalisation to adopt since it is a very contested concept in the social sciences. The second hurdle will be to evaluate the evidence, since globalisation has sparked a large body of literature some of which has been widely attacked as:

> steeped in oversimplification, exaggeration and wishful thinking... conceptually inexact, empirically thin, historically and culturally illiterate, normatively shallow and politically naïve. (Scholte 2000: 1)

So, with little consensus and much political and economic literature that is highly speculative, it will not be an easy matter to arrive at the definition of globalisation that can help us understand the paradigm in which the language question will develop in the twenty-first century. It does seem essential to attempt this, however, because the failure to deal in depth with the developing political and economic dimensions of globalisation is what has undermined some of the work on global English in the past.

The divergence of views on what globalisation might actually be is extreme. One group of social scientists sees globalisation as a civilising force which promotes modernity and prosperity (cf. Levitt 1983; Ohmae 1990 and 1995; Wriston 1992; Guéhenno 1995). An opposing group portrays it as a destructive force born of unfettered Capitalism and dehumanising technology (cf. Callinicos 1994; Greider 1997; Rodrik 1997; Mittelman 2000). Some economists take an extreme view and suggest that the world now has the capacity to act as a single economic unit (cf. Luard 1990; Ohmae 1995; Castells 1996; Albrow 1997). Others are sceptical and remind us that history is cyclical and that, arguably, foreign trade represented as great a proportion of states' economic activity in 1900 as in 2000 (cf. Gordon 1988; Hirst and Thompson 1996; Wade 1996; Weiss 1998). Some social theorists argue that advocacy and pressure groups now act in a completely transnational way with environmental pressure groups, rights groups, women's liberation movements, unconstrained by borders (cf. Robertson 1992; Albrow 1997; Guidry, Kennedy and Zald 2000;). Others remind us that this is hardly new; the struggle for female suffrage, the abolition of slavery and the rights of trade unions were fought for by international movements (Keck and Sikkink 1998). The debate about the long-term effects is equally fractured and there is no consensus on whether globalisation will be pernicious or beneficial in economic and political terms. The jury is still out, and it may well be that the final outcome of globalisation will be judged a complex mixture of benefit and harm.

One aspect of globalisation, however, is not contested. The group that characterises the phenomenon as the conquest of geographical space and real-time interaction on a global scale (cf. Giddens 1990; Mittelman 1996; Held *et al.* 1999) has clear evidence to illustrate that the multidirectional cross border flows of goods, services, money, people, information and culture are going faster and further than ever before. The difference in rate and kind between the contacts that accompany globalisation and those provoked by imperialism and world trade in the past are clear. Flows from one part of the globe to another are almost instantaneous. All those who possess the hardware and have access to the electricity that permits use of audio-visual and information technology are constantly informed of what is taking place in other parts of the world. It is essential to underscore the necessity for such a proviso. In discussing the flow and networks of globalisation that audio-visual and information technologies have made possible, it would be wise to remember the claim that was prevalent in the late 1990s: that there were as many telephone lines in Manhattan as there were in the whole of Africa. Globalisation is thus far an affair that touches elites far more than other groups, and having access to the technology divides the world into the haves and have-nots.[1] However, for the former, for those with access, feelings of involvement are now increasingly global; the images of famine, drought, flood, earthquake and war from all continents are in our living rooms and news is presented as if from the global village. The immediate knowledge of events elsewhere in the world changes us psychologically and it is difficult to be detached when we see conflict, protest or disaster in real time. This is actuality not history, and we are within a time frame where our reaction could conceivably affect events.

In the programmes that promote fantasy rather than the real world, viewers also share experience. Soap operas from one part of the globe may be watched in another, causing us to resolve some of our dilemmas and review some of our emotions through the filter of a shared fiction. Sports programmes often have a global audience. If we know nothing else about our neighbours, we know their sports teams.

Moreover, the group involved in this is growing fast. The expansion in availability of information technology is phenomenal and recent surveys suggest that one in five of the world's population will soon have access to the Internet (NUA 2002) and that 514 million people already have an email address (NUA 2002). In parts of the world where there has been low participation (e.g. Africa and South America), Internet access is increasing at about 20 per cent a year (NUA 2002) which suggests that disparities may narrow if not close. Only the most isolated communities are *completely* untouched by this phenomenon. The cyber café has penetrated to some remote places and the proportion of humanity *totally* unaffected by television or film becomes an ever smaller minority. Thus new ideas, new theories, new approaches, new techniques, whether helpful or harmful, can be disseminated to enormous numbers very quickly. In short, with the provisos noted above, these technologies have redrawn the imagined communities that we construct. Anderson's (1983) idea that we perceive ourselves as part of the national group as we read the daily national newspaper or the latest fiction in the national language may no longer hold to the same extent as in the recent past. We may be just as disposed to construct our identities in relation to the transnational networks we belong to as we cross former boundaries for our information, contacts and exchanges. The satellite television channels we watch, the websites we access, the email groups we belong to may well be as influential in the construction of group identity as our national media. Once there is access to audio-visual and information technologies, it is only language that constrains the choice of news source and virtual group. The old system in which national media disseminated national news in the national language is slowly disappearing and as it does so, a powerful shaper of national identity disappears too.

Another undisputed facet of globalisation is the spread of the neo-liberal economic model that we began to discuss in the previous chapter. In the wake of the fall of Communism, economic and political pressure have been brought to bear on states to adopt this model and there has been global (re)structuring of both private and public enterprise within the Capitalist paradigm. However, economic globalisation does not necessarily mean economic convergence. The gap between the poorest and the richest state has widened considerably despite the general move to a single economic system; the disparity in per capita income was five times as great in 1990 as in 1870 (Guillen 2001). The financial crises in south-east Asia in the final years of the last century and in South America in the first years of this have brought criticism of the Western development model and of US-led policies seen to be 'insensitive if not malevolent' (Gordon 2001: 129). However, although the subsistence peasant farmer has far from disappeared, some 50 000–60 000 multinational corporations and enterprises now account for between 20 per cent and 30 per cent of world output and perhaps as much as 60 per cent of all world trade. In the view of some, these are historically unique; they are not national firms working internationally but organisations that coordinate production and distribution transnationally without this being for the exclusive benefit of any one centre (Held *et al.* 1999). Globalisation has not meant that the economic system treats us all equally but it has meant that one global system affects the vast majority of humanity.

Globalisation has brought about some convergence in political expectations (Meyer *et al.* 1997). People in most societies now expect that there will be state effort to provide some education for the young, some welfare provision including health care and old age support, a degree of respect for basic human rights and the rule of law. Where this does not yet exist, there are lobbies to demand them. Where societies do not have democratic representation this too is an increasingly common demand; where oligarchic or autocratic authority remain they are increasingly challenged. There is a heated debate over the ability of globalisation and market economies to deliver these expectations (Rodrik 1997; Mishra 1999; Guillen 2001). Some authorities claim that ability to provide the welfare now expected depends on a move to the liberal model and others maintain market economies restrict welfare systems. On the one hand, it is argued that they are the only systems which generate enough wealth to do so; on the other, they are held not to promote the societal solidarity necessary for general acceptance of welfare responsibility. However, divergence here does not result from lack of information. The advances in audiovisual and information technologies and their continual spread throughout societies have aided the circulation of ideas and knowledge in ways that change society as profoundly as the invention of writing and printing did in the past.

Globalisation is also definable as an erosion of the sovereignty of states and the growth of international organisations. The tendency is towards an agreed common core of rights and duties that govern the individual's relationship with the state, and an increasing propensity for international courts, organisations and institutions to superimpose international standards in political life (Sorenson 2002). As rights and the rule of law are accepted as a common platform, states that fail to respect the rights of minorities on their territory, or who contravene the minimum standards of the international community in terms of the rule of law, are increasingly likely to find themselves sanctioned in some way (Jett 1999). However, the process is not yet uniform and some states remain undisciplined while others are constrained to comply; the discrepancies are related to the power of the state in question and whether the big political players see chastisement as politically expedient or not (Richmond 2002).

For a period at the end of the last century, globalisation in the guise of global Capitalism seemed to have no challengers. The disappearance of Communism as a force and the apparent victory of the Western worldview led to the claim that there were no alternatives to free market neo-liberalism and the democratic paradigm.[2] This was a state from which the human race could not progress and against which there was no opposing force. In the intervening decade this analysis has been revealed as a simplistic[3] view and alternatives to the American Capitalist vision clearly do exist. However, the challenges (militant Islam, Balkan nationalism) that have surfaced have, up till now, been faced down by the 'Western world', either in the form of action by the United States supported by some of its allies or by action taken under the aegis of the NATO or the Western lobby in the United Nations.

In the light of these various developments, it is difficult to agree with those sceptics who contest globalisation as a phenomenon; it may not be so developed as some hyperglobalist commentators imagine; it is, however, a greater force than the minimalist position allows. And while the jury may still be out on which groups will actually benefit from globalisation, there is no real doubt that the extensity of global networks, the intensity of the interconnectedness and the velocity of flows are all greatly increased in the last decades. The political scientist, David Held expressed it in the following way:

> Globalisation can best be understood as a process or a set of processes rather than a singular condition. It does not reflect a simple linear developmental logic, nor does it prefigure a world society or a world community. Rather it reflects the emergence of interregional networks and systems of interaction and exchange. (Held 1999: 27)

We can be fairly sure that whatever other outcomes result from globalisation, greater contact between language groups is an indisputable and major effect of the phenomenon.

8.2 The weakening of the state

So, having accepted that there is increased activity at the trans- and supranational level which may have a language effect, is there any evidence that there is a parallel weakening of the nation state system, that would contribute to such change bottom-up as well as top-down? One clear signal of postnationalism is seen in the numerous pressures that undermine the absolute sovereignty of the state.

Scholte (2000) summed up how the situation appeared to be evolving at the beginning of the twenty-first century. He argued that, although national governments retain an important role in governance, globalisation has caused several shifts in how they exercise it. First, the affective hold of the state over its citizens has loosened in a world where radio, satellite television, telephone and internet contact do not halt at the state boundaries. Such contacts have allowed various non-territorial identities and communities to develop alongside the national. Second, this process has been exacerbated as the acceptance of free market philosophy and the concept of individual responsibility weakens the relationship between citizen and the state, with the latter ceasing to be cradle to grave protector and provider of health care, education, nutrition, minimum income and other welfare. Third, the legal hold of states over their citizens has loosened in a world where citizens can appeal to international courts and rulers be held to account for crimes against humanity committed on their sovereign territory. Fourth, the state is no longer sheltering its domestic market to the same degree, as general pressure for free trade and the power of transnational corporations (TNCs) make protectionism impossible.[4] Fifth, wars are much more likely to be civil war within the state than conflict between states.[5] This is in part because of economic global interconnectedness which is a strong disincentive to interstate strife for powerful groups and in part because of the power and terribleness of the arms in states' arsenals.

Events since the publication of Scholte's book mean that this last claim has to be rethought or at least recalibrated. But certainly the firepower that the United States exhibited in the Afghan and Iraq wars confirms one part of the thesis. However, even if only part of Scholte's analysis holds, we are still witnessing a loss of the distinctive nature of the nation state. It will no longer be the main source of identity, the prime welfare provider for its citizens, a sovereign territory where no outside force may intervene, a closed domestic market with high boundary fences and the principal protector of its people in interstate conflict.

There seems to be a reasonable case to be made that the world is moving into a postnational period where systems and societal relationships are increasingly configured on a supranational rather than a national scale. Hence we should also expect major changes in language use, as the need for media for communication is increasingly at the supranational or transnational level rather than at the national level.

8.3 The exceptions to postnationalism

Of course, there are exceptions to this trend towards these postnational patterns of governance, interaction, orientation and association and a global community of communication. The various cultural, political, economic and scientific aspects of globalisation discussed above are not penetrating all societies at the same rate.

It is also true that many groups are nation building as enthusiastically today as at any time in the past. After the break up of the USSR, its constituent parts have engaged in nation building in very similar ways to those described in Part I of the book. Much of the fracturing into states occurred according to ethnic nationalist criteria, and where the proposed polities have not followed these lines there has been conflict. Groups that do not see their natural home in the state in which they find themselves have fought to secede, either to be reunited with groups with which they do identify (e.g. the Armenians of Nagorno–Karabakh) or to be fully independent on their own (e.g. the Chechens). In former Yugoslavia, similar ambitions led to war as the state fractured along ethnic lines and the central power opposed its dismantling. In Western Europe, the process has been less violent but no less significant. Old centralised nation states like Spain and the United Kindom agreed to high degrees of autonomy for groups within state boundaries. The great difference between this nation building in the late twentieth and early twenty-first centuries and that of previous eras is that it is taking place in a macro context which is much less favourable to the enterprise. The phenomenon of small autonomies and new nation building is a subject to which we will return in Part III of the book.

But before leaving the subject of exceptions to postnationalism, it is necessary to note one further anomaly. Ironically, the loss of distinctive national identity and state sovereignty seems to apply less to the United States, itself than to other states. Is there a case to be made that the United States is less affected by globalisation than the rest of us? Some of the most robust resistance to globalisation comes from within the United States itself. As the remaining and only superpower, the United States dominates in a number of key areas but is not reciprocally dominated. The US government is able to guards its sovereignty and autonomy in the classic manner of the nation state. The national group exerts pressure on its members to be patriotic in a way that has become increasingly more difficult in many other Western states. Even the English only debate seems redolent of a former era. Returning to some of evidence presented to support the arguments in Chapter 7, we can see that it also upholds the thesis that the United States is not as profoundly affected by globalisation as many other groups, whether the phenomenon is interpreted as 'flows and contacts' or as 'constraints and pressures'.

First, American pre-eminence in media networks and entertainment industry has caused the flows to be away from it and not to it. American cultural products are a major export but there is no equivalent volume of imports.[6] Most Americans do not regularly experience the cultural products of other language groups, even dubbed or in translation. American patterns of identity are thus not highly influenced either by seeing the cultural creation of the Other or by seeing themselves reflected in the eye of the Other.

Second, the United States appears to be protected from some of the material effects of economic globalisation. Large companies from outside the United States tend to be TNCs because the size of their domestic markets drives them to cross borders. Large companies based in the United States have an enormous domestic market to be exploited before they need to consider transnational activities and so a high proportion of companies do not expand into foreign markets to survive.[7] The domestic market is aided by a certain amount of pressure on domestic consumers to choose US goods in preference to foreign imports as a mark of patriotism.[8] Moreover, in a number of industries the US government has legislated for a degree of protectionism.[9] Thus with large sales within the domestic market and a government that protects certain industries, the US domestic economy exhibits many of the features of a national economy pre-globalisation.

Third, the United States is the only superpower, the dominant member in political alliances and groupings, and the most puissant player in international institutions. In the role of global law enforcer, the United States, with its allies, challenges the sovereignty of those who act against global interest but there is currently no power that can challenge US sovereignty. As we saw in Chapter 7, the American government resists any diminishing of its own freedom to act as a sovereign power and this has been most apparent in the debate about unfettered industrial growth and unrestricted consumption. In particular, the United States has not been willing to accept the constraints inherent in the consensus that has built around several ecological issues that affect the whole of humanity.

Fourth, developments in the political sphere may well be causing increased isolation. The attack on 11 September 2001 and the growing fear of terrorism in the intervening period have heightened patriotism and may have caused Americans to turn inward. The drop in numbers travelling abroad[10] as a result of fears for personal safety can only exacerbate retreat from the international and global.

Fifth, the reluctance of North Americans to experiment with supranational regional governance is part and parcel of these current attitudes towards political independence. The North American Free Trade Association (NAFTA) remains solely economic with no political dimension, and studies of North American opinion have found that:

> The European subordination of national identity and values in the pursuit of greater economic advantages seems to neither be necessary nor desired in North America. (EKOS 2003)

Consequently, the United States could be said to be bucking the trend and retaining many of the attributes of the nation state. It is interesting that in the current 'English only' debate within the United States itself, many in the establishment elites have taken a stance clearly within the nineteenth-century nation-building mould and have argued against any public space for the languages of other constituent groups (cf. Gonzalez 2001). Thus we appear to be witnessing asymmetric developments within globalisation: loss of economic autonomy and political sovereignty for many states; continuing economic autonomy and political sovereignty together with the survival of some elements of traditional 'one nation, one territory, one language' nationalism for the United States.[11]

8.4   Opposition to English spread: questions of justice and equity

Thus in the opening years of the twenty-first century we have a situation where a globalising world is using the US paradigm and the English language, but where Americans seem to participate only where this is of clear advantage to them and opt out where it is not. It is little wonder that this situation of ascendancy and imbalance has led to intense irritation and anti-American feeling. I have explored it here because it is, no doubt, one of the causes for the strong reactions to the spread of English in many quarters. A growing body of scholarly literature sets out to demonstrate that the English language is imposed through a complex ideological process of dominant discourses linked to this pursuit of Anglo-Saxon self-interest (e.g. Tollefson 1991; Phillipson 1992; Calvet 1993; Pennycook 1995; Hagège 1996[12]) and fuelled by an inward-looking hegemon refusing to engage with the rest of the world in a multilateral way, resulting in disadvantageous language practices being imposed on poorer countries (Tollefson 1991 and 1995; Blommaert 1999; Skutnabb-Kangas 2000). It is these oppositional discourses that we shall now consider and evaluate whether they have had effect in the wider community.[13]

8.4.1   Critical Theory

Given the association of English with British colonialism and American extreme free market Capitalism, it is not surprising that much of the literature that opposes or questions the spread of English comes from the Marxist and Critical Theory tradition.

Critical Theory, which originated in the Frankfurt School,[14] takes the stance that research cannot be neutral. From this perspective Critical Theorists set out to marry the empiricism of the social sciences with morality. Their main contribution has been first to clarify the socially constructed character of society, revealing how ruling social groups propagate their world view to justify inequalities in social arrangements, and second to identify and enlist those in society whose interests would be served by social change. Critical Theory clearly has much to contribute in the area of language, and this dimension is highly developed in the work of Jürgen Habermas. Habermas' theory of communicative action presents contemporary Capitalism as a set of systems that colonise people's lives. The systems are economic and political. The economic system is mediated by money and the political by language.

Other major social theorists such as the Postmodernist French philosopher, Michel Foucault, developed theories based on similar premises. Foucault's work sought to uncover the historical construction of certain discourses and to uncover the connections between them and political 'realities'. He pointed to the increasing importance of ideology as a mechanism of power in societies where overt control is no longer possible and ascribes a central role to discourse as the main tool of persuasion that ensures modern forms of power. This development was in direct contradiction to mainstream Linguistics whose proponents had long felt themselves to be in an academic discipline that was apolitical. The legacy of the Saussurean approach had been to study language as a free standing system; the legacy of the Behaviourists had been to associate the study of language to the individual and to psychology rather than to the group and to sociology.

The philosophical underpinning of both Critical Theory and Postmodernism seemed to offer insights for a number of politically aware linguists who reacted against apolitical approaches, and, by the late 1980s, the numbers working within the paradigm influenced by Critical Theory were such that one can begin to talk of the Critical Linguistics school. Critical Linguists turned to a consideration of 'the relationships among language, power and inequality, which are held to be central concepts for understanding language and society' (Tollefson 2002: 4). They wanted to understand the social and political effects of particular language policies and practices, to make clear how such policies and practices were often presented as inevitable by elites who benefited from the *status quo* and to investigate how they disadvantaged individuals and groups who had little influence over the linguistic dimension of public life and who had to function within systems where their own languages were not valid. Critical Linguistics involved activism: linguists were seen 'as responsible not only for understanding how dominant social groups use language for establishing and maintaining social hierarchies, but also for investigating ways to alter those hierarchies' (Tollefson 2002: 4). Thus the main scholars under this umbrella see themselves as involved and implicated. They do not believe in the value, or even the possibility, of reporting dispassionately on events. They are engaged in the processes which they studied and analysed.

The first published work from this research paradigm had a national focus and examined the links between language policies and practices and inequalities of class, region, and ethnicity/nationality. The focus was on the distinction within the nation state between elites that knew and used prestige standard versions of the national language and groups who mastered the variety less well. Pierre Bourdieu, the French social theorist, was among the first to examine how elites practise a kind of Weberian social closure in language use and protect the cultural capital that accrues to them through knowledge and use of the standard language (Bourdieu 1982, 1991, 2001). Norman Fairclough and Roger Fowler, under the general inspiration of Halliday's work, spearheaded the Critical Linguistics approach in the United Kingdom, dissecting the way language is employed to produce, maintain and change the social relations of power and to permit the domination of some people by others (Fairclough 1989). Fairclough's focus was in the first instance the reproduction of class relationships within the society but his more recent work examines how discourses that reproduce ideology circulate globally (Fairclough 2002).[15] Jim Tollefson in the United States was primarily concerned with the situation of linguistic minorities produced by policies which enshrine a single national language in a state but he also extended his work to examine the role of English in the developing world. He attacked modernisation theory in its claims that 'Western societies provide the most effective model for "underdeveloped" societies attempting to reproduce the achievements of industrialisation' (Tollefson 1991: 82). Assessing the export of the model as problematic and as contributing to economic and political inequalities, he then turned to the language in which the process takes place. He does not claim that the spread of English is responsible for inequalities but he argues that it institutionalises the gap between sectors and establishes a significant practical barrier for anyone seeking to move from one to the other. He thus attacks those who argue that English is 'merely a practical tool for development rather than a mechanism for establishing and institutionalising unequal social relationships' (Tollefson 1991: 85).

Robert Phillipson (1992), following this tradition, describes postcolonialism as a process in which actual colonialism was replaced by virtual colonialism based on language and expresses clear disapproval of the role of English as lingua franca. He assembles extracts from marketing and policy briefs from the British Council and other promoters of English to reveal the political and economic purposes of the English-speaking centre in promoting the language.[16] He concludes that globalisation is a form of imperialism only differentiated by the extent to which those dominated are hoodwinked into seeing some benefit to themselves and do not rebel against the system. He maintains that the states of the 'periphery' are uniformly stifled by the power centres of globalisation.

It is not surprising that he, together with a number of other Critical Linguists who have followed his lead, have based much of their thinking on analysis of hegemony described by the work of the Italian Communist, Gramsci. Gramsci identified hegemony as a process in which a ruling class succeeded in persuading the other classes of society to accept its own moral, political and cultural values. Policy which can be presented as for the good of all allowed elites to win consent to their domination and thus obviated the need for the hegemony to be underpinned by coercion and might (Gramsci 1971; Joll 1977; Sassoon 1980; Bellamy and Schechter 1993). Gramsci's analysis focused on workers in a Capitalist state who accepted their own evident exploitation and weak economic position within that system because civil society had obtained the general consent of the population to the general direction imposed by the dominant groups. The workers had been convinced that to an extent the system benefited them too:

> This consent is 'historically' caused by the prestige and consequent confidence which the dominant group enjoys because of its position and function in the world of production. (Gramsci 1971: 13)

The concept of hegemony permits us to explain why language shift happened so easily within nationalism. Desire to join with prestige groups in the hope of sharing their advantage worked alongside all the other pressures for change to the national standard.

Hegemony appears to be working in the same way in globalisation. The concept explains why on the whole, English is increasing as the prime medium in all transnational political domains without coercion. The acceptance of English in its lingua franca role is consensual. There is little actual direction or compulsion, except for the dominant groups' refusal to communicate in any other medium. Non-native speakers of English believe that they can share the advantages that accrue through having that language if they acquire it. The data[17] show overwhelmingly that groups are changing linguistic practices and that increasing numbers of non-English speakers are adding English to their repertoire to ensure participation and inclusion in new developments.

Many Critical Linguists see the confidence, prestige and persuasiveness of the dominant English-speaking groups in globalisation as a lure for the rest of the world. For them globalisation only differs in degree and not in kind from imperialism and both are characterised by exploitation (Phillipson 1992). For this group the concept of hegemony and the consensus it has obtained start to explain why non-English speakers accept the move to English to permit global activity even where it puts them at a relative disadvantage in communication. They tend to see those who do not accept that they are exploited as dupes.

Others reject the idea that all those that choose to use English to enter the structures, flows and exchanges of globalisation are victims. Phillipson has been attacked for being overly deterministic and reductionist[18] on the language issue, and for failing to recognise that language users are not eternal victims and eventually own the languages that they adopt (Brutt-Griffler 2002; Canagarajah 1999). According to Canagarajah, the discourses of English are far from unitary and as the language is appropriated, the power of the 'centre' is diluted or usurped. In an optimistic reading globalisation may yet be democratised, and English may have a role to play in the process. Holborow (1999), from a Marxist perspective, argues that it is simply inaccurate to portray states that employ English in some functions as dupes, since the choices they have made have allowed them to realise their own projects sometimes in direct contradiction to interests of the English-speaking centre. The East Asian Economic Caucus (EAEC) is one example of a group where a utilitarian decision to use English for planning and negotiation[19] has allowed it to further its interests, mostly at the expense of the United States. Despite some reverses among members, the EAEC has clearly been able to increase the standard of living that it can offer citizens by moving towards regional cooperation and entering the global system (Gordon 2001). Critics respond that this does not change the argument. An elite English-speaking class works in tandem with global institutions and business, aids their spread and penetration, and accrues benefits for itself. The great mass do not profit and are victims. The difficulty is to know where this leads on the language question. Can participation increase within society as English spreads vertically or should there be insistence on using the national language in institutions and business to permit greater participation? (Tollefson 1991).

Critical Linguists believe that language policy and planning can help in recalibrating power within society. Much work from the tradition (e.g. Phillipson 2000) provides insightful analysis of the way that English is associated with the reproduction and the legitimating of power, both as the language of a dominant speech community internationally and as the language of elites in national contexts. However, to go the next step in Critical Linguistic tradition and to claim that this can be changed by policy seems untenable. Such a claim flies in the face of one of the central tenets of this book: that the success of a lingua franca relies on factors largely outside the control of individual governments and certainly outside the control of the language industries. Phillipson, for example, argues that for

> English to be a force for democracy and human rights much needs to change in North countries as much as in the South and in North–South relations. Language policy could and should play an important role in such a transition. (Phillipson 2000: 102)

No doubt Phillipson is correct about North-South relations; I question, however, that language policy could be an agent in change. To stand against the forces of globalisation by rejecting the English language seems to me to be the tail wagging the dog. And all the evidence to date suggests that governments are unable to legislate top-down about acquisition of lingua francas. Although language learning on an ideological basis was achieved in nation building, this was because top-down and bottom-up movements coincided: the spread of the national language was central to nation building; acquisition of the language was useful for individual success and social mobility. Such dual pressure is not present for any policy that tries to limit English-language spread. Many believe that one's likelihood of profiting from the global market, of finding employment within a transnational corporation, of informing oneself through global news, of participating in global culture or of influencing global regulatory bodies or enlisting their aid depends in the first instance on one's ability to communicate in the languages that dominate in global systems, institutions, relationships and contacts. Any national policy trying to limit citizens' acquisition of competence in English, the 'necessary if not sufficient' prerequisite for access to influential power networks, global economic structures, and new scientific and technological developments, would be flouted. Whether or not the desire to learn English is the product of hegemonic processes or the outcome of rational choice it will be impossible to deflect people's determination by legislation and policy. The Europeans have already demonstrated that.

Unsurprisingly, Critical Linguists oppose the argument that English can be viewed as utilitarian, simply a public good that permits progress. In a landmark text for teachers of English to speakers of other languages (TESOL), Alistair Pennycook (1994) examines the discourse that has constructed English as an international language as neutral, beneficial and natural. He examines how accepting English affects the learners, putting them into a new position within the social order. Peoples' relationships with Capitalism, Modernity, Democracy, Aid and Education are mostly mediated through English. Pennycook's critique of the role of English in the Capitalist system opposes the optimistic view that English could be a neutral medium for modernisation, progress and prosperity. He demonstrates how English 'helps to legitimate the contemporary world order' and is used as a 'gatekeeper' to the glittering prizes of Capitalism. Pennycook takes a highly Foucauldian view of the issues, seeing discursive practices as wholly constitutive of social systems and the very object of conflict (Foucault 1972). Because of this, he has a tendency to underplay the socio-politico-economic dimension of power formation (Holborow 1999). I do not want to deny that discursive practices and the elaboration of ideology are constitutive of the present linguistic situation, but I do believe, along with Holborow, that this is only a partial truth. Power relationships are constituted through force and money as well as through discourse and these three actually dovetail in a complex way. Moreover, the Postmodern discursive model tends to lead authors to concentrate on the top-down imposition of ideology and to neglect the very strong and widespread bottom-up demand to enter and be part of the process. To see those who want to be part of global networks, structures and flows as completely hoodwinked by hegemonic manipulation from the heartland of Capitalism denies agency to the vast majority. It is difficult to accept that the individual subject is never competent and that their motivations and rationales do not sometimes develop from a dispassionate assessment of the opportunities open to them and the constraints operating on them.

The limitation of these oppositional approaches is clear from the solutions suggested. Phillipson seems to be proposing linguistic nationalism as a strategy for combating the linguistic neo-imperialism of English-speaking centres. This, however, fails to take into account how recent nation building has developed. Sorenson (2002) recognises that the problems of recently constituted states derive in part from world market dependence, but he also lists the contributory internal problems: weak administration and institutions, rule based on coercion rather than the law and low levels of social cohesion. He directs our attention to the failings of the new nationalisms and reminds us that, even where nationalism has been a success in its own terms, as in some nineteenth-century nationalism, the outcomes have been far from universally beneficial. In the contest between the evils of (linguistic) nationalism and the evils of (linguistic) globalisation, the choice would not seem to be as clear cut as Phillipson's solutions suggest.

Pennycook (1995, 2000b), on the other hand, is clear that English cannot be extirpated. He is realistic in his appraisal of the constraints on those who wish to affect linguistic practices and relations and insightful in his insistence that language cannot be reified. He argues for a 'principled Postmodernism' that can respond to the ethical and political questions that the present linguistic state of affairs produces. His thesis is that, while use of English cannot be neutral, since it plays a part in the maintenance of elites, neither does it have any essentialist characteristic (Pennycook 1994). It can be appropriated and become the property of those who use it. He argues that 'English offers a community of speakers through which oppositional positions can be taken up' (1994: 326). Positioning himself in the tradition of Critical Pedagogy (Freire's idea that education can work for social change), he calls on the teaching profession to be combative against systems that are pernicious:

> If English is the major language through which the forces of neo-colonial exploitation operate, it is also the language through which common counter-articulations can perhaps most effectively be made. (Pennycook 1994: 326)

However, because of his reluctance to deal with the political and economic context, he does not confront all the constitutive factors identified by some commentators (Holborow 1999). Furthermore, his relativist approach has been seen as a brake on action, and his plan to resist in the classroom, to struggle in 'local contexts' does not really address the fundamental issue: the need for a lingua franca for a globalising world and for the flows, networks and structures of an increasingly postnational system. In spite of this criticism, Pennycook's work has opened the debate in the ELT sector and there is an influential group that could be seen as Pennycookian. Canagarajah, another key scholar, builds on the concept of appropriation and shows the processes by which a language comes to belong as much to speakers in its new sites as to speakers in its traditional sites (1999).

Other writers are not so optimistic. They focus on the undoubted difficulties that a second language education medium presents to the individual student (Tollefson 2002; Skutnabb-Kangas 2000) and highlight the injustice inherent in lingua franca relations, where the language of the powerful group is imposed on the less powerful. They argue that educational preparation to use that language will not necessarily bring second-language learners to equality with those for whom it is a first language, and, in competition for work or access to education, there will not be a level playing field (Tollefson 1991). They argue that use of English in education may hinder learning, because students do not master it sufficiently well, and this will contribute to school failure (Skutnabb-Kangas 2000). They show how English medium secondary education acts as an effective class filter and ensures that only an elite group completes schooling (Mazrui and Mazrui 1998). However, this argument does not acknowledge the fact that education is already delivered through a second language for enormous numbers. Since the majority of the world's languages do not have a written form, speakers of these languages are always educated in another language,[20] if they receive education and acquire literacy. The language rights issue in education is thus more complex than the simple choice of global lingua franca versus mother tongue, and we shall return to this in Part III.

8.5 The need for a global language

In other disciplines of academia, scholars have been discussing the fundamental dilemmas for justice, where subjects in a multilingual world want transcendence and channels for communication. Van Parijs' (2002) and Pool's (1991) work on linguistic justice draws from a Rawlsian concept of fairness. I think that going back to this basic philosophical framework is very useful because it lays bare the stark choices which are not always apparent in the detail of case study. Pool argues that there are only two alternatives to ensure even-handedness in a multilingual situation and bring into being a community of communication. The first is for everyone to learn everyone else's language. The second is for everyone to learn a language which is external to the group.[21]

Bilingual studies (Appel and Muysken 1987; Hamers and Blanc 1989; Romaine 1995; Li Wei 2000) have been consistent in showing that mutual learning of languages is never the course chosen; social bilingualism is always asymmetric, with the weaker group learning the language of the more powerful for the reasons of force, money and prestige discussed at length above.

Studies of artificial languages show that the neutral solution is also difficult to achieve. In the five decades before the First World War, the European scientific community debated the alternatives for communication after national languages had replaced Latin as the media for scientific research.[22] The favoured solution during this period was a planned lingua franca that could act as an auxiliary language of scholarship for scientific exchange. A number of international languages were in fact invented from first principles. The movement had weighty backing among eminent scientists (e.g. Ostwald) and linguists (e.g. Jespersen) but eventually came to nothing.[23] Today artificial languages such as Esperanto are completely out of favour as the dismissal of attempts by its supporters to have the language adopted by the EU has shown (Wright 2000a).

In globalisation, communication needs cannot be met by Pool's first solution, the learning of all other languages, and is equally unlikely to be solved by the second. The adoption of an artificial language failed to become practice even at the moment that was most propitious, when the idea had widespread support. A third alternative, machine translation, is also not delivering a solution. The enterprise has proved to be much harder than early predictions suggested. The results so far have been disappointing and it would be optimistic to expect the advances necessary to resolve intergroup communication problems in the near future (Schwatzl 2001).

The language question is, at present, resolving itself through the principles of lingua franca adoption, discussed in earlier chapters, and English is the solution for the present and for the foreseeable future. The arguments in the literature which regret English dominance are comprehensible, but the very fact that this opposition is presented in English to an English-using audience shows the existence of English as a common medium is not irrevocably linked to any world view. In fact, it is possible to build a strong case that a common language, if necessary English, is fundamental to the healthy development of future political arrangements.

Where structures of production, knowledge, finance and security are organised at the global level (Strange 1996) and where social, political and economic relations are not constrained by borders, one can contend that the existence of a widely spread lingua franca is a public good. We all recognise that policing corruption, restraining unfair practices, evening out glaring inequalities with some redistribution or protection, protecting public goods such as non-renewable resources and the environment, or enforcing the rule of law even-handedly have proved to be immensely difficult to achieve, even within national communities, where there are political structures to aid and interconnectedness to encourage the endeavour. Achieving justice at global level is proving even more problematic, largely because such structures and the interconnectedness they promote are not present and it is this absence of political control that the opponents and critics of globalisation have rightly condemned. To fill this vacuum, it is actually very useful to have a language that permits a forum where exchange, challenge and condemnation can start to take place. Building a political superstructure will be dependent on the existence of a community of communication, without which there would be inner circles of inclusion and outer circles of exclusion. The moral agents that could start to constrain the excesses of free market Capitalism and ruthless competition are language dependent. Whereas force backed by might and money can function without language, force and control through consensus needs communication.

To make economic globalisation human we need increasingly thick interconnectedness, in the hope that we can reproduce at the global level some of the vertical integration and society-wide cohesion that was one of the positive outcomes of nationalism. It is difficult to conceive how this could happen without mutual knowledge and exchange and this would be piecemeal without the development of a community of communication. It is difficult to conceive how the unacceptable side of economic and political globalisation could ever be contained if the victims remained linguistically fractured and unable to build global networks of resistance.

The school of thought that attacks those who see English as able to fulfil this role as neo-colonialist, pro-Capitalist and triumphalist has got to come up with something else, and not just a retreat into Steiner's 'zones of silence'. If the spread of English is also the medium of counter discourses to contain the unwanted aspects of globalisation, as suggested by Pennycook and Canagarajah, then it can become the means by which regulation and redistribution could be negotiated and a constraining consensus built. Its use as a medium for a forum allows us to start building the structures necessary for democratic control. A language will always have ideological associations, but these derive from the way it is employed by its speakers. To think otherwise would be very deterministic and would misunderstand the very nature of language. We should not reify language in this debate. It is only a medium for its speakers.

In this argument, a common language is a public good from which all benefit. Van Parijs (2002) argues that in an ideal world, the costs for this universal public good should be shared more equitably. At the present moment the system is asymmetric. Both the opportunity costs involved in second-language acquisition and the financial costs of teachers, books and classroom space are borne by those who learn English as a lingua franca. Those societies whose citizens acquire it in childhood socialisation are spared the burden of formal acquisition. Van Parijs argues that such asymmetry is not inevitable and makes a radical suggestion, that is extremely idealistic but highly defensible in terms of justice. He argues that since all societies benefit from a common language, those that already possess the language should help to underwrite the financial costs of acquisition in other societies. As a redistributive strategy it starts to address the exploitation inherent in others' need to learn English, exposed by Phillipson, but it is unlikely to find much support in a market-driven world in general and the hard-edged business environment of English Language Teaching (ELT) in particular.

8.6 One language or several?

It seems clear that status planning and lingua francas do not seem compatible; it has been impossible to promote or constrain the spread of lingua francas in any but totalitarian societies. Is it then also the case that any kind of corpus planning to maintain the unitary nature of the language is equally ineffectual? There is a key tension here since the nature of unconstrained linguistic development is centrifugal and leads towards heteroglossia but the utility of English as a lingua franca is that its enormous numbers of speakers can communicate. This section will consider briefly how cohesive the community of communication can hope to be and how questions of ownership and appropriation may make the language more acceptable to individual users but of less utility to them and other speakers. The issues of standard and pluricentricism need to be addressed.

Kachru (1985) created a framework of three concentric circles to categorise users of English. The inner circle consists of societies where English is the medium of public and private life and where English is overwhelmingly the first language of speakers.[24] The outer circle represents societies where English is used by the state as an official language, although it may not be the first language of all citizens, or where English has a significant role as an additional language, in education for example.[25] In many of these states distinctive forms of English are developing which are increasingly accepted as the appropriate local norm (e.g. Singlish, Nigerian English). Pakir (1999) has termed this process linguistic globalisation. Kachru's third circle is a rapidly expanding circle consisting of those states whose members use English for international communication.

Leitner (1992) is just one among many linguists who have challenged the Kachru model. He identifies the tensions within each of the categories and questions whether there are systematic differences among speakers from different circles. Yano, conducting a similar review of Kachru's categories ten years later, confirmed Leitner's analysis. These divisions may be unhelpful since the metaphor assigns speakers to a hierarchy that may not exist. The scientist from a country categorised as outer circle may be working and publishing in English at the highest level of language competence; the rural agriculturalist in a state where English is used extensively in its institutions and in its towns may have minimal knowledge or none. The concentric circle image does, however, suggest penetration and concentration within a society as a whole which is perhaps where it is most useful. Moreover, the concentric circle classification alerts us to where there may be appropriation and thus the elaboration of differing norms. In the outer circle, where English is learnt as a foreign language and used intergroup, there are rarely clearly differentiated forms of the language (Yano 2001), except in the case of imperfect learning and interference, as different forms of interlanguage arise. This is, perhaps a short-term phenomenon. In the future, certain aspects of interlanguage could become fixed and general, particularly where teachers in the expanding circle are statistically unlikely to be native speakers of English and where English is used mostly in interaction among those for whom it is an additional language.

There is thus no guarantee that English users will maintain mutual intelligibility let alone common norms. Indeed outer circle varieties are already exhibiting a high degree of divergence. The appropriation of the language that Pennycook and Canagarajah saw as the way of reconciling learners to the need to acquire English leads to domestication and ultimately to fracturing, particularly where the language becomes a medium for creativity. Attempts to impose inner circle standards are unlikely to be universally acceptable. When the conservative strand in British linguistics made the case for an acceptance of a single linguistic norm, that of British English (Quirk 1985), there was strong resistance to such direction. Kachru summed up the outer circle position:

> In my view, the global diffusion of English has taken an interesting turn: the native speakers of this language have lost the exclusive prerogative to control its standardization; in fact, if current statistics are any indication they have become a minority. This sociolinguistic fact must be accepted and its implications recognized. (Kachru 1985: 30)

Svartvik (1985) speaking as a member of the expanding circle of English as Foreign Language (EFL) users was, however, dismissive of Kachru's thesis:

> The current gigantic investment in the English language in countries such as mine (Sweden) is really defensible only as long as the acquired skill can be put to good use as a means of international communication. ... There can be no question of an English speaking community or fellowship among Swedish speakers of English. ... Their norm is the native speaker norm. ... They are not norm-producing groups ... The strong argument in favour of English as an international medium is that it is the most widely used language but it will remain usefully so only as long as it remains intercomprehensible. (Svartvik 1985: 33)

This position continues to be strongly represented within the countries where English has only lingua franca functions. The 2002 TESOL conference in Paris took the issue of linguistic imperialism as a starting point for a round table discussion and this subject revealed very strong support for the centre standard model. These teachers reported that their learners only wanted a tool and that any process of appropriation would be against their interests in that it deprived them of some of the speakers with whom they counted on being able to communicate.[26]

However, the situation may be different where English has a role intra as well as intergroup. The Indian speakers of English, that Berns (1992) reports on, have learnt English to talk in the main to other Indians and to gain access to higher education within their own society. She discusses the sound reasons for such a group to develop a variety which marks them as distinct and contributes to intragroup cohesion and identity. However, this viewpoint looks back to the nation state past and to the construction of identity rooted in territory. Henceforth, it may well be that identity will derive from the transnational networks that are interest and work based and which cross territorial frontiers. These may generate socio-professional varieties which transcend geographical location. Indeed in the view of Jenkins (2000) and Seidelhofer (2000), transnational professional varieties of English can already be identified.

Now, if an economically powerful and influential, international group saw the need to promote a norm to maintain intelligibility, there is the possibility that the provenance of the standardisation might make it more acceptable. Standard International English could develop in a community of communication which did not derive from just one national group or just one of the three concentric circles.

8.7   Conclusion

The evidence outlined in this chapter that the role of English in globalisation derives from more than the usual reasons for adopting a lingua franca. It is not only being learnt because it gives access to the power and prestige of a centre, but because it enables the flows, networks and structures of an increasingly postnational system. It is the medium that allows individuals to transcend their group membership, and this is what people appear to want to do. The second is that there is very little room for manoeuvre. One may see the spread of English as a hegemonic process in which those who are handicapped contribute to their own disadvantage by accepting to join the community of communication. Or one may be optimistic that the spread of English may provide the means to build the forums in which the political control of the new systems can be negotiated. Or one may see the limits of the spread as creating a global division between those participating in the structure, flows and networks of globalisation and those that cannot. No matter which stance one takes, one thing is clear. The choice of language is dictated by forces outside the control of national policymakers and cannot be countered by any anti-globalisation bloc. Trying to counter a consensus that has built worldwide will not be possible from any one quarter. Status planning at the global level does not appear from any of the available evidence to be a sensible or a useful activity. As Kachru has said 'English ... comes through the channels which bypass the strategies devised by language planners' (Kachru 1994: 137).

English spread is clearly happening, but the winners and losers in the process may not be as clear cut as Marxist and Critical theorists pretend.

There may be some truth in Fishman's description of the current spread of English as the 'democratisation of a formerly elitist resource' (Fishman 1996: 7), if we view it from the perspective of Braudel's *longue durée*. At the present time Fishman seems optimistic since the speakers and learners of English are not yet the masses of the non-English speaking world but its elites and would be elites. The spread of English has been like much of globalisation, a phenomenon that has as yet really only touched and benefited the middle and urban classes of the developing world. However, Grin (1999), may well be prophetic when he claims that in some settings English is on the way to becoming a banal and unremarkable skill like literacy. He argues that competence in English is no longer exclusive cultural capital since so many now have it. He reports a kind of democratisation in the European context whereby English language competence has become 'necessary but not sufficient, a basic requirement for a whole raft of professions, activities and memberships'. It cannot be a tool for social closure since it is so widespread, but it does provide a medium for the common ground that humanity must develop in so interconnected a world. And its very banality and generalisation must suggest a shift in power balance as monoglot English native speakers become a minority group in a community of communication where the vast majority is using English as a lingua franca.

Part III

Renaissance and Revitalisation in Small Language Communities

9
New Discourse, New Legal Instruments and a New Political Context for Minorities[1] and their Languages

As we have seen, Western political traditions have been a powerful factor in the linguistic homogenisation of populations. Nationalism promoted the creation of large communities of communication. A minority of these retained a measure of pluralism but in the majority there was relentless eradication of linguistic difference in order to achieve that community. In the last half century the homogenisation process has continued with the structures of globalisation encouraging an ever larger community of communication. Over the same time period, however, we have also witnessed a growing and energetic movement to halt, counter and reverse linguistic convergence. Will Kymlicka has suggested that the recent expansion of minority rights thinking and legislation, of which this is part, can be seen as a defensive response to nation state building (2001: 2). Reaction to the assimilatory policies of some nationalisms may well be among the causes of this expansion, but there is perhaps as much reason to believe that the trigger for renaissance has been different postnational facets of globalisation.

It would be wise not to claim too much too soon. Certainly, nation building still takes place, with linguistic difference suppressed in the cause of national unity. Majorities who subscribe to the national ideal can still be enlisted to put pressure on those who do not. The process has not been thrown into reverse entirely. Where nationalism continues to be a major force there is still majority rejection of minority language use in the public sphere. The case of the United States shows how a period of nationalism and heightened patriotism can make plurilingualism more difficult to promote. In the United States, the ideal of linguistic homogeneity remains a major preoccupation (Woon and Zolberg 1999) and, by 2002 the English only movement had gained enough support for official monolingualism to be enshrined in recent legislation in 22 states.[2] Kymlicka's 'defensive response to nationalism' does seem to have been checked in the United States at the present moment, at least as far as language is concerned.

On the other hand, where a state is in the process of relinquishing some sovereignty and economic autonomy, in order to join a supranational regional group for prosperity and security purposes, then it may also pull back from the dogged pursuit of national homogeneity, if this is the price it is asked to pay for entry. Where a government makes application to join such a group, policies for homogenisation within the nation may seem less necessary. In addition, the practice among the other states in the supranational regional group may be to accord minority rights and thus there will be pressure on new applicants to apply minimum standards. The Turkish government is in this situation. Anxious to join the EU, it has bowed to European pressure to curb its aggressive assimilatory policies with respect to the Kurds.[3] It is thus regionalisation, pressure from the supranational level, from outside the nation state, that has caused Turkey to start to change policy. It has not been the Kurds' long refusal to assimilate to Turkish nationalism that has brought about change in Turkish attitudes and legislation. It is Turkey's need to show the international community that it is moving towards the international code on minorities that is influencing its first moves to acceptance of diversity.

The proposal in this chapter is going to be that supranationalism and globalisation are associated with the current spread of minority rights, including language rights. These two phenomena can be seen to be opening up space for difference in ways that the nation state system does not accommodate and would not tolerate. A number of developments have made this possible. First, formal exchanges within the institutions of supranationalism and globalisation have inaugurated a system where basic human rights are widely recognised and where minority rights are increasingly accepted. It is no longer legitimate to pursue state cohesion by policies designed to eradicate difference and impose assimilation where these contravene such rights. International law has been continually strengthened in order to protect minorities from exclusion, ill treatment and disadvantage. To uphold the new philosophy and laws, there has been intervention in the internal affairs of states.[4] Second, globalisation in economic and defence spheres removes many of the old obstacles to autonomy and independence for small territorial groups. There is no need to be part of a state to have access to a market or to be defended by a sizeable army. These state functions are now increasingly organised at the supranational level, where there are common markets like the EU and defence organisations like NATO. This removes the need for small groups to accept the pressures to assimilate culturally and linguistically in order to ensure the political and economic umbrella of a large state. Third, the sheer enormity of globalisation makes a return to the local for roots, identity and community more likely, and is perhaps a kind of psychological necessity. The global community may be too vast and amorphous for it to fulfil the individual's need to belong. In the past, the nation state was often the focus of belonging, reinforced in the school curriculum, in national service and in the banal nationalism of daily life. Loyalty to the nation state was often demanded as an exclusive loyalty. Patriotic feeling towards the national group could not be extensive nor multilayered with other allegiance. This kind of nationalism has weakened in many countries. The pathological nationalisms of the twentieth century demonstrated the danger of the concept and the increasing exchanges, contacts and flows of transport and telecommunications, audio–visual and information technology have dismantled the boundary fences between national communities.

In a world where nationalism is weakening, if not yet disappearing, there is thus a space where new patterns of identity for the new situation will develop. And while some of the strands for these new patterns may come from the supranational level, some may well come from the old local identities that were eclipsed in national times. Now, under less pressure to assume national identity in an exclusive way, individuals may be more likely to conceive themselves as multilayered, with their position in local communities as well as their participation in global networks contributing with nationality to their whole identity.

Minority rights,[5] fracturing national territory and layered patterns of identity are recent phenomena and we cannot be sure how these new settings will affect language behaviour in the long term. However, one thing is likely: the multiforums of the different layers may mean that the medium most appropriate in different environments will not necessarily be the same and this may protect the bi- or multilingualisms that still exist and even favour a return to linguistic pluralism. This chapter will attempt to see what evidence there is for such speculation. It deals first with the development of the discourse of minority rights, then presents the legislation and legal instruments that this has produced. The final chapters review the effects of the legal framework and new societal attitudes. These can be seen to have been instrumental in the peaceful devolutionary processes to be observed in many parts of Europe. Spain is taken as the case study. There the rights of autochthonous minorities have been recognised as the centralised nation state has reconfigured to cede much political autonomy to regions and to open up the public space to the other languages of Spain. The legal framework and new societal attitudes can also be seen to be contributing factors in the increased demand to protect small languages from extinction. The case studies here are three reports from linguists in the field (the north east of China, the Andes and Sicily) whose work demonstrates the challenges and problems of minority maintenance.

9.1   The discourses of liberty, equality, fairness and justice

9.1.1   Liberty

The liberal strand of the Western political and philosophical tradition suggests that the basic rule for society should be that each member of it be permitted to exercise the greatest liberty consistent with doing no harm to others or depriving them of their liberty.[6] Liberalism prioritises the freedom of the individual and insists that s/he be liberated from any inherited status or ascribed condition. Twentieth-century legislation on human rights has been highly influenced by this position and rights have been enshrined as individual rights.

Liberals have thus had little interest in accommodating the public expression and institutionalisation of ethnic diversity since this entails group rights. This is the case with language, since the right to use one's language is only meaningful if accorded to a group as a whole. Maintenance of language difference is held to be at odds with the entitlement of the individual to remain within or to exit from the community as s/he desires. In this conception of rights, it is the prerogative of individuals to conceive of the good life as they wish and not to accept the defined path that would accompany obligatory membership of a defined group.

The inadequacy of this liberal thinking is, of course, that the individual is never outside society, and so the refusal to protect a minority group because it imprisons members inside the group becomes default imprisonment within the majority group, rather than the protection of choice for the individual. This is particularly salient in language. For example, a national government may refuse to provide state education through the minority language, using the argument that to do so would be a group right that would constrain all minority members to be educated through it whether they chose to be or not. However, since education must be delivered through a medium and since this medium cannot be infinitely variable, the state will always treat pupils as a group when it designates the language(s) of instruction.

The crux of the issue, and the difficulty for liberals, is that language is not easily translated as an individual right. The right to use one's own language is not simply the right to speak it when and where one wants but also the right to be understood and to understand, and that is a constraint on interlocutors and affects their rights in turn. The freedom of individuals to use whichever language they choose is circumscribed by the competence and choices of others. Constraining another person to use one's language to ensure your right has implications for their rights. Language is *de facto* a group right whether acknowledged as such or not.

When this is recognised, the liberal position that claims neutrality in language matters is untenable. Choosing to deliver education in the state language is to treat the individual as a member of a group just as much as when the decision is to employ a minority language. And as Kymlicka (2001: 283) has pointed out, there is no *moral* basis to policies that 'automatically privilege majority or state nationalism over minority nationalism'.

9.1.2 Fraternity

The communitarian counter argument to the liberal position denies that the individual is autonomous. On the contrary, members of a society are embedded in their society and 'inherit a way of life that defines their good for them' (Kymlicka 2001: 19). To privilege individual autonomy would be destructive of community. Communitarianism underpins a number of different ideologies from socialism, through nation-statism, to minority group ethnicism. Within the nation state the influence of communitarian philosophy is clear. Difference is a threat to the state and a disadvantage to the individual. In consequence, a melting pot strategy is seen as necessary to build a larger, inclusive community and to eradicate difference and with it inequality. None of this is conceived as an attack on minority individuals. Indeed the opposite is usually held to be true. Homogenisation is seen to be in everyone's interest. Where minorities are not integrated, this creates a 'problem' and a likely site of tension or inequity, leading to disloyalty and persecution. Where they are integrated, there can be cohesion and social mobility.

Elites of minorities seeking devolution or increased rights often take a very similar stance to national elites on the issue of language and homogeneity within the group. The state and its minorities may actually be distinguished only by the ability to implement policy rather than by a difference in the philosophy that underpins it. Minorities may also wish to promote internal cohesion and maintain distance from other groups. They traditionally see liberals' defence of moral individualism and individual autonomy as a threat to the group's right to maintain group distinction. If freedom to choose permits the individual to deny that distinction and exit the group, then the collective is weakened.

Despite their apparent differences, both the liberal and communitarian traditions see the right of minorities to participate in political forums as best served by linguistic assimilation. Assimilation has one of its clearest expressions in French Republicanism, which from Jacobinism on was concerned to spread French so that all could participate in the revolution. Minorities were held to be obscurantist and anti-progress and eradication of their languages an essential part of the extirpation of counter-revolutionary ideas. In the British liberal tradition there were surprisingly similar sentiments. John Stuart Mill had little time for Breton nationalists who would not give up their particularism to be part of a greater whole or the French Canadians who kept their language and thus put a brake on the construction of a democratic and more equal society:

> Among a people without fellow feelings, especially if they read and speak different languages, the united public opinion necessary to the workings of representative institutions cannot exist. (Mill 1861/1972: 230)

This strand of reasoning continues to the present and many socialists believe that communities must have a common language if there is to be the solidarity necessary for the welfare state. Both socialists and liberals see a linguistically homogeneous population as providing the united public opinion and common purpose necessary for the working of liberal institutions (cf. Mallinson 1980; Miller and Walzer 1995). This is, of course, a defensible position. Any democratic political process requires a community of communication. When current literature refers to the tolerance of the old empires in linguistic matters and asks nostalgically if we could not learn from them (de Varennes 1996; Kymlicka 2001) this seems to have been forgotten. To hold the Ottoman or Austro-Hungarian Empires up as a model seems to ignore the fundamental point that imperial rulers were not required to consult the ruled and were not legitimated by them. Communication was circumscribed and the political process had no need of a forum. Tolerance of language difference was one small advantage in an otherwise thoroughly disadvantageous system. The basic conundrum remains to find a way for speakers of different languages to cooperate through negotiation and at the same time safeguard the specificity of their community.

9.1.3   Equality

Western political philosophy and practice have been moving steadily towards egalitarianism since the Virginia Bill of Rights (1776) and the *Declaration of the Rights of Man* (1789). Both documents called for a number of human rights without distinction as to race, sex, language or religion. The abolition of slavery, the enfranchisement of populations, decolonisation, feminism are all movements pushing forward along this trajectory. Despite the clear benefits of these developments there is, however, an argument that liberation movements are fundamentally flawed. John Rawls (2001) reveals the inherent bias of much former thinking on equality. He argues that the extension of privileges from those at the top of the hierarchy to those lower down, just as long as these latter accept the rules imposed by the former, may not serve the cause of equality. He shows that this was the model in much of the recalibration of the master/servant, colonist/colonised, patriarch/subservient woman, majority/minority imbalances undertaken during the Modern period. Rawls suggests that a different approach would serve fairness better. Rather than promoting the extension of privilege, political philosophers should return to first principles and conceive equality without recourse to history. The argument is as follows: if a group were to negotiate the distribution of rights and privileges among its constituent parts without knowing which of the constituent parts they in fact belonged to, members would be concerned to achieve the most equitable distribution of goods and the fairest possible arrangement of society. There would be no lobbying from interest groups, no pressure from powerful sections, no hierarchical outcomes. No one would appeal to history to demand differential treatment. No weight would accrue to the *status quo*.

This philosophical perspective is, of course, utopian but also very revealing when applied to the issue of language rights for minorities. Going back to first principles will disclose how language use is always the result of past and present power relationships and the prestige that results from them. It would expose how the 'commonsense' argument for language choice and use is rooted in acceptance of the differentials inherent in the *status quo*. For example, the classic liberal response to the problem of language minorities has been to practise benign neglect, that is, to allow any group to organise their group life in the language that they choose.[7] Since the language of the institutions and forums of the state results from past or present power, benign neglect must always be a reinforcement of that power. Together with blindness to group difference it favours the majority because it encourages a default language, which is always that of the majority.

Thus Rawlsian fairness demands that the relationship among language groups be worked out from first principles. *Laissez faire* policies mean that the languages of power and prestige will eventually take over in all situations of contact. Benign neglect, and the accompanying claim of blindedness to group difference, are always *de facto* support for the language of the group that is already dominant and, if this is not acceptable, then there must be some form of protection for the language of minority groups. As the French revolutionary, Lacordaire, pointed out, where no law constrains, the rule of might prevails:

> Entre le fort et le faible, entre le riche et le pauvre, entre le maître et le serviteur, c'est la liberté qui opprime et la loi qui affranchit.[8]

Rawls' suggestion also undermines the division made between autochthonous and allochthonous groups. The former are held to have greater claim to minority rights because their ancestors had a prior claim to the territory and had been incorporated by force or diktat into states. Thus to accord them language rights is to correct an historical injustice. Allochthonous groups are held to have migrated by choice and thus cannot ask the host state to accommodate their linguistic distinction. Applying Rawls' criterion that there be no recourse to history, however, might make us more accommodating of migrant groups. It is difficult to see why the right to education in one's first language can be a right dependent on the level of injustice suffered by one's ancestors. Children from migrant groups may well have the greater practical need for bilingual arrangements because of levels of language competence in their first and second languages.

9.1.4 Justice

To give other languages equal space would demand an elaboration of the concept of even-handedness in the according of language rights. In an attempt to find some templates for this, language freedoms have been compared to religious freedoms. In some ways there are parallels. Like a common language, a common set of religious beliefs is social glue. But in other ways there is little to be gained from the comparison. Whereas a state can be secular, it cannot avoid using a language for its institutions and forums. A state can take an ecumenical approach with religious beliefs and, as the main religions have considerable moral overlap, emphasise what is common; languages, on the other hand, particularly in the case of the written languages of the law and administration, are systems complete in themselves that fill the space. Where one language is used in an institution, a second language can only be admitted in a hierarchically inferior position, as the translation of documents or interpretation of speech. Within institutions, language does seem to be a zero sum game.

Achieving even-handedness for language users is a profound moral problem. When we view language as a means of communicating with the greatest number, having available the largest possible body of knowledge, gaining access to power and choosing social mobility, it would be a scandal if language policy worked against an individual or a group and prevented them acquiring the language that fulfilled these functions in the most efficient way. However, when we view language as an expression of our identity, as our link with our heritage, as a privileged way of cementing group solidarity, as a component of our deepest self, 'the spectacles through which we identify experiences as valuable' (Dworkin 1985: 228), the shaper of 'us as group member', then it would be an affront to basic human rights to support any policy that endangered or eradicated the language that fulfills these functions. Kymlicka (2001: 210) argues that individuals not only need access to information, the education that allows them to reflectively evaluate it and freedom of expression and association to act on it, but also 'access to a societal culture' in order to make sense of it in terms that are relevant to them. Thus we need the liberty to go out in the world and the liberty to retain the elements of our condition that maintain our integrity and make us what we are.

For these dual purposes we may need different codes. The only solution would seem to be to educate for both levels of involvement, to make personal bilingualism a social norm and diglossia a societal commonplace. However, a number of commentators have attacked the idea as facile[9] and they are correct in drawing attention to the numerous difficulties inherent in embracing bilingualism and diglossia as a solution. Diglossia is typically asymmetrical and thus demands more from minorities than majorities. A bilingual speaker often has to address the central dilemma of trading maintenance of the home language against greater use of and competence in the language that may be more economically profitable. Bilingualism is a tricky balancing act for the individual, and rarely stable within populations (Romaine 1995). Clear functional differentiation and secure financial support for the weaker language are the most basic of requirements and other protective mechanisms will probably be necessary.

There, do not, however, seem to be many other viable options available to reconcile the contradictory demands of protecting the primary community of communication and building the larger. Fishman (2001) maintains that those wishing to maintain minority languages or reverse the language shift away from them (RLSers) are realists:

> (M)ost RLSers are not by any means aiming at a 'return to the golden past' when the interaction between peoples was minimal and, therefore, when local differences could be easily maintained. (Fishman 2001: 6)

and that they accept the bilingual/diglossic solution as the only course feasible within modern society:

> (N)ot only is globalisation/modernisation as a whole not rejected, but an internal societal re-allocation of languages to functions is pursued that will also be partially acceptive of the culturally stronger, Big Brother language. (Fishman 2001: 7)

9.2   Human rights; language rights

The legal sphere has developed in parallel with political philosophy and there has been a gradual move from a very strict adherence to the belief that rights must be individual rights to an awareness that where fundamental language rights are concerned (the right to express oneself freely in the medium one knows best, the right to understand and be understood) there must be some acceptance of group rights. However, the process has been slow and is still incomplete. The legal instruments to protect minority language rights have taken time to develop and are still a matter of some debate.

9.2.1   Individual rights for minority members

Minority rights have their foundation in the legislation to protect human rights developed in the mid-twentieth century, which was prompted in part by the widespread horror felt in reaction to the events of the Second World War and a general desire to guard vulnerable minorities against a repeat of abuses and atrocities (Eide 1996; Simon 2000; Baehr 2001).

There was no specific mention of minority rights in the Charter of the United Nations (1945) nor in its Universal Declaration of Human Rights (1948). No provision was made for minorities because the early view 'was that if the non-discrimination provisions were effectively implemented, special provisions for the rights of minorities would not be necessary' (UNHCR nd). The provision for the individual protected individual members of the group: the Universal Declaration of Human Rights states that:

> everyone is entitled to all rights and freedoms ... without distinction of any kind such as ... language. (Article 2 Paragraph 1)

This is often categorised as a 'negative' right, in the tradition of language blindness and benign neglect discussed above. It is certainly a limited right in that it protects the individual from discrimination because they speak a certain language, but does not safeguard or guarantee use of the language. This has been made abundantly clear in the cases brought that invoke the right to use one's own language that it seems to accord. To cite just one example, the European Commission on Human Rights ruled in 1965 that the right to freedom of expression was not transgressed where Belgian citizens were refused documentation on municipal matters in French, because linguistic freedom does not guarantee the duty of authorities to deal in that language (de Varennes 1996). Freedom of expression in this interpretation is a right that can be used to stop persecution and guarantee the private exercise of the freedom but it does not contribute positively to minority language maintenance.

But maintenance of language was not the object of the exercise. The climate post 1945 was highly influenced by the strong representation of the liberal tradition in powerful sectors in the United Nations. In addition, minority rights were tainted by recent history (Simon 2000). The actions taken by the Nazis on behalf of German-speaking minorities were regularly evoked as reasons against repeating the experiment of minority group protection included in the treaties at the end of the First World War (Janics 1982).[10] This was the first time minorities had been protected in international law (Thompson 2001) and the instrument had been hijacked.

International laws designed to prevent discrimination against individual minority members, developed independently in different sectors. They were held to provide the legal instruments necessary to challenge linguistic discrimination and make a dedicated law unnecessary. The International Labour Organisation Convention (1958) gave the framework to challenge unfair distinction in employment. The UNESCO Convention against Discrimination in Education (1960) was designed to set standards of equal access. The International Convention on the Elimination of all Forms of Racial Discrimination (1965), the UNESCO Declaration on Race and Racial Prejudice (1978), the declaration on the Elimination of All Forms of Intolerance and of Discrimination based on Religion or Belief (1981), the Convention on the Rights of the Child (1989) and the Protection of the Rights of Indigenous and Tribal Populations (ILO 1989) were all possible instruments.

A number of non-discrimination clauses were also included in all the basic regional human rights documents. In Europe, these were the affair of the

Council of Europe (European Convention for the Protection of Human Rights and Fundamental Freedoms, the European Social Charter and the Framework Convention of National Minorities) and the Conference on Security and Cooperation in Europe[11] (Document of the Copenhagen Meeting of the Conference on the Human Dimension), in America, the Organisation of American States (the American Convention on Human Rights), and in Africa, the Organisation of African Unity (the African Charter on Human and Peoples' Rights).

Some acceptance of the group dimension of minority rights is contained in Article 27 of the UN's International Covenant on Civil and Political Rights (1966). This is the most widely accepted legally binding provision for the rights of minorities as such (UNHCR nd), and recognises that an individual right may have little meaning unless enjoyed in community with others:

> In those states in which ethnic religious or linguistic minorities exist, persons belonging to such minorities shall not be denied the right *in community with the other members of their group* to enjoy their own culture to profess and practise their own religion or to use their own language. (UN 1966. Author's italics)

9.2.2 A limited acceptance of group rights

Capotorti,[12] special rapporteur of the UN Sub-Commission on the Prevention of Discrimination and Protection of Minorities, attempted to define the concept of minority for the United Nations. He proposed that a 'numerically inferior group' in a 'non-dominant position' but being nationals of a state would constitute a minority if it possessed 'ethnic, religious or linguistic characteristics differing from those of the rest of the population and could show, if only implicitly, a sense of solidarity, directed towards preserving their culture, traditions, religion or language'. This was not adopted by the Commission on Human Rights. The stumbling blocks to acceptance of minority as a legal concept was the fear that both minority and majority elites could use it to rein in the right of the individual to move between groups (Simon 2000).

It was only in 1992 that a United Nations declaration addressed the special rights of minorities in a separate document. The Declaration on the Rights of Persons Belonging to National or Ethnic, Religious and Linguistic Minorities (1992) is a new departure; in addition to the usual negative freedoms, this text clearly covers positive freedoms, requiring governments to promote as well as protect the identity of minority groups.[13] Article 1 states that:

> States shall protect the existence and the national or ethnic, cultural, religious and linguistic identity of minorities within their respective territories and shall encourage conditions for the promotion of that identity.

This implies positive duties for the state, in particular that there should be policies to protect and promote the language. Within the detail of the Declaration there is overt direction on how this should be accomplished. Article 4.3 requires governments to allow minorities adequate opportunities to learn their mother tongue or have instruction in their mother tongue. Other articles give implicit direction on language. Articles 2.2 and 2.3 require governments to aid minorities to participate in public life and share in decisions which affect them on the national and regional levels. These articles infer that political debate must be in a language which minorities can understand. In the commercial sphere, Article 4.5 requires states to make it possible for minorities to participate fully in the economic progress and development in their country, which again presupposes that there will be no language barrier.

The date of the Declaration (1992) is significant. The evolution in philosophy can be traced in part to the political events of the early 1990s (Phillips 1995). The conflicts arising among groups in the former Communist states had brought pressure to bear on the international community to accept that 'measures were needed in order to better protect persons belonging to minorities from discrimination' (UNHCR nd). Thus, following the 1992 declaration, there were other initiatives at UN level. The post of United Nations High Commissioner for Human Rights was created in 1993 and has been *de facto* a guardian of minority rights since then.[14] A United Nations Working Group on Minorities[15] was set up in 1995 (Thompson 2001). One of the working group's key tasks was to define the groups that could claim minority status to benefit from international legislation and from programmes developed by UN agencies such as UNESCO, UNDP and WHO.

The legal definition of minority continues to be problematic but despite this theoretical problem, legislation and resulting good practice are developing for those who find themselves in a minority position. The regional institutions that set the new standards for minorities and framed new legislation in Europe are the Council of Europe, with membership from the whole of Europe, the European Union, whose membership to date has come only from Western Europe[16] and the OSCE which has focused on minority protection in the east of the continent.

9.2.2.1 Council of Europe

The Council of Europe has been the most energetic in framing legislation for minority protection. Its Framework Convention for the Protection of National Minorities which entered into force on 1 February 1998 was a legally binding multilateral instrument for the protection of national minorities in Europe. The Convention is not concerned with individual problems and the Council of Europe has no mechanism to deal with individual complaints. It works rather by monitoring the safeguards provided by the state structure to protect rights. The Council of Europe observes and oversees[17] the implementation of the policy and practice in all the states that have signed up to the Convention but has paid particular attention to south-east Europe where recent history has made the minority issue of immense importance.[18]

The linguistic freedoms that the Convention supported were largely symbolic, including use of one's own name, the public display of information of a private nature and the signposting of place names in the minority language. The use of the minority language in public, for example, in administration or education, was evoked as an ideal but there were no concrete plans for action.[19] This was provided within a parallel piece of legislation, the European Charter for Regional or Minority Languages, which came into force the same year (1/03/1998).

The Charter promoted the use of regional or minority languages in education and the media and urged their use in judicial and administrative settings, economic and social life and cultural activities. States that signed up to the Charter had to agree to introduce the minority language in a minimum number of functions across these categories. The Charter marks a distinct development in legislation, in that it not only contains a non-discrimination clause concerning the use of minority languages, but also sets out to provide active support for their introduction, use and maintenance.

Because this is active promotion of minority languages, far fewer states have signed up to guarantee the positive language rights provided for by the Charter (17) compared to the number prepared to agree to the largely negative language rights guaranteed by the Framework Convention (35).[20] Signing a document that would ensure the right of minority speakers to use their language in the national public space was a step too far for many governments, even though the Charter spells out in very clear terms in its preamble that the protection and encouragement of regional or minority languages should not be to the detriment of the official languages and should not obviate the need to learn them.

It is perhaps too early to say whether the Charter for Regional or Minority Languages will have an extensive effect.[21] States have considerable leeway in the language support and provision that they agree to. The minimum level is quite modest. In any case the Charter may not actually be instituting change but only reflecting it. It has so far been adopted by those states that were moving towards greater autonomy for regional groups in any case (e.g. Spain and the United Kingdom) but has been resisted in states which still retain a high degree of centralisation (e.g. France).[22]

The Charter clearly discriminates between the rights of autochthonous and allochthonous minorities. The numerous members of minorities constituted by immigration are excluded from support for their home languages. The philosophical underpinning for the distinction seems to be premised on the appeal to history mentioned above and makes no concession to the dual need of the individual to be able to use the language of primary socialisation and the language of wider opportunity for self-actualisation and to ensure both primary community solidarity and openness and contact with the wider world. Nonetheless, despite its deficiencies, the Charter marks a big advance in minority language rights provision.

9.2.2.2   The European Union

The European Union has played a lesser role in minority protection because in strict legal terms the area is outside its jurisdiction. However, as with many other issues, both the Commission and the Parliament have ventured into the area ahead of a clear mandate to do so (Wright 2000a). This has resulted in the passing of a number of Resolutions. Despite having little legal bite because of their lack of status in law, these have been surprisingly influential and can be seen to have contributed to the discernible change in attitudes.

In 1981, the European Parliament Resolution on a Community Charter of Regional Languages and Cultures (Arfé Resolution) called on member state governments and on regional and local authorities to enact a number of measures to support and promote regional and minority languages particularly in the domains of education, mass communication, public life and social affairs.[23] This had little immediate effect on the member states since the area is outside the competence of the European Parliament and it could only exhort not direct. However, it did open the way for the creation of an organisation which could speak and act on behalf of minority language groups at European level. The European Bureau of Lesser Used Languages (EBLUL) was established in 1982, financed in the main by the Commission[24] with a brief to defend and promote the linguistic rights of speakers of regional or minority languages.

The next major initiative on behalf of minority languages was the 1987 Resolution on the Languages and Cultures of the Regional and Ethnic Minorities in the European Community (Kuijpers Resolution) 1987. The Kuijpers Resolution was more ambitious and wide-ranging than the original Arfé Resolution, 'calling for specific actions which might be taken in different areas' (Ó Riagáin 2001). In the wake of the report the Commission and EBLUL established Mercator,[25] a network of three research and documentation centres dealing with the regional and minority languages spoken by more than 40 million citizens of the EU.

EBLUL was particularly successful in establishing communication, contacts and exchanges among minority communities, resulting in the creation of a powerful lobby, which played an important part in bringing the European political classes to accept a legal and political framework for the promotion of lesser used languages. After the Council of Europe launched its Charter for Regional or Minority Languages in 1992, the European Parliament threw its full support behind it, passing a Resolution (Killilea Resolution) calling on states to sign it so that there would be a legal framework for minority language provision. When the vote was taken on the Resolution in February

1994 there was massive support. As Ó Riagáin observed

> (This) landslide vote in favour of the most ambitious resolution yet to be put to the Parliament in favour of lesser used languages, serves as a yard-stick in assessing the positive shift in public opinion in favour of linguistic diversity. (Ó Riagáin 2001: 1: 10)

It also shows a growing consensus among the political classes in Europe that group rights might be necessary to ensure some liberties.

There is some interweaving here with the growing acceptance of subsidiarity. The conventional way of seeing the citizen and the state as the sole parties in any political arrangement is undermined by the concept of subsidiarity. Subsidiarity is a political theory developed in the EU that requires decisions to be taken as close to the citizens concerned as possible. One of the motivations for subsidiarity was the desire of national politicians to block power amassing at the supranational level. It was, however, seized upon by groups at substate level who argued that the process could be extended to regions. Where accepted at other levels than the national, subsidiarity makes it possible for arrangements to be different for different subsets of citizens, that is, for groups.

The sub-state level of organisation is recognised in the Council of the Regions, established in 1995. As yet, it is a relatively new body which has not made much impact on the European political landscape. However, the existence of a level of governance that can give territorial minority groups political expression and provide for links across borders is yet another sign of the move away from the unity of the nation state.

Despite these small advances towards minority protection and empowerment, it cannot be argued that it is part of the *acquis* (Community law and practice that are inviolable). None of these resolutions is legally binding (von Toggenburg 2001). However, there is constant movement towards such a situation. The Amsterdam Treaty (1997) introduced a provision for extending non-discrimination (Article 13) and the Nice Treaty (2000) produced the European Charter of Fundamental Rights, which included a specific commitment to respect linguistic diversity (Article 22):

> The Union shall respect cultural, religious and linguistic diversity

Respect has been taken to imply more than negative freedoms (Giordan 2003).

Further developments suggest that there will be significant advance in this area in the near future. On 15 December 2001, the European Council approved the Laeken Declaration on the Future of the European Union, which included a decision to set up a broad-based Convention to pave the way for the reform of the EU. With the establishment of the Convention, the EU governments accepted that the earlier practice of reforming the Union by Inter-Governmental Conferences had failed and that, with the prospect of enlargement, perhaps to 30 members, the queries about democratic legitimacy and transparency of the present institutions, the role of national parliaments, the efficiency of decision making and the workings of the institutions needed to be resolved.

The Convention on the European Union is still consulting and debating as I write, but it is already clear that the 40 million plus citizens of the Union (EBLUL 2002) who speak a minority language wish to use the new institutional design for the Union, to produce a more democratic political system for them. Minority speakers are anxious to see how Article 22 of the European Charter of Fundamental Rights will be reflected in the new constitution.

The groups that have shown a commitment to the rights of minorities to use their languages in the public European space are continuing to lobby during this period of consultation. The European Parliament remains one of the organs, which is most willing to press on language questions, and the MEP for South Tyrol, Michl Ebner, presented a report to the European Parliament's Committee on Culture, Youth, Education, the Media and Sport on 8 July 2003, on the ways in which the European Commission could help preserve the languages of minorities in the EU, in the context of enlargement and cultural diversity. It included a motion for a European Parliament resolution to call on the Commission to establish a European Agency for Linguistic Diversity and Language Learning. This will be voted on in a European Parliament Plenary session in autumn 2003.

The European Bureau for Lesser Used Languages has also continued to apply pressure. A Recommendation from its plenary meeting in June 2002 asked that:

> European identity and European citizenship as defined by the Treaty on European Union incorporate the notion of cultural and linguistic diversity. For speakers of regional or minority languages, the notion of European citizenship has an important dimension only if the European Union effectively respects its lesser-used languages as an important part of – and an added value to – the European heritage and culture. (Council Ljouwert/Final Doc 150602)

The Bureau also asked for a financial commitment from the European Union to make it possible to enact any policy adopted.

The EU has already had some effect in the area of linguistic minority rights, moving from a mild expression of support for minority heritage to more muscular political protection expressed in terms of anti-discrimination. At present, the enlargement of the Community seems set to give increased impetus to the movement. Resolving issues of minority discontent is seen as central to peaceful development, and this view has led to pressure on accession countries to deal with minority issues before joining. As the new entrants are subject to minimum standards for minority rights, it will be difficult for existing members to retain any policy or arrangements seen as discriminatory. For example, it will be problematical for states such as Greece and France to maintain centralist policies and Jacobin practices.

9.2.2.3 *The Organisation for Security and Cooperation in Europe (OSCE)*

The third body involved in the safeguarding of minority rights in Europe is the OSCE. With 55 participating states in Europe, Central Asia and North America, the OSCE is the world's largest regional security organisation. It states its purpose as preventing conflict, managing crisis and rehabilitating where conflict has taken place.

The OSCE began as the Conference on Security and Cooperation in Europe (CSCE), an organisation which widened its scope and remit after the fall of Communism. In the Charter of Paris for a New Europe (1990) participating heads of state and government declared their support for the equal rights of peoples and their right to self-determination in conformity with the Charter of the United Nations and with the relevant norms of international law, although it was clear that self-determination was to be seen as subject to the principle of the territorial integrity of states (Shaw 1997). The Copenhagen Human Dimension meeting (June 1990) took this declaration a step further and marks a watershed in minority rights. At the outset of the meeting some Western governments were wary of touching on the issue of minorities, arguing that consensus was unlikely and that consequently it would be futile to establish a committee for minority issues. However, a group of Central European states led by Hungary insisted on establishing a working group to deal with the area. The conference ended by approving a set of agreements on national minorities that once again shows how the general trend is from 'negative' freedoms (there will be no interference) to recognition that there should be positive promotion of minority attributes. The Copenhagen Recommendations reiterated the rights of national minorities to express, preserve and develop their identity, use their mother tongue, establish their own educational, cultural and religious institutions, profess and practise their religion, disseminate information in their mother tongue and establish and maintain organisations or associations. In addition, the recommendations called on the state to create the conditions that make these rights possible. Shaw (1997) says that this protection is so significant that some Western governments have since regretted this move and have attempted to place limitations.

At the Geneva Expert meeting (1991) minority rights were significantly strengthened from another direction. The meeting pronounced on the limits of state sovereignty in this area:

> Issues concerning national minorities, as well as compliance with international obligations and commitments concerning the rights of persons belonging to them, are matters of legitimate international concern and

consequently do not constitute exclusively an internal affair of the respective state. (Chapter II)

The rationale for this interventionist stance is that OSCE participant countries are concerned to foresee where intergroup conflict might arise and where an agreed response and course of action could pre-empt violence. The belief is that security derives in part from an appreciation that laws and their enactment are just and evenhanded. From this perspective, the absolute right of the state to deal with its own minorities as it sees fit is no longer acceptable.

Since 1991, the OSCE has continued to promote the rights of minorities, paying particular attention to areas of democratisation and governance and to the educational measures necessary for minorities to participate fully in the political process. It has published its common positions in the Hague Recommendations regarding the education rights of national minorities (1996), the Oslo Recommendations regarding the linguistic rights of national minorities (1998) and the Lund Recommendations on the effective participation of minorities in public life (1999) and in a set of guidelines to assist national minority participation in the electoral process (2001). The OSCE has appointed a High Commissioner on national minorities who is charged with promoting dialogue between potential adversaries, encouraging mutual confidence and finding solutions to intergroup tensions.

However, the High Commissioner is not an ombudsman and will not deal with individual cases. The purpose of the post is to open channels between groups and foresee the injustices and inequalities that could cause conflict, not to respond to individual grievance. The OSCE has this in common with the minority protection provided by the Council of Europe and the EU. The framework in all three institutions has constituted itself to deal with group rights and will not become involved at the level of the individual.

9.2.2.4   The limits of pluralism

Thus there is undoubtedly a growing common core of shared values in this domain within Europe:

> (T)he rule of law, democracy, human rights, including the rights of persons belonging to minorities, tolerance and a pluralistic society ... are values that are widely accepted from OSCE documents to Council of Europe treaties, as well as part of the political criteria for admission of new states to the European Union. The observance of these values is no longer a matter of choice, but a political and – in the case of human rights – a legal imperative. (de Varennes 2001: 6)

Those European minorities whose governments are signatories to the Charter and Framework have a concrete right enshrined in international and European law to use their language and can make representation, backed by case law to have state authorities use their language in dealings with them. Majority populations seem to be in support of a rolling back of the homogenising tendencies of the state. For example, the English majority seem to have accepted devolution for Wales, Scotland and Northern Ireland without difficulty and the signature and ratification of the Charter for Regional or Minority Languages, recognising Welsh, Irish Gaelic, Scots Gaelic, Ullans and Lallans[26] as languages of the public space has largely gone unremarked.

However, although the majority in the United Kingdom may have accepted autochthonous rights without much comment, this is not the case where immigrant minorities are concerned. At government level, policy-making still seeks linguistic conformity for allochthonous populations. Worried that immigrant groups are not assimilating as completely and as quickly as it would like, the Labour government set out to pass legislation in its second term of office that would enshrine in law the duty of the immigrant to learn English to *an agreed level of competence*.[27] To recognise the languages of the allochthonous communities in the same way in which autochthonous languages have recently been recognised would be currently politically unacceptable to many of the majority population and many in the political class. It would also be extremely difficult in practical terms. Before the French *Conseil constitutionnel* forbade the ratification of the Charter, the French had planned to recognise 75 languages, making no distinction between autochthonous and allochthonous communities. Cynics suggested that this was one way of ensuring that nothing substantial would be done for any single group, since the difficulties of making space for 75 languages in public life would be insuperable (Wright 2000b).

The discourse of assimilation is still widely heard.[28] So although the one language, one country, one territory philosophy is under attack in Western Europe from the new rights philosophy, we should be clear that linguistic space is only opening up for territorial rather than migrant groups.

Whether this remains so or not is difficult to predict. The Committee on Human Rights, the treaty monitoring body, published General Comment No. 23, in 1994 ruling that the applicability of Article 27 cannot be held to apply simply to autochthonous groups. This protection must be for all:

> Just as they need not be nationals or citizens, they need not be permanent residents. Thus, migrant workers or even visitors in a State party constituting such minorities are entitled not to be denied the exercise of those rights.

However, whether this commitment to the largely negative rights of Article 27 (such as freedom from interference) will be extended to positive rights (such as funding for education in a child's mother tongue) is far from sure. Opinion on this is divided, even sometimes in one and the same commentator. On the one hand, the group harm approach that tests the withholding of language rights, according to the degree of harm that would cause,[29] clearly makes it pressing to provide services in the language of the migrant community. New arrivals may not all be competent in the majority language. In contrast, all members of a territorial minority are likely to be bilingual (Simon 2000). On the other hand, given the operational difficulties of providing support for all, in the highly multilingual setting of Europe's cities, the provision of information and services in all languages is probably not realisable (Simon 2000). The challenge of respecting language rights in complex plurilingual societies will be the subject of Chapters 10 and 11.

10
The Fragmentation of the Old Nation States and the Rise of Small Nations

The minorities that are examples of successful linguistic renaissance are often territorial minorities large enough and cohesive enough to have claimed and to have gained a degree of autonomy. They are often termed nations without states (Guibernau 1999). Within the states in which they are embedded they have often replicated some of the linguistic aspects of nation building, if on a smaller scale.

10.1 The historical moment

We saw in Part I, that nineteenth-century politicians held that the state should be of a certain size because it was essential for a polity to be politically and economically autonomous. The country needed a population large enough to provide an army able to defend it and a domestic market of a size that would allow it to be self-sufficient. This meant that the philosophy of self-determination of peoples was always a compromise since states were judged to be viable or not on demographic grounds, and so were often amalgamations of groups felt to be too small to manage alone. Aspirations for independence could rarely be fully met. Thus groups such as the Czechs and the Slovaks were joined together to form Czechoslovakia and the southern Slavs to create Yugoslavia.

If, as I argued in Part II, the nation state system appears to be weakening, what effect might this have on the minority question? Two of the reasons for incorporation are no longer applicable. First, the size of the domestic market was important when nation states were economically isolated. However, as free trade becomes the norm, the size of the national market becomes largely irrelevant as it is no longer protected and no longer has to stand alone. And in Europe, where the European Economic Community has established a supranational common market and a common currency, this imperative for nation states to have a certain population mass has disappeared completely because of the change in states' economies. The supranational regional grouping provides the economic umbrella which was once the role of the state. Second, defence of the state has become an international affair. The UN system provides some guarantee that the international community will not tolerate invasion of a small country by a large one.[1] In Europe once again these developments have gone a stage further. Most European countries belong to NATO which guarantees their defence. In addition, by signing the Treaty on EU (the Maastricht Treaty) in 1992, member states pooled some of their sovereign political power in the justice and foreign policy pillars of the EU. Mutual defence and common military projects were a part of this.[2]

In Europe, this move from the national to the international, transnational and supranational seems to have opened up space for the region, the province or the district. In the new climate and in response to the realisation that a group did not need to be of a certain size for political and economic survival, minorities that had been incorporated into the nation states of Europe in previous centuries made moves to regain some autonomy or independence.

The extent of this pressure for devolution was a surprise to some (cf. Kupchan 1995; Özkirimli 2000), because one current of thought held that once modernisation and a certain level of economic development had been achieved, people would stop mobilising along ethno-cultural lines within the nation state. However, this proved to be a false prediction and a number of European countries have witnessed a renaissance of local identity politics which refuses the old model where a supposedly homogeneous people was ruled from the capital. Sur (1997) argues that the state is today being brought into question and that the internal homogeneity of the nation is challenged:

> National identity itself is being put to the test by regional-level demands, minority rights issues, cross-border relations, immigration, disrupted societies, and growing opposition between the rich and the poor. (Sur 1997: 421)

There have been differing degrees of consent to this challenge from the national centres. In some settings, autochthonous minorities within the various states have succeeded in having their differences formally recognised and in gaining a measure of political autonomy in a peaceful process of devolution or independence. In others, there has been violent conflict between capital and minority when the latter demanded independence and the former refused to grant it. In a third group, peaceful devolution of power has been accompanied by violence emanating from a minority within the minority that wants complete independence

Significant devolution of powers has taken place in Spain and in the United Kingdom. In Spain, the new constitution (1978) devolved some power to 17 Autonomous Communities. In the United Kingdom, Wales gained its own assembly, Scotland its own parliament after referenda in 1997. In Northern

Ireland, the Good Friday Agreement provides for complex power-sharing in an assembly.[3] In both the Basque Autonomous Community and in Northern Ireland there is a faction that wants to move to complete independence from Madrid and London and is prepared to fight to do so. However, in other Spanish and British communities devolution is progressing peacefully.

In Belgium, the 1994 constitution introduced more federal organisation of domestic affairs. Flemings and Walloons drew apart as unitary structures were dismantled. Education, the judiciary and administration became the affair of each community.[4] Central government had a reduced number of responsibilities, mostly to do with Belgium's relations with the wider world. The Czechs and Slovaks took this process one step further and ended their association completely. In 1993, they became two fully independent and separate states.[5]

The failure of Communism was the catalyst for the fracturing of the USSR. The Baltic States seceded in 1991 and became entirely independent.[6] Other groups became independent but agreed to retain links in a loose association, the Commonwealth of Independent States.[7] Yet other groups wanted independence but Moscow blocked their secession by force (e.g. the 1994 insurrection and subsequent war in Chechnya).

If demands for autonomy and independence have spread because the times are more propitious for the survival of the small polity, devolution and secession have perhaps been granted more readily than in the past because central governments have assessed the situation in the light of globalising trends and become more willing to contemplate some decentralising of the state. Many governments have ceded some power in the hope that devolution will prevent secession. Where states have continued to maintain the integrity of the state as completely inviolable, the decoupling process has often been violent, as in the Balkans and the Caucasus.

In each of the cases of devolution, secession or decoupling mentioned above there has been some linguistic effect. Status planning has strengthened the position of the group language in the institutions of the state. This has happened on a continuum, extending from minimal changes (the introduction of the group language to be learnt as a subject at school) to a complete language revolution (the adoption of the group language in every setting and power function to replace the former national language). Corpus planning has been undertaken to differentiate the language from neighbours on the dialect continuum (e.g. Slovakian), and to reach agreement on a common written standard (e.g. Basque). Acquisition planning has included the production of teaching materials so that the language can appear on the school curriculum (e.g. Scots/Ullans). Even where the outcome of the struggle for separate statehood was profoundly uncertain, language policy and planning were undertaken at an early stage in the process. For example, work on a new Bosnian dictionary to differentiate Bosnian lexis as much as possible from

Croatian and Serbian started in the mid 1990s, actually during the Bosnian conflict and under the shells (Levinger 1998).

The interesting point for the present argument is that in essence there seem to be few material differences between what is being undertaken in these new autonomies and independent states and what was undertaken by the nation builders in the past two centuries. In some cases, the desire for linguistic homogeneity in the public life of the new polity is as intense as any example from the past.

10.2 Spain as a case study

Events in Spain over the past quarter century are a good illustration of the devolutionary process and the restitution of languages that had been eclipsed in the nation building era. The Spanish case is a clear example of how history is evoked as the justification for the restitution of autochthonous languages in the public space. To understand the historical reasons put forward for the claiming of language rights, we shall need to look at the incorporation of Basque, Catalan and Galician speakers[8] into the Spanish state. Catalans, Basques and Galicians resisted the state's assimilatory policies in various ways and to different degrees. Because of this, the reintroduction of Basque, Catalan and Galician to public and official life following autonomy has given rise to different problems and challenges. However, policymakers and planners in all three Autonomies have acted in some respects as if they were nation building.

10.2.1 Catalan

10.2.1.1 *The historical background*

In the Middle Ages Catalonia had been an autonomous territory in the Kingdom of Aragon, which was on the frontier with Muslim Spain, and often took on the role of defender of the Christian world. Aragon was expansionist, acquiring extensive possessions around the western Mediterranean littoral. It was also a cultural centre which attracted interest and emulation in northern Europe (Nelde *et al.* 1996). Aragon's incorporation into the Kingdom of Spain was by marriage not through conquest,[9] and, as a kingdom joining with another through the personal union of their monarchs, the provinces of Aragon retained the autonomy which they had previously enjoyed (Kamen 1991). The Catalans lost much of this liberty in 1716, when Philip IV, the first Bourbon monarch of Spain, began a process of centralisation on the French model. In the cause of homogenisation and unification, he banned most Catalan institutions, customs and laws and restricted the public use of Catalan (the Decree of Nova Planta).

In the eighteenth and nineteenth centuries Catalonia was politically weak, but it was also, increasingly, an economic success. The only Mediterranean region to industrialise on the model of northern Europe at the end of the nineteenth and beginning of the twentieth century, it became the industrial powerhouse of Spain and attracted workers from all over Spain, as well as southern France (Esteva Fabregat 1975; Conversi 1997). Catalonia was also buoyant on the cultural front. Catalan artists and intellectuals went through a period of intense creativity in the second half of the nineteenth century. In the middle of the century, the *Renaixença* re-established the prestige of Catalan literature and touched all the Catalan-speaking areas, from Roussillon in France to the Balearics. The *Modernista* movement of the late nineteenth century found its expression in the plastic arts, particularly architecture. At the turn of the century, Barcelona was again at the forefront of artistic and intellectual innovation with the movement *Noucentisme*. Against such a background of industrial muscle and cultural vitality, it was inevitable that Catalan self-confidence would be strong and the desire for autonomy crystallise.

In the late nineteenth century Spain lost the last of its colonies, and with them went some of the reasons that the Catalans had for remaining part of the Spanish state.[10] Led by Prat de la Riba, they entered into negotiations with Madrid for political autonomy. Their arguments were given muscle by mass demonstrations.[11] After the successful conclusion of the negotiations, Catalans governed themselves with a certain degree of political independence from 1913 onwards, in the arrangement known as the Mancomunitat. This autonomy included a private school system in which the Catalan language was the medium of instruction. The Mancomunitat was short-lived, ending in 1923 when General Miguel Primo de Rivera took power in Madrid. His dictatorship presaged what would happen under Franco and the Catalans lost all the rights they had acquired. Catalan organisations were suppressed and the language banned in the public space.

The dictatorship lasted only seven years and by 1931 the republic had been reestablished. The Catalans had agreed to participate if the principle of self-determination for Catalonia was accepted. The Generalitat, the autonomous government of Catalonia, was dominated by the Left in this period and became a laboratory for all kinds of social experiments. Socialism and federalism seemed set to extend within Spain after the victory of the Popular Front government in February 1936. This was halted by the military revolt led by General Franco. After their victory in the Civil War, the Francoists were most repressive in areas like Catalonia where socialism and regionalism had been entrenched (Hansen 1977). Coercion and persecution both played a role in Madrid's pursuit of a strong, centralised and unitary state. The Catalan language was banned, Catalan books burnt, Catalan medium education abolished and civil servants caught using it punished.

However Catalans did not give up their language. In the years of the worst repression they practised it in the family and by the 1960s the vigorous civil society of Catalonia was beginning to reintroduce the language to public life in a variety of modest ways.[12] For example, in 1970, the General Law in Education allowed teaching of Catalan.

By the time Franco died in 1975, Francoism was losing its middle class support. Spain was isolated politically and economically. The state was ineligible to join the EU because it was not a democracy and was estranged from the mainstream in Europe. The economy was in decline with 30 per cent inflation and one million unemployed in 1975. The regime could either prepare to counter revolt or reform itself. The political class chose the latter course (Guibernau 2002). Thus both Francoist reformers and anti-Francoists were the authors of the 1978 Spanish Constitution, a consensual document that emerged after the first democratic elections in 1977. Trying to reconcile so many points of view, it both recognised the autonomy of national groups such as the Catalans and at the same time underscored the indissoluble unity of the Spanish nation. There was an inevitable tension in these arrangements.

The Spanish Constitution (1978) made Catalonia an Autonomous Community and in 1979 the Autonomy Statute for Catalonia made Catalan an official language in the Autonomy alongside Castilian. In 1978 teaching in Catalan was authorised with some restrictions. The 1983 Language Act set the framework for the reinstatement of the language in all functions and domains, and most significantly as the main language of education.

On the evidence of the short history above, the Catalans are clearly the aggrieved party. A centralising monarchy attempted to assimilate a separate cultural group. This group lost their political autonomy but flourished as a cultural centre and as an industrial powerhouse. It regained autonomy in the early twentieth century only to lose it twice to dictators who took power in Madrid. The second military coup led to a bitter civil war in which the Catalans suffered greatly in many ways: physically, materially and psychologically. After the end of Francoism, the Catalans regained their autonomy and set about reinstating their language and reviving their culture. This seems linguistic justice.

10.2.1.2   *The problems of historic linguistic justice*

Things are never that simple however, and achieving linguistic justice has proved a highly complex affair. The history of Catalonia is instructive, because it illustrates how difficult it is to be even-handed in the matter of language policy. There are two problems that have arisen along with the fully defensible reinstatement of Catalan as the language of Catalonia. The first concerns the mix of population of Catalan territory. As Catalan has become the language of education, the language of some of the media, the language of administration, the language of the judiciary, the language of the workplace, the language shift made the situation of non-Catalan speakers difficult. Catalonia is an industrial area and workers in the factories have always come from all over Spain. This was particularly true during the Franco period when there was a conscious effort to dilute Catalan nationalism with in-migration, but there has been a constant inflow since the nineteenth century (Comet I Codina 1990). A frequent argument for the assimilation of immigrants is that those who migrate voluntarily will have weighed cultural and linguistic heritage against economic advantage and will have accepted that language shift may be necessary to make the migration a success. This was not the case for those who came from other parts of Spain to Catalonia. They saw their actions as a move within their own nation state and their own group, not migration to an area where they would need to move language to be full members of the society. Thus there has been resentment against Catalan revivalism.[13] However, in the early 1980s this group had to temper its resistance as mass demonstrations in the streets of Barcelona to demand Catalanisation showed that unless there were concessions in this area the Catalans were likely to move to a demand for complete independence. The integration of the *castellans* proceeded, with immersion education in Catalan. In 1998 another set of Catalan language laws took Catalanisation yet further. The language shift in public life has occasioned much resentment among some Spaniards from other parts of Spain living and working in Catalonia. The Castilian medium press, particularly the right wing Madrid daily newspaper, *ABC*, provides a forum for Castilian speakers' discontent and reveals the indignation and bitterness that this reversal of the language relationship has caused among those who now feel themselves disadvantaged (Hoffmann 1996; Hoffmann 2000). Catalonia's language laws have been the object of many complaints to the Spanish Ombudsman but so far without success (Poggeschi 2000).

Catalans argue that concessions to Castilian speakers cannot be made if they wish to ensure that they can continue to use their language in their public space. They argue that since the Spanish Constitution imposes a duty on all Spaniards to know the national language, no Catalan speaker is educated to be monolingual in Catalan. Strubell (2001) remarks on the high level of Castilian competence recorded among Catalans and reminds us that, since Catalans can always communicate with each other in Castilian, they often do so, particularly where their interlocutors' language background is unknown. Strubell notes that language choice seems to be of little concern to the bilingual younger generation and that this insouciance of Catalan–Castilian bilinguals may prove the biggest threat to the full reinstatement and revitalisation of Catalan. First, past experience suggests that balanced bilingualism is unlikely to be stable over time:

> To defy history, leading people to believe that we shall be the first to maintain the balanced coexistence of two languages in a given territory, is an error which will be paid for dearly. (Prats *et al.* 1990: 23, translated Strubell 2001: 265)

Second, the proximity of Castilian and Catalan in linguistic terms means that there are often high levels of borrowing and interference from one language when the other is spoken. Strubell (2001) reports that some convergence of the languages has already been noted. What will be maintained may not be Catalan in its traditional sense:

> There is a danger of the specific features of Catalan in phonetics, in grammar and syntax, and in lexicon, gradually being lost, and of Catalan becoming, in effect, a mere dialect of another language (Spanish). (Strubell 2001: 277)

Supporters of Catalan are thus very aware that they need to protect and promote the language. They are acting in the classic ways. Corpus planning is very evident. There is an official terminology service to supply neologisms, halt borrowings and maintain the 'purity' of the language. There is a telephone service to 'answer doubts about official Catalan usage' (Pym 1999). Sociolinguistics, Catalan studies and Catalan linguistics are well funded departments in the universities.

Catalan activists are militant about the need to protect the fragile roots of new language practice and many believe that this cannot be done with too many concessions to Castilian. This has meant that the laws and their implementation have been quite forceful and can seem quite illiberal from an outsiders' perspective.[14] This is, of course, an illustration of the theoretical point made in Chapter 9. Had the Generalitat taken a less vigorous approach it would have been tantamount to supporting the Castilian status quo.

However, where Catalan strategies and initiatives have been effective, they have edged Catalonia towards the kinds of assimilatory policies that the Catalans refused to countenance from Madrid. Catalan nationalism suffers from the same dilemma that dogs French Republicanism. It is a very inclusive nationalism. Jordi Pujol, the main theorist of the moderate Catalan nationalist party Convergència I Unió and president of the Generalitat until 2003,[15] famously defined a Catalan as 'someone who lives and works in Catalonia and who wants to be a Catalan' (Pujol 1980, quoted in Guibernau 1997: 91). Thus one can become a Catalan by assimilation. In one reading, this is admirable, in the way that French Republicanism is admirable. In another reading, it can be attacked as hegemonic. Inclusion can also be intolerance and eradication of difference. It was inevitable that the campaign for normalisation (i.e. to extend use of Catalan to all spheres where Castilian was used previously) would be experienced as an assault on their liberties by those who did not understand Catalan easily or speak it fluently. Castilian speakers can, of course, learn Catalan, but this is not an easy solution and there may be lost years, even a lost generation, before the gap closes. In Catalonia, monolingual Castilian speakers are becoming a new minority. They suffer from a lack of cultural capital in the new situation, in the way of all minorities. Such minority status is intensified where Catalan speakers and Catalan–Castilian bilinguals practise Weberian social closure to redress balance and promote the group that was formerly disadvantaged.[16]

The process of Catalan nation building is a new phenomenon in that the CiU does not demand full independence and the party that does (Esquerra Republicana de Catalunya) remains a minority (Guibernau 2002). However, the Catalans continue to press for recognition of their status as a different nation (Barcelona Declaration 1998) and argue that they have a right to an institutional presence in the EU and other international organisations (2001 Catalan Self-Government Report). Catalonia seems to be representative of a new phenomenon of the post EU era, nation building at regional level. Catalans differ from old style nationalists in that their attitudes to sovereignty are less rigid, and their associations at the supranational level are fluid and open. However, there are distinct parallels when it comes to promoting a cohesive community of communication within the group. Here attitudes are less open. One can see old style nationalism, for example, in the discourse that presents large families among the Castilian-speaking group as a demographic threat (Fieldwork 1997). One can understand why the Generalitat feels that 'the only hope for Catalan is to recruit new speakers among the immigrant groups' (Strubell 2001: 269). This comes perilously close, however, to the nation building policies that Catalans rejected for themselves.

The second major problem arises because of the Catalan desire for critical mass. Catalonia is only one of seven areas in which Catalan, or a dialect very close to Catalan, is spoken. The areas where Catalan is spoken in Spain are Catalonia, the Balearic islands, the north and east of Valencia and the western counties of Aragon. Outside Spain, Catalan is the official language of Andorra, was the language of Roussillon in southern France and is present in one town in Sardinia (Alghero). The enthusiasm in Barcelona to get these areas to band together and use their combined weight to achieve greater recognition[17] for the language has had mixed results, with some groups being ready to follow the Generalitat's lead and others unwilling to be satellites to a centre that they do not recognise as their own. The relationships among these disparate Catalan speakers are illustrative of all the difficulties that I have discussed in theoretical terms in other parts of the book.

For Catalonia, the Balearic islands, Valencia and Aragon to agree to work together in the Spanish context a precondition has to be fulfilled. They have to accept that they speak one language, and this has not been the case. For nearly two decades, the Balearic islands were not willing to subsume their linguistic particularism into the whole in order to give weight to a Catalanism which they saw as Barcelona dominated. However, the coalition government that came to power in September 1999 took a different line, and a declaration of cultural unity signed in March 2000 and an agreement on language policy cooperation has led to collaboration and common programmes. It is significant that one of the collaborative projects is the digitalisation of the

Diccionari català–valencià–balear produced between 1901 and 1962 by the Balearic linguists Antoni Maria Alcover and Francesc de Borja Moll. This is illustrative of the Generalitat's awareness of the unacceptability of imposing a norm from the centre and its comparative sophistication in sociolinguistic matters compared with other states.

However, even such soft pedalling has not been enough to gain the cooperation of all Valencians, among whom there is solid resistance to attempts by the Catalans to pull them into the Catalan-speaking group. This has led to resentment in Barcelona that these speakers are so obdurate in denying a common linguistic heritage and great suspicion in Valencia that the Catalans want them to assimilate in the way that national centres have traditionally asked of regions on the periphery. This perennial problem of language boundaries is underlined by two adjacent passages in Comet I Codina (1990). In the first, he recounts that a school handbook written by a Jesuit teacher in 1939 denied the existence of separate languages in Spain apart from Spanish (Castilian) and Basque. Catalan was categorised as a dialect of Spanish. In the second, he appears to be repeating the error at the Catalan level, claiming that Valencian is the same as Catalan.[18] He quotes the similarities in the two versions of the constitution as evidence that the Valencians are making too much of the slight differences between the languages. The point here is surely election; the Catalans did not wish their language to be seen as a dialect of Spanish and the Valencians do not want their language to be categorised as a dialect of Catalan.[19] This is not primarily a linguistic matter and has nothing to do with the similarities or lack of similarity between the varieties. The Valencians do not see Barcelona as their centre. The history of Valencia has contributed to a different identity which with few exceptions does not recognise the leading role of Catalonia within the Països Catalans (Poggeschi 2000). The dilemma is not particular to Spain and to Catalonia. As Sur remarks:

> Each minority, upon closer analysis, tends to integrate several others into itself in such a way that this logic of Russian dolls can lead to indefinite fragmentation. (Sur 1997: 429)

Relations with Aragon seem less fraught, particularly since the leader of the Autonomous Community of Aragon since 1999, Marcelino Iglesias Ricou comes from the Catalan-speaking part of Aragon, la Franja. For the majority of Aragonese, cooperation with Barcelona is not of major importance because the five counties (83 villages) where Catalan is spoken make up only a small percentage of the Autonomy, unlike Valencia where over half the population is concerned. However, in 1997, those that were concerned came together to campaign against the incursion of Catalan[20] and asked that if a local language were to be made co-official in Aragon that it should be their 'own language and culture', that is to say, Aragonese.

Outside Spain the situation of Catalan speakers in the three areas is very different. In Andorra, Catalan is the official language of the state,[21] despite which a continuing shift to Castilian has been noted (Mercator news report May 2002). In Alghero, Catalan is recognised as one of the twelve minority languages or dialects of Italy and can be used in the municipality's official documents and taught in the municipality's schools as a heritage language. In Roussillon, the language is permitted only as an option in the state secondary system and allowed as a medium of instruction in private primary schools. There has recently been a heated debate on the position of minorities and minority languages within the French state. This was provoked by France signing and then failing to ratify the Charter for Regional or Minority Languages and by the demand of the Breton medium Diwan schools to have state funding. The widespread interest in this question and the acrimony with which citizens exchanged views revealed that the French are in the majority still marked by Jacobin centralism and a belief in a French medium universalism that eschews all regionalism as tribalism. The position of Catalan in Roussillon is therefore parlous. Few learn it, few speak it and were this to be its only homeland, then Catalan would be among the languages in danger of extinction.

As it is, Catalan is far from dying out. It may be spoken by as many as 10.8 million people (Generalitat 2000). These figures make Catalan the seventh largest language in the EU and have fuelled the Catalans' argument that it should be included as an official language of that organisation. It has the largest number of speakers of the 36 languages considered to be regional or minority in the EU and from this position champions the cause of linguistic minority rights. But of course, as we have seen, because it is such a successful language in terms of numbers of speakers, domains of use and variety of functions, it is also seen as a hegemony, impinging on the linguistic rights of others, ambitious to install a muscular monolingualism within Catalonian public life, working to assimilate speakers of different varieties of the language to the Barcelona dialect and imposing a language shift on Castilian speakers who live in Catalonia through immersion education.

10.2.2   Basque

Catalan nationalists used language as a central unifying factor, a core value in the way this term is employed by Smolicz (1988) in his study of maintenance of language and national identity among immigrant groups and Edwards (1985) in his work on language and identity in history. Conversi (1997) in an in-depth study of language and nationalism in the Spanish context contrasts Catalan foregrounding of language with the relatively minor role that language has played in Basque nationalism. It is rather religion and race that have been promoted as the core values that could unite Basques. This was understandable because language has been more problematic as a unifying factor in the Basque areas. First, until work in the 1960s, there was no standard Basque and the seven varieties that have been identified in the Basque-Navarrese area are not all mutually comprehensible. The standard, Euskera batúa, is still not universally acceptable (Hoffmann 1996). Second, competence in Basque became associated with rural poverty unlike Catalan, which never entirely disappeared as the language of the commercial, industrial, professional and intellectual middle classes. In the Basque country the urban population and the middle classes had mostly moved to Castilian and the heartland of the language was the rural population.[22] Because of this, knowledge of Basque was not widespread among members of the early nationalist movement who were mainly town born and middle class. Indeed, even Sabino Arana, the architect of Basque nationalism, did not acquire Basque as a child in his family but as an adult through study. Basque was, therefore, far more typical of languages eclipsed by European nation building. The elite had shifted to the language of the capital and those who retained the original language were in a diglossic situation needing to use the language of the capital both with central authorities and with their own urban elites.

Since the concepts that the Basques have evoked for unity have been race and blood, they exemplify the ethnic tradition in nationalism. In contrast to the tradition of civic nationalism in Catalonia, where one can become Catalan by learning the language, adopting the culture and living and working as a Catalan, one is born into the Basque nation, one does not become Basque. Thus, in the early nationalist movement language learning was not encouraged among non-Basques and language competence was used as a barrier to protect the autochthonous population from infiltration by outsiders (Conversi 1997). In fact the language's own term for Basque is *Euskaldun* which means someone who possesses the Basque language (Allières 1986). Hence the legacy for Basque nationalism bequeathed by Arana has been a certain racial exclusivity and a desire to exclude outsiders from becoming Basque speakers.

The stress on ethnicity was perhaps inevitable. The Basques are the archetypal autochthonous group, living on this territory and remaining cohesive over millennia, as the conservation of the language demonstrates. However, immigration to the industrial areas in the Basque country in the nineteenth and twentieth centuries had an immense effect on this cohesion, mixing newcomers into the population and negating the claim that the Basques are a single people in a single space. It is perhaps not coincidental that ETA's origins coincided with the peak of immigration (Conversi 1997). The overtly racist theories of Arana and the early nationalists[23] are rejected by all the present day Basque nationalist political parties but the legacy of the early period has conditioned the nationalist movement and it is not difficult to find expression of sentiments close to the Aranist tradition among Basque-speaking, grassroots supporters. The legacy of the past is exclusivity rather than the inclusion of the Catalans.

Those committed to the spread of Basque in the Autonomous Community of the Basque Country encounter the classic problems of nation building and language. The first is to gain acceptance of the standard in all quarters. Euskera batúa is based on educated Guipizkoa Basque and speakers of other varieties, for example, Bizkaia Basque, find many aspects alien (Hoffmann 1996). Of course, as we have noted before, accepting a standard or rejecting it is in part a political decision. Heteroglossia is a feature of all living language and whether we accept a different linguistic variety may have as much to do with our attitude towards the speakers as with actual linguistic differences along the dialect continuum.

The second problem concerns persuading all those Basques who live in regions outside the heartland of the Autonomous Community of the Basque Country and who could be part of the Basque revivalist movement that they want to be included. There are Basques in the south-west of France and in Navarre. To gain the numbers of speakers that would give weight to their language and culture externally and ensure its survival internally those engaged in the revitalisation and normalisation of Basque would like to work with both groups. A similar situation pertains, however, to that described for Catalan. The French do not manifest more than a moderate interest in their Basque identity. They celebrate it by cultural maintenance, mainly dance and song. There are a limited number of Basque medium private primary schools. As a movement, Basque nationalism is not a major force in France, and many Basques in France would subscribe to the French model of civic nationalism and describe themselves as French. The Navarrese, for their part, are wary of exchanging centralism practised by Madrid for centralism practised by Bilbao. The hesitation and reluctance in the French Basque Country and in Navarre may have much to do with the radical nature of Basque nationalism. ETA may have recruited a certain group of disaffected young men (Ignatieff 1994), but it has alienated a large proportion of the general population. Many Basques, particularly in France, are suspicious of what they see as an exclusive, extremist and violent nationalism harnessed with radical Marxism (cf. Conversi 1997). On the other hand, Madrid's treatment of the Basques has sometimes been extremely repressive, which has had the effect of uniting the group[24] and encouraging their desire to learn the language.

The last problem is the practical difficulty of acquiring the language. Basque is so far from Castilian and French, that speakers of these languages must expect to devote a much longer period of study to learning it than they would to Catalan, where the Romance family resemblance makes acquiring comprehension, if not fluent production, a reasonably easy ambition to achieve. Thus, there may be no danger that the distinctiveness of the language will fade in contact with adjacent languages on the continuum, but there is the possibility that the alien nature of the language is too great a hurdle for some Romance speakers.

Despite these problems, competence in Basque is on the rise in the two Spanish Autonomies according to both official census data and individual research (Azurmendi *et al.* 2001). Using Fishman's grid for Reversing Language Shift (1991) Azurmendi *et al.* report that there is significant if not linear progression along the continuum that Fishman devised. They conclude that in the Basque Autonomous Community (BAC), which is the heartland of regeneration, Basque is now used in numerous formal functions that will guarantee its survival. In the classic nation building tradition, Basque has been introduced into the areas where the state has some leverage, for example, education, media and political life, and is encouraged in civil society and industry and commerce. In the BAC, the language is increasingly reported as the habitual language of family interaction, an important development since intergenerational transmission is the key to regeneration (Fishman 1991). The other significant development is the rise in Basque immersion schooling for families where the language is not the home language. During the 1990s participants in Basque medium schooling in the BAC passed the 50 per cent threshold, a much higher figure than the proportion of the population that claims to be first language speakers of Basque. The Navarrese (NAC) are trailing in the reversal of language shift although the numbers of Basque speakers has risen in the NAC too, if in a more modest way and more slowly. The French Basque country is still reporting attrition.

Azurmendi *et al.* (2001) report on the ongoing conflict among those who support a radical programme of Basquisation, those who would like to stem or even reverse the trend to Basque and a third and minor group that would like to devise a system of symmetrical bilingualism where Basque and Castilian remain in balance. Nothing is as yet resolved and it would be encouraging in linguistic rights terms to think that the last option could be possible. Historical precedent does not encourage us, however, to expect symmetrical bilingualism to endure. The doyens of the discipline are in agreement on this. Romaine (1995) reminds us that historically no group has maintained two languages for the same functions. Fishman (2001) sees functional differentiation and diglossia as the only feasible way to maintain societal bilingualism.

10.2.3   Galician

Galicia gained similar status to Catalonia and the Basque Country as an Autonomous Community in the 1978 Constitution. However, although the Galician language has been recognised as official alongside Castilian within the Community, Galician is in a slightly different situation from that of either Catalan or Basque.

In contrast to Catalan, Galician was not the language of a national patrician class, the language of a confident and prosperous bourgeoisie nor the medium for artistic movements that had gained international recognition. In a largely farming and fishing community it was the widespread medium of oral communication, that is, the language of a rural peasantry. It had no history as the language of local administration, education, military conscription, local media or local arts. Although there had been a Galician nationalist movement since the nineteenth century, it had not provoked a cultural movement. Even Rosalía de Castro, the best known Galician author, wrote mostly in Castilian. Others, from Alfonso the Wise in the thirteenth century to Lorca in the twentieth, did produce some poems in Galician, but the volume of such work is small (Hoffmann 1996). So, because Galician was primarily a spoken language without a strong literary tradition, there was no settled written form which could immediately be employed as a language of government and administration in the Autonomy and as a medium of education. The Galicians were faced with a problem of standardisation and codification, as in the Basque case.

The first step in the linguistic normalisation process was not undertaken until the 1980s. Although Galicia had been granted some autonomy at the time of the Second Republic, the onset of the Civil War had meant no formal language planning had taken place. Galician is a language on the Romance dialect continuum, a bridge between Portuguese in the west and Castilian in the east. The debate on standardisation divided between those who saw alignment with Portuguese as a way of giving Galician a ready made standard and the benefits accruing from the rootedness and prestige of a national language and those who wanted to make the language linguistically distinct. A third group that speaks castrapo, a variety of Galician very close to Castilian, was not taken into consideration in the debate as the aim was to differentiate usage from Castilian. Hoffmann (1996) recounts the struggle of the different factions to have their solution accepted. Failure to agree produced two sets of orthographic norms.

The standardisation of Galician had not only a geographical hurdle but also class distinctions to overcome. In the classic way of minority languages in Europe, the language had become associated with older, poorer, rural speakers. It had existed in a situation of typical diglossia, being used in all the usual functions of an L language with Castilian fulfilling all the H functions. Hence Galician had very low prestige. Now, in emulation of Catalonia and the Basque Country, it was seen as necessary to promote the Autonomous Community as linguistically and culturally distinct and to encourage a language shift in the Castilian-speaking towns and middle classes. For this to happen Galician had to lose its former characterisation as the language of rural poverty. This meant that the solution for standardisation had to take account of what would be acceptable to these urban groups. The standard, Gallego normalizado, was thus based largely on the language of intellectual activists, who had sometimes acquired it as a second language. However, as they were educated urban speakers, theirs was held to be a variety that could become a prestige language (Hoffmann 1996).

This left the traditional Galician speakers who in their majority were rural and did not speak such a variety as minority speakers once again. Indeed they were now arguably a double minority, neither at home in the prestige variety of Galician nor mother tongue speakers of Castilian. Green (1994) terms this a situation of double jeopardy. As Hoffmann says:

> Having to accept and acquire literacy in this new form may well be perceived as an alienating element. Culturally it is probably hard for them (rural Galician speakers) to recognise *gallego normalizado* as part of their heritage. Yet not accepting it bears some risk too. Social mobility and migration (both into urban areas and through urban sprawl into the countryside) brings with them increased contact with Castilian Spanish as well as with the new Standard Galician....One thing seems sure: constant conflict with these two varieties will remind rural speakers that they use neither of them well. (Hoffmann 1996: 82)

Bratt Paulston (1994) made the same point for the dialects of the Occitan continuum. She notes that the written form of Occitan is sometimes so divergent from the spoken dialects that the speakers feel as alienated from it as they do from French.

The position of Galician is very precarious. Since Galician has not traditionally been the means of social advancement, the reasons for the urban elite to learn it have been slight. The well-entrenched rural varieties that were the expression of a certain identity may be undermined by the top-down imposition of a prestige standard. Where this form is not close enough to the former to count as the original language of local group solidarity Galician maintenance may be weakened, and the language be in a more parlous position than if there had been no state intervention and support. Strubell (2001) has shown how disturbing the functional distribution of two languages can affect the vitality of the weaker language, which no longer has a clearly defined space.

10.5 Conclusions

Spain provides three extremely illuminating case studies which reveal how much the enactment of language rights is problematic. Renaissance of a language that has been eclipsed is to be welcomed, particularly when it is the expressed wish of the majority of the population affected. There will, however, always be those whom the new practice marginalises or excludes, whether these individuals are speakers of a variety of the language which is distant from the standard chosen or speakers of another language entirely who find themselves through historical circumstances on the territory, and yet are not part of the linguistic tradition being restored. A review of any of the other cases of devolution or secession mentioned at the beginning of the chapter would reveal similar difficulties. Langman (2002) shows how the Hungarian-speaking minority have been under pressure to assimilate linguistically in the new state of Slovakia, whose elites are set on classic nation building. Fevre, Denney and Borland (1997) discuss how the English-speaking southern Welsh are at a disadvantage in the new power structures of post devolution Wales. Ozolins (1999) gives an account of the situation in Latvia and Estonia where the large Russian-speaking minorities need to acquire competence in Latvian and Estonian to become citizens.

The case studies also illustrate how the problem of centre and periphery are endemic to the concept of community of communication. Those geographically distant from the heartland of a standardised official language and linguistically divergent may turn towards that language or turn away. Efforts from the centre to maintain the community as unitary will always be experienced as hegemonic. This seems to be an issue no matter how small the language community. Agreement on the standard form can be a difficulty even in the extreme case of a language with so few speakers that it is about to die out. Furbee and Stanley (2002) report on the difficulties of getting the last speakers of Chiwere to agree on a form so that it could be recorded, and suggest that in general:

> (t)he decline of Native American languages was hastened by the competition among families for speaking the best version of the language to the denigration of other family dialects. ... (P)rogress cannot be made on preservation because no matter who initiates the effort, other groups will question the person's claim to act. (Furbee and Stanley 2002: 114)

The final point to be made is to ask whether the Catalan, Basque and Galician situation is actually a new phenomenon. Is it the enactment of linguistic rights within a devolutionary process or is it simply a second phase of self-determination and nation building, this time on a smaller scale? Is it merely the phenomenon of the smaller Russian doll? On the evidence there seems to be little reason to see what has been achieved in these cases of devolution and independence as a model for human rights for minority language speakers. The proponents of rights for their own minorities have not been concerned with minority rights *per se*. Not even the Catalans, highly aware of the theoretical work on minority rights throughout the world and capable of showing great solidarity[25] with minorities in other parts of Europe, have been protective of the language rights of others in their proximity or even in their midst. The issue of the recognition of Valencian has already been mentioned. It is also worth noting that there is no systematic offer of Arabic and Berber, even as school subjects, to the minorities of Moroccan and West African origin in Catalonia.[26]

In Chapter 9, I discussed the zero sum nature of language. Where one language is embedded in a role and is the medium of institutions, another can only be present as a translation or an alternative. Complete equality is enormously difficult to arrange. And where one group's language rights are restored, this often has negative effects for another group. The case of Spain amply illustrates the difficulties inherent in the language rights issue.

11
Endangered Languages

This chapter of the book deals with all the other languages of the world, languages that are neither the official language of a state or of a region or a province nor important trading languages or intergroup lingua franca. This is an enormous topic because most of the world's 6000[1] or so languages fall into this category. And most of these can be considered in danger.

Although, at first sight, the contexts of minority languages as disparate as the three case studies in this chapter (the Albanian spoken in Sicily, the language of hunter–gatherers on the north-west frontier of China and the language of subsistence farmers in the Bolivian Altiplano) might appear to have little in common, on closer examination it becomes evident that some of the pressures on them are similar and the speakers' experiences comparable. The processes of nation building and globalisation discussed in the earlier chapters of this book are at the root of these pressures. Indeed, as we have seen, nationalism is one of the main reasons why small groups come to be conceived as minorities and nation building is where they are put under most pressure to become bilingual or to shift language. As education, modern state administration, modern forms of media and new technologies enter settings where the local language has no written form and only small numbers of speakers, it is easy to understand how difficult maintenance of the local language can become and how strong the pressure to shift entirely. Romaine (2002) reminds us of the four key reasons why so many languages are in an endangered position:

> Fewer than 4 per cent of the world's languages have any kind of official status in the countries where they are spoken...most languages are unwritten, not recognised officially, restricted to local community and home functions and spoken by very small groups of people.... (Romaine 2002: 01)

Given the external pressures on speakers and the likely choices that they will make, under these pressures, a number of these languages are likely to die out completely. Krauss (1992) suggests that the number to disappear might be in the region of 4000, or two-thirds of the languages currently spoken. Hale (1998) and Woodbury (1998) believe that only 600 out of the 6000 plus present languages are fully secure.

Crystal (2000) poses three questions that arise from this prediction: Should we care? Can anything be done? Should anything be done? To which one could add, if there is something to be done, are scholars and practitioners of LPLP the right people to do it? Can behaviour be influenced through policymaking? This chapter examines some of the reasons advanced for language maintenance and protection, and then reviews some of the issues in three different case studies where there has been policy and planning to promote and protect an endangered language.

11.1   Should we care?

There are several arguments advanced as reasons why humanity as a whole should not let languages disappear. We shall look at the strength of evidence for each one and then move to what can be done if we accept the arguments. The arguments can be categorised under a number of headings. The first is that diversity is good *per se*, in the way that bio-diversity is good. Second, language maintenance allows members of a group to remain in touch with their own history and cultural heritage. Third, language is an essential element of identity that should be respected. Fourth, languages constitute an irreplaceable resource for humanity.

11.1.1   Language diversity is good *per se*

The hypothesis developed by the American linguists, Franz Boas, Edward Sapir and Benjamin Whorf, mentioned in Chapter 1, is a cornerstone of the argument that language diversity is good *per se*. Their fieldwork among Native Americans led to the development of the theory that groups develop their languages in reaction to and in relation with their different bio-niches and that group experiences mediated through language allow them to develop particular worldviews. The way that the lexis and syntax of a language develops encourages its speakers to interact and portray experience in a certain way:

> (T)he background linguistic system (in other words the grammar) of each language is not merely a reproducing instrument for voicing ideas, but rather is itself the shaper of ideas, the program and guide for the individual's mental activity, for his analysis of impressions, for his synthesis of mental stock in trade. Formulation of ideas is not an independent process, strictly rational in the old sense, but is part of a particular grammar, and differs, from slightly to greatly, between different grammars. We dissect nature along different lines laid down by our native languages.

The categories and types that we isolate from the world of phenomena we do not find there because they stare every observer in the face; on the contrary, the world is presented in a kaleidoscopic flux of impressions which has to be organized by our minds – and this means largely by the linguistic systems in our minds. (Whorf 1956: 212–13)

This led Whorf to a highly determinist position:

(N)o individual is free to describe nature with absolute impartiality but is constrained to certain modes of interpretation even while he thinks himself most free ... We are thus introduced to a new principle of relativity, which holds that all observers are not led by the same physical evidence to the same picture of the universe, unless their linguistic backgrounds are similar or can be calibrated. (Whorf 1956: 214)

This means that Whorf believed that some concepts are ultimately untranslatable. Sapir was slightly more cautious. He is quite categorical that national characteristics (which he terms group temperament) and language have no intimate connection and that language and culture have no causal relationship. He did, however, advance the idea that there can be no thought without language, and that human ability to conceptualise arises as the language faculty is refined (Sapir 1921: 15). Because of this, it is argued, humans are very much at the mercy of the particular language which has become the medium of expression for their society, and they interpret through the veil of their language or according to the framework it proposes. Sapir believed, however, that in terms of complexity, the language of the cultivated Frenchman and the South African Bushman are in essence perfectly comparable although different (Sapir 1921: 22). Moreover, he held that speakers of differing languages are never imprisoned in their language, because all languages have the potential to be elaborated and concepts adopted.

The ecolinguistics school, which has developed in the last decades, begins from this premise that there is a strong relation between a language and a worldview. A central claim is that certain languages are perfectly adapted to communicating certain values and attitudes. For example, the languages of pre-industrial societies are held to promote respect for the natural world (Mühlhäusler 2001). In contrast, Standard Average European languages (SAE)[2] deal with industrialisation and the pollution it causes with a semantic imprecision that fudges, euphemisms that mislead and an absence of terms that can direct attention to certain important processes. Mühlhäusler argues that the languages of the big polluting states allow them to systematically underestimate and play down the consequences of dangerous practices. Chawla (2001) compares lexis from Native American languages and English to illustrate how language frames what we see and how we act in our relations to the natural world. He explains how Cherokee and Pueblo extend kinship terms to nature and claims that:

> (B)ecause of these beliefs, Indians have traditionally treated the inanimate and animate world with awe and concern in ways that do not indiscriminately damage the natural environment. (Chawla 2001: 118)

He contrasts this with an analysis of English, where he concludes that its individualising tendencies contribute to English speakers' failure to see the environment holistically and exacerbate their propensity to act for egotistical advantage, even when this may be against the greater good. Influenced by a scientific worldview, they interpret the Cherokees' anthropomorphic attributions to the animate and inanimate world as superstition and dismiss them.

The ecolinguistic literature generally tends to assume a close and essential relation between language and knowledge. Accordingly, when intergenerational language transmission breaks down and a language disappears, there is likely to be a serious loss of inherited knowledge. The argument is that any reduction of language diversity diminishes the adaptational strength of our species because it lowers the pool of knowledge from which we can draw (Bernard 1992).

This would only be the case if the strong Whorfian claim that translation is ultimately impossible were true. However, translation is possible. The very fact that Mühlhäusler and Chawla can point out that Westerners ignore important aspects of the environment, and that new ways of expressing our experience might change how we behave towards it, exemplifies Sapir's claim that elaboration and adaptability are always possible. Speakers of SAE could gain insights from peoples whose languages make the need to respect the environment more explicit. If a certain language does not have the lexis for a particular subject, it can be borrowed or invented. If it does not have a particular structure, it can be developed. If there is a particular way of reasoning or conceiving a topic in a language, it can be copied. If precise ways of talking about the ecosystem make speakers more aware of diversity and of damage and encourage them to be active stewards of biological and ecological diversity, then these can be copied and learnt.

The argument that protecting languages where relationships are encapsulated in particular ways might make us more respectful of nature is a weak one for the preservation of the language. We would have to believe that there was an essential relationship between the language and the concepts expressed for the argument to hold. However, many people do take this line. Skutnabb–Kangas argues that the language/concept link is never fully translatable:

> Traditional knowledge may indeed linger even after a native language is lost, but the richness and diversity of that knowledge cannot survive even one generation of language loss. (Skutnabb-Kangas 2000: 259)

But, if we take a non-essentialist position, we cannot use this argument for the preservation of the language. There is no reason why the insightful framing of other languages could not be imported into SAE languages if their speakers decided to develop the competence to reflect different ecological positions. The question is not whether it can be done but whether it will be done. Are SAE speakers being alerted to the way that their languages obfuscate and mislead in environmental affairs by the ecology lobby? Yes, they are. Articles from the ecolinguistic group are doing so. Whether such awareness will result in more careful linguistic formulation in other languages and more ecologically aware behaviour are further developments and not at all inevitable. Certainly there are precedents for believing that language change may be associated with change in other behaviour and attitudes. The feminist movement argued that aspects of practice in the SAE languages contributed to patriarchal attitudes. A reworking of terms and structures to change this was advocated as a way of changing attitudes, influencing behaviour in relationships and promoting greater equality in society. In another example, the anti-vivisection lobby points out that the impersonal constructions of English scientific discourse may well contribute to the desensitising necessary for researchers to function in the laboratory (Kahn 2001). Campaigners argue that if those engaged in vivisection were forced to articulate what they were actually doing, then they might feel less comfortable doing it.

There is an important point here for small language survival, because, if the argument is valid, it could just as easily be used against minority languages. Anyone adopting a strong Whorfian position, whereby languages are not 'interchangeable' (Mithun 1998), would have also to accept that a group could never transcend its position, could not learn from others more advanced in some area, through translation. According to this logic, to profit fully from advances in cognition, new concepts in technology, novel art forms and so on, members of the small group would need to acquire the language in which they had been developed, with the consequent risk of language shift.

There is also a wider claim from the ecolinguists. Parallels have been drawn between linguistic diversity and bio-diversity. Extrapolating from the ecological mainstream, they argue that diversity is good *per se*, and that the multiplicity of languages contributes to the health of an environment. This seems to be a metaphor that cannot be taken too far and one that is difficult to support with evidence. Adaptation to an environment is positive, and can be shown to be so in the case of language. Mühlhäusler points out that

> Languages over time become fine-tuned to particular environmental conditions. It is language that allows people to become efficient users of the environment. But it takes time to get to know a place. (Mühlhäusler in a university newspaper interview 1998, quoted by Skutnabb-Kangas 2001: 259)

But language diversity can also be seen as contrary to human well-being. Although Crystal (2000) and Skutnabb-Kangas (2000) cite the Mexican myth that holds that the goddess Iatiku created different language groups so that they could not quarrel, it is difficult to find examples from history where incomprehension safeguarded peaceful coexistence. There is more data to confirm the view expressed by George Steiner, already mentioned in the introduction to this book:

> Time and again linguistic differences and the profoundly exasperating inability of human beings to understand each other have bred hatred and reciprocal contempt. … In short: languages have been throughout human history zones of silence to other men and razor edges of division. (Steiner 1998: 58)[3]

Most importantly perhaps, too much reliance on parallels with the natural world raises the spectre of 'survival of the fittest'. This aspect of the biological metaphor is not compelling if we want to argue for the preservation of languages under threat.

Thus, the ecolinguistic case seems to rest on analogies that do not fully hold, on a conviction that language and thought are so inextricably linked that worldviews cannot be understood outside the language group where they originate, and that languages are ultimately untranslatable. The claim that a language may provide insights and make relationships evident is probably true, but it does not furnish a sufficient reason to maintain a language, where a group is shifting language for its own project. The argument does not stand on its own unless one has accepted the strong Whorfian position.

11.1.2 Language, history and group continuity

Another reason advanced for preserving languages is so that the past remains contactable:

> With language loss the link with the recorded and transmitted cultural legacy is broken. (Bourhis 2001: 6)

Where languages have a stable standard, the written form allows access to the group's past, beyond living ancestors. The texts of former generations are available for their descendants, because the language does not change substantially. In some groups too rigid adherence to historical norms sometimes causes problems. Where a written standard has been based on the literary forms of an earlier period, there will be some distance between the written and the modern spoken language, with all the difficulties this entails for universal literacy. This was what occurred in Italy and Greece where early standardisation drew from the canon of a past golden era. The diglossia and social exclusion it can cause may be seen as a high price to pay to maintain historical continuity. In other cases the planners of the written standard may have consciously broken with the past in order to simplify or to align the language with a new ideology. This was the case with the alphabet reform in Turkey, and the change has made old texts inaccessible for modern Turkish readers.[4]

If the language has no written form, the texts of the group are passed on in the oral tradition. The data on how oral transmission is affected by language shift is not extensive and, as yet, is inconclusive. Eades (1988: 97) finds that Australian Aboriginal people maintain 'significant Aboriginal and social aspects' and 'distinctively Aboriginal interpretations and meanings' even when their language of interaction is English. Woodbury (1998), commenting on Eades, agrees that content and style can be transported from language to language, but wonders what is left out. Jocks (1998) gives an account of Native American religious ceremonies in which he tries to evaluate how far those who participate in translated ceremonies can experience the event in the same way as those who speak Kanien'kéha, the language used in the rituals he studied. He concludes that, although translation is possible, something is inevitably lost in translation.

This may be true but Jocks' research on these translated/interpreted ceremonies itself provides just one example to show that group history, memory and knowledge can be preserved even when there is language shift. Whether or not they will be preserved will depend on group attitudes to past organisation of the society and its values and attitudes. Memory may be jettisoned along with the language if there is a strong modernising current in the group. It will also depend on the group composition during and after shift. If there is dispersal, penetration and mixing, then opportunities and occasions for the transfer of group history, memory and knowledge may be fewer. It is not inevitable, however, and the core of ideas and values can survive a change in the language that carries them as they can survive a change in the speaker that expresses them.

In another branch of linguistics there is a long tradition of research into one aspect of linguistic continuity. Historical linguists track lexis in language shift where groups are conquered and assimilated, tracing a word through a set of languages to show patterns of contact and how words passed from one language to another as goods or ideas were exchanged.[5] There is usually a trace of substratum groups in the language and the gene pool of a people (Cavalli-Sforza 2000). It is, of course, of little comfort to a conquered and decimated group to know that elements of their language, perhaps along with some of their genes, survived, incorporated into the new society. This is a very weak form of language maintenance! However, the fact that there are more languages that have died out than are now spoken means that it is a very widespread phenomenon. These previous languages survive in the vocabulary of the languages that come after. Naturally, topography is particularly likely to bear witness to former speakers on the territory.

For there to be no legacy from a language that is eclipsed to the language that supersedes it suggests conscious repression of the transfer process. Where there is no trace of a language in situations of contact, the reasons are sometimes to be found in paranoid attitudes among the dominant group and fear among the subordinate. Humphrey (1989) discusses how speakers of Buryat, in south-east Siberia, avoided importing Buryat terms into Russian in order not to offend the Soviet authorities by using Mongolisms. This was a widespread reaction among local political elites who were aware of Stalin's fear of pan-Mongol nationalism. They would not risk misrepresenting themselves as unorthodox in a dangerous political period and so rejected code-switching and tag-switching when speaking Russian. This was one of the factors that halted the process of borrowing and mixing and maintained strict compartmentalisation of the languages.

11.1.3 Language and identity

The third reason advanced for maintaining languages is that a language is a component of identity and that the disappearance of the language of a group has immense repercussions for healthy self-regard (Crystal 2000). Language is a robust marker of group membership and one that is not easily changed. It is one of the stronger markers of identity because there are cognitive as well as psychological barriers to be overcome when individuals shift language. An outsider cannot decide to join a linguistically distinct group simply by willing it. The apprenticeship before being able to make the change will be long and possibly hard. Particularly in the case of an adult learner, it may never be complete. The strong post-structuralist argument that language is contingent falls apart when we witness the difficulties that individuals have when they are forced to shift language.

This is not to reify or essentialise language: the relative difficulty of changing language group does not mean that it cannot be done, only that it is done with difficulty. There is nothing intrinsic about language and identity: they can both shift: they can both be hybrid; they can both be layered. That being said, if a group views membership of their language group as essential to their identity and believes their society would be fundamentally altered in ways that they do not want by language shift, then it seems their perfect right to couple identity and language. As May (2002) argues, even if language is a contingent factor of identity, that is not to say that it is not experienced as significant for or constitutive of identity. The strongest argument for taking the necessary institutional decisions to support maintenance of a language has to be because its individual speakers wish to do so.

However, the problem then arises that language maintenance cannot be an individual decision. An individual does not want to be the only person maintaining a language. S/he wants the group to maintain the language so that s/he can function in that language within it. In Chapter 9 we considered whether language rights can be seen as individual rights or whether they are *de facto* a kind of group right. The point is fundamental to the identity issue. Using the language of a group is a kind of social glue. Where speakers are part of a small language group and know only that language then their repertoire constrains them to social commerce within that group, often limits their choice of marriage partner and usually dictates where they can work. If the group's concern to maintain solidarity and continuity placed a limitation on the other languages that members may learn, this would be an infringement of individual rights. However, discouraging the learning of other languages may seem to group leaders the only way to preserve group language in the face of economic and political pressures on individuals to shift.[6]

There are several dilemmas here. On the one hand, it would be invidious if the individual's right to acquire a language that gives access to higher levels of education and allows social and geographical mobility were curtailed in any way to encourage language maintenance among the group.[7] On the other hand, the decision of individuals to acquire a language that is instrumentally more useful affects not just them but the group as a whole, because each individual decision to acquire a dominant language (L2) has an incremental effect and makes maintenance of the dominated languages (L1) more difficult. In the best case scenario, learning the L2 leads to personal bilingualism and societal diglossia. The L1 may not develop the lexis necessary for many domains but remains secure in the private spheres. In the worst case scenario for language maintenance, the L2 penetrates the private sphere as well and there is personal and family shift. Where there is education in a standard language and where there is scope for social and geographical mobility, there may be exit from the language group, and then numbers of the group may dwindle and those remaining become isolated. This has always happened. It is the scale of the phenomenon, which is the new development:

> If members of a subordinate population have the opportunity to learn the language of the dominant group, some or all of them will usually do so. ... It seems that it is not so much the tendency to learn a dominant group language which has increased a great deal in modern times, but rather the opportunity to do so, and concomitantly and more importantly for linguistic diversity, the tendency to abandon one's ancestral language in the process. (Dorian 1998: 5)

The second problem is concerned with freedom of choice. It is difficult for individuals to choose the language(s) in which they are socialised and educated since this happens in childhood. The adults responsible for the socialisation and education of the younger generation determine the medium. The literature abounds with numerous examples of how the decision of parents or educators to socialise and educate in the majority language has been experienced as deprivation, exclusion and loss by those for whom the choice was made (Dorian 1998; Mithun 1998; Crystal 2000). Hale (1998) believes that not being taught the language of one's group can even give rise to grief. On the other side, a major theme in all literature is the individual who rails against the constraints of the primary group and struggles to transcend them. Literature may gloss over the linguistic dimension of this but transcendence mostly involves language acquisition. The fundamental problem is that the choice of language(s) of socialisation and education is not one that individuals can make for themselves.

Before leaving the subject, there is perhaps one further point to be made about the contingency of the link between identity and language. Does group identity survive when the group no longer speaks its ancestral language? For example, can the southern, mainly non-Welsh-speaking Welsh claim equivalent Welshness to those in the north-west where the Welsh language is more widely spoken? Can immigrants who assimilate linguistically in the host country maintain their identity? Clearly in the first case there will be different contributing factors to what makes these two groups see themselves as Welsh, but they may be no less powerful. The powerful factor in the cultural vitality of both groups may be the fact that both are cohesive groups that continue to be a majority in their settings. This is not the case in the second situation. Identification with the land of origin may continue to be very strong and maintained through religious practices or cultural maintenance in diet and dress, even where, given the need to survive and the hope of prospering in the new environment, there is linguistic accommodation. However, where there is complete loss of the original language of the group in a situation of migration this must affect identity, because new language behaviour will affect patterns of contact. Migrant groups in the United States have tended to shift language within three generations (Fishman 1977b) and this has happened in some cases of migration into Europe. In such cases contact between grandparents and grandchildren is cut, and, at the very least, a new, hyphenated identity becomes likely for the younger group.

It seems unproblematic to suggest that where there is language change there will be changing identity. This is not to agree with the Whorfian notion that a language carries other aspects of the culture in a particular way and makes likely certain ways of being and that a change of language necessarily affects that. It is to recognise that patterns of association are central to identity formation. Where individuals acquire the medium that opens the door to other groups, diverse contacts and different influences, it is difficult not to accept that identity will be altered. Very few who become members of new networks and who are exposed to new ideas will not change their perception of their identity in some way. Bourdieu's concept of *habitus* describes the process: the embodied meanings of groups do not determine how individuals act but they provide an influential frame of reference. To acquire more embodied meanings is to widen and alter frames of reference.

11.1.4   Diversity as a research resource

Another argument from those who are striving to save endangered languages is that they are an irreplaceable source of information on the way that the human brain processes thought. If every linguistic system finds a slightly different way for individuals to conceptualise, reason, communicate, be expressive and so on, then the loss of one way takes away a building block that might allow us to understand the process more clearly. Thus preserving the thousands of human languages that currently exist may help scholars to understand how language works. Hale (1998) says categorically that the loss of linguistic diversity will be a loss to scholarship. Like Mühlhäusler (1996), Fill (1993), and a selection of contributors to Dascal (1992, 1995), he contends that we must have as much data from as many languages as possible to reveal how language works. Every language that is lost is one less example of the phenomenon, and with it may go a particular feature that exists nowhere else. At the same time, linguists argue that the more languages available for study, the more likely the search for the universals of language will be successful:

> While a major goal of linguistic science is to define the grammars of all natural languages, attainment of that goal is severely hampered, some would say impossible, in the absence of linguistic diversity. If English were the only language on the face of the earth, we could not know literally hundreds of things which are permitted, even predicted, by universal grammar and accidentally missing in English, or any other single language. (Hale 1998: 192)

Further research data comes from the fact that the languages of people in apparently simple societies are as complex in linguistic terms as the languages of societies, which are much more technologically and socially elaborate. Hale (1998) claims that so-called simple societies should be seen as rich in mental wealth with respect to language formulation and ritual interaction. Difference among groups is very revealing about deep and surface levels of the evolution of the human brain. However, it would be naïve to think that the needs of scholarly research alone could ever be a compelling reason for a group in the process of shift to reassess their behaviour and change tack.

11.2   What can we do?

11.2.1   Describing the problem

The first step is to recognise and describe the problem. The sheer scale and speed of language shift and loss have led to heightened interest in the fate of the smaller languages of the world in the last two decades. Linguists started making it the focus of major international meetings as, for example, in the conferences on maintenance and loss of minority languages, held in Noordwijkerhout, the Netherlands, in 1988 and 1992, the conference on language endangerment held at Dartmouth College in the United States in 1995, and the conference on language rights in Hong Kong in 1996. In 1993, UNESCO set up the 'Endangered Languages Project', a programme to record the world's disappearing languages before their last speakers died. Funding has been made increasingly available through organisations such as the Foundation for Endangered Languages and the Endangered Language Fund. Individual programmes to protect, maintain or revitalise particular endangered language groups have proliferated.[8]

A growing number of linguists have made the position of endangered languages and policy reactions to endangerment their specialism. Representative scholarship can be found in edited volumes by Dorian (1989), Fase, Jaspaert and Kroon (1992), Grenoble and Whaley (1998) and Fishman (2001).

Numerous typologies have been developed to describe the different situations along the continuum of endangerment and to identify the variables that lead to the disappearance of a language. Conflating them[9] gives a five-point scale indicating the declining probability of survival.

1. Language groups that are viable and unproblematic. These languages will survive.
2. Language groups that are viable although small. On demographic grounds these languages could be considered to have too few speakers to sustain them, but are likely to survive because of the presence of other factors. The reasons for expecting survival could derive from the isolation of the community, the traditional and conservative nature of the society, the high status of the community relative to neighbouring groups, the value placed on language as a marker of identity, and so on.
3. Language groups whose future is uncertain in the long term. In these cases, past experience suggests that the languages will die out if nothing changes. Speakers do not appear to be committed to the language, perhaps because they feel that they are socially and economically disadvantaged by maintaining it. Peer pressure to use the language is weak. Typically, child speakers are fewer than adults in number as families pursue social mobility through shift.
4. Language groups that are contracting now. The languages are in imminent danger of disappearing. The younger generation have been educated through another medium and have shifted. The youngest monolingual speakers are aged 50+.
5. Groups that have shifted. The languages are either nearly extinct or completely extinct. In the former, the tiny number of surviving monolingual speakers are very old. In the latter all mother tongue speakers have died. The language may survive in written or recorded form but it is now a dead language.

11.2.2   Responses to language loss

Languages can cease to be spoken for two reasons: the group that speaks the language ceases to exist or the group that speaks the language shifts to another language. The first case implies the destruction of the speaker or the speakers' habitat. This was what happened in the genocide that took place in some European colonisation and what happened in Ireland in the famines of the nineteenth century or in the Sahel in the famines of the late twentieth century. Language death was a side effect of exploitation, war and genocide or catastrophe; as the safety of a people was threatened so was its language. Such language death must have occurred frequently in history as small weak groups were conquered and displaced by larger and stronger peoples or as natural disasters struck. Whether groups were physically wiped out or became too small to exist as a separate society, their languages disappeared. Pagel (1995) suggests that perhaps 100000 languages may have once been spoken by humans and have since disappeared, probably in a violent way.

The second case is mutation not extinction. Here one group (A) in contact with a second (B) disappears as a discrete group because it makes the shift to B's language. This can also result from oppression, but in other kinds of contact there can be an element of choice. The reasons are usually to be found in the imbalance of economic and political power between the two, but the pressure can also derive from more positive reasons: marriage, educational opportunity, professional advancement, economic advantage. The shift can happen with or without overt pressure from the more powerful group.

The violence of obliteration in the first case and the large degree of external coercion and pressure found in a good deal of the second has coloured much recent scholarship in the area. It is perhaps in consequence that some of the language rights literature treats those who become bilingual or who shift from a smaller to a bigger language as pawns in globalisation or capitalist economics or dupes of nationalism. There is sometimes a lack of recognition that it may be a considered and conscious decision to accept language shift as the price to pay for a desired move from one's original group to the wider world. Depending on the individual situation, shift can be associated with transcendence rather than tragic loss. However, to date, understanding aspirations and transcendence does not seem to have attracted as much research interest as understanding coercive pressures and loss. More investigation of pull factors would be a very useful contribution to this debate.

More emphasis on this focus would also remind scholars and planners that the objects of LPLP are also agents, and their choices are ultimately decisive in determining how language behaviour develops. Speakers themselves are the ultimate arbiters of language revitalisation, and the other players need to be sensitive if they aspire to play a role. The academic community can put the case and identify the variables but ultimately language maintenance is not their choice and they can only help if they are asked to do so.

The activists of the minority group may have to compromise on goals if the rest of the group is not committed to language revitalisation, and accepts shift and mutation of identity to further other goals. A central government, that supports its minorities, needs to understand the process it implements, if it is not to have unlooked for results. These points are illustrated in the case studies discussed below.

The position that a language group finds itself on the continuum and an understanding of its aspirations will determine what action can be taken to maintain or revitalise the language. There are three possible options:[10]

The first is to do nothing; accept changes in language use as normal. Such a philosophy would perhaps reflect Edwards' (1985: 86) assertion that it is natural for language use to change, and 'more reasonable to consider group and individual identity altering... than it is to see the abandonment of original or static positions as decay or loss'. Language will adapt as speakers are in contact with others or in new situations. Those holding this position would say that the dynamic and accommodating nature of language and its users will always counter any attempt to preserve a language as if it were an artefact in a museum, frozen in its present state for all time.[11] The argument is also that one cannot pressurise people to give up life chances to revitalise or preserve a language and that there has to be a reason beyond a simple desire to conserve.

The second option is to turn to scholarship. Linguists can preserve the language, by documenting and recording as much data as possible. Then, if the endangered language disappears as practice, it can still survive as knowledge and system. People will know about it, even if no one uses it as a medium. The arguments for such activities are, as discussed in 11.1.4, that they safeguard linguistic diversity and contribute to a knowledge base for language universals. The Western idea that knowledge in and of itself is valuable is at work here. Some[12] would see an implicit ethical problem in the fact that such scholarly activity is likely to be of little immediate benefit to the remaining speakers, who may feel their ownership of the language under threat, as well as the language itself.

The third option is to attempt some sort of language salvage, revitalisation, or maintenance programme, depending on the position of the language on the continuum of vitality. This would include language development strategies, such as producing a written form of the language; encouraging acquisition of the language and literacy in it; using it as a medium of education; funding and encouraging literary production; translating government and administrative documents into it; funding media in it; requiring business and commerce to make their services available in it; and other such tactics.

A number of the strategies for revitalisation will need the approval of the state and may require changes in state law. Their implementation will need extensive financial support from general taxation. Revitalisation of a minority language is language policymaking and language planning at a local level and the activities encompassed by it are the status planning, corpus planning and acquisition planning usually undertaken by the state: that is to say, designating the language as a medium in certain institutions (status planning); making the language fit for that purpose, by codifying and standardising it (corpus planning), and finally educating speakers to use it in both written and spoken forms (acquisition planning). Where an organ of civil society undertakes the role of promoting the language, then it will need to do so under the aegis of the state. Little can happen here if the governing elite or the dominant group is opposed to extended use of the minority language or subscribes to the civic ideology of the 'neutral' state.[13] The activity may be judged balkanisation rather than a beneficial promotion of diversity.

This has led a number of sociolinguists to argue that official support for a language should be a key component of language maintenance (Bourhis 2001; Skutnabb-Kangas 2000). Other scholars concede that this is true, but warn against too great a reliance on official intervention. Fishman stressed that top-down policies cannot compensate for lack of bottom-up support and that use in the family is ultimately more important than use in institutions:

> Endangered languages become such because of the lack of informal intergenerational transmission and informal daily life support, not because they are not being taught in schools. (Fishman 1997: 190)

Nettle and Romaine (2000: 39–40) agree and believe that state support for the language and culture of a group relatively lacking in power does not necessarily ensure the reproduction of a language unless other measures are in place to ensure intergenerational transmission at home. Romaine (2002) wrote elsewhere that:

> looking to schools and declarations of official status to assist endangered languages is much like looking for one's lost keys under the lamp post because that is where the most light appears to shine, rather than because that is where they have been lost. Just as it is easier to see under the lamp post it is far easier to establish schools and declare a language official than to get families to speak a threatened language to their children. Yet only the latter will guarantee transmission. (Romaine 2002: 04)

If use in the home is the key to language maintenance, community activists who want to maintain a language have to address the problems of status linked to minority language use and the advantage bound up with majority language use. Grillo (1989) believes that the attitudes of majorities towards minority groups can often be categorised as an 'ideology of contempt'. Basing his analysis on languages in Europe, he concluded that any language that is not a language of state or power is despised by non-speakers and that this attitude is sometimes transferred to its speakers. In consequence, those who are not part of the dominant majority may want to shift to acquire prestige (Joseph 1987). Nettle and Romaine (2000) suggest that conferring power and thus prestige on a minority language group is one of the surest ways of reversing language decline.

However, conferring power and prestige through designating a language an official language may still not be sufficient to reverse decline. The relative failure of Irish revitalisation in Ireland is one illustration of Fishman's point that official language promotion needs the backing of families committed to intergenerational transmission and private use of the language (Ó'Laoire 1996).

11.2.3 The variables in maintenance and loss

Edwards (1992) suggests, in a predictive typology, the sites where prestige is located. The wide variety of variables that he identifies as playing a role and the difficulty of altering circumstances in some of them is a clear indication of the limitations of LPLP.

Edwards distinguishes 33 elements that favour language maintenance. The best case scenarios fall broadly into the following areas:

1. The group is demographically secure, concentrated in an area, with a tradition of endogamy and little in or out migration.
2. The geographical situation protects the integrity of the group and inhibits contact.
3. The socio-economic status of speakers is high and a range of employment opportunities is available within the group, in the group language.
4. The group has achieved political recognition, rights and a degree of autonomy. Some political life takes place in the language. Dominant and other groups have a positive attitude towards the minority group.
5. The group is cohesive, practising a single religion and maintaining cultural practices in the group language.
6. All generations of the group have high levels of competence in the group language, which is the habitual language of the home and transmitted intergenerationally.
7. The language has a standard written form and speakers are literate in it. It is used in literary production, education and the media.

There are a number of variables in this list that no amount of state support or group effort could affect. Geographical settings that isolate the group and belief systems that discourage any exit from the group, in particular exogamy, will always help maintenance, but cannot be planned for. A large, healthy group that provides a choice of marriage partners and an attractive bio-niche that supplies all the material needs of the group are basic human desiderata. They will aid language maintenance if they promote stability and lessen the reasons to pursue prosperity and general human happiness outside the group.

Other variables depend heavily on the will of central government. If the dominant group agrees to a measure of devolution and autonomy, this will make a significant contribution to minority language maintenance. Where central government relaxes its hold and the group achieves a measure of political control over their institutions, use of the minority language can become the medium for the police, the judiciary, the civil administration, in education and democratic forums with significant effects on language revitalisation. No centralised societal arrangement maintains the language over time in the same way. Bourhis (2001) is one among many who has demonstrated that even pluralism leads to language shift in the long term, because social mobility in a pluralist society still requires that minorities learn the dominant language.

The third set of variables in the typology derives from the economic value attached to knowing and using the language. The central role of economics in language maintenance is twofold. Where the group sees itself as a group and defends its interests as a group, there are positive effects for solidarity and group language maintenance. Where interests are defended successfully, it remains possible to live economic life in the minority language. Where the minority language is used in business and industry, the language is an economic asset and becomes a language which non-speakers want to acquire. Recent events in Wales illustrate how this can happen. Devolution for Wales (1997), building on the Welsh Language Act (1993), led to a legal framework for language revitalisation. Government departments were required to make services available in Welsh as well as English. Business and commerce followed the lead of local government and took the voluntary decision to provide bilingual services, seeing this as advantageous in a situation of national self-confidence and enthusiasm. With more and more employment hinging on bilingual competence, bilinguals increasingly found themselves in a position of economic advantage. English monolingual families became more willing to choose bilingual education for their children. The results of the 2001 census record that there has already been a growth in those claiming knowledge and use of Welsh. The economic advantage of knowing Welsh, allied to an increasingly positive image of the nation, seems to have affected patterns of identity with many identifying themselves as Welsh rather than British, and exhibiting this orientation by choosing to learn and speak Welsh.

Other variables have also contributed to the vitality of the Welsh language. Cohesion in the informal networks of civil society, in religion, cultural production, sports has been influential for revitalisation. There is also a tradition of pride in history and culture within the group, and a custom of using the language for literature, in particular song and poetry. However, these elements were present in the years when there was a decline in the use of Welsh and a language shift to English that seemed irreversible. They do not appear to have been adequate on their own to ensure language survival. Economic and political factors seem to have been necessary to halt the shift to English monolingualism.

11.3 The problems of small groups and language maintenance

These are dispiriting findings for all those committed to maintaining the language of their group, but who have no prospect of achieving the political independence and socio-economic buoyancy that seem to guarantee success. The evidence seems to be building incontrovertibly that many of the tactics suggested for language maintenance and language revitalisation are not materially different from those undertaken in nation building, if perhaps on a smaller scale.

Now, out of the 4500 or so groups whose languages are threatened, few are engaged in struggles for self-determination. Few are large enough to have the political clout to gain autonomy or to sustain it. Many have no aspirations to do so. Many are penetrated by other speakers and to achieve autonomy and then employ the strategies of nation building would simply produce new inequalities. The kind of solutions developed in nationalism are not appropriate where groups are nested one inside the other like the proverbial Russian doll. There will need to be new solutions other than endless fracturing. We shall return to this in the conclusion. Before doing so, let us look at three case studies that illustrate how difficult it would be to implement the kind of strategies for reversing language shift and revitalising language that sociolinguists often suggest, for example Fishman and others in Fishman (2001).

11.3.1 Development and the end of isolation

Many small languages have survived because of the isolation of their speakers. Lindsay Whaley (2002) documents how development and the end of isolation have caused language shift among the Oroqen, a group living on the north-west frontier of China. The Oroqen were originally a nomadic hunter-gatherer people, organised in a number of clans, that arrived in the frontier area of the Hinggan mountains sometime in the seventeenth century. Whaley cites sources that estimate their number at around 4000 before the Second World War.

Under the Communist regime, their situation altered radically. In the first decades of the PRC, there were positive attitudes to minorities and minority rights were enshrined in legislation. These rights were based on the territorial principle and resulted in the creation of autonomous regions, prefectures and counties for minority groups. The Oroqen were allotted the Oroqen Autonomous Banner, and thus became a group identified with a clearly defined territory for the first time. The Chinese government instituted a number of measures to raise the standard of living of minorities, including the provision of health care and education. One aspect of this policy was the settlement of nomads so that children could be schooled. The Oroqen ceased being nomadic in the late 1950s and began to settle in villages (Whaley 2002).

Other aspects of Modernity altered traditional ways. In order to exploit natural resources, the Beijing government sent large numbers of workers into the area, mostly Han Chinese. To transport resources and products out of the area, Beijing built roads and rail track. The new infrastructure and industrial activity had a number of effects. In particular, the increased population density and the network of roads affected the Oroqen hunting grounds. It became more difficult to live by the old methods and increasingly easy to live by the new. In a few decades, the Oroqen went from living through hunting to participating in the PRC economic system, from being an isolated group, numerically dominant in the area, to a tiny minority (1 per cent) in most of the villages and cities that they inhabit (Whaley 2002).

By its own criteria, the state treated minorities well in a number of ways. First, secondary education was free for them and there were quotas to guarantee minimum minority numbers at university. A relatively high proportion of Oroqen thus went through the Chinese education system. Second, the Oroqen, like other minorities, were exempt from the national one child per family policy. Third, to encourage them to settle, many Oroqen were housed in government built houses, which were of good standard for the region. These various advantages meant that the Oroqen became relatively pro-government and never felt the need to mobilise as a group to defend their interests.[14] They also gave the group relative prosperity and standing which have been incentives to non-Oroqen to marry into the group. The Oroqen found themselves in a classic melting pot situation and there has been a massive language shift from Oroqen to Chinese in a few decades.

As the Oroqen have become conscious that their language is not being transmitted to the next generation, there have been some initiatives for basic Oroqen language classes in school and on children's television to give the children of the community some familiarity with, if not competence in, Oroqen. These have not been an unqualified success, mainly because Oroqen is a collection of dialects rather than a unitary language with a standard written form. The acquisition programmes have each based their course on one of the dialects and this has alienated other Oroqen groups who do not recognise their own idiom in the form taught.[15] This is the problem experienced by the Galicians and the Basques discussed in Chapter 10, and indeed wherever speakers of a set of dialects acquire a standard language that must serve them all. Some of the group will be speakers of a variety far from the norm adopted and, unless there is a compelling reason for accepting it, may not do so. Standardisation may be rejected by those who do not recognise it as their speech.

The case study illustrates how even where the political elite of a state has shown some support for minorities,[16] there can still be language shift. Whaley believes that it may even have been the government's treatment of them as a minority group that actually weakened their identity patterns and made assimilation more likely. As highly independent and fluid hunter groups, speaking related dialects of the Oroqen language, they did not originally see themselves as a unified group. The various policies of the PRC, however, treated them as if they were. Being conceived as an entity was as much a new development for the Oroqen, as settlement, work in a cash economy, education, intermarriage and all the other innovations that they have experienced. Now language revitalisation also requires them to see themselves as unified. It may not happen if the very recognition of group membership itself constitutes a break with the past.

11.3.2 The disappearance of a language and its speakers

The language in the next case study is as endangered as the Oroqen dialects but the reasons for this are quite different. The Uru of Iru-Itu in the Bolivian Altiplano did not lose their language because of economic development but through lack of it. The community where it was spoken almost disappeared after a period of natural disaster and hardship.

The Uru live on the banks of the river that flows between Lake Titicaca and Lake Poopo, surrounded by Aymara-speaking peoples. There are three Uru languages/dialects, Uchumataqu, Murato and Chipaya, and they appear to be distinct from surrounding languages (Muysken 2002).

The Uchumataqu community was decimated after a three-year drought between 1939 and 1942, which caused death and dispersal. 'In 1942 only six men and a few women, all elderly remained' (Muysken 2002, quoting Vellard (1954). The tiny size of the group and the fact that the women were past childbearing age meant that the men who had remained sought wives outside the group. These women were Aymara-speaking and this became the main language used in the new families. Muysken (2002), again drawing from Vellard (1954), suggests that in the area the prestige of Aymara was then higher than that of Uchumataqu, the dialect of Uru spoken by the community. The mothers did not raise their children to speak 'a despised dialect' (Vellard 1954: 93).

In 2001, Pieter Muysken worked with the villagers to record what elements of the language the community could remember.[17] He reports that there are no speakers for whom Uchumataqu is a first language and the reconstruction depended on the memories of those who have passive or partial knowledge of the language. Muysken records that there was little consensus and much imprecision among his informants. There were unbridgeable gaps where memories failed and some lexis could not be recalled. Those who remembered some of the language had experienced the fundamental problem of maintaining competence in a situation of shift. De Bot (2001) suggests that language loss is a spiral. If there are few opportunities to use the language because of dwindling numbers of interlocutors and decreasing domains, there will be loss of language ability deriving from the shrinking occasions when the speaker employs the language. It will take longer to retrieve words for objects in the language that is undergoing attrition, which insecurity in itself discourages use of the language. There is a demographic point at which this process begins. The process is then immensely difficult to reverse. The critical mass factor not only affects competence in the language but motivation to improve competence. If there are few interlocutors and few domains, why maintain the language?

In this situation it is interesting to speculate why the Uru are taking steps to revitalise Uchumataqu. Muysken suggests a possible motivation. The Uru have been part of the tremendous labour migration from the Altiplano. This migration is seasonal rather than definitive and those involved return regularly. The contact with the wider world has given both the desire and finance for modernisation. Iru Itu is no longer a poor community, but amongst the most prosperous and innovative in the region, 'looked upon with some jealousy and respect by their Aymara neighbours' (Muysken 2002). There is now reason to feel proud of group membership. Moreover, there has been significant ethnic mobilisation in Bolivian politics since the mid-1990s in which the neighbouring Aymara have been major players. In their turn, the Uru are becoming more self-aware, either because of rivalry with or emulation of the Aymara. Desire to remember the language and record it may reflect a new pride in group membership. Muysken recognises the limits of what can be done:

> It would not be a purely automatic and unconscious reversal of a process of language shift, of course. That shift took place much too long ago for that, and the language is too far gone. It would be a conscious effort to give the language its place alongside, not in place of, Aymara and Spanish. It would involve the activities of a small group of cultural brokers, community leaders, and be linked to processes such as folklorisation and musealisation of Uru culture. It would also need to be a modern development, relying on literacy and possibly even on modern media. For some, this makes the possible revitalisation of Uru unreal, artificial or suspect. However, it may be the way in which many such revitalisation processes take place in different parts of the world. Situations such as that of the Uru and the Uchumataqu language cast doubt on traditional notions of authenticity and spontaneity, and show that even rural communities are capable of 'language planning'.[18] (Muysken 2002: 313–14)

Muysken does not mention another possible factor that may be contributing to this desire for revitalisation among the Uru. Those who work outside the village are in contact not with Aymara speakers but with

Spanish, possibly English, speakers. There may be a possibility that where the language that one needs for work is far removed from the cultural base, the desire to cultivate a language of identity becomes stronger. This seems to be an effect associated with globalisation and is an issue to which I will return in the conclusion.

11.3.3 Status and literacy

The third example of an endangered language is taken from a study carried out by Eda Derhemi in Europe. Piana Arbresh is a dialect of the variety of Albanian currently spoken in five communities in Sicily.[19] The Arbresh-speaking population in Piana degli Albanesi numbers about 7000 (Derhemi 2002). Arbresh has been the language of the community for the past 500 years, since the Albanians came to settle in Sicily. Derhemi suggests that the reasons for its survival derive in part from the fact that the Albanians were Orthodox Christians among a Catholic population. They maintained their religion and practised endogamy, which kept them a separate and cohesive group. Other factors encouraging maintenance included the relative prosperity of the group; the issue of status worked for the minority rather than against it, since the Albanians were rather contemptuous of the rural Sicilian majority and dissociated themselves from the surrounding population. The prosperity and confidence of the Piana degli Albanesi group contributed to the survival of Albanian in the town and may be the significant variable missing in the other centres where Albanians settled, but which have not conserved the language into the twenty-first century.[20]

Arbresh speakers appear to be in a much stronger position of language vitality than either the Oroqen or the Uru. Despite their centuries long contact with Italian/Sicilian speakers, they have conserved their language and maintained stable diglossia. In addition, a recent law passed by central government[21] gives them legal instruments to strengthen their position and puts them in a position to promote Arbresh in new settings. In particular the new[22] laws make it possible to use Arbresh in school. The status and prestige of the language appear undiminished.

Derhemi reports, however, a general perception in Piana degli Albanesi that the use of Arbresh is declining, both in the number of domains in which it is used and among younger speakers. Having witnessed 'the semi-speakers or non-proficient Arbresh speakers' in other communities, community leaders have expressed their determination to work to stem attrition in Piana itself (Derhemi 2002).

The principal course of action in the language maintenance programme was to be courses in and through Arbresh in the schools. This had the support of the majority of parents according to a survey conducted in 2001 (Derhemi 2002). Arbresh would be used in the earliest years of primary education as the language of school socialisation, which would formalise a practice that already existed as teachers provided a bilingual bridge for

Arbresh-speaking children. In addition, older students would be able to acquire literacy in Arbresh in more advanced classes.

Despite these various indicators of the vitality of Arbresh, there are two obstacles which need to be overcome if the language is to survive in the long term. The first problem is the absence of an agreed standard written language, which means that the educational initiatives have been delayed whilst the community comes to an agreement on what this should be. At the moment there are two camps: those who believe that a standard should be developed for the 7000 Arbresh speakers in Sicily and those who argue that it makes more sense to adopt the written standard of Albania, which already exists and which gives access to wider sources and contacts, and an extensive literature.

All descriptions of the present dilemma show parallels to the case of the Galicians, described in Chapter 10. The ready-made standard is exterior and slightly alien. Opponents to its adoption reason that there is little point in struggling to conserve a language if what is conserved is not the group's language but another, which, although close in many ways, is alien in others. They argue that the differences between standard Albanian and Arbresh cannot be treated as negligible and that adopting it would create a situation of double diglossia for Arbresh speakers. The other solution, to codify and standardise Arbresh has also attracted strong criticism. The problem is that the project was assigned to a small group of scholars and poets who did not consult widely (Fieldwork Italy 2002). The result is a highly literary standard that would need to be introduced top-down to speakers. The few school texts produced in it so far have been ill received. Teachers report that their pupils found the language difficult to understand and did not relate it to what they actually spoke (Derhemi 2002). The controversy and the subsequent slow rate of progress in producing texts is a key reason for the slow implementation of the educational initiative. Moreover, informants (Fieldwork Italy 2002) suggest that the highly public arguments are likely to drive those families where use of Arbresh is fading even further away from the language.

This brings us to the second problem for language maintenance in the group. The point has been made several times in this text, that perceptions of status and prestige are key to intergenerational transmission and language loyalty. Among Arbresh speakers a very keen pride in group membership seems to have been a major reason for the survival of the language. In much of the twentieth century contact with Albanians from Albania was minimal and in the Communist period links were cut entirely. Since the opening up of Albania, Italians' attitudes towards their neighbours across the Adriatic have fluctuated. In 1997 there was widespread support for those opposing the regime and a warm reception for the first refugees who crossed the Adriatic in small boats to leave the crumbling Communist regime. In the years since then, many Albanians, particularly young men, have entered

Italy, mostly in search of work and mostly without the papers to allow them to do so. Their difficult position in the margins of economic activity has produced an impression among the Italian majority that they are employed illegally in the black economy and may even be involved in criminal activities. Italian prejudice against Albanians has grown with the result that, however justified or unjustified this attitude may be, seeking association with Albania, Albanian and Albanians may have become less attractive at the present time.[23] Semi-speakers of Arbresh may be less motivated to take steps to improve their competence and to work to maintain the Arbresh-speaking community in Piana degli Albanesi, if they feel the language associates them with a community that is the object of majority suspicion or racism.

11.4 The difficulties of implementing universal linguistic rights

Bratt Paulston (1997: 82) suggests that claims for universal language rights may 'merely serve to weaken potential rights since many claimed rights patently cannot be enforced in some situations'. The three studies in this chapter demonstrate that many of the strategies suggested for language revitalisation (Fishman 2001) are not an option for the Uru, the Oroqen, or even possibly for the Sicilian Arbresh speakers. These groups cannot copy language groups that have fought their way out of subjugation and which are commonly held up as models. The Welsh, the Catalans, the Basques that I have used as examples of successful revitalisation of 'minority' languages are not in the same situation as the Uru and the Oroqen. The languages of the latter are among the 4500 under threat; the former are not. Even Arbresh speakers, with some legal recognition in Italy, larger and more concentrated numbers of speakers, and closely related to a language which is national and official in another state, are not in a comparable position. There is a continuum along which the likelihood of revitalising or maintaining a language grows, closely related to whether the group takes or is accorded some measure of political independence. The probability of maintaining the language diminishes for many practical reasons of *doability* as well as conscious repression.

Without the political muscle to gain separate development, minorities depend entirely on dominant majorities being ready and willing to confer on the language of the weaker group the necessary prestige (Grillo 1989) and utility (May 2002) for long-term stable bilingualism. If majorities refuse to accept arrangements that allow languages to coexist within the same space, minorities with little power can do little to fight their case. Of the four ideological approaches to dealing with a multicultural/multilingual state,[24] even pluralism which is founded on equality and even-handedness and which is the most favourable to minorities cannot guarantee bilingualism and minority language survival.

Pluralist regimes ensure that minorities enjoy freedom from interference and provide positive support, for instance, by funding the cultural and linguistic activities of the minority in the same way that it does for the majority. The pluralism ideology works with the concept of 'reasonable accommodation' (Bourhis 2001: 11) and it is assumed that the cultures of the dominant majority and that of linguistic minorities will be more or less transformed by the sustained contact between these communities:

> However, it is acknowledged that by virtue of their weaker vitality position, linguistic minorities are more likely to be transformed by such contact in the long run, than is likely to be the case for the dominant majority. (Bourhis 2001: 11)

Thus, in practice, even pluralism may not be robust enough to change perceptions of prestige within and towards the weaker group and maintain distinction.

A number of scholars have pointed out the symbolic nature of much policymaking in pluralism. Schiffman (1996) suggests that central authorities of the state are often cynical in that they grant status to languages that are fast disappearing. Where a policy appears to be accommodating linguistic pluralism, it is often symbolic and little actual planning follows from the declaration. May (2001) criticises pluralist policymaking for often being grandiose but delivering little. It rarely changes the power relationships. Romaine (2002) cites the Native American Languages Act of 1990 as a classic example of a policy where the rhetoric is not reflected in measures to implement the law. She also notes that where official support comes too late, after the community has ceased to transmit the language, there is no threat to the *status quo*. This is probably why it is allowed to happen and may account for an apparent increase in support for pluralism. So we should be aware that state support for minority language maintenance may be meant to be token.

The other state ideologies found in multilingual states either reject language rights or, where they appear more supportive may actually derive from rather sinister reasons. Civic and assimilationist ideologies both promote the language of the dominant group, along with its culture, attitudes and core values, although the rhetoric of the former sounds more egalitarian. Their inclusivity leads to an intolerance of difference. Ethno-nationalist ideology may support language rights for minorities living among the majority, but the price the latter pay for this will often be exclusion.[25] The minority may be marginalised, or in the worst cases, held in enclaves (apartheid, reserves), expelled (ethnic cleansing) or even physically eliminated (genocide) (Bourhis 2001). It is the separate development required in a system of apartheid or reserves that allows the language of the minority group to be taught within the group. Indeed it serves the marginalisation and differentiation desired.

Language provision for allochthonous minorities can help to prepare an immigrant group for return to the country of origin when they are no longer required as a workforce.

There is thus a fundamental dilemma; the more desirable current state ideologies all encourage linguistic shift in the minority group. The alternative, marginalisation within the state, is a high price to pay for language maintenance. In the setting of the strong state, the only way to acquire the prestige necessary for maintenance without marginalisation, seems to be to go it alone. The coexistence of languages without hierarchy is claimed for certain societies where language is exclusively oral and interaction face to face (Fairhead 1994), but it does not seem an option where there is a strong state or a literate culture. Even where stable bilingualism can be maintained there is still diglossia. The hierarchical arrangement of languages seems to be the price that societies pay for universal literacy and education, social mobility and free movement of citizens, and an inclusive political system and democratic participation. The interesting question to ask is whether there will be any change in this, if the state weakens as structures become more global.

12
Conclusion

Identity and community; communication and transcendence

In a book published posthumously in 1998, Ernest Gellner compared the two major competing visions of society in modern thought:

> On the one hand there is atomistic individualism which sees the individual building his cognitive world (and indeed any other) by orderly, step by step, individual effort, possibly maintaining cooperative relationships with others similarly engaged, but without this fundamentally affecting the nature of the enterprise, which in the end is solitary. ...
>
> On the other hand, there is romantic organism, which sees the community or the ongoing tradition as the real unit, transcending the individual, who only finds the possibility of fulfilment and creativity and thought, even or especially of identity itself, within that community. (Gellner 1998: 181)

Each of these visions of society takes a very distinctive view of the nature of humanity. People are either individualists accepting membership of a community in a contractual spirit, but reserving the right to choose what they want from their society and to exit from it if it suits them to do so, or they are social animals who can only find fulfilment through participating in and belonging to their distinctive culture. To leave the group would attract censure from other members and would be seen as contrary to the individual's own interest.

The first of these two traditions, which prioritises the individual, has developed into the dominant strand of Western philosophy, growing in importance since the Renaissance.[1] Today, it underpins neo-liberal philosophy and all the positions which believe that individuals are free to judge for themselves, and that there are no cognitive hierarchies or authorities. Gellner argued that, as an explanation, individualism grossly misrepresents the human condition, both in terms of the historical development of humanity and with regard to its social organisation. He believed that people were not individualistic at an early stage in history. They needed a basis for obligation and cooperation, a worldview that integrated the natural and the social, a communal source of symbolism to give meaning to existence. He held that individualism conspicuously fails to provide for these needs. The prioritising of the individual is peculiar to a few particular settings.

On the other hand, the rival position, romantic communalism, recognises that society does exist, that life is lived in terms of shared ideas, concepts and values. Communalism makes every undertaking a 'team game', anchors the individual to the group and the place and provides for belonging and continuity through myths of origin and ancestors. But, according to Gellner,[2] communalism is based on equally false premises and rules for living that are not always conducive to human happiness either. In particular, the idea that the beliefs, attitudes, norms, ways of doing things of the group are sacrosanct and cannot be challenged imprisons and constrains members. Communalists by looking inward and placing a high value on conservation and tradition have usually stifled the spheres of cognition and production.

Gellner concludes his analysis of these two competing philosophies by claiming that they are not as mutually exclusive as their respective supporters contend. He believes that our modern experience is actually communalism shot through with the transcendence that can come with the freedoms of individualism. He believes that this made the modern world, and when people:

> began to think as individuals, and to break up their world as an intellectual exercise, that they also broke through the erstwhile limits on cognition and production. It was then that the great scientific and economic revolutions took place. (Gellner 1998: 183)

He concludes that the 'possibility of transcendence of cultural limits is a fact; it is the single most important fact about human life' (Gellner 1998: 187).

I have explained Gellner's position at some length because it seems to me that his reconciliation of these two philosophical positions can be extended into the domain of language and are useful for the present discussion. He makes clear that there are necessary compromises if we are to remain anchored within our group (to fulfil our needs for identity, stability and belonging) and at the same time respond to ambitions of transcending our community (to fulfil our needs for self-actualisation, cognition and exploration). Could his description of the way

> mankind has shifted, and is continuing to shift from relatively self-contained communities to a wider community endowed with powerful knowledge which works more or less in terms of norms conveyed by the individualist model. (Gellner 1998: 188)

be used as a framework to explain what is happening and what could happen in language groups? Many of us are shifting between small or medium communities of communication and the wider communities of global networks and flows. The key question is whether the phenomena of a spreading lingua franca and global networks can be reconciled to a growing desire to conserve community and traditional ways of meaning, or whether they are competing phenomena that cannot easily coexist.

Given that so many of us are products of 'one people, one territory, one language' nationalism, the possibility of a dual language regime seems idealistic, but perhaps there are reasons to believe that we may be in a period where the blocks to solving language problems in this way may be fewer.

The first reason to believe that there may have been a paradigm shift is political. A number of political scientists have advanced the argument that the political organisation of twenty-first-century Europe, with its overlapping authorities and multilayered loyalties, mirrors in some ways the essential characteristics of medieval Europe where no ruler had total sovereignty (Bull 1977; Held *et al.* 1999). In this prenational model, the monarch had to share authority with vassals below, and with the Pope and, in many cases, the Holy Roman Emperor above. Can governance in the twenty-first century be seen to be returning in some respects to this arrangement? Certainly power is no longer concentrated *solely* at the level of the state. National governments share their authority with regional and world organisations and with sub-state or sub-national institutions. In tandem with this development, the concept of sovereignty has been challenged and with it the right of the state to command exclusive loyalty. If these changes strengthen, deepen and spread, 'then a neo-medieval form of universal political order might be said to have emerged' (Bull 1977: 255).

In the quarter of a century since this speculation first circulated, it has become more likely[3] ... And if there are indeed such parallels between these two otherwise disparate sets of political arrangements, are there useful insights to be gained from remembering the linguistic arrangements of the medieval order? They provide a model of how language works with multilayered authority. In medieval Europe, the political arrangements made it necessary for those who interacted at European level to acquire the various media that allowed them to do so. A lingua franca allowed contact among clerics and scholars. All those not part of those circles practised the language of their immediate group. The state took a *laissez-faire* attitude towards language acquisition and practice. Now we could argue that there may come to be some parallels between language use in the twenty-first century and Medieval language communities. On the one hand, those who are part of the structures involved with regional and world authorities or those who participate in any way in the global networks, flows and exchanges use the lingua franca of those domains, English. On the other hand, there is an increasing desire to maintain or revive traditional languages that have been eclipsed and for sub-state or sub-national groups to use them in their public space.

This implies a challenge to 'one people, one territory, one language' nationalism. However, the discussion in the preceding chapters has shown how much is predicated on experience with this national model, even when we are rejecting it. For example, English as a lingua franca is seen as a threat because it is assumed that it will replace the first language of the learner as the national language did. For example, those engaged in the revitalisation of minority languages believe they can only do so by replicating nation building policy and planning processes. For example, languages become 'endangered' because they are not used in political institutions, commercial circles or education, and speakers appear to assign little value to them if they are only used as the media of civil society and domestic life.

The reconciliation of community and transcendence might well depend on an adoption of a model that turns its back on nationalism, and re-interprets the multilayered practices of prenational societies for a postnational context. If, following the model of old Central Europe, we were to start viewing bilingualism as a prestige activity rather than a practice for the powerless, we would take the first step in a new development.

Grosjean (1982) reminded us 20 years ago that bilingualism is accepted by much of the world as the solution to language diversity. Such acceptance was then out of favour, however, in all those countries where national state ideology had taken hold. Individuals from minority groups were always under pressure both from the minority community itself and the state to become competent in the national language. Learning the national language was in the minority's interest since it served mobility and inclusion. The minority's acceptance to do so was also in the interest of the majority since it served cohesion and solidarity. So, it usually happened. But the process did not halt there. Bilingualism in nationalism was rarely stable (unless there were sinister reasons for separate development). Since national language was intertwined with patriotism, nation builders were always likely to press minorities to take the further step from second language acquisition and bilingualism to full-scale shift. Mother tongue maintenance, even with bilingualism, made the majority suspect schismatic tendencies among autochthonous minorities and inadequate loyalty among allochthonous groups.

In addition to the ideological pressures working against bilingualism, there are also all the practical difficulties that were discussed in Chapter 9. In the situations where language becomes a zero sum game (medium of education, law courts, political process, commercial negotiations) the competition between national language and minority language was always unequal.

Now in the new situation where the need to act at supra-, inter-, transnational level has entered the equation, members of minorities who wish to maintain their first language and have access to global networks are faced with the need to manage personal trilingualism. In some ways this is even more problematic than bilingualism, in that there are now even more languages available for use in each domain. However, this apparent complication may also lead to simplification. Certainly, the competition between the minority language and the lingua franca is different in kind from that between national and minority language, since the two functions of the first pair are more clearly demarcated than in the second. Learning and speaking the language of wider communication is different from learning and speaking the national language. Both may be acts of transcendence, allowing the individual to move outside the primary group. Instrumental motivation may fuel both, as individuals make the decision to acquire the language to fulfil personal ambitions, access higher education and interact on a wider stage. The difference lies in the integrative motivation at play. The big difference between minorities who learn the national language and those who learn English as a language of international communication in order to transcend the group is that the former are involved in a process of integration as well. The latter are primarily 'individualists accepting membership of a community in a contractual spirit, but reserving the right to choose what they want from it and to exit from it if it suits them to do so' (Gellner 1998: 181). There might perhaps be an element of integrative motivation towards the ideologies of globalisation and it would be foolish to believe that the actors and agencies of globalisation could be culturally neutral. The big difference, however, is that there is no central global group systematically requiring cultural and linguistic integration. The supranational level has no consistent interest in issues of group identity and loyalty. The loyalty that the state requires of citizens has no parallel at global level.

Are there any indications that the global lingua franca is replacing the national language as language of transcendence for speakers from smaller language groups? Since some power is now located at a supra-or international level, the international lingua franca may be adequate to serve the individual's project for mobility and inclusion if ambition is to act on a wider stage. Going to the capital to realise ambitions may occur less frequently if governance is diffuse. The instrumental reasons to master and use the national language diminish as those to learn English increase.

There is thus a theoretical possibility that minority language speakers will opt for English-minority language bilingualism over national-minority language bilingualism in the future if they have a choice. In Europe there are an estimated 40 million who belong to minority language groups and who could find themselves in this position. There might be some enthusiasm for this from those groups that have had a stormy relationship with their majority groups and national elites.[4]

One might expect to see further renaissance and revitalisation of local languages as small groups seek ways of affirming their identity in a global environment, and do not find that affirmation in the national. One can appreciate how local language medium communalism could be attractive in a context where transcendence of the group can be assured by a lingua franca. Such bilingualism would be relatively stable since the subsequent pressure to shift that occurs in the national model would not occur and because English in its lingua franca form would not necessarily develop in affective domains and so encroach to fulfil the needs of community.

The residual legacy of nationalism, the perception that bilingualism[5] is a disadvantage and is to be avoided, is fading as more people become bilingual to function at supra- and international level. National majorities in non-English-speaking countries are now increasingly likely to be bilingual. Even English native speakers have a clear need to develop bidialectal skills to maintain their own language of community in all its first language complexity and to learn to communicate effectively in International English.

This is all, of course, highly speculative. Such a globalised future, where identity is served by membership of small language groups and communication is catered for as an ever-larger percentage of populations learn the current lingua franca presupposes a withering of the state in its present form, and the process could still move into reverse.

If the scenario that I am sketching out does prove to have some substance, however, the differentiation enshrined in the role of the two languages makes it hopeful that the resulting bilingualism will be stable. As Romaine (1995) has pointed out, bilingualism does not continue across generations unless the role of the two languages is differentiated and they are reserved for different functions that do not overlap. The language of wider diffusion is linked to well delineated formal domains and is removed from the affective purposes that are the role of the mother tongue or first language. These are separated out with the result that the language of the group remains the language of identity and is protected, in a way that was never possible when minorities were being incorporated into nations. There are of course disadvantages: power issues remain and there are linguistic effects. For example, the diglossic nature of the arrangement means that only English would develop the lexis for certain formal domains.

Kymlicka (1995) dismisses the idea that generalised bilingualism could disaggregate the functions of language into language for identity and language for communication in this way. I would agree with him that it is impossible to compartmentalise totally language of culture and language of utility. All languages in one's repertoire will have elements of each aspect within them. However, in a world where there are advantages in gaining access to the wider world and where, at the same time, individuals exhibit a profound desire to maintain their affective links with the groups into which they were socialised, it seems likely that many might come to choose this differentiated bilingualism rather than any of the alternatives. The two possible monolingual scenarios would be totally unacceptable. The first, linguistic convergence at the supranational level and a shift to global English would destroy the cohesion of communities and might be the path to anomie (Baehr 2001) if English supplants rather than supplements other languages. Eggington (2001) warns that replacement would mean cultural impoverishment with the subtractive domination of a monoculture and the victory of raw Capitalism with the institutionalisation of hierarchies and a 'never to have' class. The second, limiting or refusing the lingua franca, confines members within the group and makes fracture more likely if those who want to bridge the two worlds are prevented from doing so. Only a minority of communities could maintain the isolation necessary for this. Moreover, isolation is never undertaken for the sole aim of protecting language; it is always dependent on other variables.

All monolingual solutions either dismiss the importance of transcending cultural limits or reject community and ongoing tradition as central to fulfilment, creativity and identity. Only a bilingual solution goes any way to supplying a solution: the group language provides for socialisation, rootedness, continuity and identity and the language of wider diffusion allows access to higher education, to international networks, to information in the international arena, to social and geographical mobility.

Human beings have always moulded language to their ends. In the past the medium of the group was sometimes used to bar entry, to maintain difference. The one good thing about English and globalisation is that there is no actual exclusion. There may be all the advantages that accrue to those who possess the language of power and there may be a hierarchy that puts non-native speakers in a weaker position, but, as the language is taken up in more and more sites, the advantages are spread more widely. And unlike most goods, they are not even spread more thinly. In many ways language is much easier to deal with than other commodities. Unlike almost every other resource, it is inexhaustible. As Auguste Comte pointed out, language is a kind of wealth that everyone can use without diminishing the store. The more it is used the more useful it becomes and no one individual can exhaust the allotment of another (cited in Bourdieu 1991: 42). Grin (1999) has made the useful suggestion that we should treat English as we do literacy. Competence in it opens up access to knowledge and understanding. And just as we would not see written language as a threat to spoken, so, if the roles are clearly differentiated, the lingua franca ought not to impinge on the language of community.

Fishman (2002) warns against talk of English as 'a killer language' and 'linguistic genocide'. He suggests that there is too much reliance on metaphor in sociolinguistics and that it makes for imprecise conceptualisation. These terms push us to misplace agency. A language can *do* nothing. Only speakers can decide or not whether they will use a language. Although they always act under the influence of all the variables that we have discussed, the speakers are always the final arbiters of whether a language survives or not.

Perhaps this is where the scholars of LPLP can be most useful, monitoring what people are doing and want to do. This is the plea that Fishman (2002) made recently. He said that the field will only really fulfil its potential when we have the critical mass of case study knowledge that will allow us to aggregate the particular to get a clear view of the general. To extend his call for more empirical work, I would also petition for more targeted investigation of how the three levels (global/national/local) are developing and interacting linguistically. It is only when we have more evidence that we will be able to judge if there is a leaking away from the national in language practice as there is in other spheres of activity.

The other plea that I would make is for more work on reconceptualising the key ideas of the subject area. As I have researched and written this book, it has become clear how much current work on lingua francas, linguistic rights and endangered languages is still framed by the nationalist paradigm even though we may actually be moving beyond the national model. Without reconceptualisation, and influenced by the language and nationalism model, Gellner's reconciliation seems idealistic, naïve and impossible. If we start to move beyond, it glimmers as a possibility which could contribute to coexistence and general well-being.

Notes

1 Introduction

1. A common accusation. Wierzbicka is one among many who charge him with this. She says that 'Chomsky's thoughts on the subject of lexical universals are based on speculative reflection rather than on any empirical investigations' (Wierzbicka 1992: 6).
2. There was always some self-questioning within the group. See, for example, Rubin and Jernudd (1971).
3. Migration was temporarily halted by the oil crises of the mid-1970s that put the world into recession and made Western governments seek to stem the tide of labour from Asia, Africa and the Caribbean.
4. See the special edition of *MOST* (2003).
5. The term Ecolinguistics was coined by Haugen (1972) to refer to the societal arrangements necessary if languages are to be preserved.
6. For a review of some of the analytical work recently carried out see Fill (2001) and Goatly (2001).
7. Together with two other major themes of LPLP, language and migration and language and colonisation. I have not dealt with these two themes at length in this book. This is, in part, because of considerations of space and cohesion, but also because there is already a very rich literature in both areas.

2 From Language Continuum to Linguistic Mosaic: European Language Communities from the Feudal Period to the Age of Nationalism

1. Hroch (1985) wrote an influential comparative study of civic and ethnic nations in the late 1960s which was published in German and Czech. It was not available in English translation until 1985. For a fuller discussion of civic and ethnic nations, see Wright (2000a).
2. One can speculate that the language patterns described prevailed for the ten centuries between the end of the Roman Empire and the beginning of the Modern period. There is, of course, less evidence for language practices in the earlier period and the argument is based largely on the Late Medieval period (1200–1500) where contemporary accounts exist, but where, perhaps, the isolation of peasants on the land was lessening.
3. This differed in different parts of the continent, dropping to 60% in the Netherlands and in Italy and rising to 95% + in Ireland, Scotland, Scandinavia and the Slavic East (Fossier 1970). Singman (1999) suggests that the low level of technology and poor health of the peasant class made agriculture very hungry for manpower.
4. There are, of course, exceptions. In periods of demographic growth, some members of the agricultural class took part in the clearing of new lands. For example, as the Teutonic knights conquered East Prussia they recruited a peasant population from western Europe to farm the new lands (Davis 1988).

5. Fossier (1970) points out that this was a restriction designed to guarantee that the children born to serfs belonged indisputably to the master of the parents. Serfdom was dying out in many parts of Europe by 1300 although it lingered in England well into the century and resurfaced in the east of the continent as German settlers colonised Slav lands (Nicholas 1999). Bourin and Durand (1998) discuss the difficulty of marrying those outside one's own *seigneurie* which persisted until very late in the period in the lands under French control.

6. Where other classes mentioned them the picture tends to be disparaging and stereotypical (Singman 1999).

7. The definition of feudal in this chapter is based on Bloch (1962): a subject peasantry, widespread use of the fief instead of a salary; a specialised warrior class with ties of obedience and protection; fragmentation of authority.

8. For the history of this period see Bideleux and Jeffries (1998).

9. For numerous examples see the *Biographical Dictionary of the Late Medieval Age* (Drees, C. (ed.) *The Late Medieval Age of Crisis and Renewal, 1300–1500: A Biographical Dictionary*, Westport, CT: Greenwood Press 2001).

10. 'In the Middle Ages the people of Western Europe regarded themselves as a single society, which they often likened to the seamless robe of Christ' (Davis 1988: 350).

11. Although the Latin term *nationes* was used, for example, in the Sorbonne, it simply indicated the locality one came from, in a much more limited geographical sense than the modern term *nationality* (Seton-Watson 1977; Greenfeld 1992).

12. See below; the French king starts to address the problem with the Edict of Villers–Cotterêts (1539) and the English king with the Act of Union (1536).

13. The few exceptions to this that have been recorded are the speeches to fighting forces, with perhaps the most famous example being the Serments de Strasbourg (842) where Charlemagne's grandsons swore oaths before their respective armies in the vernaculars of the two armies (lingua romana and lingua teudisca).

14. Increasingly armies became professionalised and paid from the fourteenth century (Nicholas 1999).

15. For a comprehensive review of the literature on nationalism and an explanation of the different traditions of the scholarship in the area see Özkirimli (2000).

16. Hroch (1985) includes Russia as one of the early state nations but I have left it out because it seems to me that the attitude of the Czars to their subjects was entirely in the mould of feudal monarchs and that the Russian state remained very much an agricultural society where the aspects of Modernity described here and seen to be contributory to the growth of nationalism did not occur until a later date.

17. There were minor adjustments to the boundary between France and Italy in 1947.

18. Between 1128 and 1279, the House of Burgundy took the crown and reconquered the territory that was to become Portugal. There is a general consensus that this happened mainly because Castile was too busy elsewhere to oppose the Portuguese:

> The question of the roots of Portuguese individuality and the formation of a separate monarchy in the southwest has provoked considerable discussion. The two great Portuguese historians of the nineteenth century, Alexandre Herculano and Oliveira Martins, considered Portuguese independence somewhat accidental, the consequence of fortuitous political developments in the twelfth century. (Payne 1976: 113)

19. The English monarchy retained only Calais. This was ceded to France in 1559 at the Treaty of Cateau–Cambresis.

20. The Treaties of Aix-la-Chapelle (1668) and Nijmegen (1678) set the frontier between France and the Flemish north. In 1860 the south-eastern frontier of France was extended to include Nice and Savoy. Alsace, Lorraine and Franche-Comté were conquered in the seventeenth and eighteenth centuries although subsequently lost and conquered again.

21. This was not always unpopular. Nordman (1998) charts the history of local rivalries in the Cerdagne and notes that the Franco-Spanish border was welcomed by some groups as a way of differentiating themselves from their neighbours and rivals.

22. For example the Cathars who would not convert to Catholicism were massacred at Montsegur in 1244. For example the Muslims of Granada conquered in 1492 were forcibly converted under the direction of Francisco Jiménez de Cisneros (1436–1517). In the same year the Spanish monarchy ordered the expulsion of all Spanish Jews.

23. The rise of the idea of sovereignty was favourable to the development of the state nations but stemmed the process whereby subject peoples could break away from larger polities. The rise of the ethnic nation states did not begin, in part because of this, until the nineteenth century (Cobban 1969).

24. Although territory continued to be conquered and lost in Europe, this concern to stop any one player becoming too powerful helped stabilise frontiers since rulers understood the sanctions if they challenged the balance. The race for colonies and the intra-European conflicts outside Europe both contravene this point and reinforce it. Changes of boundaries outside Europe were not seen in the same light, although the desire to retain the overall balance of power in colonial conquest remained.

25. Anderson (1983) has termed this variety print language but it is in many cases (e.g. French and English) identical with the language of the court and the capital and I would argue that the prestige deriving from its associations was a key factor in the choice of variety. If printers were principally driven by profit they are likely to have set out to secure the most prosperous market segments. It seems unnecessary then to call it print language in these states, since it does not develop separately.

26. The phenomenon was not solely in Protestant areas. A growing desire for access to the Bible meant that it was translated into the vernacular in Catholic countries too. Welsh was the only non-state language of Protestant Europe to become the medium of a published Bible within a century of the Reformation. The Irish did not get their own Bible until 1690; the Scots had to wait until 1801 for their Gaelic Bible, long after the Highland clearances and massive emigration had almost emptied the country of its Gaelic speakers. Interestingly, both Wyclif and Huss had translated the Scriptures, but, before the advent of printing, this had not had great impact.

27. Patriotism was, of course, republican vocabulary and it is slightly anachronistic to employ it here, but the term expresses the point.

28. Documentary evidence for this comes from texts such as Elizabeth I's Charter to Sir Walter Raleigh (1584). The race to discover parts of the world hitherto unknown to Europeans and to grab resources and claim colonies caused acute rivalry between monarchs and the colonisation race deepened the demarcation lines between their states. The last time the Europeans had set out *en masse* to take territory on other continents had been the Crusades. Although the desire for personal wealth and advancement may have been just as much the motivation for

the individuals who went to the Crusades as it was for those who went to take lands in Asia, Africa and the Americas, the discourses that authorise the two enterprises have very different emphases. The texts that defend the Crusades evoke the idea of the brotherhood of European knights engaged in a common cause, to secure the Holy Land for Christendom. The texts that defend the right of conquest in the new world also cloak territorial ambition in the mission to spread Christianity, but at the same time they defend the endeavour as being in the *national* interest. The adventurers had the support of the Christian monarchs to take these lands in their name, and their piracy was presented as a patriotic endeavour for the *greater good of the country*. The reports of the conflicts between these soldiers of adventure show how the protagonists defined themselves and their rivals according to *nationality*.

The same process was happening in all the Absolutist states. In Russia there was the development of unswerving loyalty and direct attachment to the person of the tsar 'by God's will the sole power-holder and head of the church' (Szporluk 1990: 2).

29. A number of historians make the case that the seeds of such centralisation and bureaucratisation can be traced to earlier eras (e.g. Davis 1988).
30. For a discussion of the role of language in democracy see Wright (2000a).
31. The methodology is contested but it is clear that whatever the actual statistics, the Abbé Grégoire found extreme linguistic diversity.
32. See the debate in the French press (October–December 2001) on the funding of Breton medium schools for contemporary expressions of this stance.
33. Elias (1996) points out that the lack of clear frontiers, the absence of a single dominant dynasty and the shifting power centres of the German-speaking world gave it a very different perspective compared with the French- and English-speaking groups.
34. It would be anachronistic in the view of some commentators (Breuilly 1982) to see Herder as a nationalist. Nonetheless, his work became the cornerstone of nationalist theory.
35. The theory of the primordial nature of nations has been highly contested. In the academic community there are few who do not see both nation states and state nations as the direct consequence of the political actions and decisions of elite groups under the pressures of modernity. Belief in ethnic nationalism is almost entirely confined to activists.
36. Or *Standardsprache,* as it is now often termed in a desire to move away from hierarchical connotations.
37. For example, Victor-Emmanuel had no qualms about gifting Nice and its county to Napoleon III in exchange for his support against the Austrians, despite the fact that the town was the birthplace of one of the key architects of Italian nationalism, Garibaldi. Most Niçois were actually in agreement, seeing France as a better commercial prospect and their cultural and linguistic ties as dispensable (Wright 2002).
38. Nairn's view reflects a widely held position that nations are constructed by elites who have to persuade the proto-nation to see itself as such and so bid for independence. The argument suggests that no independence movement would arise spontaneously without some intellectual inspiration and moulding.
39. This is exemplified by the change of policy in the French Revolution described above. The acceptance of diversity and the agreement to customise the message soon changed to a concerted effort to make French citizens French speakers.

40. As, for example, in the large numbers of Hungarian speakers incorporated into Romania and Yugoslavia, and German speakers into Italy to ensure the continued weakness of Hungary and Austria.
41. This linguistic similarity did not prove enough for lasting association and on 1 January 1993 the Czechs and Slovaks split to form two states.
42. After the Second World War, a number of international institutions, regimes and supranational organisations began to alter the strict system of national autonomy described here. The second section of the book deals with this and the effect on language use that this has caused.
43. These were a cause and effect of the Great Depression. The United States passed the Smoot–Hawley Tariff Act to raise tariffs on imports by nearly 60%. Sixty countries retaliated and ultimately all were hurt by the downturn in trade that was caused by competitive devaluation and protective tariffs. Keynes was one of the first to alert the public to this: 'Each nation in an effort to improve its relative position takes measures injurious to the absolute prosperity of its neighbours' (Keynes 1932).
44. Where natural and political borders did not coincide this made economic life difficult. Before 1860 Nice and its county suffered from this. It could trade within Piedmont–Savoy without border taxes but with immense difficulty since the routes were over high mountain passes where no good roads existed, or it could trade with France which was physically easy in that there was only the river Var to cross but for which there were heavy duties. This was perhaps the major reason for the decision taken by the Niçois to accept their inclusion in France.
45. Media and mass culture were of course only to be contained within national boundaries for a very limited period and the processes of globalisation have since changed this description.

3 Language Planning in State Nations and Nation States

1. This is akin to the points made by Paul Brass about vertical integration and elite permeability. He argues that the sufficient conditions for the growth of national sentiment are the existence of a means to communicate the selected symbols of identity to other social classes, a socially mobilised population open to the message and the absence of intense class cleavage or other difficulties of communication between elites and other social groups and classes (Brass 1991).
2. See, for example, the discussion in Burke *et al.* (2000: 249) and in Milroy and Milroy (1985).
3. This was the case for both the Breton and Welsh nobility (Ager 1997). Joseph (1987) discusses how, before the national period, those societies which associated power with literacy often cultivated the mystic, enigmatic and esoteric in order to restrict entry to the few.
4. A recent change in the law (September 2002) has just raised some restrictions in Turkey. Now privately run schools can teach Kurdish. A number of restrictions mean that this is likely to affect only a small part of the Kurdish group.
5. 'In Florina (northern Greece) where most ethnic Macedonians live, four ethnic Macedonians were put on trial in September 1998 for 'inciting citizens to commit acts of violence'. The charges stem from an incident in September 1995 when a mob led by the mayor attacked and ransacked the offices of the ethnic Macedonian Rainbow party after the four defendants hung a sign in Greek and in Macedonian stating 'Rainbow–Florina Committee'. Those who attacked the

offices were never indicted, although a complaint was filed by the Rainbow party. However, the party was prosecuted for using the Macedonian language on the sign. The party was acquitted on 15 September due to intense international pressure (*Human Rights Watch Report* 1999).

6. While some officials in the United Nations, the Russian Government, and members of the local ethnic Russian community continued to criticise the Estonian Citizenship Law as discriminatory, notably for its Estonian language requirements, the Organisation for Security and Cooperation in Europe (OSCE) as well as other international fact-finding organisations, including the Finnish Helsinki Committee, ruled that the Citizenship Law conformed to international standards. However, the Estonian language requirement has blocked and delayed applications for citizenship. The Government has established language-training centres, but there is a lack of qualified teachers, financial resources and training materials. Since 1999, Ethnic Russian deputies in the State Assembly must be Estonian speakers. Estonian law prohibits the use of any foreign language on public signs, advertisements, and notices, including election posters (US Bureau of Democracy, Human Rights, and Labor 2001).

7. In its refusal to ratify the Council of Europe's Charter for Regional Minority Languages signed in 1999.

8. In the wake of signing the Maastricht Treaty and in a situation of increasing transnational exchange the French government felt the need to make the status of French in France explicit. A sentence was inserted in Article 2 of the Constitution of 4 October 1958: *La langue de la République est le français.*

9. Spain, on the other hand, is a state nation which ruled on its official language at an early stage. Castilian was declared the language of state in 1714. It was far from being the language adopted throughout the territory and among all social classes at that time. Article 3 of the 1978 Spanish Constitution reiterates that Castilian is the official language of the State.

10. The bilingual cantons of Fribourg and Valais/Wallis (French and German) and trilingual Graubünden (German, Italian and Romansh).

11. The claim for Irish to be a distinct variety of English is supported by the recent analysis of a southern Irish corpus collected by researchers at Limerick University at the turn of the twentieth/twenty-first century.

12. For the whole country. There were censuses in Lower Rhine, Upper Rhine and Moselle in 1946 and 1962.

13. The thesis is weakened by the fact that countries of immigration ask the language question on their censuses. There is, of course, a need to have this data for educational provision. Interestingly, in 1980 the US census amended its question on respondents' mother tongue to ask whether the respondent and household spoke English and how well.

14. There is some dissension over the provenance of some of the texts ascribed to Mikhail Bakhtin (1895–1975), Pavel Medvedev (1891–1938) and Valentin Voloshinov (1884–1936?). These men met and discussed as part of the same circles in the early Soviet period (1918–28). The authorship of some work may have been collaboration (Morris 1994).

15. Thomas (1991) records how individual linguists often spearheaded the drive to elaborate, extend and purify the language in the nationalist cause, how they grouped together in informal associations and then as the project succeeded, how the state recognised their work and funded their work in institutes.

16. In particular by the introduction of three new vowel forms into the written language ä, ö and å.

17. Because of the development of two standards in Norway. Bokmal is used in the eastern parts and cities, and Nynorsk is used mostly in the western and rural parts of Norway.

18. For a discussion of Slovakian attitudes towards nationhood in general and language in particular in the period between the founding of the state and Slovakian autonomy under the Third Reich, see Karpat (1993). For a review of the same period from a Czech perspective, see Slapnicka (1993).

19. Discussed in more depth in Chapter 7.

20. In July 1917, Pašiæ and the Yugoslav Committee issued the so-called Corfu Declaration, which declared that a postwar state would be a united Kingdom of the Serbs, Croats and Slovenes, under the Karageorgevic dynasty, with common citizenship for Serbs, Croats and Slovenes, equality in religion, and the use of both alphabets, Latin and Cyrillic.

21. Those who argue that there is only one Serbo-Croatian say that the two languages were standardised as a unitary language by Vuk Stefanovic Karadzic in the first half of the nineteenth century. Croatians maintain that Croatian standardisation started in the early seventeenth century (Katièiæ 1997).

22. The oldest written form of a Slavic language is Old Church Slavonic. It is generally believed that St. Cyril invented Glagolitic, and that Cyrillic which is named after him was developed by some of his students.

23. See Franolić (1983) and Katičić (1997) for the history of discussions and in particular the positions taken at the Vienna Literary Convention 1850.

24. There is no consensus on the influence of audio–visual media. Milroy and Milroy (1985) believe that spread of the RP accent in the United Kingdom has not been an outcome of exposure to television, recording that viewers do not accommodate to models. Cheshire, Kerswill and Williams (2002), on the other hand, accept that television may have an effect on pronunciation, since rising intonation among younger age groups is becoming general. They suggest that this comes from imitation of speakers in the large number of Australian soaps offered to that age group in the 1990s.

25. See Joseph (1987) for a full discussion of this point. Also Haugen (1972: 325) who argues that:

> Language exists only in the mind of its users, and it only functions in relating these users to one another and to nature, i.e. to their social and natural environment.

26. I hesitate to give an exact date because it is under dispute. Edwards (1985) cites sources, which give 1582, 1572 and 1546. This is perhaps understandable as there were a number of literary groups in the city which concerned themselves with language and which predate the interest of the Medicis.

27. Even though there is general scholarly agreement that the dictionaries produced by the Académie have been long in coming and have not always been at the cutting edge of lexicography (Hall 1974).

28. The popularity of spelling bees in the United States testifies to a similar folk acceptance of the need to master the national language correctly.

29. There are claims that dictionary making moved from prescription to description long before this but, as Benson (2001: 9) points out, while lexicographers continue to adjudicate on the acceptability of words, the process remains essentially prescriptive.

30. Only contemporary borrowings from High German were held to be particularly offensive; older loan words from Low German were more acceptable perhaps because they were not recognised as borrowings (Karker 1983).

31. This was the conclusion arrived at in debate at the Globe conference, held in Warsaw in September 2002. A number of papers and responses from the floor made this point.

32. For example the tax levied on foreign words in shop signs from 1923 onwards in Italy (Lepschy and Lepschy 1988).

33. Chapter 6 includes a discussion of the (mostly unsuccessful) attempts of the French government to restrict borrowing from English in the last half of the twentieth century.

34. At the time when Prussia was educating 1 in 6 of its population only 1 in 12 of the population in England was engaged in education (Report on 'Proportion of scholars in elementary schools to whole population' recorded in Arnold (1865–67/1964)).

35. Concern to teach children the rights and duties of citizenship in the Republic and 'guard against ignorance' was a constant. In 1848, the Minister of Education, Carnot, sent a circular to exhort teachers to present the Republican cause. Teachers were asked to prepare manuals modelled on the Catholic catechism. After 1870, such manuals became a core of the Third Republic's basic educational provision (Harrigan 1980).

36. In the event, it was not education alone that decided the shift to the standard language. General conscription and military service in the trenches of Northern France during the First World War seems to have been a major factor in the universal adoption of French (Wright 2000a).

37. The link between nationalism, industrialisation (and education) was formerly discussed in the writings of Bauer (1924) and Marx (1976).

38. Gellner has been attacked as overly functionalist (cf. Özkirimli 2000) but the reasoning that there was a relationship between language, education and industrialisation seems to fit the evidence available. At the very least, there is nothing to show that industrialisation and urbanisation worked against nationalism; in numerous cases, they seemed to accompany it.

39. Industrialisation also contributed to language shift in other ways as well, because it pulled workers from the country into urban centres, which eventually became linguistic melting pots eradicating dialectal difference and promoting convergence to the national language. This was, however, a lengthy and complex process. For a discussion of these complexities in England, see Joyce (1991).

40. Groups from different parts of the German-speaking world (in its widest definition) had migrated to the area from the twelfth century onwards and had maintained their language over centuries.

41. Croatia had come under Hungarian tutelage in 1091 and speakers from the southern Slav continuum had migrated north after the Turkish invasion and settlement of their lands.

42. Speakers of Romanian had migrated west from the fourteenth century.

43. Slovaks and other Slavic populations had moved into the Carpathian mountains fleeing the Tartar invasions of the thirteenth century.

44. The Jesuits were the dominant teaching order. From 1599, the *Ratio studiorum* (the statutes of Jesuit education) set the syllabus and medium for Jesuit schools. Latin played a major role. Kurdybacha (1973: 133) says of the parallel

situation in Poland:

> These (Jesuit) schools taught the young people mainly Latin, overburdened them with rhetoric, and kept them busy with elaborate religious ceremonies.

45. This was not true for Protestant German speakers of course and even the Catholic German speakers were more likely to have had vernacular education at secondary level.
46. Even though the Declaration of Independence 14 April 1849 paved the way for a draft constitution, which would have included the rights of minorities.
47. In 1831, Magyar competence was necessary to become a lawyer. In 1838, Magyar became the official language of the Diet. In 1839, it became the language of bureaucracy in its internal communication. In 1844, it became the official language of secondary schooling.
48. After the First World War, the Treaty of Trianon (1920) redrew the frontiers of the Hungarian state. Much reduced in size, the population was more homogeneous and the minorities that remained were at the least bilingual (Hevizi 2002).
49. Breuilly rather cynically suggests the opposite. He maintains that intensified communication can actually increase conflict (Breuilly 1982). Whether this is true or not it was obviously not an argument that weighed with European nation builders.
50. As seems to be the case in the Romanian repression of Hungarian, as well as the Turkish repression of Kurdish and the Greek repression of Macedonian mentioned at the beginning of the chapter.
51. This is particularly clear in the case of the eastern provinces of present day France. In the century 1850–1950, the population of this area was alternately French, German, French, German, French. Documenting the period post 1870 and post 1918, Hartweg (1993) shows how the language issue dominated political incorporation and participation. Even where there might have been some acceptance of membership of the new group, language barriers prevented enactment of that membership.

4 Nation Building in the Wake of Colonialism: Old Concepts in New Settings

1. Ethnologue Report for Indonesia, Summer Institute of Linguistics (2001). (This figure does not take into account the full linguistic diversity of Papua.) On some islands, particularly along the coastal plains, these are interrelated languages and dialects spaced along dialect continua and mutually comprehensible although geographical, social and functional restrictions distinguish them. However, many languages of Indonesia are substantially different from their geographical neighbours. The geographical conditions that permitted the isolation necessary for the survival of hunter–gatherer societies also allowed language groups to develop without outside contact and thus without exchange or convergence.
2. There are differences of opinion here because it is difficult to decide if languages are discrete within the dialect continua.
3. For example, Rivers State in Nigeria is typical. The area only has languages from one phylum (Niger–Congo) but there are two major families with significant subdivisions and communication without bilingualism is impossible.

4. The counter argument has been that these statistics are not conclusive and that homogeneous African countries are in the same economic difficulties. There are other important factors and variables, and, as ever, it is difficult to distinguish cause and effect in this area (cf. Joseph 1987). However, economic analysts are still reporting the same relationship thirty years on. Laitin reports that:

> Correlation analysis involving all counties of the world suggests that there is a positive statistical relationship between societies with diverse speech communities and low level economic development ... Scholars who provide policy advice accept these results and argue that economic development presupposes settlement of the language question and therefore depends on agreement on a single national language. (Laitin 1992: 54)

Mazrui and Mazrui (1998) suggest that it would be foolish to totally ignore the suggested correlation and that further investigation is clearly needed.

5. There are of course exceptions. The Ethiopic script used for Amharic in the north dates from the first millennium BC, when the Sabaean people (of the southwest corner of the Arabian Peninsula) began immigrating across the Red Sea to Ethiopia, bringing with them their language and its writing tradition. There were also written forms of African languages in West Africa where the Ajami script (based on Arabic) was used for Kanuri, Fulfude and Nupe from the early Modern period onwards.

6. The feasibility of providing mother tongue education in multilingual situations is discussed at length in Part III.

7. Colonial languages as languages of wider diffusion allowed access to ideas in science and technology developed in the West. The new national elites had been educated in these languages. Given this, it was inevitable that much would be borrowed from the European tradition and perhaps also inevitable that much of that borrowing would not be translated. Thus, for example, not only is basic law still based on European principles in many states, but also these laws are often expressed entirely in European languages. Borrowing has entailed both the concept and its linguistic expression (Mazrui and Mazrui 1998).

8. Since there was no written tradition for most indigenous languages there was no prestige alternative. Mazrui and Mazrui (1998) contend that the absence of clearly dominant indigenous languages led to weak linguistic nationalism and explains why African states have accepted the languages of former colonial powers as official languages.

9. This is now generally accepted in the field. Laitin (1992) among others makes the same point.

10. For many years European linguists had portrayed Swahili as a pidgin that had developed along the coast to facilitate exchange between the Bantu peoples who lived there and the Arabs that came to trade and ultimately to settle and rule (see, for example, Whiteley 1971). Bantu was held to be the base language, providing the phonological features and grammatical structures and Arabic the lexifier. This description was contested by Tanzanian scholars (e.g. Shariff 1979) and by Western scholars, after Hinnebusch *et al.* (1981) had carried out more careful linguistic analysis.

11. In the colonies of the British Empire, the British encouraged separate development. Their philosophy was not to destroy all former institutions but to build on them or rule through them, for example, the emirates of Northern Nigeria and

the Kabakaship of Buganda. The policy of some indirect rule through local chiefs thus helped to perpetuate the ethnic divisions of the territory. Education where it existed tended to be culturally relative and ethnically specific and so again maintained differences. Mazrui and Tidy (1984) categorise British colonial rule as racially arrogant, in that the colonisers insisted on distance between themselves and those they colonised, but culturally tolerant, in that they respected diversity and custom. French governance, on the other hand, was culturally arrogant, in that they imposed the French model on those they ruled and expected assimilation where they educated. In this, they left no space for difference, but were perhaps less racist than the British and other Germanic groups present in Africa (Mazrui and Tidy 1984). In consequence, the elites of those countries that had formerly been under French rule were arguably more cohesive in terms of language and culture than those that had been under British rule. Mazrui (1978) suggests that, despite the supposed contrasts between British eclecticism and French doctrinaire policies, by the end of the colonial period both colonial powers were educating a small intelligentsia who were then fluent in either English or French.

12. There had been some groundwork by Dr L. Krapf who produced a word list and grammar between 1842 and 1860, published 1882 and Bishop Steere who published the *Handbook of the Swahili language* in 1870. The inter-territorial language (Swahili) committee was set up in 1930 to establish a standard for educational purposes in Kenya, Tanganyila, Uganda and Zanzibar. The committee favoured the variety of Swahili from Zanzibar. In 1948, the work came under the control of the East African High Commission (Howell 1976).

13. Standardisation of language is always problematic. Ansre (1974) recounts how Doke, the Bantu scholar, participating in the standardisation of Shona, decided to amalgamate several varieties to construct a unified literary language, grammar and dictionary. Lexical items from the varieties chosen were accepted but discouraged from a number of others. The language was to be used in the bureaucracy, for police exams, for missionaries. 'Shona became the language that everyone writes and no-one speaks' quoted by Ansre (1974: 383).

14. From that period onwards the scholarly literature often uses the Swahili term for the language, Kiswahili.

15. The aim of *Ujamaa* was to make the people and country self-reliant through a combination of traditional values of cooperation with socialism. *Ujamaa* entailed putting people into 'communes' so they could have access to education and medical facilities, and to make collective farming, based on the Chinese model, possible. This resulted in nearly ten million people being moved. It was believed that once an agricultural basis was formed industrial development would follow. The whole process, especially the communal farming, was not popular with many Tanzanians and was resisted. A fall in productivity at home and of commodity prices on world markets, coupled with less foreign aid and an increase in national debt led to economic disaster. *Ujamaa* began to crumble in the late 1970s and was abandoned in the mid-1980s. Despite being, ultimately, an economic disaster, *Ujamaa* did help raise health and education standards and helped impose Swahili as the national language of the one-party state.

16. In contrast, in Kenya, the political languages are Swahili and English which means competence in both is necessary and participation is restricted. According to Mazrui and Mazrui (1998) this may have ensured educated politicians but it was very restrictive democratically.

17. The government tried repeatedly to change the medium of secondary education to Swahili, but always met with resistance from the university in particular and

the elite in general. The shift never took place. For a full discussion of the reasons, see Mafu (2001).

18. There is no space here to discuss this at length. However, it is worth noting that the IMF and other Western institutions blamed economic problems on domestic mismanagement whereas the Tanzanians saw their difficult situation as deriving in large part from external forces over which they had no control. The value of coffee on the world market was halved over the course of the 1980s, for example.

19. Tanzania is one of the world's poorest countries. Around half of the population lives below the poverty line, one in six children die before the age of five, and almost one-third of the population will not live until the age of forty (Oxfam 1998). Tanzania has a GNP of $280 and a debt burden of $35 per capita (World Bank 2002).

20. Sometimes through English or French, sometimes in a local or regional language. The difficulties of this are discussed in Parts II and III at some length.

21. In Tanzania, the elite never transferred entirely to Swahili. Secondary and higher education remained in English despite continual efforts from socialist and nationalist groups. In colonial times Swahili medium education had provoked the reaction from the African middle class to demand 'English as their political right' (Ansre 1974).

22. Mazrui (2001) suggests that Africa westernised without modernising and acquired the trappings of modernity without the substance, which explains the lack of resilience to external pressures of an alien system.

23. The great trading Buddhist kingdom of Srivijaya flourished in Sumatera from the sixth/seventh to the twelfth/thirteenth centuries and, at the height of its powers, its empire reached as far as West Java and the Malay Peninsula. The Hindu kingdom of Majapahit dominated eastern Java in the last decade of the thirteenth century and succeeded in gaining allegiance from vassal states in Sumatera, the Malay Peninsula and Kalimantan. As the influence of Majapahit waned in the late fifteenth century, Malacca, an Islamic kingdom that controlled the coastal plains of East Sumatera and the Malay Peninsula and thus east–west trade lines, became the dominant regional state. In turn this kingdom fell in 1511 to the Portuguese, the first Europeans to come in search of spices (Drake 1993).

24. Irian Jaya has regained the name, Papua, since the granting of limited autonomy in 1999.

25. The Chinese pilgrim, I-Ching, recorded a visit in his notebooks (Hunter 1996).

26. See de Waard (2000) for the history of intermarriage and its effect on education, networks and linguistic practices in the Dutch colonial period. In 1893 there was a formal recognition of the division of education into Dutch medium and Malay medium.

27. De Waard (2000) records that the Vereenigde Oost–indische Compagnie (VOC) was interested primarily in profit and, therefore, economic as much as political considerations governed decisions on education. The result was very little funding for the system.

28. *Pancasila* consists of five key principles (faith in one god, humanitarianism, national unity, representative government and social justice) and prioritised the values of consensus and group unity, particularly in its vision of democracy. The principles were promoted as the basis for the contract between the citizen and the state, in much the same way that liberty, fraternity and equality are invoked in the relationship of the French state with its citizens.

29. Indonesia grew steadily, transforming itself from an agricultural backwater to a highly diversified manufacturing and export-driven state. Per-capita income

levels rose from $70 in 1966 to $900 in 1996, while the proportion of the population living below the poverty line declined from 60% to an estimated 11% over roughly the same period. The economy grew more than 7% annually from 1985 to 1996 (Ito 1998).

30. From 1524 to 1975, East Timor had been a Portuguese colony on the island of Timor. The Portuguese abruptly withdrew from Timor in 1975, leaving a power vacuum which was filled by the Marxist Fretilin party. The Indonesian Government, regarded this as a threat and invaded, overcoming Fretilin's regular forces in 1975–76. Thousands of people are believed to have died during the fighting or later starved to death. The UN never recognised Indonesia's incorporation of East Timor. In January 1999, the Indonesian government agreed to a process, under the aegis of the UN, whereby the people of East Timor would be allowed to choose between autonomy and independence through a direct ballot. In August 1999 they chose independence.

31. Soeharto's entourage benefited immensely from the economic expansion. Critics claim that the president regularly used his position to provide subsidies and tax relief for the companies of friends and family. At the end of his period in power, the family's fortune was valued between $16 billion to $35 billion in industries ranging from hotels and transportation, to banks and automobiles.

32. In December 2000 in Stockholm where Tiro was based.

33. They can play a role in the first three years of schooling. After that tuition moves to Indonesian. This is transitional bilingual education likely to lead to language shift in the individual, according to Skutnabb-Kangas (1981).

34. The 2001 census did not contain a language question and so it is difficult to see if this spread continues or not. The shortened census was attributed to financial constraints (Fieldwork 2002). These figures should be treated with some caution (Drake 1993). Self reporting in such a context may reveal as much about allegiance and identity as about language competence.

35. Indonesian is spoken as a first language in East Sumatera (Medan area), Riau Islands and Jambi, Java (Jakarta area), Western Kalimantan (Pontianac area), Sulawesi (Minahasa area), Moluccas (Ambon Island) and Indonesian Timor (Rubin 1977).

36. The main dialects of Malay spoken in Indonesia have been identified as Riau, Jakarta, Sambas, Deli, Melayu, Pasar, Borneo, Kota-waringin, Sukadana, Makakau, Irianese, Makassarese, Manadonese, Labu, Ritok, Balikpapan, Sampit, Bakumpai, West Borneo Coast Malay, Belide, Lengkayap, Aji, Daya, Mulak, Bangka, Belitung, Larantuka, Basa Kupang, Peranakan, Kutai Malay, Berau Malay, Bukit, Ambonese Malay, Bacan Malay, North Moluccan Malay, Kupang Malay, Enim, Kaur, Kayu Agung, Lematang, Lembak, Jambi Malay, Lintang, Penesak, Rawas, Sindang and Kelingi (Summer Institute of Linguistics 2001). Some of these names have alternatives and some varieties are very similar and are the subject of dispute as to whether they are the same variety or not. As is often the case in language claiming, affiliation has more to do with identity than linguistic criteria.

37. The Summer Institute of Linguistics (2001) estimates that perhaps some 80% are cognate with Indonesian although admits that further research is needed to verify the claim.

38. An example which shows that the divergence between the H and L form is not trivial can be found in the classifiers. The H form has a complex system of classifiers for flat, round, long, oblong, thin, comb-like, stem-like etc. The L form simply distinguishes between humans, animals and inanimates.

39. This was a problem in earlier nation building. The First French Republic wanted to put a French-speaking teacher into every commune but had neither the finance nor the linguistically competent workforce to implement the policy (Rickard 1989; Wright 2000a).

40. Pusat Pengembangan Penataran Guru (PPPG) initial and in-service teacher training for government schools.

41. Principally interviews at PPPG.

42. For example the Javanese, see below.

43. The teacher-training agency includes sensitisation to the problem in its initial teacher training programme and in-service development courses (interviews, PPPG 2002).

44. The educational problems in some of the provinces are profound with inadequate funding resulting in a severe lack of resources and teachers. For example, in January 2002 East Nusa Tenggara had a shortfall of 3200 teachers in its 3958 elementary, 541 junior high and 152 senior high schools (Provincial Bureau of Statistics quoted in *Jakarta Post* 10/1/2002, p. 7).

45. Moreover, English is often timetabled against classes in the local vernacular. For example, the early start programmes in English have taken the slots allotted to the study of Javanese, Sundanese, Madurese, Batak, Minang, Balinese and so on (PPPG 2001) which may also cause resentment.

46. Links between the ethnic Chinese and the Chinese state are not new. In the early twentieth century the Chinese decided to support Chinese speakers in Indonesia and funded Chinese medium schools. The Dutch reacted quickly to stop the influence and the schools closed (de Waard 2000).

47. For example, in the first eight days of 2002, thirty people were killed in a number of incidents (*Jakarta Post*, 10/01/2002).

48. The Javanese have a rich literary tradition and educated Javanese traditionally held Malay in some contempt as the language of the street (Vlekke 1959; Suroyohudoyo 1996).

49. See for example the Javanese Language Conference 22–26 October 1996 in Malang. The standardisation of Javanese for dissemination through the education system was one of the matters discussed.

50. See the advice in *Politik Bahasa* 2000. Alwi, for example, advises that code-switching *must be stopped* (2000: 13), my emphasis.

5 Transcending the Group: Languages of Contact and Lingua Francas

1. Winford (2003) remarks that 'jargon' should be used with care since it was regularly employed in the colonial period to denigrate the creoles of dominated groups. It is used here only in the sense of simplest and most basic language of contact.

2. One fragment of Sabir that still exists is incorporated into a children's rhyme from Jerusalem. The words are understood as nonsense words by the singers but are in fact Sabir numbers.

3. Linguists are, as we noted in Chapter 4, undecided as to whether it should be designated as a pidgin or not. It certainly fulfils the pidgin function and matches some of the criteria: Bazaar Malay accommodates to many groups of speakers with different mother tongues and is highly simplified compared to the literary language.

4. For a linguistic description comparing and contrasting pidgins and creoles see Romaine (1988); Arends *et al.* (1995).

5. This is a disputed point. Many creolists would argue that creole languages develop as the result of violent conflict of one kind or another, certainly social violence if not actual warfare. There is a break in social organisation and a new language develops after specific events (Muysken and Smith 1995). They would argue that this was not the case with most other languages, for example, standard average European languages. However, since the social disruption that caused language change in some settings is lost in prehistory, this point is quite difficult to resolve.

6. For a full description of the factors governing code-switching see Myers-Scotton (1988 and 1993).

7. Such as Tsotsitaal, non-standard Afrikaans with a significant mixture of English and Zulu terms, Isicamtho, Zulu (Nguni) base with lexis from English and Afrikaans (Slabbert and Myers-Scotton 1996).

8. Ferguson (1959) coined the term to apply to situations where two dialects of a single language coexisted in H and L functions, for example, Arabic and German. The definition has since been extended to apply to similar situations where the languages are not related.

9. Military service was one way to access to citizenship in the Roman Empire and the normal practice was that when soldiers from the regular *auxilia* were discharged they received Roman citizenship. However, for soldiers in the *numeri* and *cunei* drawn from the periphery of empire, such as from Britain, Germany, Syria, Africa and Dacia, this practice was not observed. Another difference between these units and the regular *auxilia* was that words of command and battle cries were in the native tongue, not in Latin. This is an early example of how citizenship and language are often linked.

10. For details of who learnt Dutch in Indonesia see Chapter 4.

11. For a discussion of the reasoning of British policymakers see Viswanathan (1989).

12. Quoted by Pennycook (2000a: 54) who also gives a very full description of, and commentary on, language policy within the British Empire.

13. Urdu became the lingua franca of northern India and ultimately developed to become a literary language which replaced Persian. Now the official language of Pakistan, written in the Arabic script with lexis influenced by the Islamic faith of its speakers and the Persian spoken by the early Mughal rulers, the language has lost much of its mutual comprehensibility with Hindi, the standardised written form which developed in India (CILT 1985).

14. The language of the army was a source of contention as the national question became acute within the empire. In the decades before the First World War, Hungarian officers demanded that they be allowed to use Magyar and disputed the emperor's right to set the language of command (Kohn 1961; Macartney 1968).

15. Those in remote and inaccessible mountain valleys often maintain their language as do homogeneous and impermeable religious sects.

16. There is disagreement on the spread of English within the British Empire. Phillipson (1992) maintains that there was a policy to push the language; Brutt-Griffler (2002) refutes this claim and shows that, on the contrary, access to the language was restricted.

17. This is not universally the case; in Bolivia and Peru missionaries tended to use Quecha (SIL website http://www.sim.org).

18. 'per totas las terras de nostre lengage son de maior autoritat li cantar de la lenga lemosina qe de neguna autra parladura' (Vidal 1342, quoted in Janson 1991: 24).

19. Moreover, members of the main religions of the world have mostly felt a duty to convert those who are not of the faith.
20. In South-East Asia, French was a major colonial lingua franca from the late eighteenth century, when Bishop Pigneau de Béhaine helped Nguyen Anh put down the Tay Son rebellion and become emperor of Vietnam, to 1954, when the Vietnamese under the leadership of Ho Chi Minh beat the French army at Dien Bien Phu, and the French withdrew from Indo-China.
21. A tiny number of students were educated in other modern foreign languages in the national language academy to maintain a skeleton group for diplomatic roles.
22. *The Repertorium Chronicarum* at Michigan State University catalogues more than 7500 manuscripts and more than 1000 books from public and private collections in Europe, the United States and Japan describing the national, political, military and ecclesiastical life of the Middle Ages. The number of chronicles from the late Medieval and early Modern period illustrates the point (www. chronica.msstate.edu).

6   French: The Rise and Fall of a Prestige Lingua Franca

1. This was not true for territory acquired on other continents. Some of the conquests and settlements of the sixteenth and seventeenth centuries were lost in the eighteenth century in wars with the British. A second wave of conquest and colonialism took place in the nineteenth century.
2. There is a possibility that French had been used in negotiations for other, earlier treaties, such as the Treaty of Utrecht, although this treaty was written in Latin.
3. This is disputed by Brunot (1967: 402). However, the likelihood is that the tendency to use French was growing, which its acceptance at Rastadt would support.
4. The influence of French in Germany and other parts of Europe and reaction to it influenced the rise of the ethno-nationalist movement discussed in Chapters 2 and 3. The writings of Herder (1744–1803) and Fichte (1762–1814) were explicit on the need to reject French influence and create a national tradition in the national language. The *Sturm und Drang* movement (c. 1765–95) had actually taken the first steps to do so.
5. With some notable exceptions. The British court was, of course, German speaking in the early Hanoverian period. Robert Walpole used Latin to communicate with the king, not having any knowledge of French or German (Walpole 1788/1924).
6. De Broglie (1986: 45) reports a survey conducted in six European states to discover which literary figures were most known, read and revered. Although there were no French writers in the first three positions (Goethe, Shakespeare and Dante) seven out of the 21 names mentioned were French.
7. The Vatican website explains that, in addition, Latin is the sacred language and Italian the working language.
8. A very old fashioned article claiming the particular suitability of French for theology is posted on the Francophonie website, http://www.francophone.net/AFI/revue/articles/2000_295.htm

> La langue française a rendez-vous avec la raison. Elle tente d'atteindre l'absolu et l'universel, au-delà de l'anecdotique et du passager, d'exprimer les concepts abstraits le plus clairement possible en transcendant les faits particuliers et contingents.

Cardinal Paul Poupard *Christianisme et francophonie* (1999).

9. Perhaps the most famous expression of this is from Rivarol's essay, *Discours sur l'universalité de la langue française*, where he claims 'ce qui n'est pas clair n'est pas français' (Rivarol 1784).

10. For example, in 1985–86, 28.5% of Spanish secondary pupils were learning French as first foreign language (reported in Calvet 1993). The 1998 Eurydice report shows that this figure dropped to 8%. This mirrors the rise in English from 71.1% (reported in Calvet 1993) to over 90% in the Eurydice report in 1996 and 96% in the 2000 report.

11. This was by no means new. As Walter (2001) has documented there has been constant exchange between French and English over several centuries.

12. The Conseil constitutionnel censured the linking of funding to publication of research in French as a contravention of the right of free speech (1994) and this aspect of the act has withered (Hagège 1996).

13. See Ager (1999) for a full discussion of this.

14. Association francophone d'amitié et de liaison provides a forum for the Francophone world for which it publishes a newsletter. Association droit de comprendre is an umbrella organisation which links ALF, DLF and other Paris based organisations.

15. There were few rulings against those who contravened the Bas–Lauriol language legislation. Only 44 of the 5834 complaints filed between 1990 and 1994 were upheld (Hagège 1996). However, between 1995 and 2000, 35 591 complaints were submitted to the DGLF. In the year 2000, the Délégation reported to Parliament that a large number of these offending parties had agreed to comply with the law, that 1886 disputes had gone to court and that 447 defendants had been found guilty (Ministère de la culture et de la communication 2000).

16. For example, Association le droit de comprendre *Les Français et leur langue en 2001*, Paris: Editions des écrivains 2001.

17. 'L'anglais est devenu une commodité au même titre que l'ordinateur ou Internet. ... Les Français doivent cesser de considérer l'anglais comme une langue étrangère.'

18. See the influential articles by Bernard Cassen in *Le Monde Diplomatique*, for example, May 2000 and November 2001.

19. Turkey has legislated to limit the number of hours of English in private primary schools to four per week. This has led to a common practice which is to have an official timetable and an actual timetable. The English language teachers stay away during inspectors' visits and the official timetable is displayed, but at all other times the actual timetable flouts the legislation (Communication with TESOL teachers, Istanbul 2002).

20. Favre d'Echallens of the Association Défense de la langue française is explicit in his contempt for those who acquire English to enhance their own status:

> For those adopting English enthusiastically, economic reasons are only an excuse, a justification of their wish to go over to the victors' camp. Forsaking one's language is the worst of crimes, the clearest admission of having decamped to the dominant group. (Favre d'Echallens 2002. Author's translation)

21. There has been a similar move to the discourse of multiculturalism and equality of languages and cultures in the documentation of the Alliance française, an institution whose prime *raison d'être* is the promotion of French. See for example, Bruézière (1983).

22. These statistics are only a rough guide since some countries notably the United Kingdom did not provide data. However, the gaps in data are consistent across the years and would not change the patterns substantially.

23. This was echoed by the Council of Europe in its Parliamentary Assembly (1998). The Council called for Europe's linguistic diversity to be preserved and protected through a wider choice of foreign languages in school curricula and a minimum of two foreign languages for all school children. The European Year of Languages (2001) was funded as part of the publicity and promotion for this.

24.

Enrolled	20 209 200
Learning English	18 089 800
Learning French	4 277 500
Learning German	2 091 200
Learning Spanish	1 698 500

Source: Eurydice Key Data on Education in Europe 1999–2000

25. The same is true of the Greek government. Firm supporters of diversity at international level, they are particularly harsh on those Greeks who would like to use their own languages in the areas which are not traditional Greek speaking and there have been recent imprisonments. See note 5, Chapter 3.
26. See note 20, chapter 5.
27. Renewing diplomatic links progressed throughout the 1990s. The United States recognised the Vietnamese state in 1995.
28. Association of South-East Asian Nations and Asia Pacific Economic Cooperation.
29. It could be argued that there is some minor infringement of the right to speak French in France. The European Commission has asked the French to bring their practice into line with European law on the labelling of foodstuffs. The Toubon legislation which demands that all labelling be in French was ruled as unnecessary for consumer protection if it is in a language that 'is easily understood by the consumer' (Ruling on chicken wings C-366/98 and Directive 2000/13/EC). The French have agreed to revise the contested legislation and were doing so as this book went to press in 2003.
30. Toubon does not accept this. He states quite categorically that he expects French policymaking to counter the variables that have caused the decline of French as a lingua franca:

> Augmenter les positions du français dans le monde reste donc plus que jamais un combat. C'est un des objectifs de cette loi. L'autre est de lutter contrer une forme de négligence, d'indifférence qui nous appartient en propre. (Interview with Hagège 1996: 157)

7 English: From Language of Empire to Language of Globalisation

1. Bailey (1991) quotes numerous sources from the sixteenth century to illustrate that English speakers in that period did not expect to use their language in international settings.
2. Only with publication and general distribution of the Bible in the vernacular was there widespread acceptance of a single variety of English, that of the south-east,

into which it had been translated. There was no English Academy as such to promote the variety of the elites and the capital. However, the process occurred in much the same way as in countries where such academies did exist; the intellectual elites pronounced on style, pronunciation and usage in a very prescriptive way. Johnson's dictionary begun in 1755 was not state sponsored but it did originate from the same preoccupations and aims and from within a similar intellectual elite class as the Academy sponsored dictionaries of other European nation states.

3. Interestingly, David Hume was also a Lallans speaker.

4. Mazrui and Mazrui (1998) point out that the policies of the governments of France and Britain might have been very different in theory, with French universalist thinking calling for a common education for all those under French administration and the British tending to the philosophy of separate development, but that in reality both colonial powers actually funded the education of only a small proportion of those they colonised.

5. The patent for electroplating that they invented was sold to Elkington in 1843 and a partnership organised with Fox and Henderson for development of their ideas for a steam engine and condenser 1847 (*Dictionary of National Biography* Vol. XVIII OUP 1917).

6. In a speech to the Birmingham and Midland Institute of which he became president he gives an account of his linguistic difficulties in early visits to England and his need to master the language (*Dictionary of National Biography* Vol. XVIII OUP 1917).

7. As we have noted elsewhere missionaries were also agents of conservation of vernaculars in that they often codified them, translated the Bible into them and taught them in literacy programmes.

8. In an address to the Berlin Academy in 1851 (reported in Bailey 1991: 109).

9. Beginning with independence of Transjordan in 1946 and ending with handover of Hong Kong to the People's Republic of China in 1997.

10. Using 'American' in this sense is contested by South Americans and other North Americans. However, there is a long tradition of using 'American' to describe residents of the United States. 'American' was used, even before 1700 to designate British subjects on the mainland of North America (Boatner 1966) and from the very early days of independence, Americans regularly used it to describe themselves. For example, 'The American is a new man' (Crevecoeur 1782). I have followed this tradition for concision while sensible of the objections.

11. The 1790 census recorded the population of European descent as 3.9 million, among which English speakers would have just constituted an absolute majority. 48% were of English descent, 19% of African descent, 12% of Scots or Scots-Irish descent, 10% of German descent. The remaining 11% were composed mainly of citizens of Welsh, French, Irish, Dutch and Swedish origin.

12. Mass immigration falls into four distinct periods, and in each the countries of origin were different.

Dates	Numbers	Provenance of largest groups
1840–90	15 million	Germany, Ireland, Britain and Scandinavia
1891–1920	18+ million	Italy, Austro-Hungarian and Russian Empires
1921–60	7.5 million	Slow down during Depression and World War
1961–2000	20 million	South and Central America (particularly Mexico), Asia

13. In the Philippines, the United States conducted a policy of English language education for all, following the French model of colonial education rather than the British (Brutt-Griffler 2002). It was not to be entirely successful and there was no language shift at the time, as the US government had hoped.
14. See note 12, chapter 7.
15. Documents conserved by the German Reformed Church bear witness to use of German until 1917. See, for example, inauguration addresses from the theological seminary published by the Office of Publications of the German Reform Church, Chambersburg, Philadelphia.
16. After the United States declared war on Germany in 1917, many states dropped the study of German from their curriculum. Nebraska's open meeting law of 1919 forbade the use of foreign languages in public, and in 1918 Governor Harding of Iowa proclaimed that

> English should and must be the only medium of instruction in public, private, denominational and other similar schools. Conversation in public places, on trains, and over the telephone should be in the English language. Let those who cannot speak or understand the English language conduct their religious worship in their home. (*New York Times*, 18/6/1918, p. 12, cited by Baron http://www2.english.uiuc.edu/baron/essays/legendar.htm)

This had an immediate effect. As many as 18 000 people were charged in the Midwest during and immediately following the First World War with violating the English-only statutes. (Crawford 1989, cited in Baron 1996). After the end of the war the language laws were declared unconstitutional by central government and removed from the state statute books.

17. Weindling (1996) shows that the role of German as a foreign language did not contract substantially after the First World War. Fewer US citizens learnt it as a heritage language as noted above, but it remained an international language of science. The rejection of German was much more marked after the Second World War as potential learners turned away from the language tainted by association with Fascism and the Holocaust.
18. Much of which is traded within the EU.
19. As these firms do much of their business within the EU, this explains in part why nearly two thirds of global Foreign Direct Investment (FDI) outflows were sourced from Europe with TNCs in the EU investing US$510 billion abroad in 1999 (WIR 2000).
20. This could be attributed to familiarity with the cultural and legal environments, access to the country's research institutions and universities and more flexible labour regulations found in the United Kingdom in comparison to continental Europe.
21. During the new technology and e-commerce boom of the late 1990s, investment grew enormously and billion dollar funds from US venture capital sources became commonplace (*Business Weekly* 21/07/2000). Groups such as Warburg Pincus, Providence Ventures and Cross Atlantic Ventures, Benchmark Partners and Carlyle Group were very active in the European market during that boom (*Business Weekly* 21/07/2000).
22. See Scholte (2000 and 2002) for a discussion of anti-globalisation movements. The worldwide explosion of financial flows and the increasing volume of transactions in the international financial system appear so far to have been principally

of benefit to the north, to the developed world and to the rich. They are not principally from one centre (the United States) to the rest of the world nor from everywhere to everywhere else.

Exchange has grown exponentially. In 1970, US$10 billion to $20 billion were exchanged every day in the world's currency market. Today, more than US$1500 billion changes hands daily (Johnson and Mayrand 2000).

23. The traditional example in many text books is the Dutch enterprise, Phillips, which has a long tradition of using English as the internal company language. It has been joined by numerous others. Amadeus, the airline reservation service for Lufthansa, Air France and Iberia has a policy that English should be the language of all internal documents. That Alstom, the part French, part British owned heavy engineering firm, uses English as company language can be explained in part by dual ownership. Policy decisions by Alcatel and Renault to use English for internal documents are more surprising. The French press rails against this trend regularly. See, for example Cassen, B. 'La langue-dollar' in *Le Monde diplomatique*, May 2000.

24. Singapore is the only ASEAN member to have English as an official language. In Singapore, English is co-official with Bahasa Malay, Mandarin Chinese and Tamil.

25. Remarked on at length in comments on papers and round table debate at the Globe Conference, Warsaw, October 2002.

26. Groups protesting in Seattle 1999 and Genoa 2001 used internet sites to inform participants and coordinate action. The interaction on the sites is predominantly in English. There is anecdotal evidence that English was the usual lingua franca in the demonstrations, among protesters from different language backgrounds.

27. This is the position in much of the French language and Arabic language press but the views are also expressed within the United States. See, for example, Chomsky (2001), Vidal (2002) and Ahmed (2002).

28. This use of overt pressure presented as a form of law enforcement has replaced the tendency to use covert methods to promote an acceptance of its values and recognition of its interests, which seems to have been US practice, particularly in South and Central America during the 1970s and 1980s.

29. In November 2000, delegates from over 160 countries met at the Hague as part of the ongoing Kyoto protocol discussions. When this round of the talks failed, the consensus in the world press was that this was 'in large part because of the U.S.'s obstructionist stance' (Coen 2001). European headlines were virulent: 'Gas-Guzzling U.S. Under Fire at Global Warming Talks' (*Agence France Presse*) 'U.S. Blamed for Climate Treaty Talks Deadlock' (*The Daily Telegraph*) 'U.S. Blocks Attempts to Cut Global Warming' (*The Independent*) 'Pollution Pact Under Threat as America Is Accused of Con Trick' (*The Times*)

30. For example, on 5 March 2002, President Bush imposed a tariff rate on steel and quotas on certain types of steel import, as a protective measure. The rest of the world was uniformly critical. In the world press during March 2002 the tone was condemnatory: Pascal Lamy for the EU was reported as saying that the 'international market is not the Wild West where every one acts as they please'. In Germany, Schroeder categorised it as an act against free world markets and contrary to the US' professed desire to deregulate investment and trade. In France, Chirac called the move 'serious and unacceptable'. The IMF, Russia, China, South Korea and Japan all censured the action.

31. As in the greater political consensus for the war in Afghanistan.

32. As in the growing practice of policing elections in states were there could be intimidation and abuse. The protection of the population and the policing of elections in East Timor is one example.

33. The EU is the most evolved of these; ASEAN along with Japan, South Korea and China may or may not become an East Asian caucus.
34. See Wright (2000a) for a discussion of UN and NATO practice in joint campaigns during the 1990s.
35. The working language of international courts is English and French. This is the practice in the International Court of Justice at the Hague and in the European Court of Human Rights in Strasbourg.
36. The official languages of the UN are Spanish, English, Chinese, Arabic, Russian and French but English dominates; in the EU there are presently 11 co-official languages but English and French are the usual working languages; the Council of Europe has two co-official languages, English and French.
37. For example, President Putin, a former KGB officer with no reason to learn English early in life, expended time and effort to acquire English after he came to the Russian presidency.
38. Paul Wolfowitz's address to the Senate Appropriations Committee, 27 February 2002, broke down the budget request to Congress into its constituent parts. $53.9 billion was assigned to RDTE (Research, Development, Test and Evaluation) out of a request for $379 billion. http://www.defenselink.mil/speeches/2002/s20020227-depsecdef.html
39. Corporate HQ in London and R&D HQ in Södertälje, Sweden, but strong presence in the United States as well. Sales in 2001 totalled US$16.5 billion, with an operating profit of $4.2 billion. http://www.astrazeneca.com/mainnav1.
40. See patterns of immigration 1840–1921 given above in note 12, chapter 7.
41. The US product is also cheap since the home market is large enough for domestic sales to cover production costs. Films can thus be sold abroad at very competitive prices (Wright 1997).
42. The defence of theses in Latin in Austrian universities until the nineteenth century is one example. The inaugural professorial lecture given by the linguist Jakob Grimm in Göttingen in 1830 is another.
43. There is much speculation about this. See, for example, Maurais and Morris (2003).

8 Language in a Postnational Era: Hegemony or Transcendence?

1. In statistics prepared for e-commerce in 2000 the top 16 countries in terms of percentage of citizens with internet access were Norway, Singapore, United States, Sweden, Canada, Finland, Australia, Denmark, New Zealand, Britain, Switzerland, Austria, Taiwan, South Korea, Belgium and Germany (NUA Internet Survey 2000 cited on http://www.eurotrash.com/Resources/globalization_statistics.html. 19, December 2001). The Middle East and the whole continent of Africa were estimated to have provided 2.3% of the global total for internet users in 2000 (*Computer Industry Almanac* cited on http://www.eurotrash.com/Resources/globalization_statistics.html. 19 December 2001).
2. Expressed most notably by the American historian, Fukuyama, who claimed that the Hegelian/Marxist view of history as leading inexorably to Communism was discredited and overtaken (Fukuyama 1989, 1992). The idea that 'history was at an end' caught the public imagination.
3. A growing body of scholarly and activist literature attacks and exposes the 'increasing dissimulation around questions concerning equity, poverty and powerlessness' (Chowdry and Nair 2002: 1).

4. This does not seem so self-evident in the wake of events in 2001 and 2002. Neo-protectionism has arisen again as an issue. See note 9.

5. Scholte (2000) reported that internal conflict has replaced interstate conflict as the major reason for war. Between 1989 and 1998, 58 out of the 61 conflicts recorded by the UN were civil wars. The reasons for this are closely bound with globalisation. Now some of the need for large territorial units has disappeared, groups incorporated within states believe it is possible to secede and survive. And global capital may exacerbate tension where a national elite and a global company join forces to the detriment of local interests. The struggle to leave has become armed conflict in a number of cases: Croatia, Bosnia, Kosovo, East Timor and so on. Scholte's argument is weakened to an extent by recent events where there has been conflict between states, although there may be an argument that the underlying trend he discerned is still at work and that the interstate conflict is in a new mould (cf. Jett 1999).

6. In 1994 US cross-border exports, including affiliated trade of audio–visual services, were about US$ 16 120 million, while imports were only US$ 136 million (UNESCO 2000).

7. This is very clear when the percentage that the United States has of world output (27% in 2000) is compared with the percentage it has of world exports (12.3% in 2000).

8. This has a long history. Lincoln is supposed to have said 'If we purchase a ton of steel rails from England for $20, then we have the rails and England the money. But if we buy a ton of steel rails from an American for $25, then America has both the rails and the money'. This is commonly quoted in US text books. See for example Czinkota (2003). The ordinary consumer is urged to patriotic consumption on sites such as http://www.howtobuyamerican.com/.

9. See note 30, chapter 7.

10. The number of US citizens holding passports has often been cited as one indicator of this national self-sufficiency. With such an enormous space, Americans travel within their own state and foreign travel has never become a majority activity. About a third of US citizens hold passports (EKOS http://www.ekos.com/studies/integration.asp).

11. The genesis of the United States as a country of immigration might well have become the cause of networks of global interconnectedness but in the event this has not had a significant effect. The majority of Americans whose families came in nineteenth- and prewar twentieth-century migration do not return on visits to the countries of origin of their families, as the small percentage of passport holders shows. The majority of Americans whose families came from non-Anglophone countries of origin in nineteenth- and prewar twentieth-century migration have shifted family language to English and competence in ancestral languages is not maintained as a matter of course. It is only members of the last wave of immigration (particularly from Central and South America) that have countered this trend.

12. The arguments of the French opposition are dealt with in Chapter 6. This body of work is slightly different to the literature under review here in that it is an opposition to the ascendancy of other states rather than an ideological critique.

13. The opposition to English appears in many languages. Because of my own linguistic limitations I have only tracked what has appeared in French and English, whether in translation or not.

14. The scholars that made up the Frankfurt school were all directly, or indirectly associated with the Institute of Social Research in Frankfurt. Theodor W. Adorno

(philosopher, sociologist and musicologist), Walter Benjamin (essayist and literary critic), Herbert Marcuse (philosopher), Max Horkheimer (philosopher and sociologist), and later, Jürgen Habermas were the core of the group. Each of these men took Karl Marx's theory of Historical Materialism as a starting point for their own work.

15. Interestingly Fairclough focuses on the message, and the medium is somewhat neglected. One infers that it is either English or mediated by English + bilinguals.
16. Phillipson's analysis of the promotion of English, *Linguistic Imperialism* (1992), is useful in that it lays bare power relationships, but ultimately unhelpful because it takes the British Council and the US agencies on their own evaluation and suggests that the spread of English results from planning and promotion.
17. See, for example, the language learning statistics in Chapter 6 and the policy decisions discussed in Chapter 4.
18. Pennycook too finds Phillipson's discussion of linguistic imperialism useful but incomplete:

> The problem here lies partly in concentrating on the imposition or non-imposition of a language as if it were an object disconnected to all the other political and cultural forces around it. (Pennycook 1994: 74)

19. For example, contacts among the East Asian Economic Caucus are often in English (Reuters and Dow Jones informants, personal communications 2001 and 2002).
20. This may be a language related to their own or completely different. Close relatedness is not always an advantage as the case studies in Chapter 10 demonstrate.
21. Pool also points out that fairness would also be served if no one was permitted to learn another language but then there would be no community of communication.
22. Members of the community such as the Nobel prize winner for chemistry, W. Ostwald, complained that gatherings in the scientific world were a 'Tower of Babel' where scientists were forced to listen and to use Swedish, German, English, Italian and French all mixed together (*Frankfürter Zeitung* 25/12/1909 cited in Rasmussen 1996).
23. For a full list of the artificial languages suggested and an account of the debate see Rasmussen (1996).
24. Leitner (1992) extended Kachru's indicative list of countries to a more comprehensive 19. Leitner did not fully agree with Kachru and argued that this inner circle contained a wider range of variation than the model allowed, and that a variety of national norms governed inner circle English language use.
25. Leitner gives 14 states where this is the case.
26. Interesting too that European TESOL teachers at this meeting, both native and non-native speakers exhibited strong allegiance to British English. The reasons for this are not at all clear, but may relate to traditional notions of prestige (Shakespeare and the English literary canon) or may be a way of circumventing the US cultural influence that, as noted above, sometimes provokes negative reaction in Europe.

9 New Discourse, New Legal Instruments and a New Political Context for Minorities and their Languages

1. Minority is a highly contested term in the social sciences. It is used here to designate groups that do not speak the majority/dominant language of a state as

their sole/first/home language. This is the definition given in the OSCE Report on the linguistic rights of persons belonging to national minorities in the OSCE area.

2. There is currently no official language policy at the national level, but 22 states have passed some form of English-only legislation during the two decades that the Official English movement has existed. The Federal 'No Child Left Behind Act' (January 2002) seems to signal an intensification in English promotion by prioritising English-language acquisition programmes over bilingual education.

3. The treatment of Kurds was one of the reasons for holding Turkey back from joining the EU (von Toggenburg 2001). Minority rights have been a criterion for all accession countries.

4. Although intervention is not uniform, and may occur in one situation and not in another where there are similarities. Many regimes continue to mistreat political and ethnic minorities without attracting intervention from the 'international community'.

5. It is necessary to recognise that the acceptance of minority rights is also not uniform and states are in different stages of signing up to and implementing them. However, the consensus at supra- and international level is for their promotion and recalcitrant states come under pressure.

6. Expressed in John Stuart Mill's *On Liberty* in the following way:

> Secondly, the principle requires liberty of tastes and pursuits; of framing the plan of our life to suit our own character; of doing as we like, subject to such consequences as may follow: without impediment from our fellow creatures, so long as what we do does not harm them, even though they should think our conduct foolish, perverse, or wrong. (Mill 1859/1996: 15)

7. If this is a right, it is a very limited right, and one which is often termed 'negative' to signal this limitation.

8. http://iquebec.ifrance.com/antescriptum/citations.htm.

9. See for example Phillipson's attack on David Crystal (Phillipson 2000) and the discussion in Kymlicka (2001). Kymlicka sees the view that minority nationalisms are defensive protests against globalisation and modernisation as a cliché (2001: 284).

10. Between the Allied and Associated Powers and new states such as Poland, Czechoslovakia, or enlarged states such as Romania and Greece.

11. The Conference on Security and Cooperation in Europe (CSCE) became the Organisation for Security and Cooperation in Europe (OSCE) in 1995.

12. For full details see UN Economic and Social Council *Discrimination against indigenous peoples. Study on treaties, agreements and other constructive arrangements between States and indigenous populations* E/CN.4/Sub.2/1995/27 Para 68. 1995.

13. Although this is a stronger instrument with regard to the rights of the group, there is no suggestion that minorities have an automatic right to self-determination. Indeed the territorial integrity and political independence of the state is repeatedly stressed.

14. The Council of Europe also has a Commissioner who has played a major role in overseeing the observance of the rights of minorities in the region.

15. Representations to the working group have come from diverse European minorities – from France, Turkey, Slovakia and Greece (Thompson 2001).

16. Ten countries accepted as applicants in December 2002, two further applicants (Romania and Bulgaria) are identified for a subsequent phase and the case of Turkey is still under review.
17. Reports are submitted by the states and Council of Europe officers undertake country visits where meetings are held with representatives of governments and representatives of civil society.
18. For example, the Council of Europe invited the countries in the region to undertake a comprehensive and thorough review of their laws, policies and practices between 2000 and 2002 in order to identify and remove all discriminatory aspects.
19. A study of the participation of minorities in decision-making processes throughout the continent has been a spin off from the Framework, but whether the language dimension is a blocking factor or not has not been investigated.
20. Both figures refer to the situation 13/12/02.
21. For a discussion of the effect of the Charter so far see Grin (2003).
22. France signed the Charter but did not ratify it. The Conseil constitutionnel ruled that it would be contrary to the constitution.
23. The only political block which voted almost solidly against the resolution was the English Tory group (Ó Riagáin 2001).
24. The rocky legal basis for EBLUL was challenged in 1998 by those opposed to the promotion of minority languages. The objection was upheld and the budget line for these activities suspended. The issue was not resolved at the time of writing in 2003.
25. The network's mission is to provide reliable objective information about the minority languages both to the majority-language populations and to the minorities themselves for whom the data provide the basis for cross-border contacts and long-term strategies. Each of the three centres has its own thematic programme and specialist role: Mercator–Education at the Fryske Akademy (Ljouwert Netherlands) studies education at all levels; Mercator–Legislation at the CIEMEN foundation (Barcelona) is concerned with language legislation and language in public administration; while Mercator–Media at the University of Wales in Aberystwyth deals with press and media including the new media. For further information see Mercator website http://www.mercator-central.org/.
26. Ulster Scots and Lowland Scots, both dialects on the West Germanic dialect continuum.
27. In 2001 the Home Secretary, David Blunkett, unveiled plans for new immigrants to take citizenship classes to give them an understanding of British democracy and culture. They would also be required to learn English before they become British citizens:

> I believe we need to educate new migrants in citizenship and help them to develop an understanding of our language, democracy and culture. (Blunkett Speech 25/10/2001. Reported in *The Guardian* 26/10/2001)

28. For example, in the British media in the aftermath of the Bradford riots in 2001. The clashes, mainly involving young urban men, were portrayed in much of the press as the result of a failure to integrate on the part of some ethnic groups. The official report commissioned by the government on the riots (Community Cohesion Review Team 11/12/2001) blamed segregation of communities.

29. Using the UNESCO Declaration on Race and Racial Prejudice (1978) to define the harm sense of discrimination.

10 The Fragmentation of the Old Nation States and the Rise of Small Nations

1. Although the invasion of Iraq seems to move us into a new era. However, this does not weaken the general argument that sovereignty is eroding in much of the world and that the nation state is not the only or even the main protector of its population.
2. Under Article 17(J7)(4), the Treaty of Amsterdam incorporated into the TEU the so-called Petersberg tasks: humanitarian and rescue tasks, peace-keeping tasks and tasks of combat forces in crisis management, including peacemaking. Common defence, policing and conflict resolution became part of the Common Foreign and Security Policy and an EU Rapid Reaction Force was planned to give the policy some meaning. In March 2003 EU forces undertook their first peacekeeping operation as a group, in Macedonia.
3. Although at time of writing in 2003, suspended and under negotiation.
4. The capital, Brussels, is the only bilingual space. In addition to the two major linguistic groups, German speakers also have some cultural and linguistic recognition in Belgium.
5. The Slovaks have since been very active in corpus planning activities to distance Slovakian from Czech. For a discussion of recent language ideology in Slovakia see Langman (2002).
6. Lithuanian, Estonian and Latvian have been reintroduced as the media for all the functions of public and official life. The large numbers of Russian speakers who came to the Baltic states during the Communist period have been constrained to acquire the language of the state that they are living in, in order to gain citizenship.
7. Twelve of the 15 former republics of the USSR make up the CIS: Armenia, Azerbaijan, Belarus, Georgia, Kazakhstan, Kyrgyzstan, Moldova, Russia, Tajikistan, Turkmenistan, Ukraine and Uzbekistan. The CIS is not a state in itself, but rather an alliance of independent states. The capital of the Commonwealth of Independent States is in Minsk, Belarus.
8. Catalan and Galician are, like Castilian, dialects from the Western Romance continuum. Linguistic gradations (semantic, syntactic, morphological and phonological change) take place over distance but there is little bunching of differences that traces linguistic frontiers definitively (Entwhistle 1936). Basque, spoken in the western Pyrenees and on the northern coast is the only language on Spanish territory that is not part of the Romance dialect continuum. Basque is not from the Indo-European family and predates it. It has been spoken in the area for centuries, probably since Neolithic times (Collins 1986). Here, in contrast, the linguistic frontiers are distinct.
9. In 1479 the two kingdoms of Castile and Aragon were united when Fernando of Aragon became king of Castile. He was already married to Queen Isabella of Castile.
10. Sixty per cent of Catalonia's exports went to Cuba and in the fight to retain the empire the Catalans backed Madrid (Conversi 1997).
11. For example, the general strike of 1909, organised mainly by Anarchists and Syndicalists to organise resistance to conscription for the war in Morocco.

This became a massive popular revolt of some violence and was quelled with ferocity. The event has became known in Catalonia as the *Setmana Tràgica*.

12. Song troupes, folk groups, scouts and youth groups, choirs, sports associations, rambling clubs and the Catholic magazine *Serra d'Or*, published in Catalan.

13. This is not a new phenomenon; in the early years of the twentieth century, Alejandro Lerroux led a populist movement against a Catalan nationalism seen as too exclusive, too highbrow and too bourgeois (Conversi 1997). McRoberts (2001) warns against going too far in this direction and reducing Catalan nationalism to class interest. He presents evidence to show that the nationalist movement is more complex than a simple dichotomy.

14. I have not covered the normalisation process in depth because it is treated in great detail in a number of publications. For a comprehensive account of language laws, resulting policy and its implementation in Catalonia see the Generalitat's website: http://cultura.gencat.net/. For recent surveys of language knowledge, use and attitudes in Catalonia and Catalan-speaking areas consult:
http://cultura.gencat.net/llengcat/noves/hm02hivern/catalana/a_villa1_5.htm
http://cultura.gencat.net/llengcat/noves/hm02hivern/catalana/a_pujol1_4.htm
http://cultura.gencat.net/llengcat/noves/hm02hivern/catalana/a_romani1_4.htm
For a critical review of the process see Valverdú (1984); Aranu and Boada (1986); Laitin (1989); Mar–Molinero (1989); Woolard (1989); Woolard and Gahng (1990); Siguan. (1991); Miller and Miller (1996); O'Donnell (1996); Boogerman Castejon (1997); Guibernau (1997); Wright (1999); Atkinson (2000). Ferrer (2000).

15. First elected 1980 and re-elected 1984, 1988, 1992, 1995 and 1999.

16. There are many examples. The case of the local administration in Sabadell is illustrative. In accordance with the Llei 1/1998 de 7 de gener de política lingüística, the town hall implemented a regulation that all business would be carried out in Catalan, with translation into Castilian for those who requested it. The opponents of the action argued that for the 49% of Sabadell inhabitants shown by survey to be Castilian speakers, this was exclusionary both in terms of employment and in terms of their ability to interact with their local administration in their preferred language without delay and hindrance (Mercator news report August 1999).

17. For example in the Generalitat's campaign to promote Catalan as a language to be used as one of the official languages of the EU.

18. The assertion that Valencia is Catalan speaking is maintained on the Generalitat website, for example, in the 2000 Language Policy Report.

19. See the Valencian law 49/1993 that ruled on name of language. The Valencian Autonomous Community consistently resists attempts to draw it into the Catalan network. A recent ruling excluded authors not born in Valencia from school programmes. This was done to avoid promoting convergence. The Catalans attacked attempts to maintain difference as 'dialectalisation' (Mercator news report February 2002).

20. Federación de Asociaciones Culturales del Aragón Oriental.

21. The main legal document is the Act on the Use of the Official Language (2001), which develops Article 2 of the Constitution.

22. Mateo and Aizpurua (2003) report data from the 1860s that suggest that the situation was different according to province. Gipuzkoa 96% Basque speakers; Bizkaia 81%; Northern Basque country 65%; Navarra 20% and Alava 10%. So Basque-speaking is related to region as well as class.

23. For a detailed examination of the elaboration of Basque nationalism as an exclusionary and essentialist philosophy see Forné (1990). For a discussion of how

research on blood groups, cranial shapes and other physical characteristics has been (mis)employed in the movement see Collins (1986).

24. This was the case in February 2003 when *Euskaldunon Egunkaria*, the Basque medium newspaper, was shut down by the Spanish Civil Guard in a dawn armed raid. This censorship before the trial of the newspaper editors has sparked protest from a wide spectrum of the population and large protest marches (*Behatokia Newsletter* February 2003. No. 4). Conversi (1997) argues that the central government has a record of treating the Basques in a violent way and that this has contributed to their own tradition of aggression.

25. The home of Lingua Pax and other international institutions.

26. In 1996 the census found that immigrants constituted only 2.02% of the population in Barcelona (Strubell 2001; Morén-Alegret 2002). By 2002, the June Mercator news report suggested that the foreign immigrant population in schools had risen to 6%, doubling the figures for 2001.

11   Endangered Languages

1. An Ethnologue survey lists 6809 languages as being spoken in the world in 2002. This number is close to the estimate of 6000 used by UNESCO in its communiqués on the languages of the world and threatened languages. Two-thirds of all languages are to be found in Asia and the Pacific (Ethnologue 2002). Islands and terrain where mountains or jungle make contact difficult are the places where language diversity is most frequently encountered. Indonesia, Papua New Guinea, Nigeria, India, Cameroon, Mexico, Zaire and Brazil are the countries with the largest numbers of languages. In temperate climates and in terrain where physical contact is much easier, there are far fewer languages. Europe, in fact, only accounts for 3% (Crystal 2000). Saudi Arabia, four times the size of Papua New Guinea, has only nine (Grimes 1992). There are question marks over these figures and there can be wide divergence in estimates. For example, Crystal (2000) suggests that a quarter of all languages are to be found in Indonesia. Ethnologue, on the other hand, lists only 726 (Ethnologue 2002). Some of this may be explained by the fact that languages are still being discovered in Irian Jaya, but the main problem is likely to be the lack of agreement on how we actually define a language and differentiate it from a neighbouring dialect.

2. Standard Average European is a term coined by Whorf.

3. Steiner's argument points perhaps to an essential but not sufficient condition for groups to coexist. Certainly the Bosnian conflict of 1992–93 and the Rwandan conflict of 1994 illustrate that a common language is no bar to conflict (Grenoble and Whaley 1998).

4. See Chapter 3.

5. See Walter (1994, 1997, 1998, 1999 and 2001).

6. Kymlicka (1995 and 2001) discusses the problem at some length. He argues that some cases where individuals exercise their rights/freedoms, can be shown to impinge on the rights/freedoms asked for by others, particularly where these latter are group dependent.

7. This does seem, however, to be the argument advanced by Skutnabb-Kangas (2000). In *Linguistic Genocide in Education*, she suggests formal education in the language of the state as harmful for young Sami, Inuit and Aborigines.

8. For a wideranging list of these see the UNESCO website or Terralingua http://cougar.ucdavis.edu/nas/terralin/endlangs.htmlvarious.

9. This is a conflation of work from a number of scholars. The main outline comes from various publications by Wurm and Krauss and the analyses in Ethnologue (Ethnologue 2002).

10. Based on a summary from the Summer Institute of Linguistics (http://www.sil.org). SIL has traditionally been involved with endangered languages. Their efforts to preserve and/or develop them stemmed from their missionary work.

11. Indeed enthusiastic preservation of a language can be a very unprogressive position. Some champions of vernaculars of the nineteenth century started from a highly essentialist position on the languages of tribal peoples. To be a member of a group whose language was to be preserved as an example of 'primitive' culture could only have been disadvantageous to such speakers.

12. See Summer Institute of Linguistics website (http://www.sil.org).

13. The civic position, that the state should pursue a policy of non-intervention and refuse state funding for any medium but the state language, is not neutral because it enshrines the *status quo*. The dominant majority continues in its role and individuals from minority groups have to assimilate if they want equality in the wider society. See Chapter 10 for further elaboration.

14. Given the state that they found themselves in, this was perhaps an intelligent decision. Whaley (2002) suggests that the Oroqen are aware of the difficulties of life in a state where the rule of law is not assured. Although the state's policy recognises minorities' specificity, it is best not to demand too much, as rights can be revoked. The Cultural Revolution was a reminder of this.

15. Furthermore, Oroqen is a language well developed for use in a traditional setting, with a lexis geared to hunting and gathering. It needs elaboration to be used in all the domains of contemporary life. It is unlikely that there will be the money and interest to support this.

16. Whaley suggests that the PRC was more assimilatory in its actions than some of its policies might indicate.

17. An interesting point about this research is the contract drawn up between the Uru and the researcher. Clearly ownership of the language was felt to be a major issue among group elders, who authorised Muysken (2002) to aid revitalisation with data collection.

18. Available as an electronic journal (http://www.unesco.org/most/vl4n2edi.htm).

19. 'The Albanian dialect of Italy, a language that now bears little resemblance to the standard language of Albania, is spoken over a wide area comprising 49 towns and villages, from the Abruzzi Appenines to the south of Italy and to Sicily. The linguistic pockets are situated mainly in mountainous or semi-mountainous regions. These communities are dispersed among seven regions (Abruzzi, Molise, Puglia, Campania, Basilicata, Calabria and Sicily) and nine provinces (Pescara, Campobasso, Avellino, Foggia, Taranto, Potenza, Cosenza, Catanzaro and Palermo)' (Euromosaic http://www.uoc.edu/euromosaic/web/document/albanes/an/i1/i1.html).

20. The rural poverty of most groups and the massive exodus they have experienced to northern industrial centres is the main difference in settings (Euromosaic http://www.uoc.edu/euromosaic/web/document/albanes/an/i1/i1.html).

21. Law 482/1999: Norme di tutela delle minoranze linguistiche storiche.

22. The Albanian language spoken in Italy is not one of the group of minority languages that enjoy the special protection of the State under Article 6 of the Italian Constitution. At regional level, however, Albanian is accorded some degree of official recognition in the autonomy statutes of Calabria, Basilicata and Molise.

23. Derhemi (2002) concedes that speakers might reject the Albanian standard for this reason.
24. Pluralism, civic nationalism, assimilation, separate development (Bourhis 2001).
25. The main difference between this ideology and the other three is that entry to the dominant group is not guaranteed for all those born in the territory (*jus soli*). Membership/citizenship is usually restricted to those who can be included through kinship ties (*jus sanguinis*).

12   Conclusion

1. Gellner sees Descartes as the precursor of individualism, and suggests that this philosophy finds its supreme expression in Hume and Kant.
2. Gellner has made the point elsewhere (1983) that the ideologists of nationalism portrayed the traditional ethnic group as the rationale for the state, but the reality was never the idealised *Gemeinschaft*, the small supportive, homogeneous community, but *Gesellschaft*, 'the chauvinistic nation state'.
3. With perhaps the exception of the United States, which as I argue in Chapter 8 is retaining many of the attributes of the sovereign nation state with high boundary fences longer than other states.
4. The groups to watch for early indications that this might be happening are the Swiss who are starting to choose English instead of one of the other official languages of Switzerland as their first foreign language in school.
5. Always making the distinction that this is minority/majority bilingualism. Some kinds of elite bilingualism escape from this negative perception entirely.

Bibliography

Abdulaziz, M. and Osinde, K. 'Sheng and Eng: development of mixed codes among urban youth in Kenya'. *International Journal of the Sociology of Language* 125 (1997), pp. 43–63.

Accademia culturale Iliria. *Dall'etnocentrismo al pluralismo Culturale*. Rome: Bardi. 2000.

Adler, H. and Menze, E. (eds), *Herder on World History: an Anthology*. London: Sharpe. 1997.

Agence universitaire de la Francophonie. *Lettres d'information du Bureau Asie-Pacifique* 2000–2001.

Ager, D. *Francophonie in the 1990s*. Clevedon: Multilingual Matters. 1996.

Ager, D. *Language, Community and the State*. Exeter: Intellect. 1997.

Ager, D. *Identity, Insecurity and Image: France and Language*. Clevedon: Multilingual Matters. 1999.

Agger, B. *Critical Social Theories*. Boulder: Westview. 1998.

Ahmad, F. *The Making of Modern Turkey*. London: Routledge. 1993.

Ahmed, N. *The War on Freedom: Why America Was Attacked September 11th 2001*. Joshua Tree, California: Tree of Life Publication. 2002.

Alberch, P. 'Language in contemporary Science: the tool and the cultural icon' in R. Chartier and P. Corsi (eds), *Sciences et langues en Europe*. Commission européenne: Forum européen de la science et de la technologie. 1996.

Albrow, M. *The Global Age*. Stanford University Press. 1997.

Alexander, N. *Language Policy and National Unity in South Africa/Azania*. Cape Town: Buchu. 1989.

Allières, J. *Les Basques* (3rd edn). Paris: Presses universitaires de France. 1986.

Alwi, H. 'Fungsi Politik Bahasa' in H. Alwi (ed.), *Politik Bahasa*. Jakarta: Pusat Bahasa. 2000.

Ammon, U. *Status Changes of Languages*. Berlin: Mouton de Gruyter. 1992.

Anderson, B. *Tolerance and the Mythology of the Javanese*. Ithaca: Cornell Monograph. 1965.

Anderson, B. *Imagined Communities*. London: Verso. 1983.

Anderson, B. *Language and Power: Exploring Political Cultures in Indonesia*. Ithaca: Cornell University Press. 1990.

Andresen, J. *Linguistics in America 1769–1924: A Critical History*. London: Routledge. 1990.

Ansre, G. 'Language policy for the promotion of national unity and understanding in West Africa'. Paper presented at the International Conference on Cultural Diversity and National Understanding within West African Countries at the University of Ife, Nigeria, December 1970.

Ansre, G. 'Language standardisation in sub-Saharan Africa' in J. Fishman (ed.), *Contributions to the Sociology of Language*. Berlin: Mouton de Gruyter. 1974.

Appel, R. and Muysken, P. *Language Contact and Bilingualism*. London: Arnold. 1987.

Aranu, J. and Boada, H. 'Languages and school in Catalonia'. *Journal of Multilingual and Multicultural Development* 7 (1986), pp. 107–22.

Arends, J. and Bruyn, A. 'Gradualist and developmental hypotheses' in J. Arends, P. Muysken and N. Smith (eds), *Pidgins and Creoles: an Introduction*. Amsterdam: John Benjamins. 1995.

Arends, J., Muysken, P. and Smith, N. *Pidgins and Creoles: an Introduction*. Amsterdam: John Benjamins. 1995.

Arnold, M. *Schools and Universities on the Continent (Report 1865–1867)*. University of Michigan Press. 1964.

Association le droit de comprendre. *Les Français et leur langue en 2001*. Paris: Editions des écrivains. 2001.

Atkinson, D. 'Language legislation in Catalonia: the politics of normalisation'. *International Journal of Iberian Studies* 13(2) (2000).

Azurmendi, M.-J., Bachoc, E. and Zabaleta, F. 'Reversing language shift: the case of Basque' in J. Fishman (ed.), *Can Threatened Languages be Saved?* Clevedon: Multilingual Matters. 2001.

Baconnier, G., Minet, A. and Soler, L. *La plume au fusil*. Toulouse: Privat. 1985.

Baehr, P. *Human Rights – Universality in Practice*. Basingstoke: Palgrave Macmillan. 2001.

Bailey, R. *Images of English*. Cambridge University Press. 1991.

Baker, C. *Foundations of Bilingual Education and Bilingualism*. Clevedon: Multilingual Matters. 1993.

Bakhtin, M. *The Dialogic Imagination* (trans. M. Holquist and C. Emerson). Austin: University of Texas Press. 1981.

Bakker, P. 'Pidgins' in J. Arends, P. Muysken and N. Smith (eds), *Pidgins and Creoles: an Introduction*. Amsterdam: John Benjamins. 1995.

Bamgbose, A. 'Pride and prejudice in multilingualism and development' in R. Fardon and G. Furniss (eds), *African Languages, Development and the State*. London: Routledge. 1994.

Banks, A. and Textor, R. *A Cross-polity Survey*. Cambridge MA: MIT Press. 1963.

Barère. *Rapport du Comité de Salut Public sur Les Idiomes*. 8 pluvose an 2.

Baron, D. 'The legendary english-only vote of 1795' http://www2.english.uiuc.edu/baron/essays/legendar.htm.

Baron, D. *Grammar and Good Taste: Reforming the American Language*. New Haven: Yale University Press. 1982.

Bauer, O. *Die Nationalitätenfrage und die Sozialdemokratie*. Vienna. 1924.

Bazin, L. 'La réforme linguistique en Turquie' in I. Fodor and C. Hagège (eds), *Language Reform. Vol. 1*. Hamburg: Buske. 1983.

Behn, J. *Römertum und Völkerwanderung*. Stuttgart: Cotta'sche. 1963.

Bellamy, R. and Schechter, D. *Gramsci and the Italian State*. Manchester University Press. 1993.

Beni, P. *L'anticrusca: parte prima*. Padua: Martini. 1612.

Benjamin, P. 'Neo-protectionism'. *Economic Aspects* XII(2) (2002), pp. 2–14.

Benson, P. *Ethnocentrism and the English Dictionary*. London: Routledge. 2001.

Beretta, M. 'The Grammar of matter: chemical nomenclature during the XVIIIth century' in R. Chartier and P. Corsi (eds), *Sciences et langues en Europe*. Commission européenne: Forum européen de la science et de la technologie. 1996.

Bernard, R. 'Preserving language diversity'. *Human Organization* 51 (1992), pp. 82–9.

Berns, M. 'Sociolinguistics and the teaching of English beyond the 1990s'. *World Englishes* 11(1) (1992), pp. 3–14.

Bickerton, D. *Dynamics of a Creole system*. Cambridge University Press. 1975.

Bickerton, D. *Roots of Language*. Ann Arbor: Karoma. 1981.

Bideleux, R. and Jeffries, I. *A History of Eastern Europe: Crisis and Change*. London: Routledge. 1998.

Billig, M. *Banal Nationalism*. Newbury: Sage. 1995.

Birken-Silverman, G. *Phonetische, morphosyntaktische und lexicalische Varianten in des palermitanischen Mundarten und im Sikuloalbanischen von Piana degli Albanesi.* Wilhelmsfeld: Gottfried Egert. 1989.

Bloch, M. *Feudal Society.* London: Routledge. 1962.

Blommaert, J. 'The metaphors of development and modernization in Tanzanian language policy and research' in R. Fardon and G. Furniss (eds), *African Languages, Development and the State.* London: Routledge. 1994a.

Blommaert, J. 'Ideology and language in Tanzania: a brief survey' in R. Herbert (ed.), *African Linguistics at the Crossroads: Papers from Kwaluseni 1st World Congress of African Linguistics.* Koln: Köppe. 1994b.

Blommaert, J. 'Language planning as a discourse on language and society: the linguistic ideology of a scholarly tradition'. *Language Problems and Language Planning* 20(3) (1996), pp. 199–222.

Blommaert, J. *State Ideology and Language in Tanzania.* Köln: Rüdiger Köppe Verlag. 1999.

Bloomfield, L. 'Literate and illiterate speech'. *American Speech* 2 (1927), pp. 432–9.

Boatner, M. *Encyclopedia of the American Revolution.* New York: McKay. 1966.

Boogerman Castejon, A. 'Educational policy, mixed discourse: response to minority learners in Catalonia'. *Language Problems and Language Planning* 21(1) (1997), pp. 20–43.

Bossuet, J. *Politique tirée des propres paroles de l'Écriture-Sainte.* Paris. 1709.

Bot, K. de. 'Language use as an interface between sociolinguistic and psycholinguistic processes in language attrition and language shift' in J. Klatter-Folmer and P. van Avermaet (eds), *Theories on Maintenance and Loss of Minority Languages.* Münster: Waxmann. 2001.

Bourdieu, P. *Ce que parler veut dire.* Paris: Fayard. 1982.

Bourdieu, P. *Language and Symbolic Power.* Cambridge: Polity Press. 1991.

Bourdieu, P. and Wacquant, L. 'New liberal speak'. *Radical Philosophy* 105 (2001).

Bourhis, R. 'Acculturation, language maintenance and language shift' in J. Klatter-Folmer and P. van Avermaet (eds), *Theories on Maintenance and Loss of Minority Languages.* Münster: Waxmann. 2001.

Bourin, M. and Durand, R. 'Strangers and neighbours' in L. Little and B. Rosenwien (eds), *Debating the Middle Ages.* Oxford: Blackwell. 1998.

Boyle, P. *Class Formation and Civil Society: the Politics of Education in Africa.* Aldershot: Ashgate. 1999.

Brass, P. *Ethnicity and Nationalism: Theory and Comparison.* Newbury: Sage. 1991.

Bratt Paulston, C. 'Linguistic minorities and language policies: four case studies' in W. Fase, K. Jaspaert and S. Kroon (eds), *Maintenance and Loss of Minority Languages.* Amsterdam: John Benjamins. 1992.

Bratt Paulston, C. *Linguistic Minorities in Multilingual Settings. Implications for Language Policies.* Amsterdam: John Benjamins. 1994.

Bratt Paulston, C. 'Language Policies and Language Rights'. *Annual Review of Anthropology* 26 (1997), pp. 73–85.

Bratt Paulston, C. 'Comment'. *International Journal of the Sociology of Language* 157 (2002), pp. 127–35.

Braudel, F. *The Mediterranean and the Mediterranean World in the Age of Philip II* (trans. S. Reynold). London: Collins. 1972.

Braudel, F. *L'identité de France. Vol 2.* Paris: Artaud. 1986.

Breiborde, L. 'Levels of analysis in sociolinguistic explanation. Bilingual codeswitching, social relations and domain theory'. *International Journal of the Sociology of Language* 39 (1983), pp. 5–43.

Breuilly, J. *Nationalism and the State*. University of Manchester Press. 1982.

Broglie, G. de. *Le français pour qu'il vive*. Paris: Gallimard. 1986.

Bruézière, M. *L'Alliance française 1883–1983: Histoire d'une institution*. Paris: Hachette. 1983.

Brumfit, C. 'The Englishness of English-using: conceptualising identities in a language sharing world'. Paper given at the Colloquium on Language and Globalisation, BAAL, Cardiff, September 2002.

Brunot, F. *Histoire de la langue française Tome IX 2eme partie*. Paris: Armand Colin. 1967.

Bruto, G. *The Necessary, Fit and Convenient Education of a Young Gentlewoman* (trans. W. P.). New York: Da Capo Press. 1969.

Brutt-Griffler, J. *World English: A Study of its Development*. Clevedon: Multilingual Matters. 2002.

Buchert, L. *Education in the Development of Tanzania 1919–1990*. London: James Currey. 1994.

Bucklin, S. *Realism and American Foreign Policy. Wilsonians and the Kennan–Morgenthau thesis*. Westport, Connecticut: Praeger. 2001.

Bull, H. *The Anarchical Society: a Study of Order in World Politics*. London: Macmillan. 1977.

Burke, L. Crowley, T. and Girvin, A. (eds), *The Routledge Language and Cultural Theory Reader*. London: Routledge. 2000.

Burke, P. 'Heu domine, adsunt Turcae: a sketch for a social history of post-medieval Latin' in P. Burke and R. Porter (eds), *Language, Self and Society: a Social History of Language*. Oxford: Blackwell. 1991.

Bush, G. *State of the Union Address*. 29 January 2002.

Callinicos, A. *Marxism and the New Imperialism*. London: Bookmarks. 1994.

Calvet, L.-J. *L'Europe et ses langues*. Paris: Plon. 1993.

Camden, W. *Remains Concerning Britain*. University of Toronto Press. 1984.

Canagarajah, S. *Resisting Linguistic Imperialism in English Language Teaching*. Oxford University Press. 1999.

Cannadine, D. 'The British Monarchy c. 1820–1977' in E. Hobsbawm and T. Ranger (eds), *The Invention of Tradition*. Cambridge University Press. 1983.

Capotorti, F. *Study on the Rights of Persons Belonging to Ethnic, Religious and Linguistic Minorities*. New York: United Nations Press. 1979.

Caput, J.-P. *L'académie française*. Paris: Presses universitaires de France. 1986.

Castells, M. *The Rise of the Network Society*. Oxford: Blackwell. 1996.

Cavalli-Sforza, L. *Genes, Peoples and Languages*. London: Allen Lane. 2000.

Chawla, S. 'Linguistics and genes, peoples and languages: philosophical roots of our environmental crisis' in A. Fill and P. Mühlhäusler (eds), *The Ecolinguistics Reader: Language, Ecology and Environment*. London: Continuum. 2001.

Cheshire, J., Kerswill, P. and Williams, A. 'Is there isomorphism between convergence in phonology, grammar and discourse features?' in P. Auer, F. Hinskens and P. Kerswill (eds), *Dialect Change: the Convergence and Divergence of Dialects in Contemporary Societies*. Cambridge University Press. 2002.

Chilton, P., Ilyin, M. and Mey, J. (eds), *Political Discourse in Transition in Europe 1989–1991*. Amsterdam: John Benjamins. 1997.

Chirac, J. *Opening Address to the 7th Francophone Summit* in Hanoi, 14 November 1997.

Chomsky, N. *Language and Mind*. New York: Harcourt Brace. 1972.

Chomsky, N. *9–11*. New York: Seven Stories Press. 2001.

Chowdhry, G. and Nair, S. (eds), *Power, Post-colonialism and International Relations: Reading Race, Gender, and Class*. London: Routledge. 2002.

CILT (Centre for Information on Language Teaching and Research). *Hindi: Language and Culture Guide*. London: CILT. 1985.

Clairis, C. 'Le cas du grec' in I. Fodor and C. Hagège (eds), *Language Reform*. Hamburg: Buske. 1983.

Clausewitz, C. von. *On War* (trans. Graham). Ware: Wordsworth. 1830/1997.

Clyne, M. *Doing and Redoing Corpus Planning*. Berlin: Mouton de Gruyter. 1997.

Clyne, M. *Language and Society in the German-speaking Countries*. Cambridge University Press. 1984.

Cobban, A. *The Nation State and National Self-determination* (2nd edn). London: Collins. 1969.

Coen, R. 'Rare, not well done: the US coverage of climate change talks'. *Extra*. March–April 2001.

Collins, R. *The Basques*. Oxford: Blackwell. 1986.

Comet, I. Codina, R. 'Minority languages in Spain' in D. Gorter, J. Hoekstra, L. Jansma and J. Ytsma (eds), *Papers for the Fourth International Conference on Minority Languages*. Clevedon: Multilingual Matters. 1990.

Conac, G., Desouches, C. and Sabourin, L. *La coopération multilatérale francophone*. Paris: Economica. 1987.

Conrad, A. 'The International Role of English: The State of the Discussion' in J. Fishman *et al.* (eds), *Post-Imperial English: Status Change in Former British and American Colonies 1940–1990*. Berlin: Mouton de Gruyter. 1996.

Conversi, D. *The Basques, the Catalans and Spain: Alternative Routes to Mobilisation*. London: Hurst. 1997.

Cooper, R. *Language Planning and Social Change*. Cambridge University Press. 1989.

Corré, A. *A Glossary of Lingua Franca*. http://www.uwm.edu/~corre/franca/go.html. 2000.

Crawford, J. *Bilingual Education: History, Politics, Theory, and Practice*. Trenton, NJ: Crane Publishing. 1989.

Crawford, J. *A Source Book on the Official English Controversy*. University of Chicago. 1992.

Crevecoeur, H. 'Letter from an American Farmer'. *Encyclopedia Britannica* 1971/1782.

Crystal, D. *Language Death*. Cambridge University Press. 2000.

Cummins, J. *Language, Power and Pedagogy*. Clevedon: Multilingual Matters. 2000.

Cummins, J. and Corson, D. *Bilingual Education*. Dordrecht: Kluwer. 1997.

Czerny, P. *The Politics of Grandeur. Ideological Aspects of de Gaulle's Foreign Policy*. Cambridge University Press. 1980.

Czinkota, M. *International Business*. Mason, Ohio: Thomson/South-Western. 2003.

Daff, M. 'Sénégal' in R. Chaudenson (ed.), *La Francophonie: représentations, réálités, perspectives*. Paris: Didier Erudition. 1991.

Daniels, R. *Coming to America. A History of Immigration and Ethnicity in American Life*. New York: Harper Collins. 1990.

Danish Ministry of Foreign Affairs. *Strategy for Danish Development Cooperation with Tanzania*. January 2002.

Dardjowidjojo, S. 'Strategies for a successful national language policy: the Indonesian case'. *International Journal of the Sociology of Language* 130 (1998), pp. 35–49.

Darwin, C. *The Descent of Man*. London: Murray. 1871.

Das Gupta, J. and Ferguson, C. 'Problems of Language Planning' in J. Rubin, B. Jernudd, J. Das Gupta, J. Fishman and C. Ferguson (eds), *Language Planning Processes*. Berlin: Mouton de Gruyter. 1977.

Dascal, M. (ed.), *The Philosophy of Language: an International Handbook of Contemporary Research. Volumes 1–3*. Berlin: Walter de Gruyter. 1992 and 1995.

Davis, R. *A History of Medieval Europe* (2nd edn). Harlow: Longman. 1988.

Déniau, X. *La Francophonie*. Paris: Gallimard. 1983.

Derhemi, E. 'The endangered Arbresh language and the importance of standardised writing for its survival. The case of Piana degli Albanesi, Sicily'. *MOST Journal on Multicultural Societies* 4(2) (2002).

Dickson, C. 'Study of Labour Market and Foreign Enterprise in Vietnam'. *Vietnam Commerce and Industry* 19(12) (1998), pp. 15–16.

Dorian, N. 'Western language ideologies and small language prospects' in L. Grenoble and L. Whaley (eds), *Endangered Languages*. Cambridge University Press. 1998.

Dorian, N. (ed.), *Investigating Obsolescence: Studies in Language Contraction and Death*. Cambridge University Press. 1989.

Drake, C. *National Integration in Indonesia*. University of Hawaii Press. 1993.

Duby, G. (ed), *Histoire de la France*. Paris: Larousse. 1987.

Dupuy, A. *Histoire chronologique de la civilisation occitane*. Lunel: Saber. 1987.

Dworkin, R. *A Matter of Principle*. Cambridge, MA: Harvard University Press. 1985.

Eades, D. 'They don't speak an Aboriginal language, or do they?' in I. Keen (ed.), *Being Black: Aboriginal Cultures in 'settled' Australia*. Canberra: Aboriginal Studies Press. 1988.

Eco, U. *The Search for the Perfect Language*. Oxford: Blackwell. 1995.

Economist. 'Goodnight Vietnam' 8 January 2000. pp. 74–6.

Edwards, J. *Language, Society and Identity*. Oxford: Blackwell. 1985.

Edwards, J. 'Sociopolitical aspects of language maintenance and loss: towards a typology of minority language situations' in W. Fase, K. Jaspaert and S. Kroon (eds), *Maintenance and Loss of Minority Languages*. Amsterdam: John Benjamins. 1992.

Edwards, J. *Multilingualism*. London: Routledge. 1994.

Eggington, W. 'Language revitalisation planning within a power/solidarity framework'. *Current Issues in Language Planning* 2(2–3) (2001), pp. 242–50.

Eide, A. 'Ethnic conflicts and minority protection: roles for the international community' in K. Rupesinghe and V. Tishkov (eds), *Ethnicity and Power in the Contemporary World*. New York: United Nations University Press. 1996.

Eldridge, P. *The Politics of Human Rights in Southeast Asia*. London: Routledge. 2002.

Elias, N. *The Germans: Power Struggles and the Development of Habitus in the Nineteenth and Twentieth centuries* (trans. Schröter). Cambridge: Polity Press. 1996.

Elugbe, B. 'Minority language development in Nigeria: a situation report on Rivers and Bendel States' in R. Fardon and G. Furniss (eds), *African Languages, Development and the State*. London: Routledge. 1994.

Entwhistle, W. *The Spanish Language*. London: Faber and Faber. 1936.

Errington, J. 'Indonesian's Development: on the state of a language of state' in B. Schieffelin, K. Woolard and P. Kroskrity (eds), *Language Ideologies: Practice and Theory*. Oxford University Press. 1998.

Esteva Fabregat, C. 'Ethnicity, social class and acculturation of immigrants in Barcelona'. *Ethnologia Europaea* 8(1) (1975), pp. 23–44.

Ethnologue website http://www.ethnologue.com/.

European Bureau For Lesser Used Languages. *Ljouwert Declaration* 15 June 2002.

Eurydice. *Key Data on Education in Europe 1995*. Edition 1996.

Eurydice. *Key Data on Education in Europe 1997*. Edition 1997.

Eurydice. *Key Data on Education in Europe 1999–2000*. Edition 2000.

Fairclough, N. *Language and Power*. Harlow: Longman. 1989.

Fairclough, N. *New Labour, New Language*. London: Routledge. 2000.

Fairhead, J. 'Healthy production and reproduction: agricultural, medical and linguistic pluralism in a Bwisha community, Eastern Zaire' in R. Fardon and G. Furniss (eds), *African Languages, Development and the State*. London: Routledge. 1994.

Fanon, F. *The Wretched of the Earth*. Harmondsworth: Penguin. 1967.

Fardon, R. and Furniss, G. (eds), *African Languages, Development and the State*. London: Routledge. 1994.

Fase. W., Jaspaert, K. and Kroon, S. (eds), *Maintenance and Loss of Minority Languages*. Amsterdam: John Benjamins. 1992.

Fatah, E. 'Otoritarianisme dan Distorsi Bahasa' in H. Alwi (ed.), *Politik Bahasa*. Jakarta: Pusat Bahasa. 2000.

Favre d'Échallens, M. 'Après l'euro, l'anglo!' *Les Echos* 3 December 2002.

Febvre, L. and Martin, H.-J. *The Coming of the Book: the Impact of Printing 1450–1800*. London: New Left Books. 1976.

Feer, R. 'Official use of the German language in Pennsylvania'. *Pennsylvania Magazine of History and Biography* 76 (1952), pp. 394–405.

Ferrer, F. 'Languages, minorities and education in Spain: the case of Catalonia'. *Comparative Education* 36(2) (2000), p. 187.

Ferguson, C. 'Diglossia' in *Word* 15. pp. 325–40. 1959.

Ferguson, C. *Language Development*. 1968 (mimeographed document quoted by Ansre (1974)).

Ferguson, C. 'Sociolinguistic settings of language planning' in J. Rubin *et al.* (eds), *Language Planning Processes*. Berlin: Mouton de Gruyter. 1977.

Fevre, R., Denney, D. and Borland, J. 'Class, status and party in the analysis of nationalism: lessons from Max Weber'. *Nations and Nationalism*. 3(4) (1997), pp. 559–79.

Fichte, J. *Reden an die deutsche Nation*. Munich: Goldmann. 1807–1808/1905.

Fill, A. *Ökolinguistik: eine Einführung*. Tübingen: Gunter Narr. 1993.

Fill, A. 'Ecolinguistics: state of the art 1998' in A. Fill and P. Mühlhäusler (eds), *The Ecolinguistics Reader: Language, Ecology and Environment*. London: Continuum. 2001.

Fishman, J. 'Language maintenance and language shift as fields of enquiry'. *Linguistics* 9 (1964), pp. 32–70.

Fishman, J. 'Introduction' in J. Fishman, C. Ferguson and J. Das Gupta (eds), *Language Problems of Developing Nations*. New York: Wiley. 1968.

Fishman, J. 'The impact of nationalism on language planning' in J. Rubin and B. Jernudd (eds), *Can Language be Planned?* University of Hawaii. 1971.

Fishman, J. *Contributions to the Sociology of Language*. Berlin: Mouton de Gruyter. 1974.

Fishman, J. *Bilingual Education: An International Sociological Perspective*. Rowley: Newbury House. 1977b.

Fishman, J. *Reversing Language Shift*. Clevedon: Multilingual Matters. 1991.

Fishman, J. *The Earliest Stages of Language Planning. The First Congress Phenomenon*. Berlin: Mouton de Gruyter. 1993.

Fishman, J. 'Introduction: some empirical and theoretical issues' in J. Fishman, A. Conrad and A. Rubal-Lopez (eds), *Post-Imperial English: Status Change in Former British and American Colonies 1940–1990*. Berlin: Manton de Gruyter. 1996.

Fishman, J. 'Maintaining languages: what works and what doesn't' in G. Cantoni (ed.), *Stabilizing Indigenous Languages*. Flagstaff: North Arizona University Press. 1997.

Fishman, J. *Can Threatened Languages be Saved?* Clevedon: Multilingual Matters. 2001.

Fishman, J. 'Introduction'. *MOST Journal on Multicultural Societies* 4(2) (2002).

Fishman, J., Ferguson, C. and Das Gupta, J. *Language Problems of Developing Nations*. New York: Wiley. 1968.

Fishman, J., Cooper, R. and Conrad, A. *The Spread of English, the Sociology of English as an Additional Language*. Rowley, MA: Newbury House. 1977.

Fishman, J., Conrad, A. and Rubal-Lopez, A. (eds), *Post-Imperial English: Status Change in Former British and American Colonies 1940–1990*. Berlin: Mouton de Gruyter. 1996.

Fodor, I. 'Hungarian: evolution, stagnation, reform and further development' in I. Fodor and C. Hagège (eds), *Language Reform*. Hamburg: Buske. 1983.

Forné, J. *Euskadi, nation et idéologie*. Paris: Editions du CNRS. 1990.

Fossier, R. *Histoire sociale de l'Occident médiéval*. Paris: Armand Colin. 1970.

Foucault, M. *The Archeology of Knowledge and Discourse on Language* (trans. S. Smith). New York: Pantheon. 1972.

Franolić, B. 'The development of literary Croatian and Serbian' in I. Fodor and C. Hagège (eds), *Language Reform Vol II*. Hamburg: Buske. 1983.

Fukuyama, F. 'The end of History?' *The National Interest*. Summer 1989.

Fukuyama, F. *The End of History and the Last Man*. London: Hamilton. 1992.

Fumaroli, M. *Quand l'Europe parlait français*. Paris: Fallois. 2001.

Furbee, N. and Stanley, L. 'A collaborative model for preparing indigenous curators of a heritage language'. *International Journal of the Sociology of Language* 154 (2002), pp. 113–28.

Gardner, R. and Lambert, W. *Attitudes and Motivation in Second Language Learning*. Rowley: Newbury House. 1972.

Gasarasi, C. 'The mass naturalisation and further integration of Rwandese refugees in Tanzania: process, problems and prospects'. *Journal of Refugee Studies* 3(2) (1990).

Gellner, E. *Nations and Nationalism*. Oxford: Blackwell. 1983.

Gellner, E. *Language and Solitude: Wittgenstein, Malinowski and the Habsburg Dilemma*. Cambridge University Press. 1998.

Generalitat de Catalunya. *Language Policy Report 2000*. http://cultura.gencat.es/llengcat/informe/angles2001/.

Giddens, A. *The Consequences of Modernity*. Cambridge: Polity Press. 1990.

Giddens, A. 'Structuration theory: past present and future' in C. Bryant and D. Jary (eds), *Giddens' Theory of Structuration: a Critical Appreciation*. London: Routledge. Pp. 201–21. 1991.

Giordan, H. 'La Politique Linguistique de la France'. Paper given at the conference *Les Enjeux d'une politique linguistique pour la France*, Nimes, France, 28 and 29 August 2003.

Giraudot, V. and Joppke, C. *Language in Migration: Controlling a New Migration World*. London: Routledge. 2001.

Goatly, A. 'Green Grammar and Grammatical Metaphor' in A. Fill and P. Mühlhäusler (eds), *The Ecolinguistics Reader: Language, Ecology and Environment*. London: Continuum. 2001.

Goldmann, K. *Transforming the European Nation State*. Newbury: Sage. 2001.

Goodman, M. 'The Portuguese element in the American Creoles' in G. Gilbert (ed.), *Pidgin and Creole Languages: Essays in Memory of John E. Reinecke*. Honolulu: University of Hawaii Press. 1987.

Gonzalez, R. (ed.), *Language Ideologies: Critical Perspectives on the Official English Movement. Volume 2. History, Theory and Policy*. New Jersey: Lawrence Erlbaum. 2001.

Gordon, D. 'The global economy: new edifice or crumbling foundation?' *New Left Review* 168 (1988).

Gordon, B. *America's Trade Follies*. London: Routledge. 2001.

Gramsci, A. *Selections from the Prison Notebooks* in Hoare and Nowell Smith (eds). London: Lawrence and Wishart. 1971.

Gramsci, A. *Selections from Cultural Writings* in Forgacs and Nowell Smith (eds). London: Lawrence and Wishart. 1985.

Grant, B. *Indonesia*. Melbourne University Press. 1996.

Grégoire, H. Abbé. *Sur la nécessité et les moyens d'anéantir les patois et d'universaliser l'usage de la langue française* presented to Parliament 16 prairial An II (4 June 1794).

Green, J. 'Language status and political aspirations: the case of Northern Spain' in M. Parry *et al.* (eds), *The Changing Voices of Europe*. Cardiff: University of Wales Press. 1994.

Greenfeld, L. *Nationalism, Five Roads to Modernity*. Cambridge, MA: Harvard University Press. 1992.

Greider, W. *One World, Ready or Not: the Manic Logic of Global Capitalism*. New York: Simon Schuster. 1997.

Grenoble, L. and Whaley, L. 'Towards a typology of language endangerment' in L. Grenoble and L. Whaley (eds), *Endangered Languages*. Cambridge University Press. 1998.

Grillo, R. 'Anthropology, language, politics' in R. Grillo (ed.), *Social Anthropology and the Politics of Language*. London: Routledge. 1989.

Grimes, B. (ed.), *Languages of the World* (14th edn). Dallas: Summer Institute of Linguistics. 1992/2000.

Grin, F. 'Language spread and linguistic diversity' in M. Kontra, R. Phillipson, T. Skutnabb Kangas and T. Varady (eds), *Language: a Right and a Resource*. Central European University Press. 1999.

Grin, F. *Language Policy Evaluation and the European Charter on Regional or Minority Languages*. Basingstoke: Palgrave Macmillan. 2003.

Grosjean, F. *Life with Two Languages: an Introduction to Bilingualism*. Cambridge, MA: Harvard University Press. 1982.

Guéhenno, J. *The End of the Nation State*. University of Minneapolis Press. 1995.

Guibernau, M. 'Nations without states: Catalonia, a case study' in M. Guibernau and J. Rex (eds), *The Ethnicity Reader: Nationalism, Multiculturalism and Migration*. Cambridge: Polity. 1997.

Guibernau, M. *Nations without States: Political Communities in the Global Age*. Cambridge: Polity. 1999.

Guibernau, M. 'Between autonomy and secession: the accommodation of Catalonia within the new democratic Spain'. *ESRC One Europe or Several Programme*. Working Paper 48/02. 2002.

Guidry, J., Kennedy, M. and Zald, M. *Globalizations and Social Movements* in J. Guidry, M. Kennedy and M. Zald (eds), *Globalizations and Social Movements: Culture, Power and the Transnational Public Sphere*. Ann Arbor: University of Michigan Press. 2000.

Guillen, M. 'Is globalization civilizing, destructive or feeble? A critique of five key debates in the social science literature'. *Annual Review of Sociology* 27 (2001), pp. 235–60.

Gumperz, J. 'Types of linguistic communities' in A. Dil (ed.), *Language and Social Groups: Essays by John J. Gumperz*. Stanford University Press. 1971/1962.

Hagège, C. *Le français et les siècles*. Paris: Odile Jacob. 1987.

Hagège, C. *Histoire d'un combat*. Paris: Michel Hagège. 1996.

Hale, K. 'On endangered languages and the importance of linguistic diversity' in L. Grenoble and L. Whaley (eds), *Endangered Languages*. Cambridge University Press. 1998.

Hall, R. *Pidgin and Creole Languages*. Ithaca: Cornell University Press. 1966.

Hall, R. *External History of the Romance Languages*. New York: Elsevier. 1974.

Halliday, M. 'New ways of meaning: the challenge to applied linguistics' in A. Fill and P. Mühlhäusler (eds), *The Ecolinguistics Reader: Language, Ecology and Environment*. London: Continuum. 2001.

Hancock, I. 'The domestic hypothesis, diffusion and componentiality. An account of Atlantic Anglophone Creole origins' in P. Muysken and N. Smith (eds), *Substrata Versus Universals in Creole Genesis*. Amsterdam: John Benjamins. 1986.

Hamers, J. and Blanc, M. *Bilinguality and Bilingualism*. Cambridge University Press. 1989.

Hamied, F. 'Pengajaran Bahasa Ansing, in H. Alwi (ed.), *Politik Bahasa*. Jakarta: Pusat Bahasa. 2000.

Hansen, E. *Rural Catalonia Under the Franco Regime*. Cambridge University Press. 1977.

Harrigan, P. *Mobility, Elites and Education in French Society of the Second Empire*. Ontario: Wilfred Laurier University Press. 1980.

Hartmann, R. *The History of Lexicography*. Amsterdam: John Benjamins. 1986.

Hartmann, R. *Teaching and Researching Lexicography*. Harlow: Longman. 2001.

Hartweg, F. 'Precarious language rights under changing governments: the case of Alsace 1850–1940' in S. Vilfan (ed.), *Ethnic Groups and Language Rights*. Aldershot: Dartmouth. 1993.

Hastings, A. *The Construction of Nationhood*. Cambridge University Press. 1997.

Haugen, E. 'Language Planning in Modern Norway' in J. Fishman (ed.), *Readings in the Sociology of Languages*. Berlin: Mouton de Gruyter. 1968.

Haugen, E. *The Ecology of Language*. Stanford University Press. 1972.

Haugen, E. 'Dialect, language and nation'. *American Anthropologist* 68 (1966), pp. 922–35.

Haust, D. *Sprachkontakt in Afrika*. Köln: Rüdiger Köppe Verlag. 1995.

Haust, D. and Dittmar, N. 'Taxonomic or functional models in the description of codeswitching. Evidence from Mandinka and Wolof in African contact situations' in R. Jacobson (ed.), *Codeswitching Worldwide*. The Hague: Mouton. 1998.

Heaton, H. *Economic History of Europe*. London: Harper and Row. 1963.

Hechter, M. *Containing Nationalism*. Oxford University Press. 2000.

Held, D., McGrew, A., Goldblatt, D. and Perraton, J. *Global Transformations*. Cambridge: Polity Press. 1999.

Hevizi, J. *Autonomies in Europe and Hungary*. Toronto: Corvinus. 2002.

Hinnebusch, T., Nurse, D. and Mould, M. *Studies in the Classification of Eastern Bantu Languages*. Hamburg: Helmut Buske. 1981.

Hirst, P. and Thompson, G. *Globalization in Question*. Cambridge: Polity Press. 1996.

Hobbes, T. *Leviathan*. Harmondsworth: Penguin. 1968.

Hobsbawn, E. 'Mass producing traditions: Europe 1870–1914' in E. Hobsbawm and T. Ranger (eds), *The Invention of Tradition*. Cambridge University Press. 1983.

Hobsbawm, E. *Nations and Nationalism Since 1780*. Cambridge University Press. 1990.

Hoffmann, C. 'Twenty years of language planning in contemporary Spain' in S. Wright (ed.), *Monolingualism and Bilingualism: Lessons from Canada and Spain*. Clevedon: Multilingual Matters. 1996.

Hoffmann, C. 'Balancing language planning and language rights: Catalonia's uneasy juggling act'. *Journal of Multilingual and Multicultural Development* 21(5) (2000), pp. 425–42.

Hohenberg, P. *The Making of Urban Europe 1000–1994*. Cambridge MA: Harvard University Press. 1995.

Holborow, M. *The Politics of English*. Newbury: Sage. 1999.

Holm, J. *Pidgins and Creoles Volume I: Theory and Structure*. Cambridge University Press. 1988.

Holm, J. *Pidgins and Creoles Volume II: Reference Survey.* Cambridge University Press. 1989.

Houston, R. *Literacy in Early Modern Europe.* Harlow: Longman. 1988.

Howell, J. *East African Community Subject Guide to Official Publications.* Washington: Library of Congress. 1976.

Hroch, M. *Social Preconditions of National Revival in Europe. A Comparative Analysis of the Social Composition of Patriotic Groups among the Smaller European Nations* (trans. B. Fowkes). Cambridge University Press. 1985.

Huda, N. 'Kedudukan dan Fungsi Bahasa Asing' in H. Alwi (ed.), *Politik Bahasa.* Jakarta: Pusat Bahasa. 2000.

Hudson, A., Chavez, E. and Bill, G. 'The many faces of language maintenance: Spanish language claiming in five South-western states' in C. Silva-Corvalán (ed.), *Spanish in Four Continents.* Georgetown University Press. 1995.

Humphrey, C. 'Janus-faced signs' in R. Grillo (ed.), *Social Anthropology and the Politics of Language.* London: Routledge. 1989.

Hunter, T. 'Ancient beginnings: the spread of Indic scripts' in A. Kumar and J. McGlynn (eds), *Illuminations: the Writing Traditions of Indonesia.* New York: Weatherhill. 1996.

Hutchinson, J. and Smith, A. *Nationalism.* Oxford University Press. 1994.

Hutton, C. *Linguistics and the Third Reich.* London: Routledge. 1999.

Hymes, D. (ed.), *Pidginization and Creolization of Languages: Proceedings of a Conference Held at the University of the West Indies, Mona, Jamaica, 1968.* Cambridge University Press. 1971.

Ignatieff, M. *Blood and Belonging.* London: Vintage. 1994.

Ito, T. Indonesia Briefing Report *Washington Post* washingtonpost.com staff. 1998.

Jakarta Post 21/12/00, p. 1. 'Hasan di Tiro in Stockholm'.

Jakarta Post 13/12/00, p. 5. 'Your Letters' Gus Tyana.

Jakarta Post 27/12/01 p. 3. 'Fear of Ethnic Nationalism'.

Jakarta Post 10/01/02, p. 7. 'Ten More Killed in fresh clashes in Aceh'.

Jakarta Post 10/01/02, p. 7. 'NTT needs more 3,200 teachers: Governor' (sic).

Jakarta Post 30/07/02. 'Is Indonesia going to lose Aceh?'

Janics, K. *Czechoslovak Policy and the Hungarian Minority 1945–1948.* Columbia University Press. 1982.

Janson, T. 'Language change and metalinguistic change: Latin to Romance and other cases' in R. Wright (ed.), *Latin and the Romance Languages in the Early Middle Ages.* Pennsylvania State University Press. 1991.

Japundžić, M. *The Croatian Glagolitic Heritage* (trans. S. Granic). Croatian Academy of America. No date.

Jenkins, J. *The Phonology of English as an International Language.* Oxford University Press. 2000.

Jernudd, B. and Das Gupta, J. 'Towards a theory of Language Planning' in J. Rubin and B. Jernudd (eds), *Can Language be Planned?* University of Hawaii. 1971.

Jernudd, B. and Rubin, J. 'Some introductory References Pertaining to Language Planning' in J. Rubin and B. Jernudd (eds), *Can Language be Planned?* University of Hawaii. 1971.

Jett, D. *Why Peacekeeping Fails.* Basingstoke: Palgrave. 1999.

Jocks, C. 'Living words and cartoon translations: Longhouse texts and the limitations of English' in L. Grenoble and L. Whaley (eds), *Endangered Languages.* Cambridge University Press. 1998.

Johns, A. 'In the language of the divine: the contribution of Arabic' in A. Kumar and J. McGlynn (eds), *Illuminations: the Writing Traditions of Indonesia.* New York: Weatherhill. 1996.

Johnson, P.-M. and Mayrand, K. 'Beyond Trade: Broadening the Globalization Governance Agenda' in J. Kirton, J. Daniels and A. Freytag (eds), *Guiding Global Order: G8 Governance in the Twenty First Century*. Aldershot: Ashgate. 2000.

Joll, J. *Gramsci*. London: Fontana. 1977.

Joseph, J. *Eloquence and Power: the Rise of Language Standards and Standard Languages*. London: Pinter. 1987.

Joseph, J. 'Linguistic Identity and the limits of global English'. Paper given at the English Language Research Seminar, University of Birmingham, UK, 12 March 2002.

Joyce, P. 'The people's English: language and class in England c 1840–1920' in P. Burke and R. Porter (eds), *Language, Self and Society: a Social History of Language*. Oxford: Blackwell. 1991.

Kachru, B. *The Alchemy of English: the Spread, Functions and Models for Non-native Varieties of English*. Oxford: Pergamon Press. 1986.

Kachru, B. 'Standards, codification and sociolinguistic realism: the English language in the outer circle' in R. Quirk and H. Widdowson (eds), *English in the World: Papers of an International Conference held to Celebrate the 50th Anniversary of the British Council*. Cambridge University Press. 1985.

Kachru, B. (ed.), *The Other Tongue. English across Cultures*. University of Illinois Press. 1982.

Kachru, B. 'Englishization and contact linguistics'. *World Englishes* 13(2) (1994), pp. 135–54.

Kahn, M. 'The passive voice of science: language abuse in the wildlife profession' in A. Fill and P. Mühlhäusler (eds), *The Ecolinguistics Reader: Language, Ecology and Environment*. London: Continuum. 2001.

Kamen, H. *Spain 1469–1714*. Harlow: Longman. 1991.

Kana, M. 'Language planning and the problem of low varieties of Indonesian' in A. Hassan (ed.), *Language Planning in South-East Asia*. Kuala Lumpur: Ministry of Education. 1994.

Karker, A. 'Language reform efforts in Denmark and Sweden' in I. Fodor and C. Hagège (eds), *Language Reform*. Hamburg: Buske. 1983.

Karpat, J. 'The transition of the Slovaks from a non-dominant ethnic group to a dominant nation' in S. Vilfan (ed.), *Ethnic Groups and Language Rights*. Aldershot: Dartmouth. 1993.

Katičić, R. 'Undoing a unified language, Bosnian, Serbian and Croatian' in M. Clyne (ed.), *Undoing and Redoing Corpus Planning*. Berlin: Mouton de Gruyter. 1997.

Keck, M. and Sikkink, K. *Activists Beyond Borders: Advocacy Networks in International Politics*. Ithaca: Cornell University Press. 1998.

Kedourie, E. *Nationalism*. Oxford: Blackwell. 1960.

Kemp, T. *Industrialisation in 19th Century Europe*. Harlow: Longman. 1969.

Kemp, T. 'Economic and social policy in France' in *Cambridge History of Europe*. Cambridge University Press. Pp. 691–738. 1989.

Keohane, R. *Power and Interdependence*. New York: Little Brown. 1977.

Keynes, J. *The World's Economic Outlook*. 1932. http://www.geocities.com/ecocorner/intelarea/jmk1.html

Kiesler, S., Walsh, J., Hesse, B. and Sproull, L. 'Returns to Science'. *Communications of the ACM* 36 (1993), pp. 90–101.

Kloss, H. '*Abstand* languages and *Ausbau* languages'. *Anthropological Linguistics* 9 (1967), pp. 29–41.

Kohn, H. *Habsburg Empire 1804–1918*. Princeton: Van Nostrand. 1961.

Kramer, J. 'Language planning in Italy' in I. Fodor and C. Hagège (eds), *Language Reform*. Hamburg: Buske. 1983.

Krauss, M. 'The world's languages in crisis'. *Language* 68 (1992), pp. 4–10.

Kubchandani, L. 'Multilingualism in India' in C. Kennedy (ed.), *Language Planning and Education*. London: George Allen. 1983.

Kupchan, C. *Nationalism and Nationalities in the New Europe*. Ithaca: Cornell University Press. 1995.

Kurdybacha, L. 'The Commission for National Education in Poland'. *History of Education* 2(2) (1973), pp. 133–47.

Kymlicka, W. *Multicultural Citizenship*. Oxford University Press. 1995.

Kymlicka, W. *Politics in the Vernacular: Nationalism, Multiculturalism and Citizenship*. Oxford University Press. 2001.

Laitin, D. *Politics Language and Thought*. University of Chicago Press. 1977.

Laitin, D. *Hegemony and Culture: Politics and Religious Change among the Yoruba*. University of Chicago Press. 1986.

Laitin, D. 'Linguistic revival: politics and culture in Catalonia'. *Comparative Studies in Society and History* 31 (1989), pp. 297–317.

Laitin, D. *Language Repertoires and State Construction in Africa*. Cambridge University Press. 1992.

Laitin, D. 'Language and nationalism in the post-Soviet Republics'. *Post-Soviet Affairs* 12 (1996), pp. 4–25.

Laitin, D. 'Language conflict and violence: or the straw that strengthened the camel's back'. *Estudio Working Paper 137*, 1999.

Langman, J. 'Mother-tongue education versus bilingual education: shifting ideologies and policies in the Republic of Slovakia'. *International Journal of the Sociology of Language* 154 (2002), pp. 47–65.

Laycock, D. 'Diversity in Melanesia: a tentative explanation' in A. Fill and P. Mühlhäusler (eds), *The Ecolinguistics Reader: Language, Ecology and Environment*. London: Continuum. 2001.

Lebrun, F. *Histoire des Catholiques en France du XVe siècle à nos jours*. Toulouse: Privat. 1980.

Leitner, G. '"Have I your permission to leave, Sir?" Die Herausforderung der neuen Formen des Englischen für die Anglistik'. *Die Neueren Sprachen* 90(1) (1991), pp. 23–38.

Leitner, G. 'English as a pluricentric language' in M. Clyne (ed.), *Pluricentric Languages*. Berlin: Mouton de Gruyter. 1992.

LePage, R. and Tabouret-Keller, A. *Acts of Identity, Creole-based Approaches to Language and Ethnicity*. Cambridge University Press. 1985.

Lepschy, A. and Lepschy, G. *The Italian Language Today* (2nd edn). London: Routledge. 1988.

Levinger, J. 'Language and identity in Bosnia-Herzegovina' in P. Chilton, M. Ilyin and J. Mey (eds), *Political Discourse in Transition in Europe 1989–1991*. Amsterdam: John Benjamins. 1998.

Levitt, T. 'The globalization of markets'. *Harvard Business Review* 61(3) (1983), pp. 92–102.

Lewis, E. 'Bilingualism and bilingual education: the ancient world to the Renaissance' in J. Fishman (ed.), *Bilingual Education*. Rowley, MA: Newbury House. 1976.

Li Wei, *The Bilingualism Reader*. London: Routledge. 2000.

Locke, J. *Two Treatises of Government*. Cambridge University Press. 1967.

Luard, E. *International Agencies: The Framework of Interdependence*. London: Macmillan. 1977.

Luard, E. *The Globalization of Politics*. London: Macmillan. 1990.

Maas, U. *Sprachpolitik und politische Sprachwissenschaft*. Frankfurt am Main: Suhrkamp. 1989.

Macartney, C. *Habsburg Empire 1790–1918*. London: Weidenfeld and Nicolson. 1968.

Mafu, S. *The Role of English in the Context of National Development (Vision 2025)*. Unpublished PhD thesis, Aston University, UK. 2001.

Magbaily Fyle, C. 'Official and unofficial attitudes and policy towards Krio as the main lingua franca in Sierra Leone' in R. Fardon and G. Furniss (eds), *African Languages, Development and the State*. London: Routledge. 1994.

Mahsun. 'Bahasa Daerah Sebagai Sarana Peningkatan Pemahaman Kondisi Kebinekaan dalam Ketunggalikaaan Masyarakat Indonesia' in H. Alwi (ed.), *Politik Bahasa*. Jakarta: Pusat Bahasa. 2000.

Mallinson, V. *The Western European Idea in Education*. Oxford: Pergamon. 1980.

Mar-Molinero, C. 'The teaching of Catalan in Catalonia'. *Journal of Multilingual and Multicultural Development* 10(4) (1989), pp. 307–27.

Marx, K. *Collected Works*. London: Lawrence and Wishart. 1976.

Mateo, M. and Aizpurua, X. *Sociolinguistic Studies Carried Out by the Deputy Ministry for Language Policy of the Basque Government* 2003. http://cultura.gencat.net/llengcat/ noves/hm02hivern/internacional/a_miren1_3.htm.

Maurais, J. and Morris, M. *Languages in a Globalising World*. Cambridge University Press. 2003.

Mauro, T. de *Storia linguistica dell'Italia unita*. Bari: Laterza. 1963.

May, S. 'It is conceiving minority language rights' in W. Kymlicka and A. Patten (eds), *Language Rights and Political Theory*. Oxford University Press. 2003.

May, S. *Language and Minority Rights: Ethnicity, Nationalism and the Politics of Language*. Harlow: Longman. 2001.

Mazrui, A. *Political Values and the Educated Class in Africa*. London: Heinemann. 1978.

Mazrui, A. 'The World Bank, the language question and the future of African education'. *Race and Class* 38(3) (1997), pp. 35–48.

Mazrui, A. 'Africa between the Meiji Restoration and the legacy of Atatürk: comparative dilemmas of modernisation' in O. Iheduru (ed.), *Contending Issues in African Development*. Westport, CT: Greenwood. 2001.

Mazrui, A. and Mazrui, A. *Swahili State and Society*. London: James Currey. 1995.

Mazrui, A. and Mazrui, A. *The Power of Babel: Language and Governance in the African Experience*. Oxford: James Currey. 1998.

Mazrui, A. and Tidy, M. *Nationalism and New States in Africa*. London: Heinemann. 1984.

McRoberts, K. *Catalonia: Nation Building without a State*. Oxford University Press. 2001.

Meyer, J., Boli, J., Thomas, G. and Ramirez, F. 'World society and the nation state'. *American Journal of Sociology* 103(1) (1997), pp. 144–81.

Michael, I. *The Teaching of English*. Cambridge University Press. 1987.

Miehle, H. Paper at the conference on Language and Culture at Atmajaya Catholic University, 24 July 2001.

Mignolo, W. *The Darker Side of the Renaissance. Literacy, Territoriality, and Colonization*. Ann Arbor: University of Michigan Press. 1995.

Mill, J.S. *Utilitarianism. On Liberty*. Ware: Wordsworth. 1859/1996.

Mill, J.S. *Consideration on Representative Government*. London: Dent. 1861/1972.

Miller, D. 'In what sense must socialism be communitarian?' *Social Philosophy and Policy* 6(2) (1989), pp. 51–73.

Miller, H. and Miller, K. 'Language policy and identity: the case of Catalonia'. *International Studies in Sociology of Education* 6(1) (1996), pp. 113–28.

Miller, D. and Walzer, M. (eds), *Pluralism, Justice, and Equality*. Oxford University Press. 1995.

Millet, Y. 'Continuité et discontinuité: cas du tchèque' in I. Fodor and C. Hagège (eds), *Language Reform*. Hamburg: Buske. 1983.

Milroy, J. and Milroy, L. *Authority in Language: Investigating Language Prescription and Standardisation*. London: Routledge. 1985.

Ministère de la culture et de la communication *Rapport au parlement sur l'application de la loi du 4 août 1994 relative à l'emploi de la langue française*. 2000.

Ministère de l'éducation nationale *Note d'information 00.40* 2000.

Ministère de l'éducation nationale *Note d'information 01.37* 2001a.

Ministère de l'éducation nationale *Note d'information 01.18* 2001b.

Mishra, R. *Globalisation and the Welfare State*. Cheltenham: Edward Elgar. 1999.

Mithun, M. 'The significance of diversity in language endangerment and preservation' in L. Grenoble and L. Whaley (eds), *Endangered Languages*. Cambridge University Press. 1998.

Mittelman, J. *Globalization: Critical Reflections*. Boulder: Lynne Reiner. 1996.

Mittelman, J. *The Globalization Syndrome*. Princeton University Press. 2000.

Moeliono, A. *Language Development and Cultivation: Alternative Approaches in Language Planning*. Canberra: Department of Linguistics. 1986.

Moeliono, A. 'Indonesian language development and cultivation' in A. Hassan (ed.), *Language Planning in South-East Asia*. Kuala Lumpur: Ministry of Education. 1994.

Montesquieu, C. *De l'esprit des lois*. Paris: Garnier. 1961 (this edn).

Moorhouse, G. *Guardian* 16/07/1964.

Morén-Alegret, R. *Integration and Resistance: the Relation of Social Organisations, Global Capital, Governments and International Immigration in Spain and Portugal*. Aldershot: Ashgate. 2002.

Morris, P. (ed.), *The Bakhtin Reader*. London: Edward Arnold. 1994.

MOST Journal on Multicultural Societies. Languages on the Internet Vol 5(3) 2003.

Mühlhäusler, P. *Pidgin and Creole Linguistics*. Oxford: Blackwell. 1986.

Mühlhäusler, P. *Linguistic Ecology: Language Change and Linguistic Imperialism in the Pacific Region*. London: Routledge. 1996.

Mühlhäusler, P. 'Babel revisited' in A. Fill and P. Mühlhäusler (eds), *The Ecolinguistics Reader: Language, Ecology and Environment*. London: Continuum. 2001.

Mulcaster, R. *The First Part of the Elementarie which Entreateth Chefelie of the Right Writing of our English Tung*. London: Vautroullier. 1582.

Murphy, C. (ed.), *Egalitarian Politics in the Age of Globalization*. Basingstoke: Palgrave Macmillan. 2002.

Muysken, P. 'Uchumataqu: research in progress on the Bolivian Altiplano'. *MOST Journal on Multicultural Societies* 4(2) (2002).

Muysken, P. and Smith, N. 'The study of pidgin and creole languages' in J. Arends, P. Muysken and N. Smith (eds), *Pidgins and Creoles: An Introduction*. Amsterdam: John Benjamins. 1995.

Myers-Scotton, C. 'Codeswitching as indexical of social negotiations' in M. Heller (ed.), *Codeswitching: Anthropological and Sociolinguistic Perspectives*. Berlin: Mouton de Gruyter. 1988.

Myers-Scotton, C. *Social Motivations for Codeswitching*. Oxford: Clarendon. 1993.

Myers-Scotton, C. 'Structural uniformities versus community differences in codeswitching' in R. Jacobson (ed.), *Codeswitching Worldwide*. Berlin: Mouton de Gruyter. 1998.

Myers-Scotton, C. *Contact Linguistics: Bilingual Encounters and Grammatical Outcomes*. Oxford University Press. 2002.

Nair-Venugopal, S. 'Language choice and communication in Malaysian business'. *World Englishes* 21(3) (2002), pp. 460–1.

Nairn, T. *The Break-up of Britain; Crisis and Neo-nationalism*. London: New Left Books. 1977.

Naro, A. 'A study on the origins of pidginization'. *Language* 54 (1978), pp. 314–47.

Nebrija, A. de *Gramática de la lengua castellana*. Madrid: Espasa-Calpe. 1492/1976.

Nelde, P., Strubell, M. and Williams, G. *Euromosaic. The Production and Reproduction of the Minority Groups of the EU*. European Commission. 1996.

Nettle, D. and Romaine, S. *Vanishing Voices: The Extinction of the World's Languages*. Oxford University Press. 2000.

Newman, I. and Waever, O. *The Future of International Relations*. London: Routledge. 1997.

Ngugi wa Thiong'o. *Decolonising the Mind: the Politics of Language in African Literature*. London: James Currey. 1986.

Nguyen Tri Dung. 'Ten years of renovation and Vietnam foreign investment'. *Vietnam Studies* 3 (1998), pp. 5–10.

Nicholas, D. *The Transformation of Europe 1300–1600*. London: Arnold. 1999.

Nordman, D. *Frontières de France: De l'espace au territoire*. Paris: Gallimard. 1998.

NUA internet surveys. www.nua.ie/surveys/. Consulted January 2002

Nyerere, J. *Freedom and Unity – Uhuru na umoja. A selection of writings 1952–1965*. Oxford University Press. 1967.

Nyerere, J. Speech celebrating the 40th anniversary of Ghana's independence, Accra, 6 March 1997.

Nyerere, J. 'The heart of Africa. Interview with J. Nyerere on Anti-Colonialism'. *New Internationalist Magazine*, 309, January–February 1999.

O'Donnell, P. ' "I'm Catalan but I'm Not a Fanatic": shifting tides in Catalan public opinion'. *Language Problems and Language Planning* 20(1) (1996), pp. 44–52.

OECD. *Report: Globalisation of Industrial R and D: Policy Issues*. 1999.

OECD. 'The global research village: how information and communication technologies affect the science system'. *Science, Technology and Industry Outlook*. 1998.

Ohmae, K. *The Borderless World*. London: Collins. 1990.

Ohmae, K. *The End of the Nation State*. New York: Free Press. 1995.

Ó Laoire, M. 'An historical perspective of the revival of Irish outside the Gaeltacht 1880–1930' in S. Wright (ed.), *Language and the State: Revitalization and Revival in Israel and Ireland*. Clevedon: Multilingual Matters. 1996.

Ó Riagáin, P. *Language Policy and Social Reproduction – Ireland 1893–1993*. Oxford University Press. 1997.

Ó Riagáin, D. 'The European Union and lesser used languages'. *MOST Journal on Multicultural Societies* 3(1) (2001).

Ougaard, M. and Higgott, R. *Towards a Global Polity*. London: Routledge. 2002.

Oxfam. *Debt Relief for Tanzania: An Opportunity for a Better Future*. Executive summary. 1998.

Ôzkirimli, U. *Theories of Nationalism: A Critical Introduction*. Basingstoke: Macmillan. 2000.

Ozolins, U. 'Between Russian and European hegemony: current language policy in the Baltic States'. *Current Issues in Language and Society* 6(1) (1999), pp. 6–48.

Pagel, M. 'Endangered languages'. Paper given at the Conservation of Endangered Languages conference, University of Bristol, 21 April 1995.

Pakir, A. 'The development of English as a glocal language. New concerns in the old saga of language teaching'. Paper given at IATEFL conference, Edinburgh, March 1999.

Parijs, P. van 'Linguistic justice'. Paper given at the workshop Linguistic Diversity and European Law, European University Institute, Florence, 12–13 November 2001.

Parijs, P. van 'Linguistic justice' in *Politics, Philosophy and Economics* 1(1) (2002).

Paulsen, F. *German Education Past and Present* (trans. Lorenz). London: Fisher Unwin. 1908.

Payne, S. *A History of Spain and Portugal*. Madison: University of Wisconsin Press. 1976.

Pennycook, A. *The Cultural Politics of English as an International Language*. Harlow: Longman. 1994.

Pennycook, A. 'English in the world; the world in English' in J. Tollefson (ed.), *Power and Inequality in Language Education*. Cambridge University Press. 1995.

Pennycook, A. 'Language, ideology and hindsight: lessons from colonial language policies' in T. Ricento (ed.), *Ideology, Politics and Language Policies: Focus on English*. Amsterdam: John Benjamins. 2000a.

Pennycook, A. 'English, politics, ideology: from colonial celebration to postcolonial performativity' in T. Ricento (ed.), *Ideology, Politics and Language Policies: Focus on English*. Amsterdam: John Benjamins. 2000b.

Pennycook, A. 'Lessons from colonial language policies' in R. Gonzalez and I. Melis (eds), *Language Ideologies Volume 2: History, Theory and Policy*. New Jersey: Erlbaum. 2001a.

Pennycook, A. *Critical Applied Linguistics: A Critical Introduction*. New Jersey: Erlbaum. 2001b.

Pentassuglia, G. 'The EU and the protection of minorities: the case of Eastern Europe'. *European Journal of International Law* 12(1) (2001).

Perl, M. 'The external language history of two English-based Creoles in Surinam'. *Zeitschrift für Anglistik und Amerikanistik* 3 (1984), pp. 241–6.

Perl, M. 'A reevaluation of the importance of early pidgin/creole Portuguese'. *Journal of Pidgin and Creole Languages* 1 (Summer) (1990), pp. 125–30.

Pham Ha. 'Practical foreign investment'. *Vietnam Commerce and Industry* 19(12) (1998), p. 13.

Phillips, A. 'Minority rights in Europe'. Paper given at the Centre for Research in Ethnic Relations, Warwick University, November 1995.

Phillipson, R. *Linguistic Imperialism*. Oxford University Press. 1992.

Phillipson, R. 'English in the new world order: variations on a theme of linguistic imperialism and World English' in T. Ricento (ed.), *Ideology, Politics and Language Policies: Focus on English*. Amsterdam: John Benjamins. 2000.

Pickering, J. *A Vocabulary of American English*. Boston, MA. 1816.

Pinker, S. *The Language Instinct*. Harmondsworth: Penguin. 1994.

Poggeschi, G. 'Linguistic rights in Spain' in F. de Varennes (ed.), *European Minorities and Languages*. The Hague: Asser. 2000.

Pollard, H. *Pioneers of Popular Education 1760–1850*. London: John Murray. 1956.

Pool, J. 'National development and language diversity' in J. Fishman (ed.), *Advances in the Sociology of Language vol. 2*. The Hague: Mouton. Pp. 213–30. 1972.

Pool, J. 'The official language problem'. *American Political Science Review* 85 (1991), pp. 495–514.

Prats, M., Rafanell, A. and Rossich, A. (eds), *El futur de la llengua catalana*. Barcelona: Empuries. 1990.

Pulcini, V. 'Attitudes towards the spread of English in Italy'. *World Englishes* 16(1) (1997), pp. 77–85.

Pym, A. 'Resplendent Catalan: what money can buy'. *The Linguist* 38(3) (1999), pp. 80–82.

Quirk, R. and Widdowson, H. *English in the World: Papers of an International Conference held to Celebrate the 50th Anniversary of the British Council.* Cambridge University Press. 1985.

Rasmussen, A. 'A la recherche d'une langue internationale de la science 1880–1914' in R. Chartier and P. Corsi (eds), *Sciences et langues en Europe.* Commission européenne: Forum européen de la science et de la technologie. 1996.

Rawls, J. *Justice as Fairness: a Restatement.* Cambridge, MA: Harvard University Press. 2001.

Rees, W. *The Union of England and Wales with a Transcript of the Act of Union.* University of Wales Press. 1937.

Ricento, T. (ed.), *Ideology, Politics and Language Policies: Focus on English.* Amsterdam: John Benjamins. 2000.

Richmond, O. *Maintaining Order, Making Peace.* Basingstoke: Palgrave Macmillan. 2002.

Rickard, P. *A History of the French Language.* London: Unwin. 1989 (2nd edn).

Ricklefs, M. *A History of Modern Indonesia since c. 1300.* Stanford University Press. 1993.

Rietbergen, P. *Europe, A Cultural History.* London: Routledge. 1998.

Rivarol, A. 'de De l'universalité de la Langue Française. Discours qui a remporté le prix à l'Académie de Berlin' in *De l'universalité européenne.* Paris Fayard 1997/1784.

Robertson, R. *Globalization: Social Theory and Global Culture.* Newbury: Sage. 1992.

Rodrik, D. *Has Globalization Gone too Far?* Washington, DC: Institute for International Economics. 1997.

Romaine, S. *Pidgin and Creole Languages.* Harlow: Longman. 1988.

Romaine, S. *Bilingualism.* Oxford: Blackwell. 1995 (2nd edn).

Romaine, S. 'The impact of language policy on endangered languages'. *MOST journal* 4(2) (2002) http://www.unesco.org/most/jmshome.htm.

Rooij, V. de 'Shaba Swahili' in J. Arends P. Muysken and N. Smith (eds), *Pidgins and Creoles: An Introduction.* Amsterdam: John Benjamins. 1995.

Rousseau, J.-J. *Du Contrat Social.* Oxford: Clarendon Press. 1972 (this edn).

Rowlinson, W. 'German education in a European context' in T. Cook (ed.), *History of Education in Europe.* London: Methuen. 1974.

Rubin, J. 'Indonesian language: planning and education' in J. Rubin *et al.* (eds), *Language Planning Processes.* The Hague: Mouton. 1977.

Rubin, J. and Jernudd, B. (eds), *Can Language be Planned?* University of Hawaii. 1971.

Rubin, J., Jernudd, B., Das Gupta, J., Fishman, J. and Ferguson, C. (eds), *Language Planning Processes.* The Hague: Mouton. 1977.

Ruffino, G. *Scuola dialetto Minoranze linguistiche – l'attività legislativa in Sicilia (1946–1992).* Palermo: Centro di studi filologici e linguistici siciliani. 1992.

Rupp, D. *An Account of the Manners of the German Inhabitants of Pennsylvania.* Philadelphia: Samuel Town. 1789. Notes added by Daniel Rupp. 1875.

Rush, B. *An Account of the Manners of the German Inhabitants of Pennsylvania.* Philadelphia: Samuel Town. 1789.

Sadec. *Asia Pacific Investment Rating Fact Sheets.* www.sadec.com, information taken November 1996 and December 1999.

Said, E. *Orientalism.* Harmondsworth: Penguin. 1978.

Salvador, G. *Lengua Española y Lenguas de España.* Barcelona: Ariel. 1987.

Salzmann, Z. 'Language Standardization in a Bilingual State: the Case of Czech and Slovak' in *Language Planning and Language Problems* 4(1) (1980), pp. 38–54.

Sapir, E. *Language: an Introduction to the Study of Speech.* New York: Harcourt Brace. 1921.

Sassoon, A. *Gramsci's Politics.* London: Cross Helm. 1980.

Saunders, R. *In Search of Woodrow Wilson: Beliefs and Behavior*. Westport, CT: Greenwood Press. 1998.

Sauvageot, A. 'Le finnois de Finlande' in I. Fodor and C. Hagège (eds), *Language Reform*. Hamburg: Buske. 1983.

Schieffelin, B., Woolard, K. and Kroskrity, P. (eds), *Language Ideologies: Practice and Theory*. Oxford University Press. 1998.

Schiffman, H. *Linguistic Culture and Language Policy*. London: Routledge. 1996.

Schlesinger, P. 'On national identity: some conceptions and misconceptions criticized'. *Social Science Information* 25(2) (1986).

Scholte, J. *International Relations of Social Change*. Buckingham: Open University Press. 1993.

Scholte, J. *Globalization: A Critical Introduction*. Basingstoke: Palgrave Macmillan. 2000.

Schremmer, D. 'Taxation and public finance in Prussia' in *Cambridge History of Europe*. Cambridge University Press. Pp. 315–464. 1989.

Schwartz, A. *A Nation in Waiting*. New South Wales: Allen and Unwin. 1999.

Schwatzl, A. *The (Im)Possibilities of Machine Translation*. Frankfurt: Peter Lang. 2001.

Sebba, M. *Contact Languages, Pidgins and Creoles*. London: Macmillan. 1997.

Seidlhofer, B. 'Mind the gap, English as a mother tongue vs. English as a lingua Franca'. *Views* 9(1) (2000), pp. 51–68.

Seidlhofer, B. 'Closing a conceptual gap: the case for a description of English as a lingua franca'. *International Journal of Applied Linguistics* 11(2) (2000), pp. 133–56.

Serban, F. 'Modernisatin de langue roumaine' in I. Fodor and C. Hagège (eds), *Language Reform Vol III*. Hamburg: Buske. 1983.

Seton-Watson, H. *Nations and States*. London: Methuen. 1977.

Shariff, I. 'Review of four centuries of Swahili verse'. *Swahili* Vol. 51/1 and 51/2. 1979.

Shaw, M. 'Peoples, territorialism and boundaries'. *European Journal of International Law* 8(3) (1997).

Siguan, M. 'The Catalan language in the educational system of Catalonia'. *International Review of Education* 37(1) (1991), pp. 87–98.

Simon, T. 'Protecting minorities in International Law'. *Pubblicazioni Centri Studi per la Pace*. 2000.

Simpson, D. *The Politics of American English 1776–1850*. Oxford University Press. 1986.

Singman, J. *Daily Life in Medieval Europe*. Westport, CT: Greenwood Press. 1999.

Skutnabb-Kangas, T. *Bilingualism or not? The Education of Minorities*. Clevedon: Multilingual Matters. 1981.

Skutnabb-Kangas, T. *Linguistic Genocide in Education or Worldwide Diversity and Human Rights*. New Jersey: Lawrence Erlbaum. 2000.

Slabbert, S. and Myers-Scotton, C. 'The structure of Tsotitaal and Iscamtho: codeswitching and identity in group identity in South African townships'. *Linguistics* 34 (1996), pp. 317–42.

Slapnicka, H. 'Majorities and minorities in an inverted position: Czechoslovakia 1918–1939' in S. Vilfan (ed.), *Ethnic Groups and Language Rights*. Aldershot: Dartmouth. 1993.

Smith, A. *National Identity*. Harmondsworth: Penguin. 1991a.

Smith, A. *The Ethnic Origins of Nations*. Oxford: Blackwell. 1991b.

Smith, A. 'Chosen peoples: why ethnic groups survive'. *Ethnic and Racial Studies* 15(3) (1992), pp. 440–9.

Smith, A. 'Gastronomy or geology? The role of nationalism in the reconstruction of nations'. *Nations and Nationalism* 1(1) (1995), pp. 3–25.

Smith, D. *The Making of Italy 1796–1866*. London: Macmillan. 1988.

Smolicz, J. 'Tradition, core values and intercultural development in plural societies'. *Ethnic and Racial Studies* 4(1) (1988), pp. 75–90.

Soejoto, I. *Draft Proposal for New English Programme*. Jakarta: PPPG. 2000.

Sorenson, G. 'The global polity and changes in statehood' in M. Ougaard and R. Higgott (eds), *Towards a Global Polity*. London: Routledge. 2002.

Steed, H. *The Hapsburg Monarchy* (2nd edn). London: Constable. 1914.

Steiner, G. *After Babel. Aspects of Language and Translation*. Oxford University Press. 1975/1998.

Strange, S. *The Retreat of the State*. Cambridge University Press. 1996.

Strong, R. *Splendour at Court: Renaissance Spectacle and Illusion*. London: Weidenfeld and Nicolson. 1973.

Strubell, M. 'Catalan a decade later' in J. Fishman (ed.), *Can Threatened Languages be Saved?* Clevedon: Multilingual Matters. 2001.

Sugiyono and Latief, A 'Sarana Uji Kemahiran Berbahasa sebagai Salah Satu Prasarana Pembangunan Bangsa' in H. Alwi (ed.), *Politik Bahasa*. Jakarta: Pusat Bahasa. 2000.

Summer Institute of Linguistics (SIL) website http://www.sil.org/.

Sur, S. 'The state between fragmentation and globalization'. *European Journal of International Law* 8(3) (1997).

Suryohudoyo, S. 'The sovereignty of beauty: classical Javanese writings' in A. Kumar and J. McGlynn (eds), *Illuminations: the Writing Traditions of Indonesia*. New York: Weatherhill. 1996.

Svartvik, J. 'Response to Braj Kachru' in R. Quirk and H. Widdowson (eds), *English in the World: Papers of an International Conference held to Celebrate the 50th Anniversary of the British Council*. Cambridge University Press. 1985.

Szporluk, R. 'The imperial legacy and the Soviet nationalities problem' in L. Hajda and M. Beissinger (eds), *The Nationalities Factor in Soviet Politics and Society*. Boulder: Westview. 1990.

Talleyrand-Périgord. *Speech to Assemblée nationale 10/9/1791*. Archives parlementaires 1re série XXX p. 472.

Tauli, V. 'The Estonian language reform' in I. Fodor and C. Hagège (eds), *Language Reform*. Hamburg: Buske. 1983.

Taylor, P. *Political Geography: World Economy, Nation State and Locality*. Harlow: Longman. 1989.

Teichova, A. 'Eastern, Central and South-Eastern Europe 1919–1939' in *Cambridge Economic History of Europe*. Cambridge University Press. 1989.

Terzani, T. *Saigon 1975: Three Days and Three Months*. Bangkok: White Lotus. 1997.

Thomanek, K. *Concepts of Urban Language in Africa*. Vienna: Beiträge für Afrikanistik. 1996.

Thomas, G. *Linguistic Purism*. Harlow: Longman. 1991.

Thomason, S. *Language Contact: an Introduction*. Edinburgh University Press. 2001.

Thompson, C. 'The protection of minorities with the United Nations' in F. de Varennes (ed.), *Minority Rights in Europe*. The Hague: Asser Press. 2001.

Todd, L. *Pidgins and Creoles* (2nd edn). London: Routledge. 1990.

Tollefson, J. *Planning Language, Planning Inequality*. Harlow: Longman. 1991.

Tollefson, J. *Power and Inequality in Language Education*. Cambridge University Press. 1995.

Tollefson, J. (ed), *Language Policies in Education*. New Jersey: Lawrence Erlbaum. 2002.

Toggenburg, G. von 'A rough orientation through a delicate relationship: the EU's endeavours for its minorities' in F. de Varennes (ed.), *Minority Rights in Europe*. The Hague: Asser Press. 2001.

Toman, J. *The Magic of a Common Languages: Jakobson, Mathesius, Trubetzkoy, and the Prague Linguistic Circle.* Cambridge, MA: MIT Press. 1995.

Trubetzkoy, N. *Polabische Studien.* Vienna: Holder-Pichler-Tempsky. 1929.

Truchot, C. 'Atelier: université et politique linguistique en Europe' at conference in the Freie Universitat, Berlin, Germany, 28–30 June 2001.

Trudgill, P. *On Dialect: Social and Geographical Perspectives.* Oxford: Blackwell. 1983.

United Nations. *Article 27 Human Rights Declaration* (HRI/GEN/1/Rev/1 at 38). 1966.

United Nations Committee on the Rights of the Child *Consideration of reports submitted by states. United Republic of Tanzania* 2000.

UNHCR Minority Rights Fact sheet 18, posted at http://www.unhchr.ch/html/menu6/2/sheets.htm nd.

US Bureau of Democracy, Human Rights, and Labor. *Country Reports on Human Rights Practices* 23 February 2001.

Valdman, A. *Pidgin and Creole Linguistics.* Bloomington: Indiana University Press. 1977.

Valverdú, F. 'A sociolinguistic history of Catalan'. *International Journal of the Sociology of Language* 47 (1984), pp. 13–29.

Varennes, de F. *Languages, Minorities and Human rights.* The Hague: Martinus Nijhoff. 1996.

Varennes, de F. (ed.), *Minority Rights in Europe.* The Hague: Asser Press. 2001.

Vavrus, F. 'Postcoloniality and English: Exploring Language Policy and the Politics of Development in Tanzania'. *TESOL Quarterly* 36(3) (2002), pp. 373–99.

Vellard, J. *Dieux et parias des Andes. Les ourous, ceux qui ne veulent pas êtres des hommes.* Paris: Éditions Émile-Paul. 1954.

Vidal, G. *Dreaming War: Blood for Oil and the Cheney-Bush Junta.* New York: Thunder's Mouth Press. 2002.

Vietnam Economic Times. 'Foreign investment by country and territory' Issue (2) 48 February 1998.

Viswanathan, G. *Masks of Conquest: Literary Study and British Rule in India.* New York: Columbia University Press. 1989.

Vlekke, B. *Nusantara: a History of Indonesia.* Chicago: Quadrangle. 1959.

Voltaire. *Lettres philosophiques ou anglaises.* 1734.

Voloshinov, V. *Marxism and the Philosophy of Language* (trans. L Matejka and I. Titunik). New York: Seminar Press. 1973.

Voloshinov, V. 'Marxism and the philosophy of language' in P. Morris (ed.), *The Bakhtin Reader.* London: Edward Arnold. 1994.

Vygotsky, L. *Thought and Language* (trans. Kozulin). Cambridge MA: MIT Press. 1986.

Waard, M. de 'Language policies in Dutch Indonesia'. *University of Pittsburgh Working Papers in Linguistics* 5 (2000), pp. 71–126.

Wade, R. 'Globalization and its limits: reports of the death of the national economy are greatly exaggerated' in S. Berger and R. Dore (eds), *National Diversity and Global Capitalism.* Ithaca: Cornell University Press. 1996.

Walpole, H. *Reminiscences Written in 1788 (Notes of Conversations with Lady Suffolk).* Oxford: Clarendon Press. 1924.

Walter, H. *Le français dans tous les sens.* Paris: Laffont. 1988.

Walter, H. *L'aventure des langues en Occident: leur origine, leur histoire et leur géographie.* Paris: Robert Laffont. 1994.

Walter, H. *L'aventure des mots venus d'ailleurs.* Paris: Robert Laffont. 1997.

Walter, H. *Le français d'ici, de là, de là-bas.* Paris: Lattès. 1998.

Walter, H 'Le français langue d'accueil' in S. Wright (ed.), *French, an Accommodating Language.* Clevedon: Multilingual Matters. 1999.

Walter, H. *Honni soit qui mal y pense*. Paris: Robert Laffont. 2001.

Walters, J. 'Socio-pragmatic processing in bilingual production and attrition' in J. Klatter-Folmer and P. van Avermaet (eds), *Theories on Maintenance and Loss of Minority Languages*. Münster: Waxmann. 2001.

Warih, D. 'Bahasa Daerah Bukan Ancaman Persatuan' in *Suara Merdeka* 20 August 2001.

Webster, N. *An American Dictionary of the English Language*. 2 vols. New York: Converse. facsimile reprint. 1967/1828.

Weimer, H. *Concise History of Education*. London: Peter Owen. 1963.

Weindling in R. Chartier and P. Corsi (eds), *Sciences et langues en Europe*. Commission européenne: Forum européen de la science et de la technologie. 1996.

Weiss, L. *State Capacity: Governing the Economy in a Global Era*. Cambridge: Polity Press. 1998.

Whaley, L. 'Can a language that never existed be saved? Coming to terms with Oroqen language revitalization'. Paper given at Sociolinguistic Symposium 14, Gent, April 2002.

Whinnom, K. *Spanish Contact. Vernaculars in the Philippine Islands*. Hong Kong University Press. 1956.

Whiteley, W. *Swahili, the Rise of a National Language*. London: Methuen. 1969.

Whiteley, W. 'Some factors influencing language policies in Eastern Africa' in J. Rubin and B. Jernudd (eds), *Can Language be planned?* University of Hawaii. 1971.

Wierzbicka, A. *Semantics, Culture and Cognition: Universal Human Concepts in Culture-specific Configurations*. Oxford University Press. 1992.

Williams, G. *Sociolinguistics a Sociological Critique*. London: Routledge. 1992.

Whorf, B. *Language, Thought, and Reality. Selected Writings of B. L. Whorf* in J. Carroll (ed.). New York: John Wiley. 1956.

Widdowson, H. 'The ownership of English'. *TESOL Quarterly* 28(2) (1994), pp. 377–81.

Winford, D. *An Introduction to Contact Linguistics*. Oxford: Blackwell. 2003.

Woodbury, A. 'Documenting rhetorical, aesthetic and expressive loss in language shift' in L. Grenoble and L. Whaley (eds), *Endangered Languages*. Cambridge University Press. 1998.

Woolard, K. *Double Talk: Bilingualism and the Politics of Ethnicity in Catalonia*. Stanford, CA: Stanford University Press. 1989.

Woolard, K. and Gahng T. 'Changing language policies and attitudes in autonomous Catalonia'. *Language in Society* 19(3) (1990), pp. 11–30.

Woon, L. and Zolberg, A. 'Why Islam is like Spanish'. *Politics and Society* 27(1) (1999), pp. 5–38.

World Bank *Poverty Analysis* 2002 http://www.worldbank.org/wbi/povertyanalysis/.

Wright, S. 'The role of the industries of communication in the formation of political identities and language loyalty'. *Plurilingua* XVIII (1997), pp. 465–74.

Wright, S (ed.) *Language, Democracy & Devolution in Catalonia*. Clevedon: Multilingual Matters. 1999.

Wright, S. *Community and Communication*. Clevedon: Multilingual Matters. 2000a.

Wright, S. 'Jacobins, regionalists and the Council of Europe's Charter for Regional and Minority Languages'. *Journal of Multilingual and Multicultural Development* 21(5) (2000b), pp. 414–25.

Wright, S. 'The renaissance of Catalan and Welsh: political causes and effects'. *Plurilingua* XXIII (2001), pp. 195–217.

Wright, S. 'Vietnam: language planning for the end of isolation' in J. Tollefson (ed.), *Language Policies in Education*. New Jersey: Lawrence Erlbaum. 2002.

Wriston, W. *The Twilight of Sovereignty*. New York: Charles Scribners. 1992.

Wurm, S. and Kincade, D. 'Taxonomy' in R. Robins and E. Uhlenbeck (eds), *Endangered Languages*. Oxford: Berg. 1991.

Wurm, S. 'Methods of language maintenance and revival' in K. Matsumura (ed.), *Studies in Endangered Languages*. Tokyo: Hituzi Syobo. 1998.

Yano, Y. 'World Englishes in 2000 and beyond'. *World Englishes* 20(2) (2001), pp. 119–31.

Zürn, M. 'Social denationalization and global governance: concepts and theoretical expectations' in M. Ougaard and R. Higgott (eds), *Towards a Global Polity*. London: Routledge. 2002.

Index

Absolutism 29–30
Abstand languages 48
academies 54–6, 97, 141, 267, 270
Aceh 11, 94–5
acquisition planning 13, 42, 61–7, 75, 78–82, 90–2, 97, 129, 169, 203, 232, 236, 276
Albania/Albanian 21, 48, 218, 239–41, 281, 282
Alghero 211
alphabets 50–2, 61, 81, 224
Andorra 211
appropriation 168, 172, 175–6,
Arabic 21, 54, 57, 61, 76–7, 84, 95, 105, 112–14, 217, 261, 266, 272–3
Aragon 210
Arbresh 239–41
army 25, 27, 78, 85, 88, 110–11, 182, 201, 266
  conscription 38
artificial languages 173
Ascoli Graziado 60
Asia Pacific Economic Cooperation 133, 272–3
assimilation 7, 10, 13, 19, 92, 111–12, 143, 182, 185, 199, 207–8, 237, 292
Association of South East Asian Nations 113
audio-visual media 53, 60–1, 102, 114, 124, 154, 158–9, 163, 193, 206, 214, 218, 231, 238, 258, 277
Ausbau languages 48–50
Australia 10,
  Aboriginal languages 224
Austro-Hungarian empire 65–6, 110
Avestan 114
Azeglio, Massimo, d' 34

Baker, Colin 10,
Basque 21, 32, 48, 203, 211–14, 278, 279, 280
  Basque-Algonquian pidgin 105
  Basque-Icelandic pidgin 105

Belgium 129–30, 203, 273
  Flemish speaking 11, 203
  French speaking 190
bilingualism 9–10, 14, 21, 90, 172, 188, 207, 214, 226, 241, 243, 247–50
Bolivia 218, 237–9
Bourdieu, Pierre 11, 44, 62, 81, 167, 227
Bourguiba, Habib 131
Bratt Paulston, Christina 97, 216, 241
Britain 8, 26, 30, 56, 62, 121, 136–40, 266, 270, 273
Brougham, Henry 62
bureaucracies 29–31, 46, 66, 81, 85, 109–10

Canada 10, 273
Canagarajah, Suresh 113, 168, 171–2, 174, 176
Capitalism 4, 114, 145–6, 149, 155, 158, 161, 165–6, 170, 174
Catalonia/Catalan 11, 37, 114, 204–12, 217, 278–9
Catholic Church/Catholicism 22–3, 28, 33, 36, 40, 113–14, 121, 155, 254, 267
census 31, 47, 55, 83, 213, 234, 257, 264, 270, 280
Chinese 94, 105–7, 110, 114–16, 235–7, 265, 272–3
Chomsky, Noam 4
Church Slavonic 23–4, 51, 114, 258
citizenship 31, 63–4, 66, 142, 196, 257–9, 266, 277–8, 282
civic nationalism 8, 31, 70, 75–6, 78, 85, 88, 92, 208, 212–13, 282
Clyne, Michael 10
codification 52–7, 75, 77–82, 88–90, 208, 215
colonialism 29, 69–75, 77, 82–3, 106–7, 112, 138, 140, 155, 167, 267
community of communication 8, 13–14, 31–42, 52, 64, 67, 85, 94, 101, 152, 163, 172–8, 186, 209, 217, 275

Communism 4, 10, 114, 116
  end of 141, 144, 148, 159, 161, 197,
    203, 273
communitarianism 185
constructivism 3–4, 54
corpus planning 13, 32, 47, 59, 97,
    124, 175, 203, 232, 278
  differentiation 48–50, 57
Corson, David 10
cosmopolitanism 61
Council of Europe 12, 191–2, 198, 269,
    273, 276–7
  Charter for Regional or Minority
    Languages 130, 193–4, 199,
    211, 257
  Framework Convention for the
    Protection of National Minorities
    192
Critical theory 165–7
Critical linguistics 166–72
Crystal, David 219, 223, 276, 280
cultural centres 113, 119, 152–6,
    204, 206
Cummins, Jim 10
Czechoslovakia/Czech Republic 22, 36,
    49–50, 147, 201, 203, 256, 258, 276

Darwin, Charles 4
Das Gupta, Jyotirindra 9
democracy 7, 13, 31–2, 40, 42, 46, 85,
    131, 139, 141, 148, 155, 170, 198,
    255, 263, 277
Derhemi, Eda 239–41
devolution 92, 94, 96, 98, 185, 199,
    202–4, 216–17, 234
dictionaries 50, 56–7, 97, 203,
    258, 262
  French 55
  Italian 55
  Johnson's 56, 270
  Websters 57, 141–2
diglossia 9, 14, 60–1, 89–90, 109, 116,
    188, 212, 215, 223, 226, 239–40,
    243, 266
diplomacy
  language of treaties 118, 143, 267
  United Nations 144
  Vietnam 131, 267, 269
divine right to rule 29
Dorian, Nancy 10

ecolinguistics 12, 220–3, 252
education 226–7, 243
  in colonial period 76, 84, 109,
    112–13, 138, 262, 270–1
  in foreign languages 72, 79–80, 82,
    92–3, 103, 114–16, 119, 121,
    124–6, 127–30, 133, 146–8, 170,
    172, 175, 260, 265, 269
  in minority or regional languages
    72, 88, 95, 98, 184, 187, 193–4,
    197–8, 205–7, 214–15, 218, 231,
    236, 239–40, 265, 277
  national 26, 32, 35, 37–8, 42–3, 49,
    52–5, 61–5, 67, 71, 78–9, 82, 85,
    90–2, 143, 234, 259–60, 262–5,
    276
Edwards, John 211, 231, 233, 258
elites
  bilingualism of 25, 30, 81, 92,
    102–3, 109, 113–15, 138, 282
  education in Africa 79–81, 261–3
  education in Indonesia 85, 90, 92–3
  education in Spain 212, 216
  globalisation 148, 158
  lingua francas 118–22, 136, 139,
    141, 147
  as linguistic model 1, 54–6, 270
  nationalism and 13, 34–5, 42, 47,
    51, 75, 185, 134, 185, 216, 255
  permeability of 13, 43, 109, 112,
    166–7, 169, 171–2, 178, 256
England 29, 139, 253, 259, 263, 270
English
  and capitalism 10, 115, 139, 144–8
  and ecolinguistics 221–2, 228
  in education 81, 92–3, 125–6, 138
  and globalisation 93, 144–56, 173–4,
    177–8,
  in the imperial period 109, 136–8,
    140–1
  as a lingua franca 11, 14–15, 165–72,
    175–8, 246–50
  opposition to English 59–60,
    165–72
  in postcolonial settings 72–3, 79–80
  standard for lingua franca 175–7,
  within the UK 30, 136–7, 199, 254
  within the US 44, 141–3, 163, 181
Engsh 108
Enlightenment 32, 62, 113, 120

equality   32, 62, 79, 93, 109, 144,
    166, 172, 186–7, 217, 222, 241,
    263, 268, 281
Estonia/Estonian   11, 44, 58, 203, 217,
    257, 278
ethnic nationalism   8, 24, 26, 32–6, 49,
    59, 66–7, 163, 212, 255
Europe   19
    devolution in   163, 183, 202
    Early Modernity   25–35, 254
    languages of   48, 107, 114, 118, 121,
        127, 136–7, 155, 232, 275, 280
    Late Modernity   36–40, 246
    Middle Ages   20–5, 253
    rights in   192–8
    transnational corporations in   146,
        271
European Union   11
    language diversity in   122, 126–30
    Lingua programmes in   128–9
    support for lesser used languages in
        192, 194–7

Fairclough, Norman   167
feudalism   20, 22–3, 26, 29, 62, 253
Fichte, Johann   8, 32, 45, 61–2, 267
Finland/Finnish   21, 48–9, 58, 105,
    129–30, 273
Fishman, Joshua   9, 111, 156, 178, 189,
    214, 229, 232–3, 235, 250–1
Foucault, Michel   166, 170
France
    education   62–3, 255
    French in   30, 254, 257, 259
    frontiers   26, 37, 260
    Grande armée   110
    national identity   24
    suppression of other languages   32,
        185, 199, 211, 253, 255
Francophonie   130–3
Free Market economics   10, 127, 144–9,
    155, 159, 161, 165, 174
French
    census   47
    in colonial period   262, 267, 271
    language academy   54–5
    in post colonial settings   72, 130–3,
        270
    as a prestige lingua franca   118–22,
        136–7, 139–40, 143, 267

prestige and vigour   133–5, 143, 272
promotion of language diversity in
    Europe   126–30
protection   122–6, 134–5, 151, 259,
    269
purism   58
frontiers   8, 21, 25–7, 36–7, 69–70, 75,
    102, 118, 146, 177, 204, 254, 255,
    260, 278

Galicia   204, 214–16, 240, 278
Gaulle, Charles de   122–3, 131
Gellner, Ernest   244–51, 259, 282
German/Germany
    in Austro-Hungarian empire   65–6,
        110, 112
    in colonies   75–6, 106, 109, 112, 262
    dialect continua   33–4, 48–9
    education   61–2, 64, 119
    ethnic nationalism in   32–3
    French in   119, 267
    industrialisation in   64
    language academy   54
    in migration   65, 142–3, 190, 259, 271
    as a prestige language   65, 114,
        139–40, 267, 269
    in religious texts   28, 49
    standard and purism   34, 54, 58–9
    unification of   33–4, 65
Globalisation   7, 10–11, 14, 45, 59, 82,
    92, 123, 131, 136, 144–50, 157–61,
    168–9, 171, 173–5, 177–8, 182, 218,
    220, 239, 248, 250, 256, 274, 276
Gramsci, Antonio   156, 167–8
Greece/Greek   21, 57, 60–1, 131, 223
    nationalism   32, 35, 44, 256, 260, 269
    prestige lingua franca   23–4, 62, 65,
        113–14, 121
Grosjean, François   247

Habermas, Jürgen   11, 166, 275
Halliday M.A.K.   1, 3–4, 167
Haugen, Einar   9, 42, 74, 252, 258
Hebrew   54, 57, 114, 141
hegemony   11, 13, 60, 147, 151–2, 156,
    167–8, 211
Herder, Johann   8, 32, 35, 57, 255, 267
Holborow, Marnie   169–70
Hornberger, Nancy   10, 12
Houphouët Felix   130

human rights 160, 182, 184, 186,
  189–91, 198–9, 217
  individual and group 182, 184,
    191–8
  linguistic 12, 13, 65, 187–8
Humboldt, Alexander 32
Hungary/Hungarian 21–2, 48–9
  and minorities 65–7, 197, 256

identity 7, 15, 227
  and language shift 134
  minority groups 225–7
  national 26, 27, 35, 38, 41, 49, 51–2,
    58, 63, 66, 67, 79, 88–9, 146, 159,
    163–4, 183, 202, 211
ideology 70–2, 77, 81, 96, 101, 114–16,
  135, 139, 142, 145, 150, 152, 165–7,
  170–2, 224, 242, 247, 278, 282
imagined community 40
imperial languages 103, 106, 108–13,
  119, 138
Indonesia/Indonesian 11, 54, 61, 71,
  73, 75, 82–96, 105, 141, 260, 263–5,
  290
industrialisation 26, 36–8, 64–5, 113,
  137, 146, 220, 259
information technology 10, 125,
  131–2, 150–1, 154, 158–9, 273
interlanguage 101, 175–6
internationalism 61
International Monetary Fund (IMF) 10,
  79, 144, 146, 263, 272
Ireland/Irish 36, 45–6, 49, 199, 230,
  233, 252, 254, 257, 270
Italy/Italian 8, 32, 34, 53–5, 58–61,
  114, 136, 211, 223, 239–41, 252–3,
  255–6, 259, 267, 270, 275, 281

Javanese 95
Jernudd, Björn 9
Johnson, Samuel 56, 270
Joseph, John 134, 256, 258
justice 165, 172–4, 183, 187, 206

Kachru, Braj 175–7, 275
Klopstock, Friedrich 32
Kontra Miklós 12
Kymlicka, Will 181, 184, 188, 249,
  276, 280
Kyoto Protocol 149, 272

Laitin, David 93, 261
language
  contact 7–14, 21, 76, 93, 101–8,
    116, 146–7, 187, 213, 216, 224,
    230–1, 238
  endangered 218–43, 251, 281
  and exclusion 5, 7, 13, 43, 109, 174,
    223, 226, 242, 250, 279
  loss/shift 7, 12, 14, 30, 38–9, 42,
    46, 51, 64–5, 68, 91, 110, 112,
    121, 125, 134, 141, 143, 168,
    179, 206–7, 211, 214–15, 218,
    221–5, 226–38, 247, 249, 259,
    263–4, 271
  and power 1, 7, 11, 20, 43–4, 46,
    48–9, 73, 103, 106, 108, 110, 112,
    118, 122, 134, 150, 152, 156,
    165–72, 177, 187–8, 232–3,
    249–50, 256, 275
Latin 23–4, 28, 30, 51, 54–5, 57, 62,
  64–6, 107, 109, 113–14, 117–19, 121,
  136, 155, 173, 258–60, 266–7, 273
Laycock, D.C. 6
Li Wei 10
liberalism 39, 67, 85, 148, 160, 183–7,
  190
lingua francas 11, 14–15, 23–4, 74, 76,
  84–5, 93, 96, 98, 101–17, 169, 173,
  175, 246–51, 266–7, 269
  English 165–72, 175–8, 272
  French 118–22
linguistic
  accommodation 7–8, 242
  convergence 7, 13, 24–5, 35, 38–45,
    48, 98, 127, 181
  determinism 3
  diversity 6, 31, 111, 122, 130, 195–6,
    219, 222, 228, 231, 255, 259
  homogenisation 24, 57, 64, 67,
    101, 181
literacy 23, 28–9, 34, 39, 43, 61–5, 68,
  78, 80–1, 84, 88, 102, 110, 119,
  142–4, 172, 216, 223, 231, 238–40,
  243, 256, 270
Lo Bianco, Joe 10

Macedonia/Macedonian 36, 44, 256–7,
  260
Malay 73, 82–96, 97, 105, 263–5, 272
Manzoni, Alessandro 60

Marxism 4, 165, 169, 177, 213, 273
May, Stephen 225, 242
migration 10, 37, 94, 193, 202, 206–7, 212, 227, 233, 238, 252, 254, 257, 260, 274
minority languages 12, 44, 65–6, 130, 167, 181–200, 211, 215, 218–43, 247–8, 277
Modernity 64–5, 72, 158, 170, 236, 253, 255, 263
Mughal empire 110, 266
Mühlhäusler, Peter 6, 104, 220–2, 228
Muysken, Pieter 7, 237–9, 281

Nation building 7–8, 17–99, 201–17
   congruence in 19, 53, 70–5
   education for 61–4
   minority languages 44, 65–7
   in postcolonial setting 70–5
   system under attack 11, 96, 161–2, 183, 201–2
   US counter current 163–5, 181
Nationalism
   symbols 35
   theories of 8, 19–41
   war 38
NATO 10, 123, 161, 182, 202, 273
Navarre 213
Nebrija 111
neo-colonialism 9, 46, 72, 167
North American aboriginal peoples
   Kanien'kéha 224
   Nez Percés 105
Northern Ireland 199, 203

Organisation for Security and Co-operation in Europe (OSCE) 12, 192, 197–8, 276
Oroqen 235–7
Orthodox Church 23, 50–1, 114, 239

Parijs, Philippe van 172, 174
Pennycook, Alistair 11, 138, 170–1, 174, 176, 266, 275
periphery 11, 25, 27, 43, 81, 91–2, 94, 210, 217, 266
Phillipson, Robert 138, 167–71, 174, 266, 275–6
pidgins 103–7, 110, 116, 137, 261, 265
Pinker, Stephen 4

pluralism 10, 35, 71, 92, 97, 181, 183, 198–200, 234, 241–2, 282
Pool, Jonathan 172–3
Portugal 21, 26, 253
postmodernism 97, 166, 170–1
postnationalism 13, 47, 82, 98, 157–78, 181, 247
prescription 2, 47, 52–7, 59, 258, 270
print capitalism 28, 34, 43
print media 39, 66, 68, 74, 81, 105, 143, 159, 206, 214, 231, 233, 256
purism 52, 55, 57–61, 77, 91

Racine, Jean 118
Rawls, John 172, 186–7
Religion
   French in the Vatican 121
   missionaries and language 76–7, 112–13, 139
   sacred languages 57, 112, 114, 117, 139, 155
   in spread of vernaculars 121
   Wars of Religion 26–8
revitalisation 8, 12, 14, 207, 213, 230–8, 241, 247–8, 281
revolution 31–2, 66, 111, 120, 131, 185, 255, 281
Ricento, Tom 10,
Richard II 22
Romaine, Suzanne 135, 214, 218, 232–3, 242, 249, 266
Romania/Romanian 49, 51–2, 58, 65, 256, 259–60, 276
Roussillon 211
Rubin, Joan 9, 74, 91, 252
Russenorsk 105–6
Russia/Russian 8, 10, 26, 34, 44, 54, 58, 115–16, 140, 144, 147, 156, 217, 225, 253, 255, 257, 272–3, 278

Sabir 105, 107, 265
Sanskrit 57, 114
Sapir, Edward 3–5, 219–21
Science
   languages of 121, 139, 143, 150–2, 271
Scotland/Scots 11, 199, 202–3, 252, 254, 277
Senghor Léopold 130
Sheng 108

Skutnabb-Kangas, Tove 12, 165, 221, 223, 264, 280
Slovakia 11, 36, 50, 201, 203, 216, 258, 276, 278
social mobility 20, 30, 43–4, 68, 81, 88, 92–3, 111–12, 170, 185, 188, 216, 229, 234, 243
sovereignty 10, 28, 36, 38, 45, 67, 70, 160–4, 182, 197, 246, 254, 278
Spain/Spanish 21, 23, 26, 44, 54, 107, 109, 111–13, 193, 204–17, 268–9, 273, 278
standard language/standardisation 8, 13, 26, 28, 34–5, 38–44, 47–60, 63, 67–8, 77, 88–91, 95, 97, 109, 125, 142, 166–8, 176–7, 211–12, 215–17, 223, 233, 240–1, 255, 258, 262, 265–6, 281
state nation 19, 26–32, 36, 43–5, 65, 67, 70, 184, 253–5, 257
status planning 13, 43, 45, 77–8, 84–5, 88, 122–6, 175, 177, 203, 232
Steiner George 5–6, 174, 223, 280
supranational governance 10–11, 14, 149, 157, 162, 182–3, 195, 201, 209, 248, 256
Swahili 54, 73, 75–82, 106, 112, 261–3
Sweden/Swedish 26, 34, 49, 54, 58, 120, 129, 176, 273
Swift Jonathan 55
Switzerland/Swiss 33–4, 45–6, 58, 132, 273, 282

Tanzania 73, 75–82, 261–3
technology 113
  languages of 139, 146, 150–2
Tollefson, Jim 10, 165–7
Toubon law 124–5, 269
trading languages 103–6
Trubetzkoy 106
Turkey/Turkish 11, 21, 43, 44, 52, 58, 61, 109, 182, 224, 256, 259–60, 268, 276

Uchumataqu 237–9
UNESCO 12, 153, 190, 192, 229, 278, 280
United Nations 10, 12, 144, 148–9, 161, 189–92, 197, 202, 257, 264, 273
Union of Soviet Socialist Republics 11, 47, 105, 123, 131, 150, 156, 163, 203, 225, 278
United States 136–79
  culture 10, 152–5, 275
  current nation building 163–5, 181
  economic power 144–8, 271–2, 274
  English only movement 44, 163
  political power 148–50
  spread of English within 141–3, 227, 257–8
  technology 150–2
universalism 4, 61, 97, 107, 120, 211, 270

Valencia 209–10
Varennes, Fernand de 12, 186, 198
Vietnam/Vietnamese 115–16, 131–3, 267, 269

welfare 32, 38–9, 160–2, 185
Welsh 30, 90, 199, 217, 227, 234, 241, 254, 256
Whaley, Lindsay 235–7
Whiteley, Wilfred 9, 76–8
Whorf, Benjamin 3–4, 73, 127, 219–23, 280
Wilhelm von 32
World Bank 79, 144, 146, 263
World Trade Organisation (WTO) 10, 144
Wyclif John 22

Yugoslavia 11, 36, 47, 50, 65, 163, 201, 256